The Complete Beginner's Photography Course

A MODULAR SYSTEM FOR SUCCESS

Ben Hawkins

ilex

An Hachette UK Company
www.hachette.co.uk

First published in the United Kingdom in 2022 by Ilex, an imprint of
Octopus Publishing Group Ltd
Carmelite House,
50 Victoria Embankment,
London EC4Y 0DZ
www.octopusbooks.co.uk
www.octopusbooksusa.com

Distributed in the US by
Hachette Book Group
1290 Avenue of the Americas,
4th & 5th Floors,
New York, NY 101014

Distributed in Canada by
Canadian Manda Group
664 Annette Street, Toronto,
Ontario, Canada M6S 2C8

Design and layout Copyright
© Octopus Publishing Group Ltd 2022
Text and illustrations Copyright
© Ben Hawkins 2022

Publisher: Alison Starling
Commissioning Editor: Richard Collins
Managing Editor: Rachel Silverlight
Editorial Assistant: Jeannie Stanley
Art Director: Ben Gardiner
Design and Illustration: Chris Robinson
Additional Photography: Adam Atkins
Picture Research: Jennifer Veall
Senior Production Manager:
Katherine Hockley

All rights reserved. No part of this work may be reproduced or utilized in any form or by any means, electronic or mechanical, including photocopying, recording or by any information storage and retrieval system, without the prior written permission of the publisher.

Ben Hawkins has asserted his right under the Copyright, Designs and Patents Act 1988 to be identified as the author of this work.

ISBN 978-1-78157-855-1

A CIP catalogue record for this book is available from the British Library.

Printed and bound in China

10 9 8 7 6 5 4 3 2 1

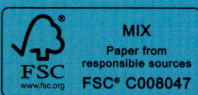

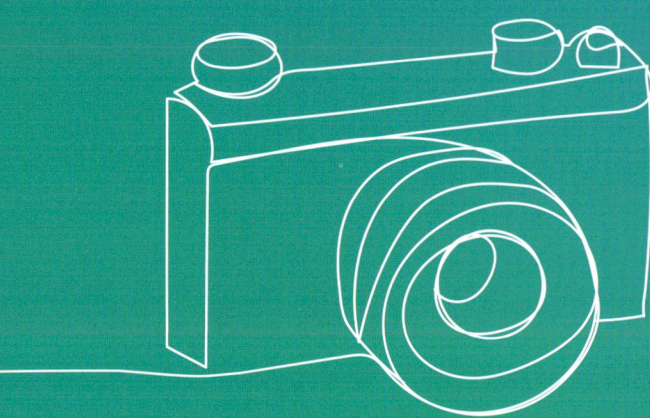

Contents

4 Your photography adventure starts here

MODULE 1: LANDSCAPES
8 Look for simplicity
14 Add a focal point
20 Create depth
26 Find natural framing
32 Inject movement
38 Get abstract
44 Use your illusion

MODULE 2: PORTRAITS
52 Start with the face
58 Add context
64 Capture kids at play
70 Create emotion with light
76 Focus on pets
82 Take a closer look at hands

MODULE 3: NATURE
90 Focus on flowers
96 Get low for grass
102 Reveal a leaf's patterns

MODULE 4: MOVEMENT
110 Capture traffic trails
116 Travel at warp speed
122 Suggest speed with blur
128 Follow a moving subject
134 Go slow with flash
140 Paint with light
146 Make a physiogram

MODULE 5: STILL LIFE
154 Make a retro classic
160 Reinvent household objects
166 Sell your products
172 Cook up a tasty dish
178 Shoot from above
184 Get abstract with *bokeh*
190 Create liquid art
196 Bend light
202 Freeze nature

MODULE 6: STREET & URBAN
210 Shoot from the hip
216 Focus on reflections
222 Frame your scenes
228 Play with shadows
234 Blur moving people
240 Look for lines & shapes
246 Isolate smaller details

252 Glossary
254 Index
256 Picture credits & Acknowledgements

Your photography adventure starts here

So, you've just bought your first 'proper' camera and want to start taking amazing photos. But of what? And how? We all experience that initial 'where to start?' moment, particularly when presented with a fancy gadget covered in buttons and dials, and it's easy to become overwhelmed. But what if there was a book that told you exactly what to shoot and how to shoot it, and all in small, bite-sized, easily digestible chunks? Well, there is, and you're holding it. Result!

Photography should be heaps of fun and hugely rewarding. It should allow you to express yourself and indulge your creative whimsies; it should inspire you to see the world in new and exciting ways; it should give you a passion and purpose. What it should never be is overly complicated or too technical. This book is here to show you that with a handful of core techniques and a basic understanding of your camera's most important modes and features (and a few overlooked and underrated ones), you can create amazing photos.

Each project starts simply and is designed to introduce you to a new technique and its basic components, walking you through the key settings and skills without getting too bogged down in the technicalities. Along the way, you'll be introduced to six fundamental genres and an arsenal of creative approaches that can be applied to just about every subject. For instance, the camera setup for flower close-ups is very similar to the one used for contemporary still life; the rules of composition are just as relevant to portraits as they are to landscapes.

On the subject of rules, the world of photography is littered with them, some of which you may already be familiar with: manual mode is best; only shoot RAW; never plonk your subject in the middle of the frame. Suffice to say I believe some rules are made to be broken, and we'll explore these suggested guidelines as we progress through the modules.

In compiling this book, I've made a few rather large assumptions. The first is that you're in possession of an entry-level DSLR or mirrorless camera. No doubt the box it came in shouted about the number of megapixels, the size of its sensor and the speed at which it can focus. This is all important stuff, but tech alone won't magically transform you into a great photographer. And despite all the noise around new cameras and their many wondrous modes and features, there really are only a dozen or so settings you need to know about – and these are mostly the same settings we'd have been talking about 25 years ago.

The second big assumption is that your DSLR or mirrorless camera was bundled with a kit lens. These small zooms typically offer a focal length of around 18–55mm, which will allow you to shoot a wide range of subjects. All projects are geared towards this, regardless of subject or style. Serious enthusiasts can get a bit sniffy about kit lenses, but they're the perfect starter lens and are capable of producing quality results when you know how.

In terms of accessories, a sturdy tripod is essential and you will soon realize why – you may think you have a steady hand, but I challenge anyone to shoot handheld at 1/30 second and get pin-sharp results. A remote shutter release and reflector would also be handy but not absolutely vital – there are workarounds and DIY solutions for both. You will also need to borrow a few everyday household items for various projects but nothing that you (or someone you know) won't have lying around. Beyond that, all you need are your eyes – develop these (and learn to trust them) and all the technology in the world won't be able to compete.

Whether you work through the modules in order or dip your toes in is up to you – each is a self-contained project that includes all the creative and technical competencies you need to complete it, with references to techniques covered elsewhere in the book where relevant. However you digest it, my hope is that you stumble on a subject or style that inspires you so much, whether ethereal landscapes or gritty street scenes, you just have to keep on shooting and refining your skills in that area. After all, even the biggest names in photography started as all-rounders in search of a niche they could call their own.

When I think back to my photographic initiation, and all those dusty old textbooks and journals I ploughed through and deciphered, I'd have killed (metaphorically speaking) for a book like this; a welcoming start-up manual that quickly shows you how without blinding you with science. We can all see amazing photos in our mind's eye, but what separates photographers from camera owners is the ability to translate these imaginary images into camera settings and real-world compositions. I truly hope you enjoy your picture-taking adventures.

MODULE SKILL RATINGS

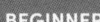

BEGINNER
An ideal entry point for your photography journey, requiring only you and your camera.

INTERMEDIATE
These modules introduce more skills and might require some basic equipment, such as a tripod.

ADVANCED
Requiring a little more patience and practice, these modules help you develop your technical skills.

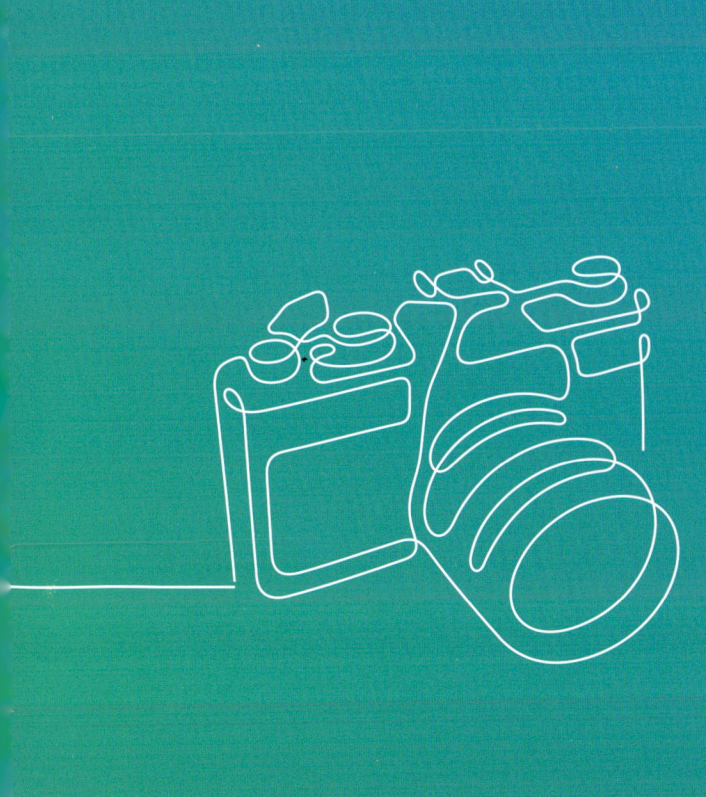

# 1 LANDSCAPES

Module 1.1
Look for simplicity

Most landscapes contain multiple elements that at first glance can appear cluttered and chaotic. Whether rural or urban, natural or human-made, these elements can overwhelm the senses and the temptation is often to want to include as many of them as possible in the frame. However, what we exclude from the picture is just as important as what we include and so our first challenge as landscape photographers is to find a visually appealing simplicity in this chaos and portray it in two dimensions. To quote a favourite lyric, 'less is more, more or less'.

In the same way that young children tend to draw scenes by reducing them to their basic elements, with a big block of blue for the sky and a big block of green for the grass, even the most complicated landscapes can be reduced to simple shapes and colours. Admittedly, some locations lend themselves to this minimalist approach more readily than others – rolling hills, deserts and sea views are particular favourites – but learn to simplify and you'll have mastered a key technique that underpins all successful landscape photography.

Once you've reduced a scene to its essential components, the next step is to balance them. Balance is a word you'll hear a lot when we talk about composition, and there are various ways to achieve this, but one of the most effective methods is to use the rule of thirds. This is a powerful device that works by dividing the frame into nine equally sized rectangles, with two horizontal lines and two vertical lines. This grid can then be used to position important elements, which in our example amounts to nothing more than a simple horizon line. Positioning the horizon along one of the two horizontal grid lines creates a visual hierarchy that emphasizes either land or sky.

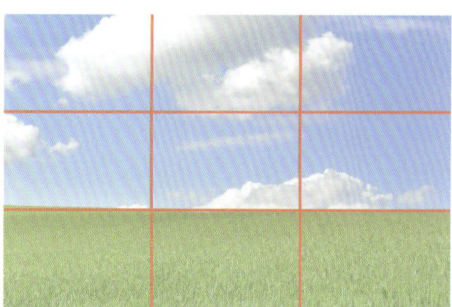

ABOVE Even the simplest of scenes can be transformed into well-balanced images.

LEFT Use the rule of thirds to position key elements such as the horizon.

DIFFICULTY ★☆☆

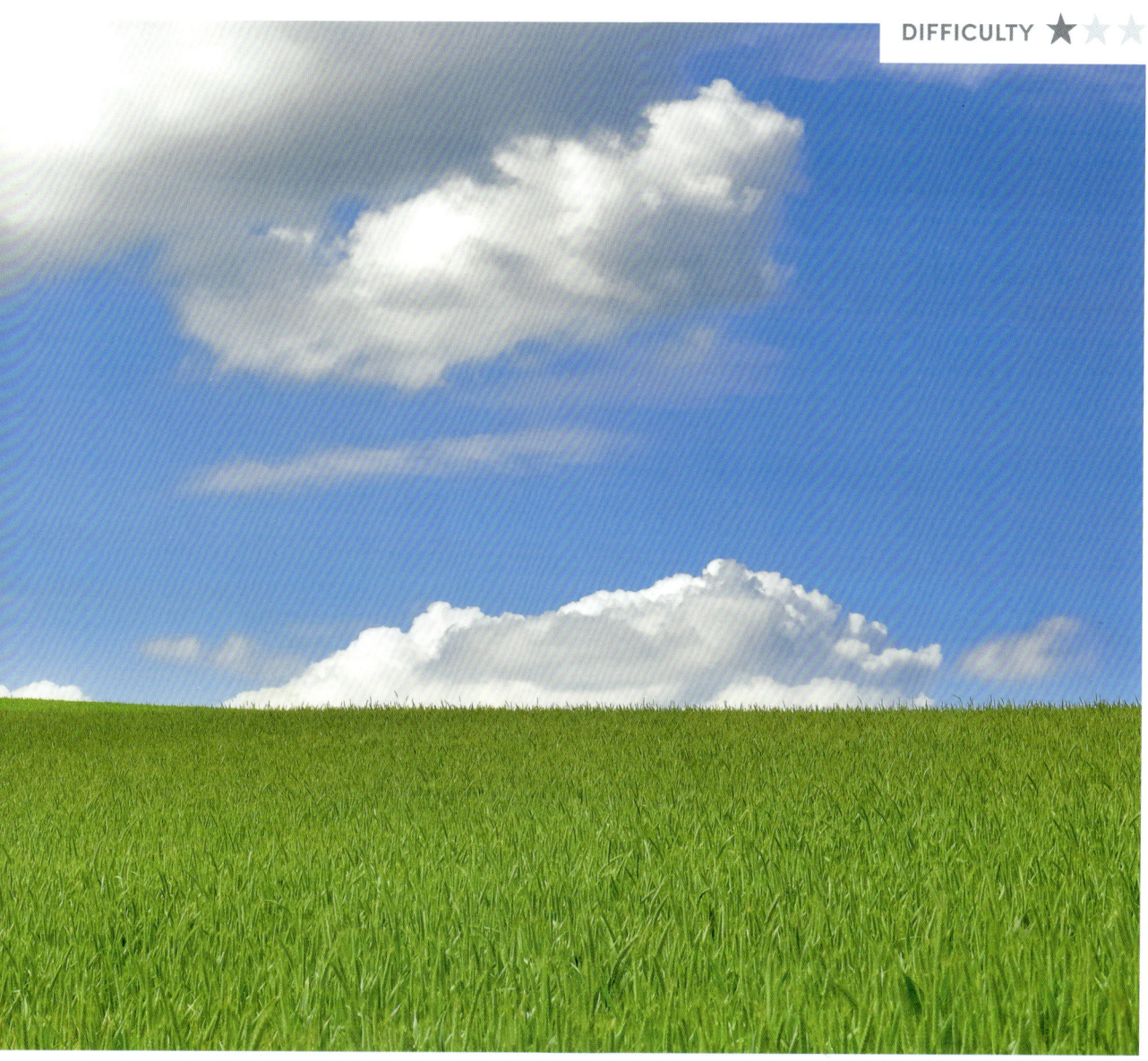

RECOMMENDED SETTINGS

- Shooting mode: **Aperture-priority**
- Aperture: ***f*/16**
- Shutter speed: **1/125sec (handheld)**
- ISO: **100**
- Focal length: **18mm**
- AF area: **Single-point AF**
- AF operation: **Single-shot AF**
- Drive mode: **Single-shot or self-timer**
- Metering mode: **Evaluative/matrix**
- White balance: **Auto or daylight/cloudy**
- Picture style: **Landscape**

Camera settings

Depth of field is a key consideration when shooting landscapes, as we typically want to achieve front-to-back sharpness and capture every little detail, so we're going to select aperture-priority, a semi-automatic shooting mode that allows us to control aperture while the camera calculates the 'best' corresponding shutter speed. This mode can be found on your camera's main mode dial, often abbreviated to A or Av. That's not to say that shutter speed is unimportant, but it certainly plays a secondary role whenever depth of field is a primary concern. Just remember to pack your tripod.

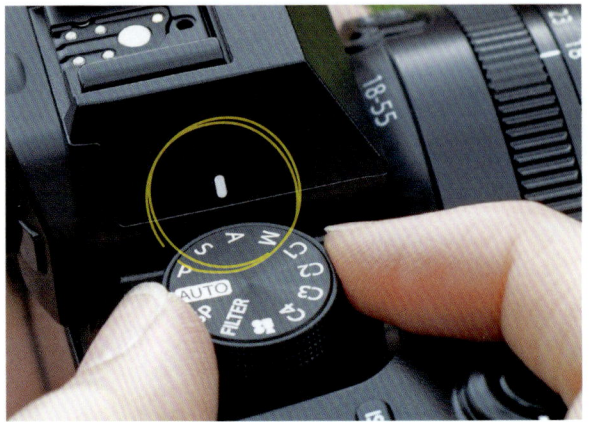

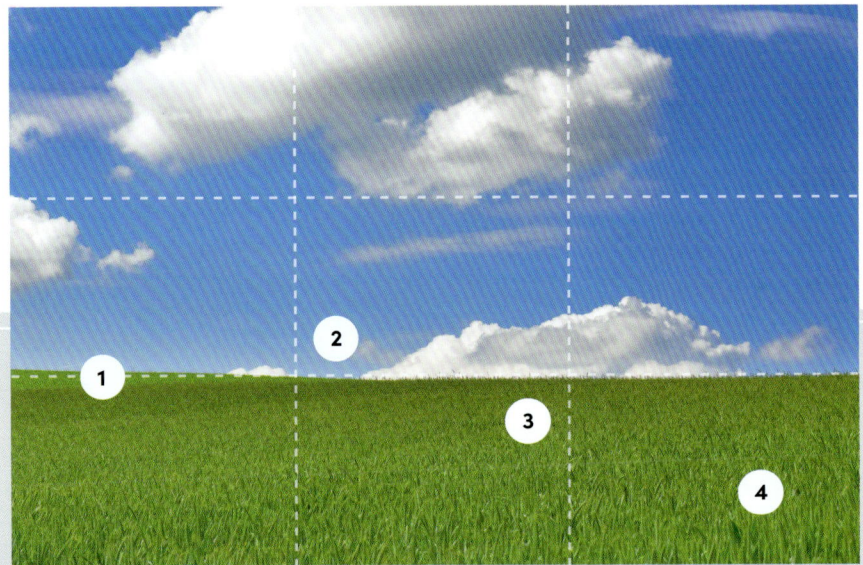

WHY THIS SHOT WORKS

1 The horizon has been carefully placed on the lower horizontal rule-of-thirds grid line, which creates a pleasing visual balance and hierarchy, with the sky occupying two thirds of the frame.

2 The colour palette may be limited, but green and blue sit next to each other on the colour wheel and create a strong and dynamic visual contrast.

3 Like coastal scenes and sand dunes, rolling hills are an ideal subject for minimalist landscapes, providing a calm, uncluttered scene that still features gentle shapes and contours.

4 By using a narrow aperture and low ISO, the photographer has maximized depth of field and image quality, resulting in front-to-back sharpness and an image packed with tiny details.

In theory, we want to select the smallest aperture available to maximize depth of field, and on most kit lenses this would be ƒ/22. However, due to an optical imperfection known as 'diffraction', which can cause a reduction in sharpness at narrow apertures, we're going to shoot at ƒ/16. This is the smallest aperture I'd recommend you use with any APS-C DSLR or mirrorless camera. As our landscape is so minimal, ƒ/16 will still provide us with plenty of depth of field and ensure that important details, such as the grass and horizon line, are crisp and well defined.

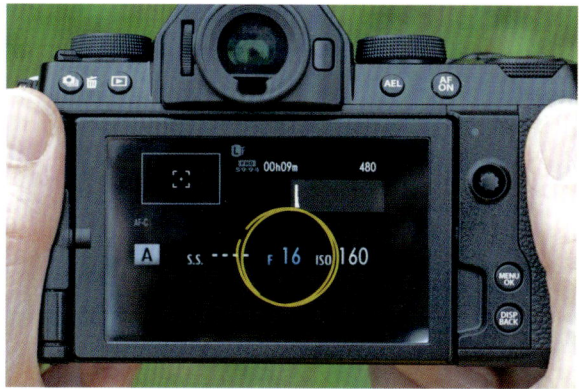

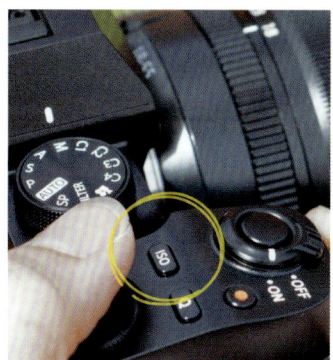 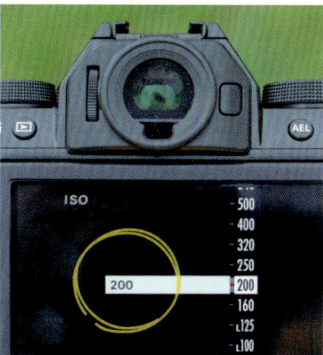

To further enhance sharpness, we also want to maximize image quality and so we're going to select the lowest ISO possible, which will either be 100 or 200 depending on the camera's make and model (some cameras even go as low as 50). Most feature a dedicated ISO button or dial, while on some you'll need to navigate the menu. The lower the ISO – and the smaller the aperture – the longer the shutter speed, which won't be a problem if your camera is firmly attached to a tripod. However, if shooting handheld is your only option, aim for a shutter speed of 1/125 second or faster. Depending on the time of day and weather, this may require a slightly higher ISO setting.

For accurate colours, auto white balance tends to be reliable in most natural lighting situations. However, if you want to take a more hands-on approach, select either the daylight preset if conditions are particularly bright and sunny, or the cloudy preset if the sky is overcast and the light more diffused. To give colours extra punch, dive into your camera's Picture Styles menu and select the Landscape preset, which will saturate all colours, but blues in particular, which is perfect for minimalist images like ours.

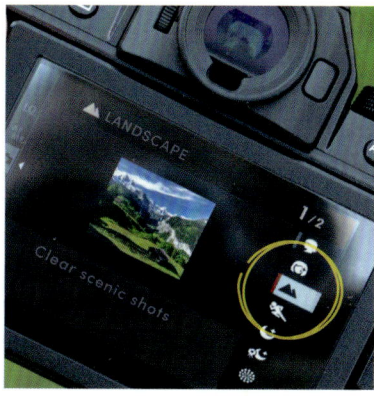

To give colours extra punch, dive into your camera's Picture Styles menu and select the Landscape preset, which will saturate all colours, but blues in particular, which is perfect for minimalist images like ours, in which the palette is limited to strong primary and secondary colours.

LOOK FOR SIMPLICITY 11

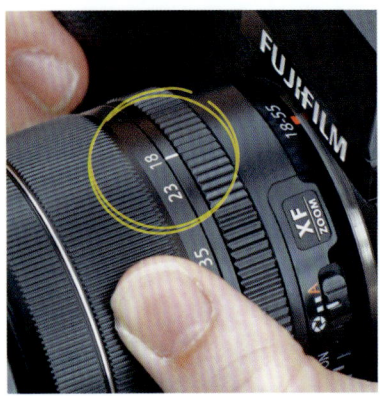

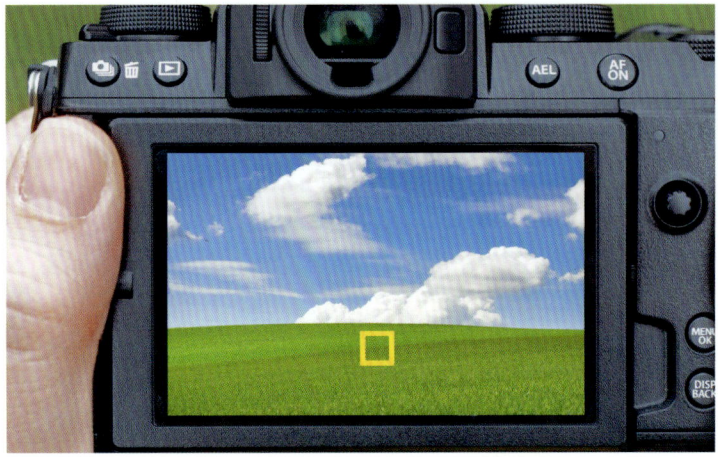

Lens settings

Wide focal lengths are often preferred for landscapes as they allow you to capture more expansive views, so zoom your kit lens all the way out to 18mm. If you find the wide-angle view this provides includes distracting elements, don't be afraid to zoom back in slightly to exclude these unwanted details from the frame. To focus, make sure your camera and/or lens are switched to autofocus (AF) and select the single-shot drive mode so that you are taking just one image at a time.

Technique

Using the single-point AF area, position your active AF point over an area of contrast roughly a third of the way into the scene – in our example, this would be one of the defined green contours just below the horizon – and gently half-press the shutter button to engage autofocus. If shooting handheld, fully press the shutter button and take your picture once focus has locked on, focusing and shooting in one smooth movement so that the camera and point of focus don't move during the split-second between actions.

If shooting with a tripod, it's good practice to switch to manual focus (MF) mode once autofocus has worked its magic, as this ensures that focus remains constant while you shoot away, and I'd also recommend you use a remote shutter release or your camera's self-timer mode to avoid any camera shake. If you find that your first image appears too light or too dark, use exposure compensation to fine-tune your exposure.

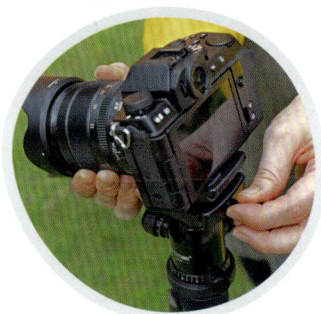

TIP

If your landscape features a particularly flat horizon, use your camera's virtual horizon (accessed via Live View) to make sure it's perfectly straight. Alternatively, invest in a hot shoe spirit level or check if your tripod has a built-in spirit level.

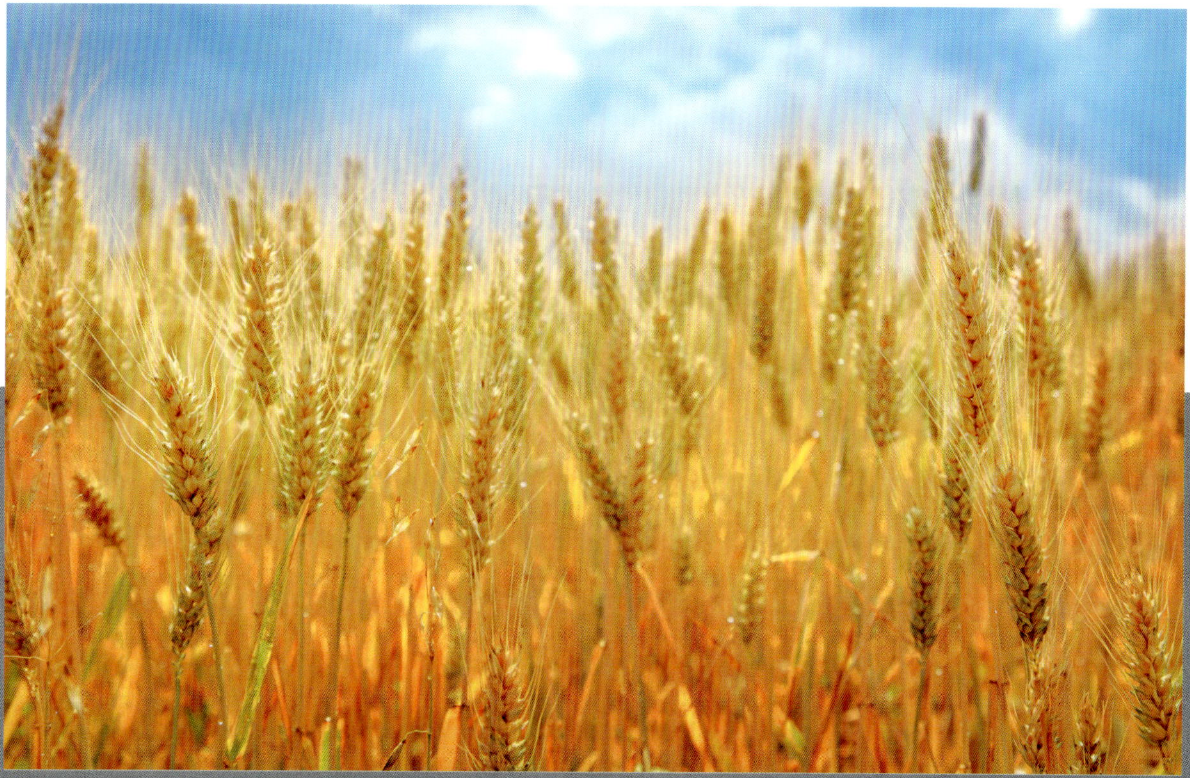

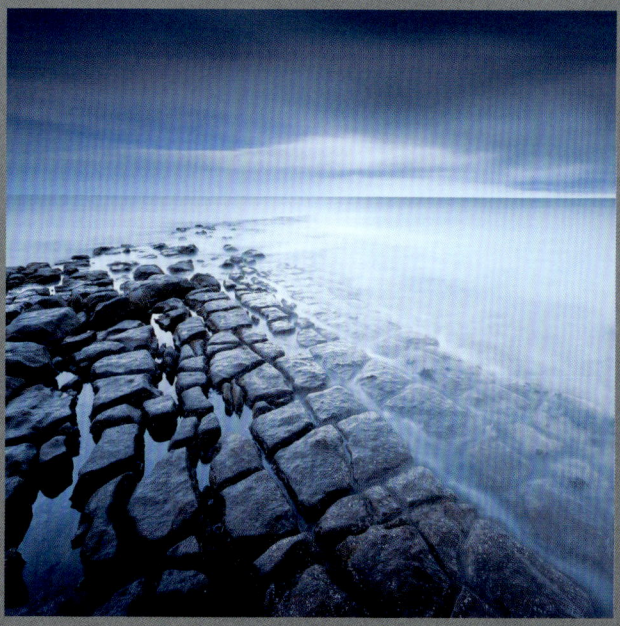

SHOOTING INSPIRATION

This technique can be employed successfully across a variety of different landscape-type shots:

ABOVE With very strong foreground interest in this field of wheat, the sky is limited to one third of the composition.

LEFT By placing the rule-of-thirds line just on the horizon, this seascape creates a strong, minimalist composition.

Module 1.2
Add a focal point

Where the first module was an exercise in reductionism and stripping our landscape's 'canvas' back to its fundamental components in a quest for visual simplicity, the second module is an exercise in adding a vital ingredient that will instinctively draw the viewer's eye to a particular object or area of your scene. Known as a focal point, this magical ingredient is effectively a photographer's way of telling the viewer where to look and what to look at, kind of like a visual tour guide pointing its finger.

A focal point doesn't necessarily need to be the largest or brightest element in the frame, but it does need to be carefully considered. Windmills, lighthouses and lone trees are all ideal subjects, and the latter in particular will change in appearance according to season, making them especially dynamic. Your focal point also needs to be carefully positioned. Children tend to draw according to hierarchy and place what they consider to be the most important part of a picture in the centre of the frame. As our visual 'language' becomes more sophisticated, we realize that off-centre compositions are often more intriguing and exciting.

Again, it's a question of visual balance and we can once again use the rule of thirds to achieve this. This versatile compositional device can be used to position more than just horizons, and it's this enhanced ability that we are going to tap into here. There are four intersections in a rule-of-thirds grid – the points at which the vertical and horizontal lines cross – and these positional markers are known as 'power points'. Place your subject on one of these power points and you instantly have a well-balanced scene with a clear focal point. Of course, images can have more than one focal point, but simplicity is so often the key to success.

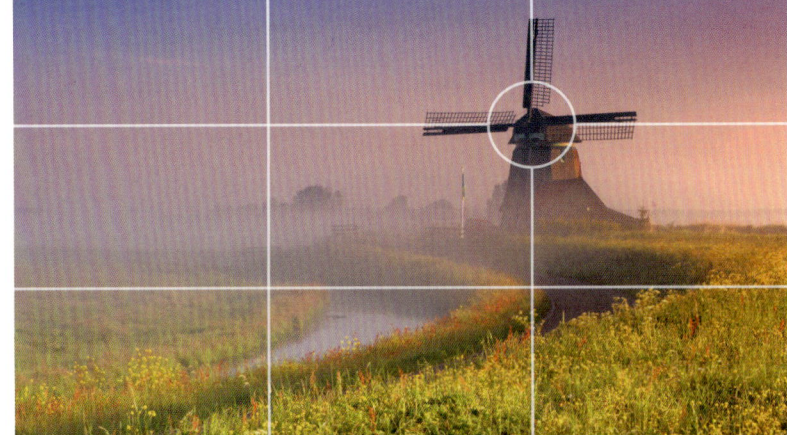

RIGHT Position your focal point on a rule-of-thirds 'power point' for maximum visual impact.

DIFFICULTY ★★★

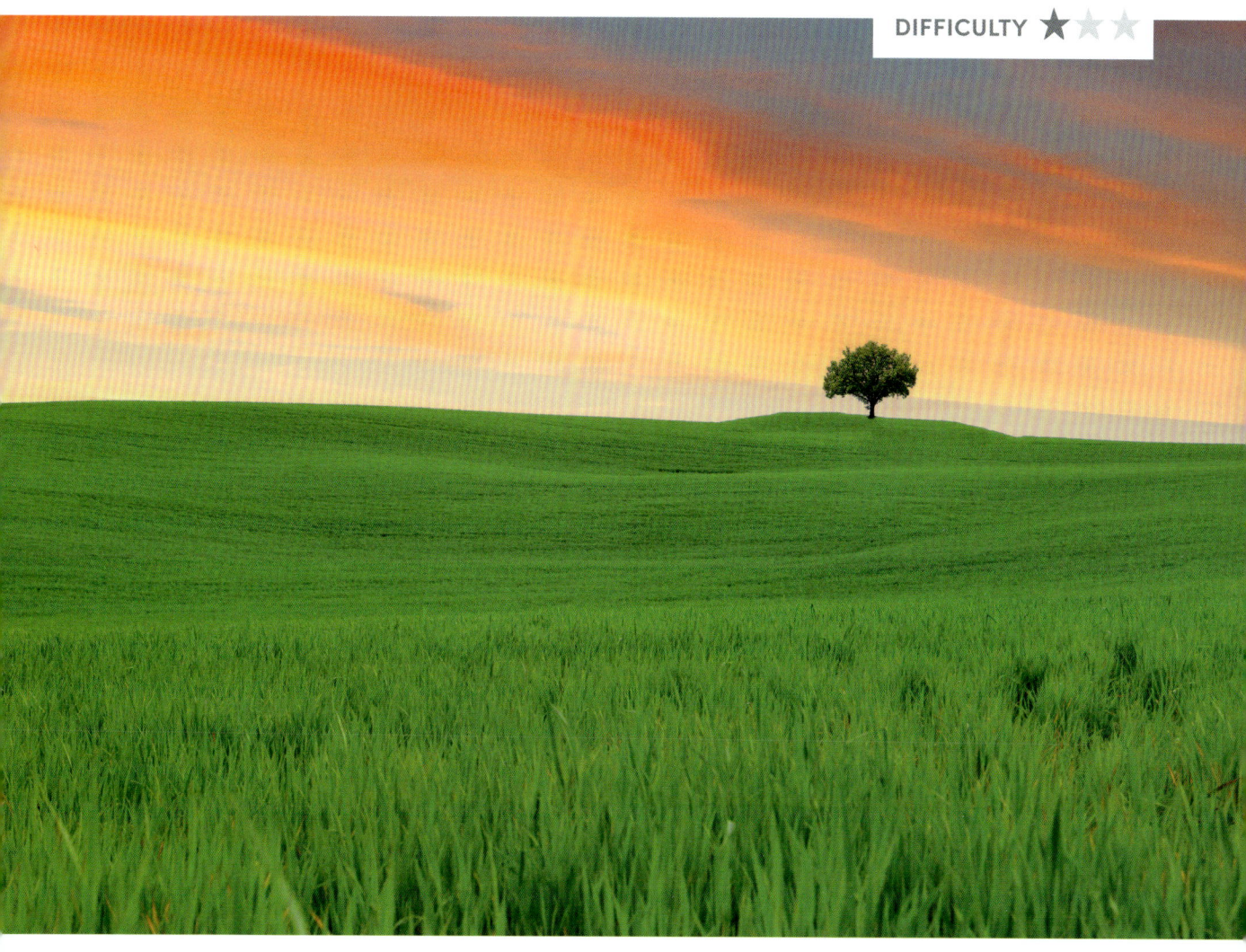

ABOVE **The inclusion of a clear and obvious focal point tells the viewer where to look first.**

RECOMMENDED SETTINGS

- Shooting mode: **Aperture-priority**
- Aperture: **f/16**
- Shutter speed: **1/125sec (handheld)**
- ISO: **100**
- Focal length: **18–55mm**
- AF area: **Single-point AF**
- AF operation: **Single-shot AF**
- Drive mode: **Single-shot or self-timer**
- Metering mode: **Evaluative/matrix**
- White balance: **Auto or daylight/cloudy**
- Picture style: **Landscape**

ADD A FOCAL POINT 15

Camera settings

Aperture should always be the most important exposure setting when shooting landscapes during the day, as it controls depth of field and front-to-back sharpness, so leave your camera in aperture-priority mode (A or Av) and leave the aperture set to ƒ/16. Consider this your default daytime landscape combination. In aperture-priority, your camera will automatically balance the exposure and so, assuming you're using a tripod, you don't need to worry about shutter speed.

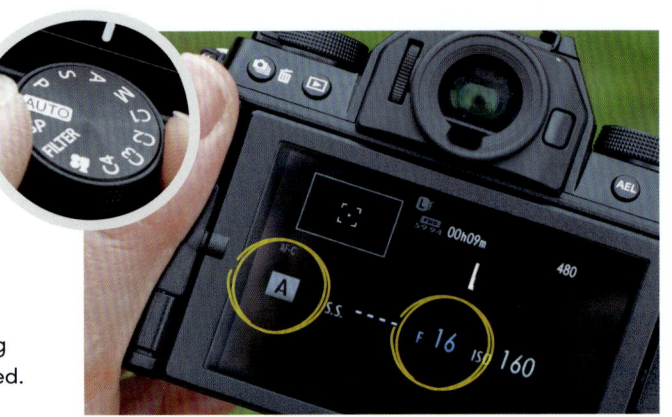

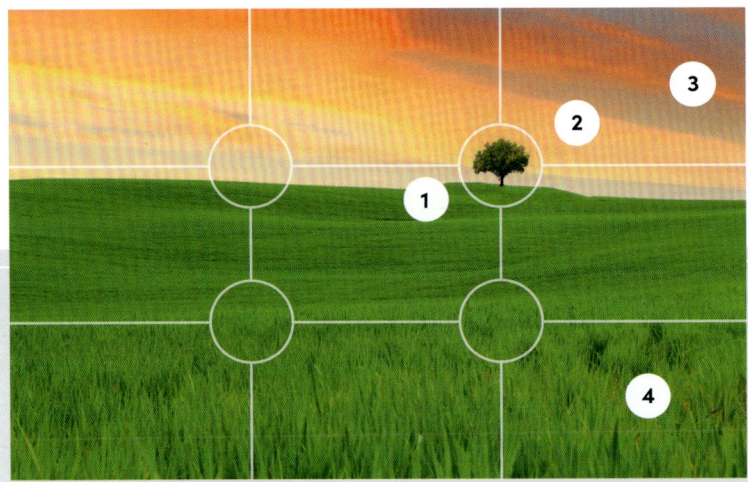

WHY THIS SHOT WORKS

1 Both horizon and focal point have been positioned according to the rule of thirds, with the skyline sitting on the upper-third horizontal grid line and the lone tree occupying the top-right power point.

2 Size isn't everything! Although the tree occupies only a small portion of the frame, its simplicity, instantly recognizable shape and isolation against such a warm sky naturally draws the eye.

3 By shooting at dusk, moments after the sun has disappeared beyond the horizon, the photographer has captured a radiant palette of reds and yellows, which contrasts perfectly with the lush green grass.

4 Using our 'default' camera and lens settings – small aperture, low ISO, wide focal length, etc. – has resulted in a classic landscape image with lots of detail and interest for the eye to explore.

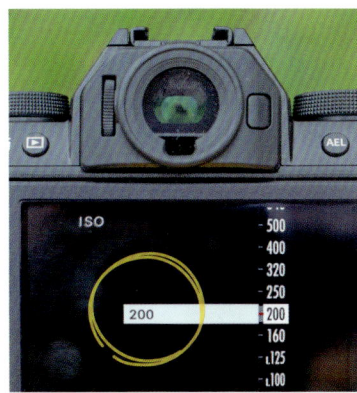

Similarly, ISO should always be set to your camera's lowest, or 'base', sensitivity value when working with a tripod, as this will produce the least amount of digital noise, so leave this set to 100 (older cameras may only go as low as ISO 200). Consider this your default ISO.

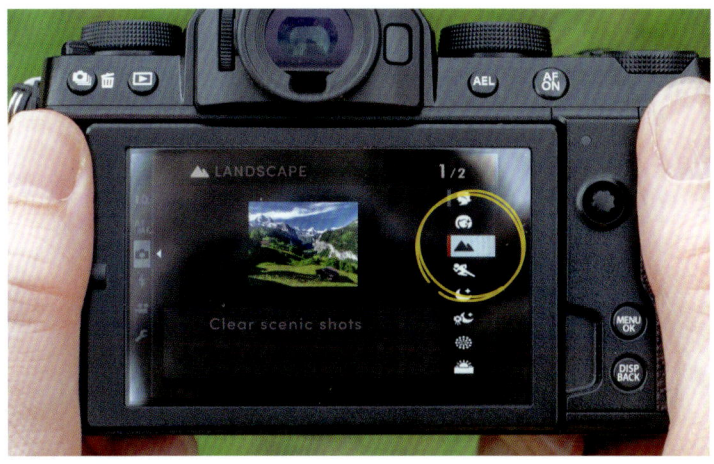

While we're discussing 'default' settings for natural light, you can also leave white balance on auto (or daylight or sunny, if you prefer) and your picture style on Landscape. This will provide you with neutral colours and a hint of extra saturation – perfect for giving Mother Nature a helping hand.

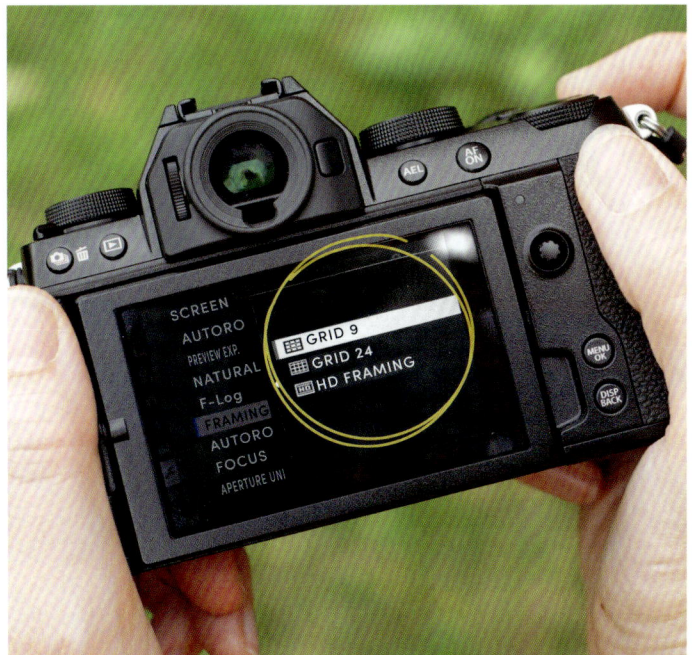

To aid composition, we're going to use a Live View feature that will help you to visualize and 'arrange' images more intuitively. Scroll through your camera's main menu and locate the grid display option. This will present you with a number of options, typically including 3x3, 6x4 and even 3x3 with diagonals. Selecting the 3x3 option will overlay a basic rule-of-thirds grid onto your camera's rear LCD screen (and viewfinder on mirrorless cameras). Now, when you find a suitable location, you can more accurately position your focal point on a power point.

ADD A FOCAL POINT 17

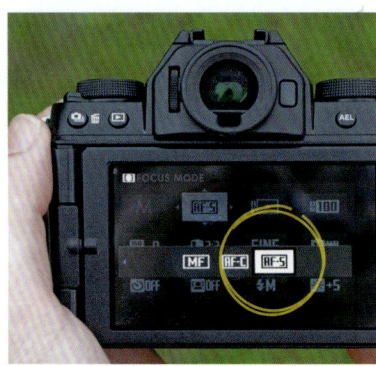

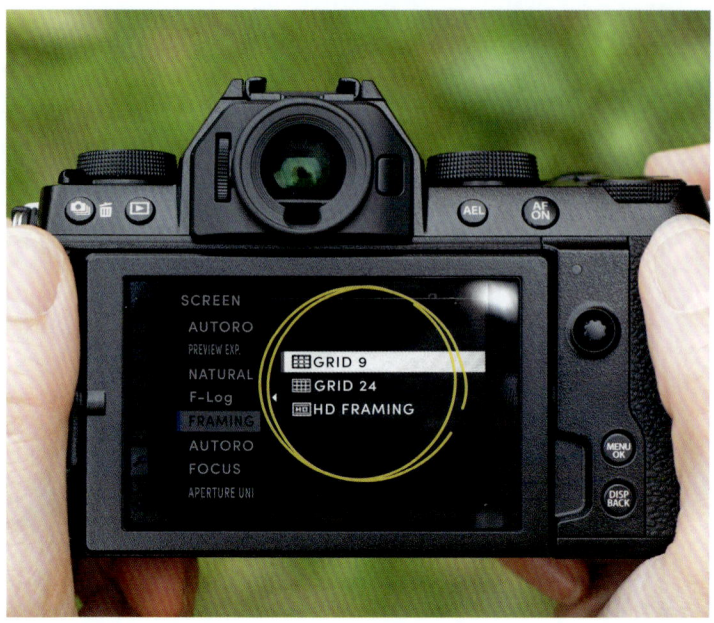

Lens settings

Start wide and zoom in if necessary. There's a famous quote by legendary photojournalist Robert Capa: 'If your pictures aren't good enough, you aren't close enough.' While Capa was talking about war photography (which, strangely, isn't a genre we'll be covering in this book), you can apply the same sentiment to landscapes and kit lenses. If at 18mm you find that your scene isn't as minimalist as you'd like it to be, zoom in until all distracting elements have been removed. If at 55mm you're still not happy, use your feet and physically move closer if you can. After all, there's no hard and fast rule that says all landscapes must be shot at wide focal lengths. Select autofocus (AF), single-point AF (AF area) and single-shot AF (AF operation) modes as your default settings.

Technique

With Live View activated and the 3x3 Grid Display selected, move your AF point directly over your focal point and half-press the shutter to acquire focus. Assuming there's enough contrast (see below), this should only take a split-second. As before, use a remote shutter release or your camera's self-timer mode to trigger the shutter – either method will eliminate any potential camera shake caused by your hand's movement – and use exposure compensation to finesse the exposure.

TIP

If your camera doesn't have a grid overlay feature, draw a rule-of-thirds grid onto an LCD-sized piece of tracing paper and hold it over the LCD when composing your image. This will help you position your focal point on a power point while taking up precisely no extra room in your camera bag.

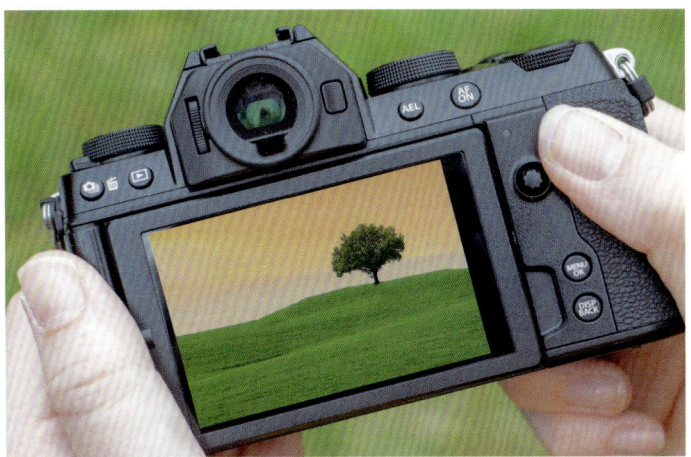

Think of your first shot as a 'test' shot and always check that your image is as sharp as possible before moving on. In my days as a magazine editor, we used the term 'thumbnail optimism' to describe the euphoria of seeing what we thought was a great image on the back of a camera only to find that it was out of focus or badly exposed on a computer screen. To avoid this, when reviewing your test shot, use the zoom/magnify button to take a much closer look, scrolling left to right and top to bottom to inspect your image in detail. This is a good habit to get into regardless of subject.

While there's no right or wrong time of day to shoot landscapes, you'll often hear enthusiasts wax lyrical about the 'golden hour' – the moments just before sunrise and just after sunset, when the sun is low in the sky and the light is at its warmest. I've always found the term a tad misleading, as in my experience the golden 'hour' usually only lasts a few minutes depending on location, time of year, weather and so on, but there's no denying that this is when light is most likely to be at its most attractive. To avoid complicated exposure issues, shoot when the sun is either just below the horizon or with it to your side – a simple way to reveal textures and accentuate shadows. And don't leave it too late – the darker the sky and the less contrast in the scene, the harder it is for AF to lock on and find focus.

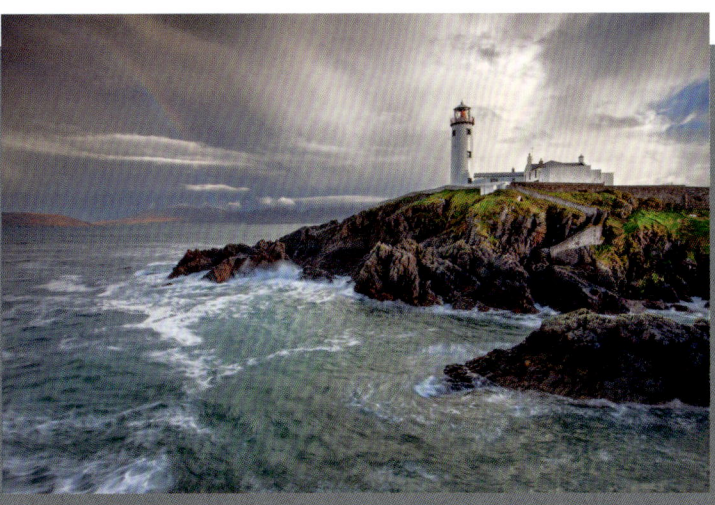

SHOOTING INSPIRATION

Focal points don't need to dominate a scene to be effective – they just need to be carefully positioned.

LEFT Placing the lighthouse on the top-right 'power point' creates a balanced composition with a strong focal point and plenty of space to explore.

Module 1.3
Create depth

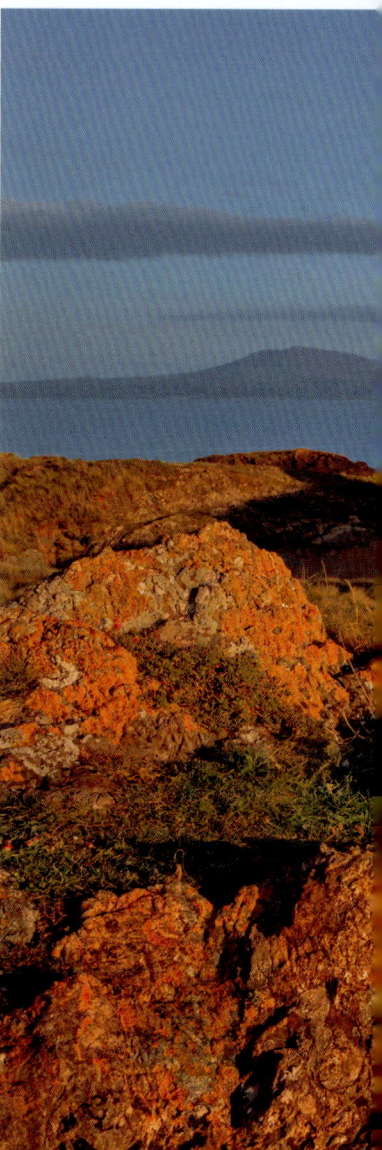

ABOVE **The gently winding stairs – our lead-in line – connects the foreground rocks to the lighthouse in the distance.**

Cameras and the human eye 'see' very differently. While we benefit from binocular vision courtesy of having two eyes and can perceive the world in three spatial dimensions – length, width and depth – cameras only have one 'eye' and so compress our three-dimensional reality into a flat two-dimensional rectangle. This fundamental difference presents photographers with a conundrum: do we attempt to capture the sense of depth that our eyes see, or do we instead focus on more two-dimensional subjects and embrace this apparent limitation?

When it comes to landscapes, the challenge is always to create a sense of depth, and there are two further compositional tools we can deploy to artfully manipulate reality: foreground interest and lead-in (or leading) lines. Foreground interest refers to the area of a scene that is closest to the camera and should act as a visual 'stepping stone' into the image, balancing near and far objects and potentially filling otherwise empty areas of the frame. Rocks and foliage are particularly effective subjects, but anything will work so long as it is relevant to the scene. Use the rule of thirds to help you position your foreground interest on a power point if possible – off-centre is almost always more interesting than dead centre.

Lead-in lines are powerful devices that take the viewer's eye on a journey through a scene, often starting at the bottom of the frame and working their way up and towards a particular area of interest. They can act as a bridge between foreground interest and focal point and can be natural or human-made. Rivers, streams and shorelines can make for effective natural lead-in lines, while paths, roads and walls are some of the most readily available manmade subjects. They can also be arrow-straight or long and winding, though diagonal lines that start in a bottom corner and converge into the distance will most obviously convey a sense of depth. Avoid positioning strong lines horizontally across the frame (with the exception of your horizon), as this will create a visual barrier that prevents the eye from travelling any farther.

DIFFICULTY ★★☆

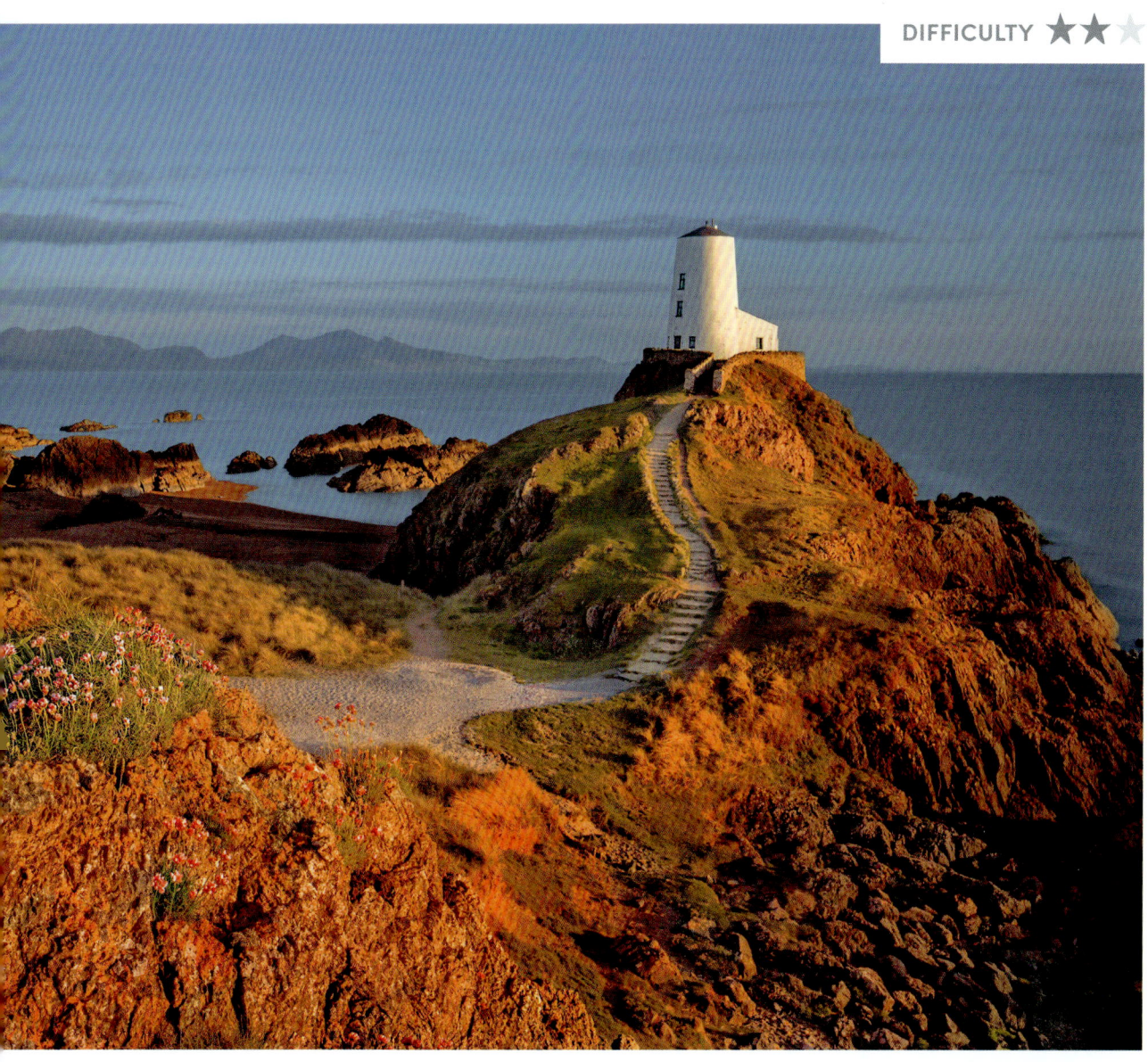

RECOMMENDED SETTINGS

- Shooting mode: **Aperture-priority**
- Aperture: **f/16**
- Shutter speed: **1/125sec (handheld)**
- ISO: **100**
- Focal length: **18mm**
- AF area: **Single-point AF**
- AF operation: **Single-shot AF**
- Drive mode: **Single-shot or self-timer**
- Metering mode: **Evaluative/matrix**
- White balance: **Auto or daylight/cloudy**
- Picture style: **Landscape**

CREATE DEPTH

Camera settings

There are always two key considerations when shooting landscapes: the creative and the mechanical. The former centres around how you interpret and compose the scene in front of you, while the latter provides the means by which you will realize your vision. While we're slowly introducing and putting into practice the creative building blocks that will allow us to more imaginatively photograph any scene, the basic camera settings we use to achieve this remain relatively unchanged, allowing us to concentrate on the importance of learning to 'see' like a photographer.

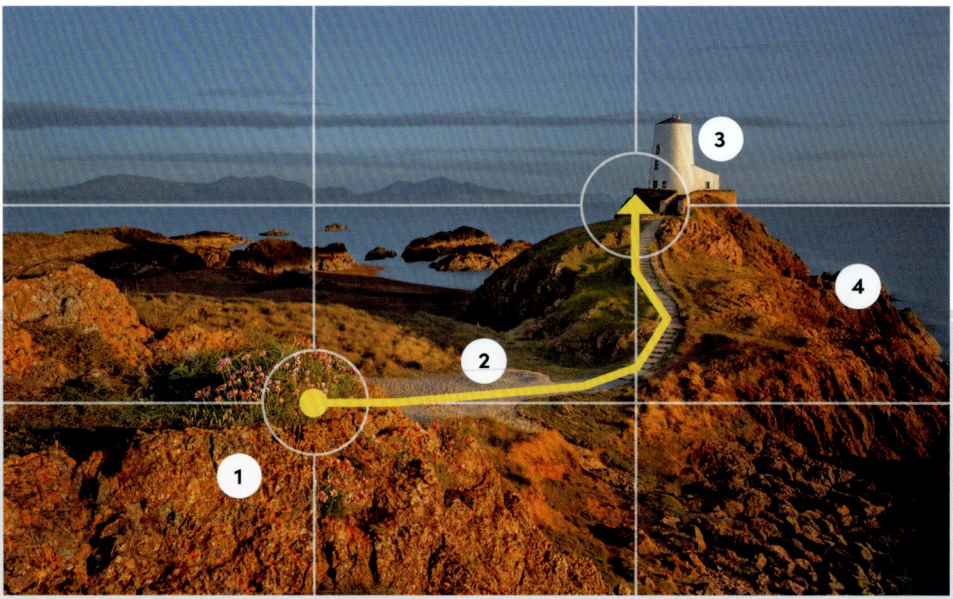

WHY THIS SHOT WORKS

1 The rocks and plants in the foreground act as visual 'stepping stones' into the landscape, creating interest in the bottom third of the frame and providing viewers with a starting point for their journey through the scene.

2 The gently winding gravel path and steps create a strong lead-in line that takes the viewer's eye from the centre of the frame to the foot of the lighthouse, adding to the sense of depth and distance.

3 Both foreground interest and focal point (Tŵr Mawr lighthouse in Anglesey, Wales if you're wondering) are positioned on power points, perfectly balancing and simplifying a potentially confusing landscape.

4 Gorgeous evening side lighting has enveloped the landscape and lighthouse in a warm glow while accentuating every little crack, colour and texture in the rocks. The lengthy shadows also add to the three-dimensional feel.

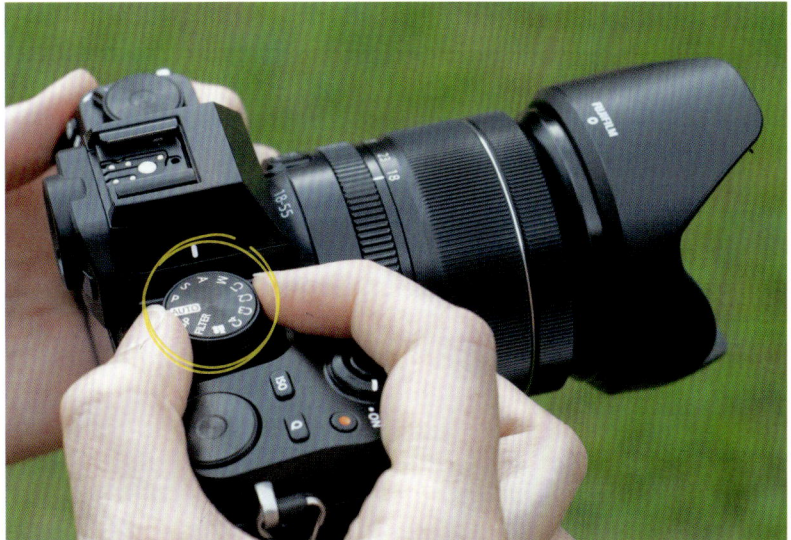

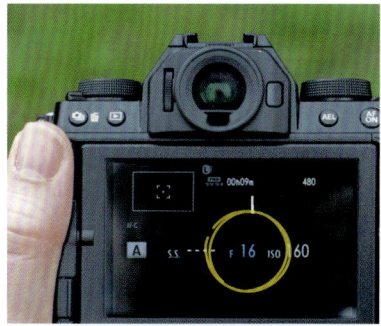

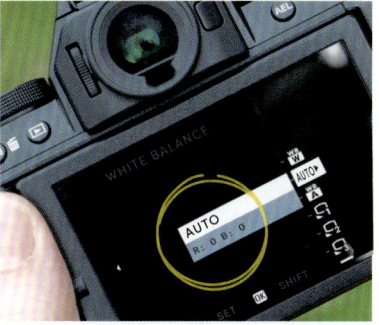

The good news is that we can use the same default camera settings we used in the previous module. Just to recap, we're going to shoot in aperture-priority mode (A or Av) with aperture set to ƒ/16, ISO should be left at its base value, white balance left on auto (or daylight or cloudy) and Picture Style set to the Landscape preset. This tried-and-tested combination will give us plenty of depth of field, the least amount of digital noise and the most neutral colours. We're also going to use the same 3x3 Grid Display option to help us compose for balance and impact.

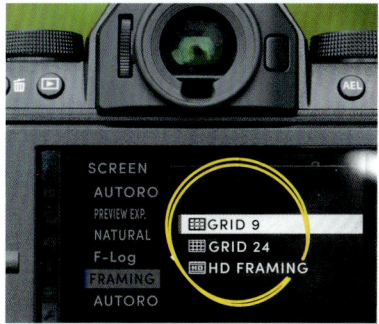

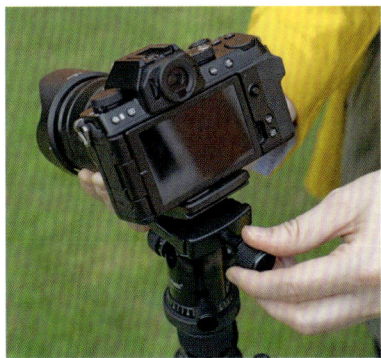

As before, shutter speeds will vary according to the available light so use a tripod whenever practical to do so.

Assuming the sun is either just below the horizon or to the side of you, I'd recommend you use your camera's evaluative or matrix metering mode (both work in the same way, but manufacturers have a penchant for using different terms to describe the same settings). This 'default' mode calculates an average exposure by measuring light from across the entire frame and when shooting in aperture-priority mode will calculate the shutter speed that best balances the exposure triangle.

CREATE DEPTH 23

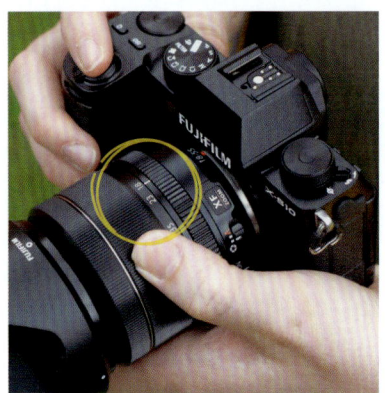

Lens settings

Your choice of focal length will have a huge effect on how prominent your foreground interest appears in the frame. Wide-angle lenses are many landscape photographers' go-to choice and for good reason – wider focal lengths exaggerate perspective while allowing you to include more foreground. Start by zooming your kit lens all the way out to 18mm, but beware – you will need to get very close to your foreground interest for it to work as an 'anchoring' point, otherwise it will appear too far away. Switch to autofocus (AF) and select single-point AF (AF area) and single-shot AF (AF operation).

Technique

Start by considering your viewpoint, which is the position and height you take your picture from. Beginners often instinctively shoot from eye level, and while there's nothing wrong with this, a higher or lower viewpoint can have quite an effect on both composition and how viewers engage with the subject or scene. Shooting from ground level increases the prominence of your foreground interest, particularly when shooting with a wide focal length, while also making it easier for viewers to 'step' into your scene. Shooting from an elevated position, on the other hand, can make foreground interest appear smaller and less important, but can also open up the landscape beyond.

Also consider your camera's orientation. So far, we have worked with the camera in a horizontal, or landscape, position by default, which is fine if many of your compositional elements run horizontally across the frame, but holding the camera upright, often referred to as its portrait orientation, is a simple yet effective way to enhance and accentuate more vertiginous subjects and foregrounds that include vertical lines. Orientation is yet another facet of composition, and despite the terms used – landscape and portrait – suggesting that certain subjects are more suited to one orientation than another, always experiment before committing to a particular view.

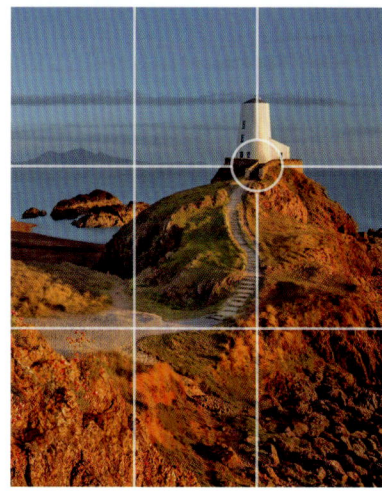

ABOVE **Portrait format places greater visual emphasis on the winding path leading to the lighthouse.**

TIP

Don't get too close to your foreground interest when shooting with a wide focal length as it's all too easy to misjudge the distance and actually hit it (and yes, I'm speaking from personal experience here). If in doubt, compose using Live View instead of the viewfinder and keep one eye on your immediate surroundings.

To focus, place your active AF point roughly one third of the way into the scene and engage AF. This is a very simple version of a very complicated focusing method called 'hyperfocal distance focusing' and is a reliable way of achieving sharp focus from front to back. The problem is that it isn't always easy to visualize where 'one third' falls when framing up an epic vista – to help, we can use apps such as PhotoPills and HyperFocal Pro, which not only calculate the hyperfocal distance (the 'one third' part) but also provide you with an augmented reality view to help you visualize where to focus.

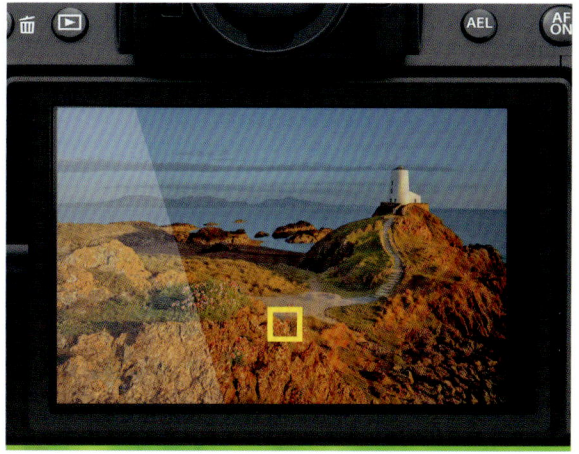

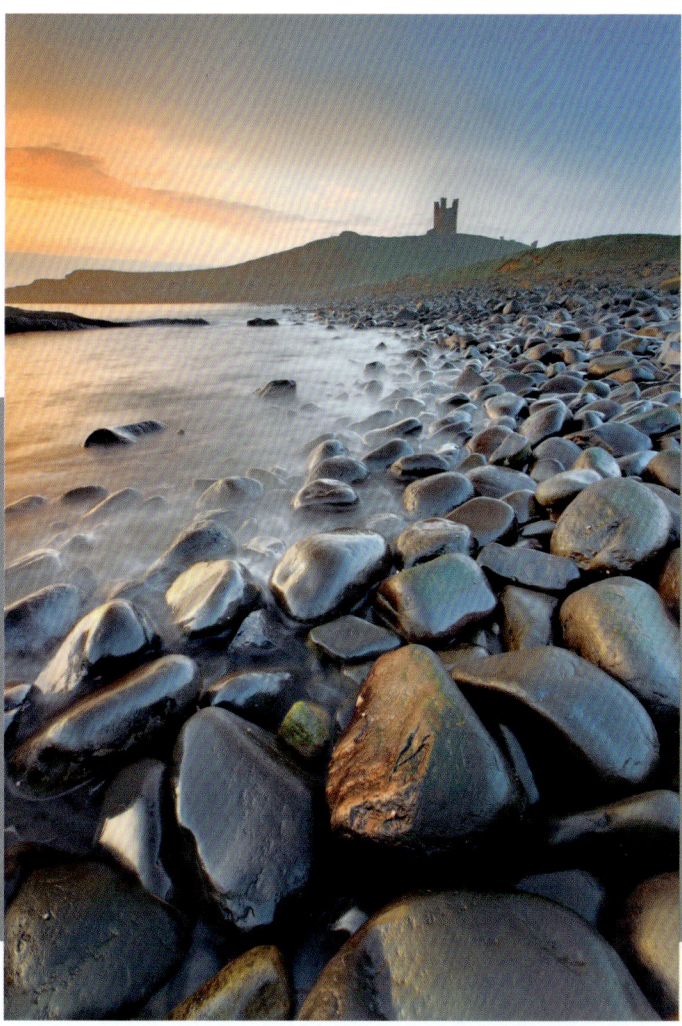

SHOOTING INSPIRATION

Lead-in lines can be straight or curved, human-made or natural, subtle or obvious.

LEFT An outgoing tide provides both an interesting foreground and momentary lead-in line that points to the castle ruins beyond.

Module 1.4
Find natural framing

The rule of thirds, foreground interest and lead-in lines are the three cornerstones of landscape composition. Master these fundamental techniques and you will be able to intuitively create images with balance and depth every time you frame up. But there is one other simple compositional device that can also help to highlight the main subject and direct the viewer's attention: natural framing. Before we move on to more creative techniques, let's explore this often overlooked yet powerful landscape mainstay.

From obvious frames such as rock arches and bridges to more implied frames such as overhanging branches and even breaks in the clouds or fog, there are all kinds of potential subjects that can be used to create frames within frames and force stronger compositions whenever there is too much open space. In our example image, for instance, the tree in the foreground obscures a large area of misty woodland and featureless sky that would add little by way of interest and intrigue. By including the tree and its overhanging branches, the photographer has not only added significant interest to this area of the frame, the visual importance of the path has also been emphasized.

The French language has a wonderfully lyrical phrase – *mise-en-scène* – that literally means 'placing on stage'. The phrase is used by filmmakers to refer to everything in front of the camera, from the framing and lighting to the set and props and more, but it is just as relevant to photography. Does the frame feel natural and seemingly random or constrained and calculated? Does the eye have room to move or is it instantly directed towards a particular object or area? Our example image feels deliberately arranged, which shows that the photographer was very conscious of composition – and the use of natural framing – when considering the *mise-en-scène*.

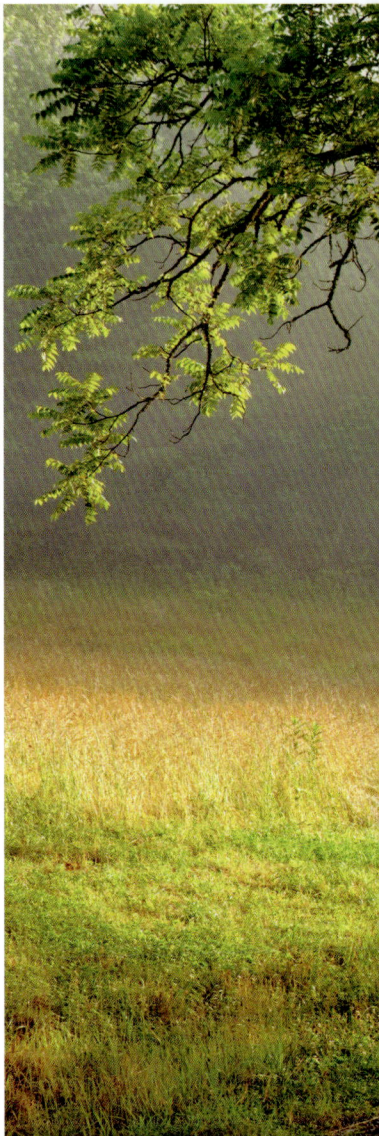

ABOVE **Try to imagine this scene without the tree and overhanging branch – it wouldn't be the most interesting of images.**

LEFT **The gap in the tangle of branches leaves the viewer in no doubt about where to look.**

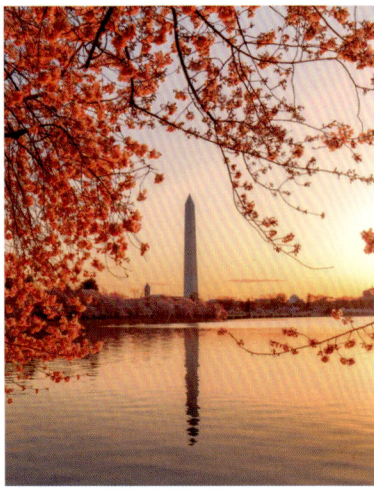

DIFFICULTY ★★☆

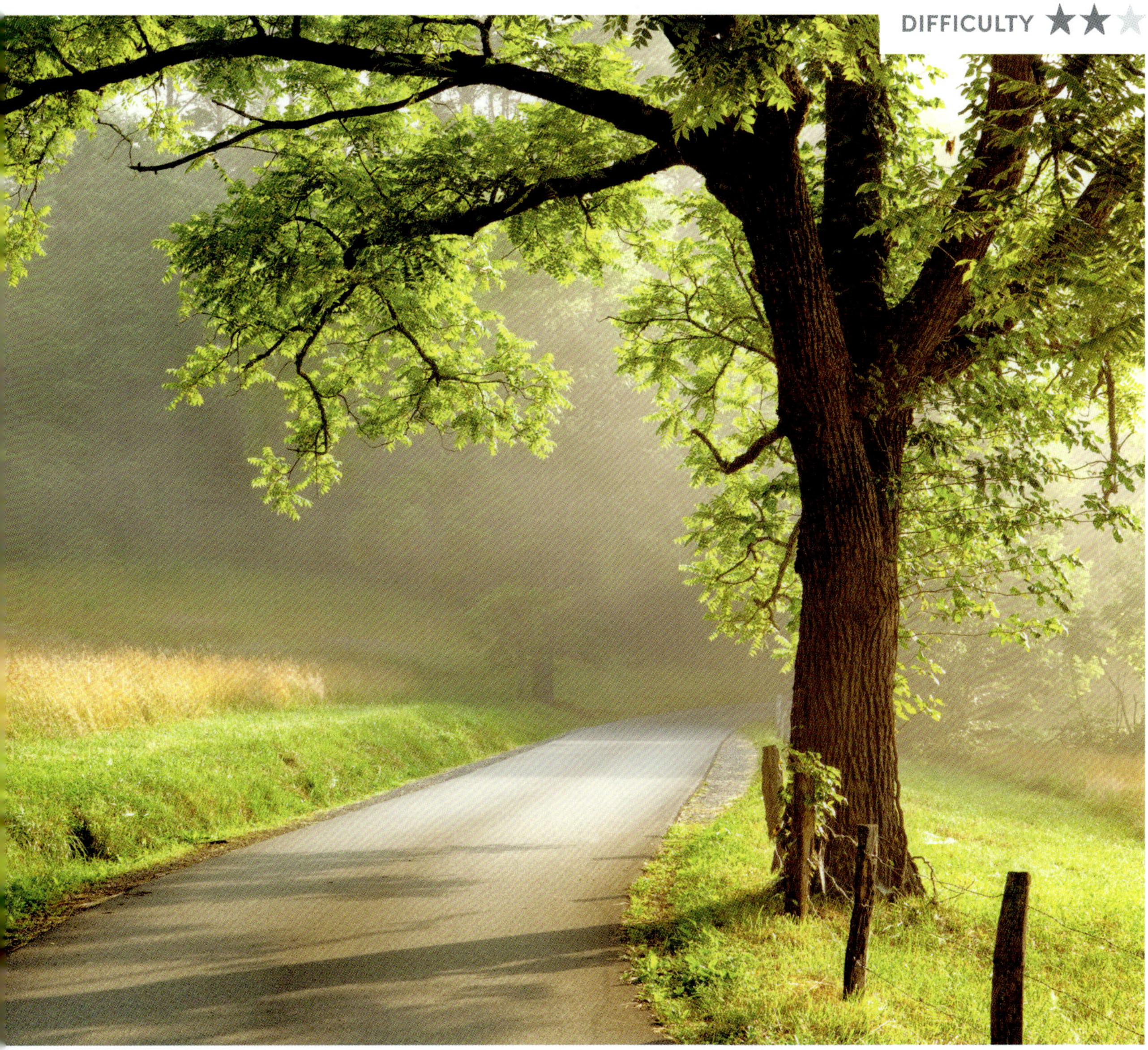

RECOMMENDED SETTINGS

- Shooting mode: **Aperture-priority**
- Aperture: **f/16**
- Shutter speed: **1/125sec (handheld)**
- ISO: **100**
- Focal length: **18–55mm**
- AF area: **Single-point AF**
- AF operation: **Single-shot AF**
- Drive mode: **Single-shot or self-timer**
- Metering mode: **Evaluative/matrix**
- White balance: **Auto or daylight/cloudy**
- Picture style: **Landscape**

FIND NATURAL FRAMING

Camera settings

The most important technical factor here is depth of field and the distance between camera and framing device. Remember that at any given aperture, two-thirds of the depth of field will fall behind the point of focus and only one-third will fall in front, but so long as your framing device sits within your zone of sharpness, it will be sharp.

In the previous module, we briefly discussed hyperfocal distance focusing and how a simplified version of it can be used to achieve front-to-back sharpness using apps such as PhotoPills and HyperFocal Pro and websites such as dofmaster.com. By entering your camera model, focal length and aperture details, these apps and websites will help you figure out whether your framing device falls within your depth of field.

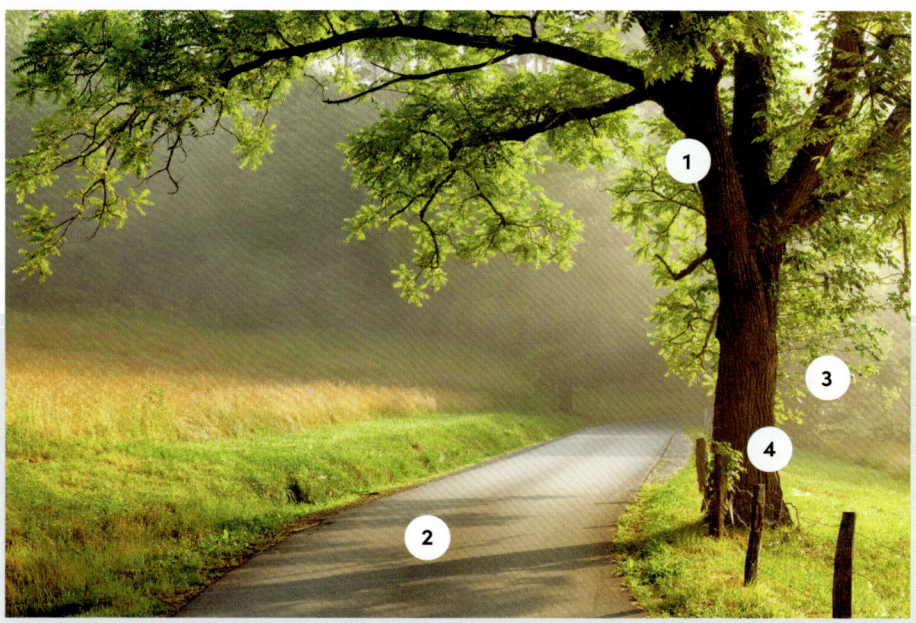

WHY THIS SHOT WORKS

1 This statuesque tree not only provides the perfect framing device for the misty country road and woodland beyond, it also adds interest to an area of the frame that would otherwise be rather empty and uninteresting.

2 The country road – as well as the grassy verge to the left and fence posts to the right – acts as a lead-in line that takes the eye from the bottom edge of the frame through the landscape and into the misty woodland.

3 Early-morning side lighting casts lengthy shadows across the country road and grass verge, adding texture and highlighting the subtle contours. It's a simple enough scene, but there is plenty of detail for the eye to explore.

4 While the colour palette is mostly limited to shades of greens and browns, the low side lighting creates enough contrast and tonal variation to retain interest throughout, with the vivid leaves in particular creating a degree of separation.

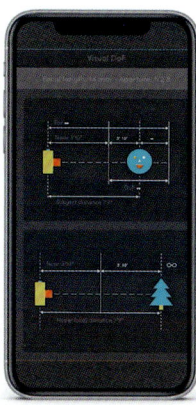

LEFT **PhotoPills and HyperFocal Pro** are powerful apps that will help you visualize where to focus.

RIGHT **DOFMaster's** depth-of-field calculator simplifies the focusing process when shooting landscapes.

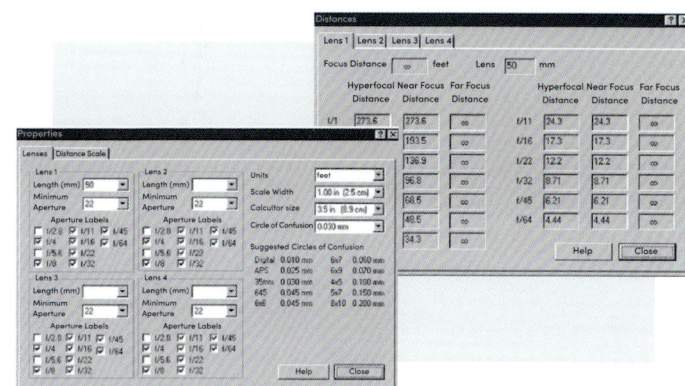

If your framing device is so close to your lens' front element that it falls outside your zone of sharpness, you have three options: increase the physical distance between camera and framing device, use a wider focal length or make a creative decision and accept that it won't be as sharp as the rest of the scene beyond.

With aperture playing such a key role here, we can once again rely on our default landscape settings (I make no apologies for sounding like a broken record!). Here they are again: aperture-priority (A or Av), f/16, ISO 100 (or base value), auto (or daylight or cloudy) white balance, landscape picture style and 3x3 Grid Display. As we're using a small aperture for a larger depth of field, a tripod is always recommended, as is evaluative or matrix metering mode.

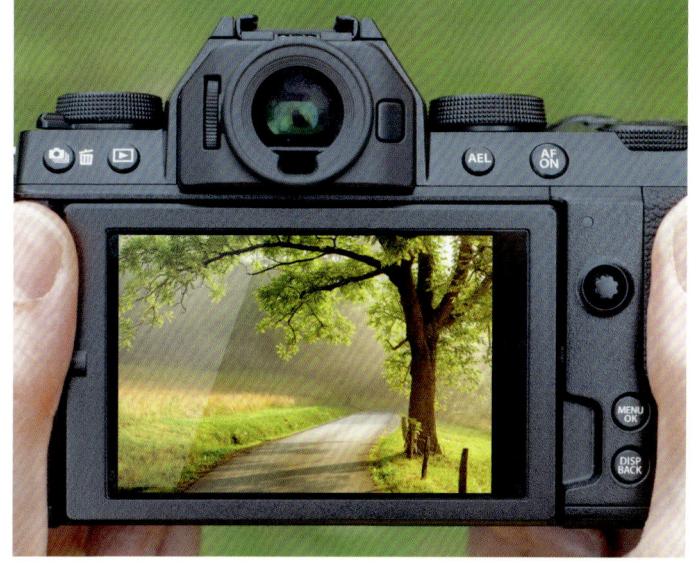

Even as an old-school film photographer weaned on a steady diet of optical viewfinders, I still find it more intuitive to compose landscapes using Live View as you can see any changes to the viewpoint, focal length and settings in real time, so activate this once your camera is mounted on a tripod. Natural framing devices don't necessarily have to conform to standard compositional rules, such as the rule of thirds, but you still need to think about where to position your horizon and focal point.

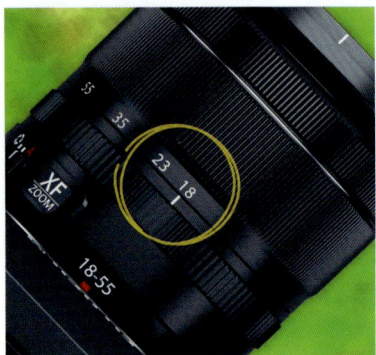

Lens settings

As with foreground interest, your focal length will determine how prominent your framing device appears in the frame, as will the distance between it and your lens' front element. Keeping in mind that wider focal lengths will make objects appear smaller and further away, while telephoto focal lengths will flatten perspective by bringing distant objects closer, start at 18mm and zoom all the way in to 55mm if a narrower field of view helps simplify a busy scene. Our default lens settings of autofocus (AF), single-point AF (AF area) and single-shot AF (AF operation) modes will work perfectly.

Technique

Natural framing devices are most effective when the device itself is thematically linked in some way to the subject being framed. This could be literal (the branches of one tree pointing to another), environmental (clouds surrounding the summit of a mountain) or tonal (pink blossom framing a pink sunset). Whatever the connection, carefully consider your viewpoint and orientation, and pay particular attention to how your framing device and focal point interact and where one 'sits' within the other. Also, consider whether you want to frame your scene on all four sides or within a circle, or just along one or two sides – there's no right or wrong here, just personal preference and artistic vision.

Once you have exhausted all creative possibilities and committed to a particular composition, it's time to attach your camera to a tripod and adjust its height. While this is a simple enough task, there are several 'best practice' techniques you can employ to make sure you are getting the best possible support. Always extend the thickest leg sections first as these are the most stable, followed by the middle sections if you need more height, and the thinnest sections only if absolutely necessary (only ever extend the centre column if the legs are fully extended). If shooting on uneven ground, adjust the height of each leg individually so that the head – the top of the tripod that screws into the camera – remains level, and push down on two legs to check stability. Finally, make sure any image stabilization (IS) features on your camera and/or lens are switched off.

TIP

Many tripods feature a hook at the bottom end of their centre column, which can be used to hang extra weight such as your camera bag for even greater stability (I've known photographers to hang gym weights!). Just don't use this technique on windy days – the ballast will act as a sail and introduce unwanted movement.

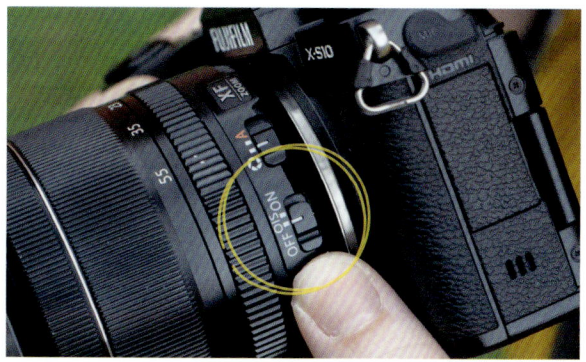 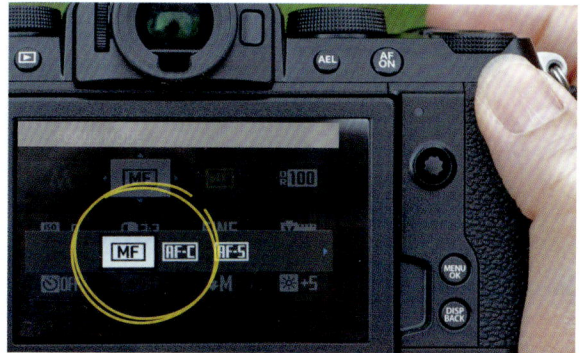

You should be well versed in the focusing technique by now – position your AF point roughly a third of the way into the scene, half-press the shutter to engage AF, and flick the AF/MF switch to MF to lock focus. Take a 'test' shot using a remote shutter release or self-timer mode, and use Live View to assess the composition and review sharpness. As always, use exposure compensation to lighten or darken the exposure.

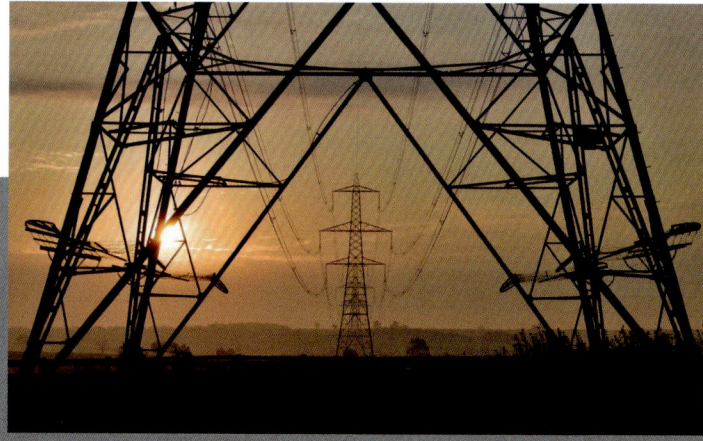

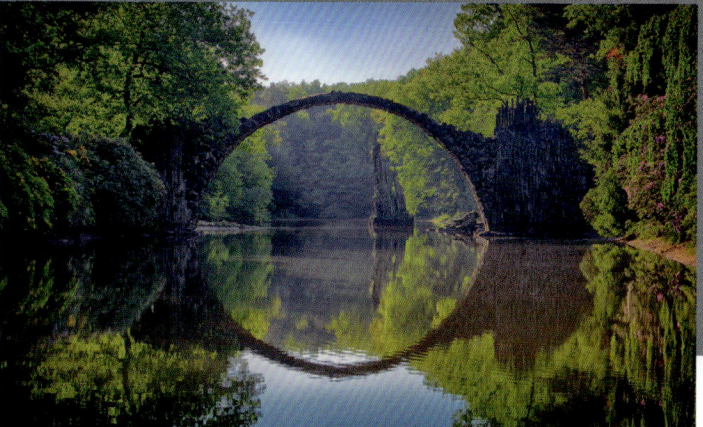

SHOOTING INSPIRATION

Once you start looking, you will find framing devices in the most unlikely of places.

ABOVE LEFT The strong geometric shapes of these electricity pylons provide a stark counterpoint to the freeflowing landscape beyond.

LEFT This bridge's mirror-like reflection creates an almost perfect O-shaped frame.

Module 1.5
Inject movement

Although we often refer to photographs as 'stills', landscapes are never as static as they might first appear. In fact, they are truly dynamic subjects – water ebbs and flows, clouds glide effortlessly across the sky and grasses dance in the gentlest of breezes. With relatively simple camera skills, we can capture this movement in our 'stills' and add another creative layer to our scenic images. Deliberate movement (as opposed to camera shake and/or poor camera technique) is called 'motion blur' and is a technique popular with wildlife and action photographers who want to convey a sense of energy and speed.

Traditional landscape photographers tend to gravitate towards certain subjects, with mountains, waterfalls, rivers, trees and the sea being particular favourites. These are all location types where movement is evident, even if that movement is as subtle as a single leaf fluttering in the wind or a small stream bubbling over shiny rocks. In our sun-kissed image of Bamburgh Castle on the wild and windy Northumberland coast in the UK, it's the motion blur in the foreground marram grass that provides the visual energy. With such a well-photographed location, techniques such as this can help your images stand out from the crowd.

There are three essential components to successful motion blur photography: shutter speed, available light and camera stability. Shutter speeds need to be slow enough to capture moving objects travelling from one position in the frame to another and while there is no such thing as a definitive 'slow' shutter speed, I'd suggest 1/60 second as a solid starting point. It's worth noting, however, that 'slow' is relative to the speed of the moving object and its distance from the camera. As shutter speeds need to be longer, light levels need to be lower and so dawn and dusk – the golden hours referred to on page 19 – are the best times to capture motion blur without the need for specialist filters. Handholding isn't an option at 1/60 second and slower, so a sturdy tripod is crucial.

DIFFICULTY ★★★

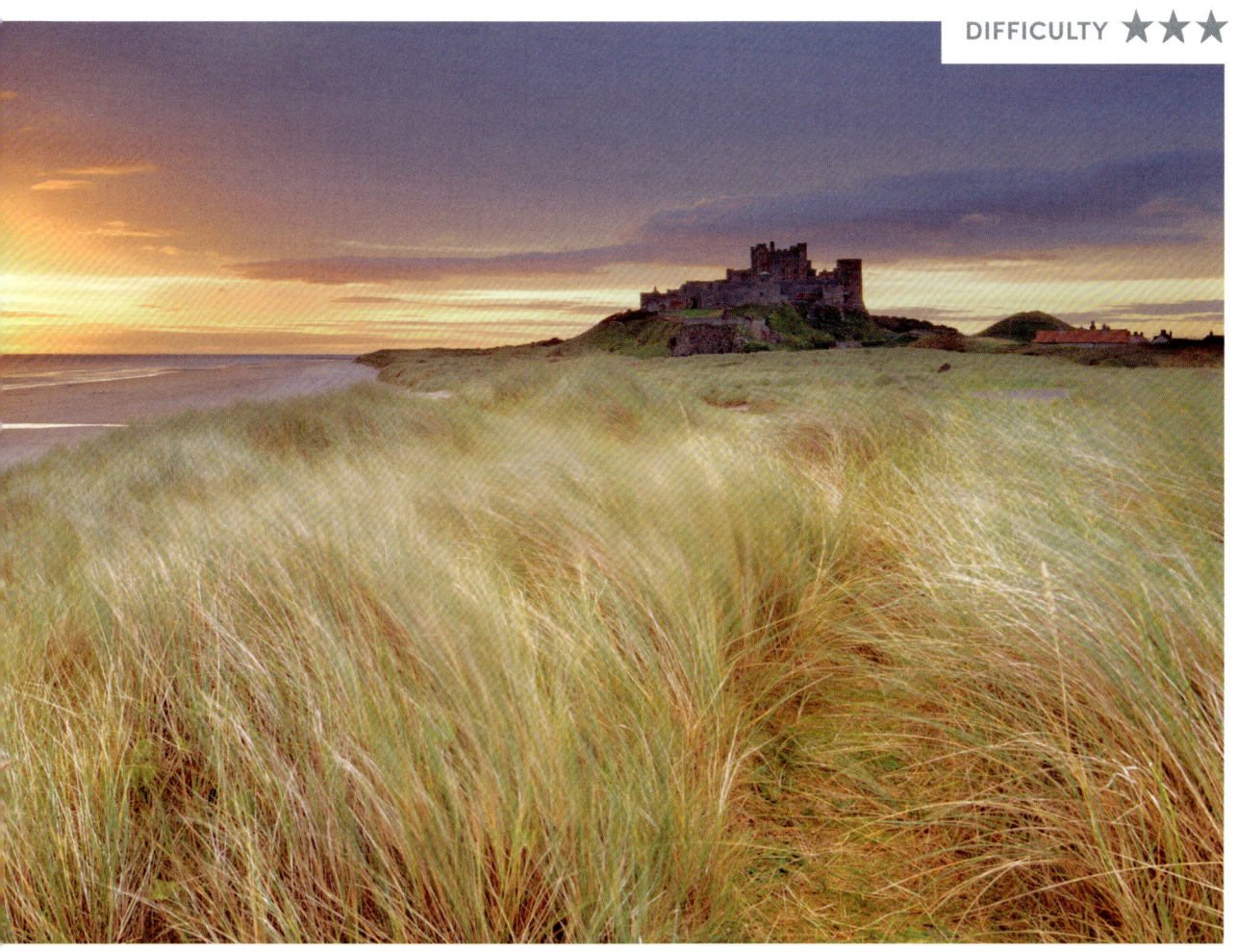

ABOVE **Even a subtle sense of movement can transform a traditional landscape image.**

RECOMMENDED SETTINGS

- Shooting mode: **Aperture-priority**
- Aperture: **ƒ/16–ƒ/22**
- Shutter speed: **1/60sec or slower**
- ISO: **100 (or 'L')**
- Focal length: **18–55mm**
- AF area: **Single-point AF**
- AF operation: **Single-shot AF**
- Drive mode: **Single-shot or self-timer**
- Metering mode: **Evaluative/matrix**
- White balance: **Auto or daylight/cloudy**
- Picture style: **Landscape**

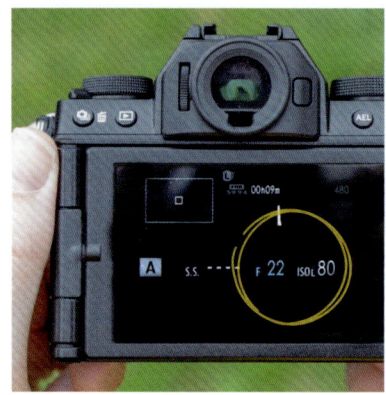

Camera settings

The aim when incorporating motion blur into your landscapes is to minimize the amount of light entering your lens and extend exposure times. As well as shooting at the ends of the day when the sun is lower in the sky, we can achieve this by using smaller apertures and lower ISOs. This is one of the reasons why we are still going to work in aperture-priority – as important as shutter speed is for this technique, this semi-automatic exposure mode allows us to control aperture and depth of field, as the usual rules of landscape photography still apply.

So far, we have stuck rigidly to f/16 as our aperture of choice and this is a sensible choice here too, although you might want to close down to f/22 if you need a longer shutter speed and are prepared to sacrifice a degree of image quality and sharpness.

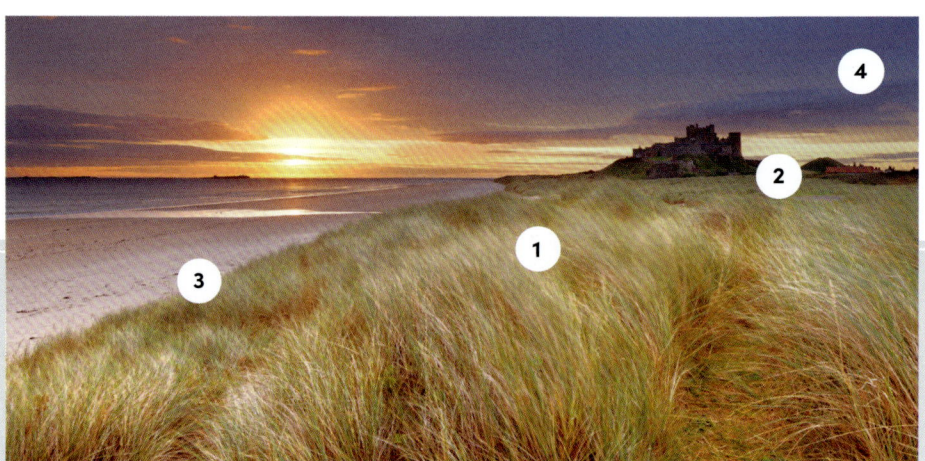

WHY THIS SHOT WORKS

1 The subtle motion blur in the foreground marram grass adds an extra creative element that helps images of well-photographed locations stand out from the crowd. You can almost feel the wind in your hair!

2 Static elements help to emphasize any motion blur caused by moving elements elsewhere in the frame. Here, the huge castle in the distance provides an unmoving counterpoint to the marram grass's ethereal sway.

3 So many lead-in lines! The shoreline, beach and subtle lines within the grassy foreground all point to the castle in the distance, moving the eye from the bottom of the frame to the focal point.

4 Just look at that sky! By shooting at dawn, moments after the sun has crept above the horizon, the photographer has captured a beautifully warm and radiant sky full of deep blues and purples.

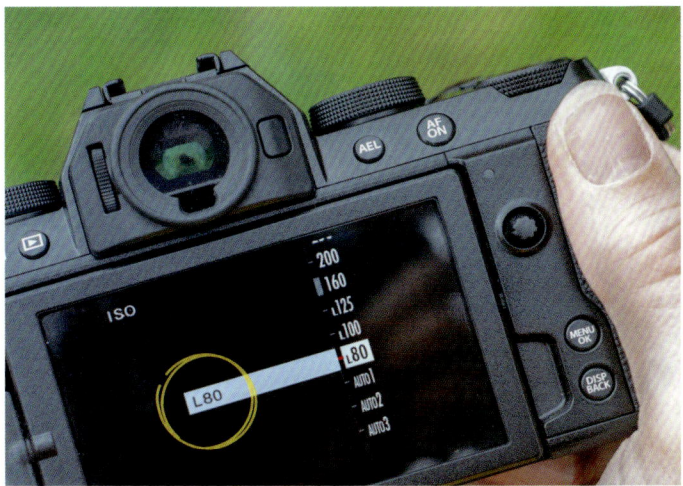
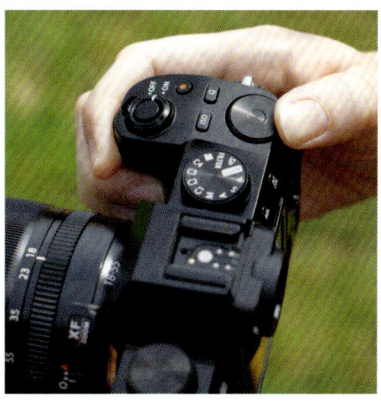

When it comes to ISO, we can explore new options. Many modern DSLRs and mirrorless cameras now feature an 'extended' ISO range, which allows you to select ISO values beyond your camera's 'native' ISO range, thanks to some clever computational wizardry. For instance, Sony's Alpha 7 III has a native ISO range of 100–51,200 and an extended ISO of 50, while Fujifilm's X-T4 has a native ISO range of 160–12,800 and an extended ISO of 80. These extended settings are found on your camera's ISO dial or in the menu, with 'L' standing for 'low'. While not a feature I would recommend you use often, now is the perfect time to set ISO to 'L' if you have the option.

There's no 'perfect' shutter speed for capturing motion blur, as it depends on the speed of your moving subject. Crashing waves in high winds move quickly and so shutter speeds between 1/60 second and 1/15 second will capture a certain amount of blur while retaining just enough shape and definition, whereas tall grasses in a gentle breeze can move almost imperceptibly and so shutter speeds of 1/8 second and slower may be needed. Experiment to find the shutter speed that matches your artistic vision (and time of day), adjusting aperture and ISO accordingly, and take plenty of shots – digital photos cost nothing, after all.

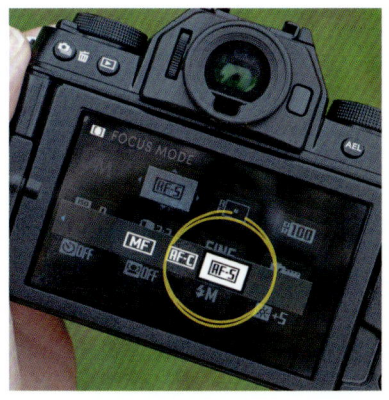

Lens settings

The same recommendations apply here as with all previous modules. If you want to capture an expansive view, start by zooming out to 18mm and slowly zooming back in to exclude any distracting elements. If your moving subject doubles up as foreground interest, as it does in some of our example photographs, remember that your focal length and the distance between it and your camera will affect how dominant it appears in your image. As always, our default lens settings of autofocus (AF), single-point AF (AF area) and single-shot AF (AF operation) modes will work just fine here.

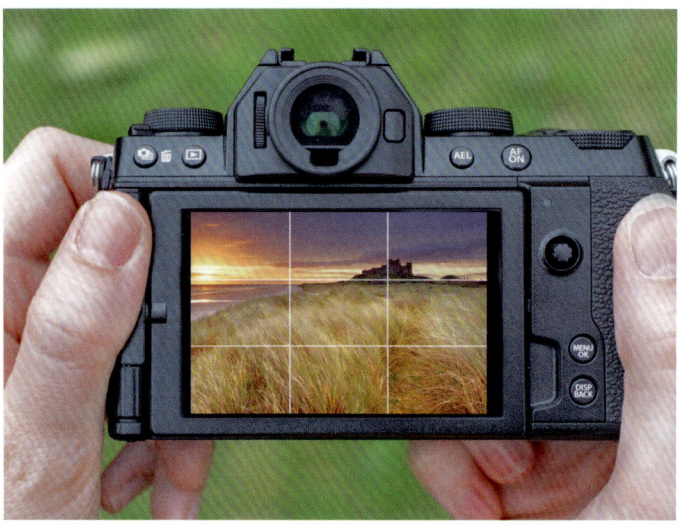

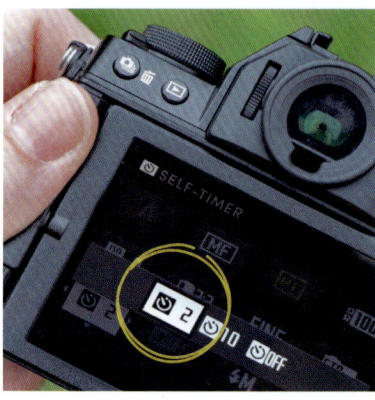

Technique

In terms of composition, this is the perfect opportunity to put everything you have learned so far into practice. Think about whether you want to emphasize land or sky and use the rule-of-thirds grid to position your horizon accordingly; draw the viewer's eye to a particular object by placing your focal point on a power point; add some foreground interest to create a visual 'stepping stone' into the image; use lead-in lines to guide the viewer's eye and create a sense of depth; think about viewpoint and consider shooting from ground level to emphasize your foreground interest; experiment with your camera's orientation, and look for any natural framing devices.

If you don't have a remote shutter release, you'll need to select your camera's self-timer. This drive mode delays the shutter by a set amount of time and alleviates any camera shake caused by manually squeezing the shutter. Most cameras have two self-timer options – 2 seconds and 10 seconds – and some even let you set your own time. When timing isn't an important factor and you want to be super-cautious, the 10-second setting is a sensible choice. When timing is important, however, the 2-second delay may be a better choice, as not all moving subjects are easy to predict.

TIP

Salt water is a photographer's worst enemy so if you decide to shoot crashing waves at the coast, waterproof your camera to protect it from splashes. Dedicated 'rain' covers are available from most photo retailers, though a simple plastic bag will suffice in emergencies. Also, always hose down your tripod when you get home, as salt water will corrode the legs and joints.

To focus, use our tried-and-trusted method of positioning your single AF point one-third of the way into the frame, using an app such as PhotoPills to help you visualize where to focus if needed. As we are using a semi-automatic exposure mode, once we have taken our 'test' shot and reviewed it on the rear LCD screen, we can use exposure compensation to tweak brightness. For instance, waterfalls in shaded gorges can appear brighter than their surroundings, which can cause overexposure (when highlights become pure white and all detail is lost). If this happens, reduce the exposure by –1 stop and try again.

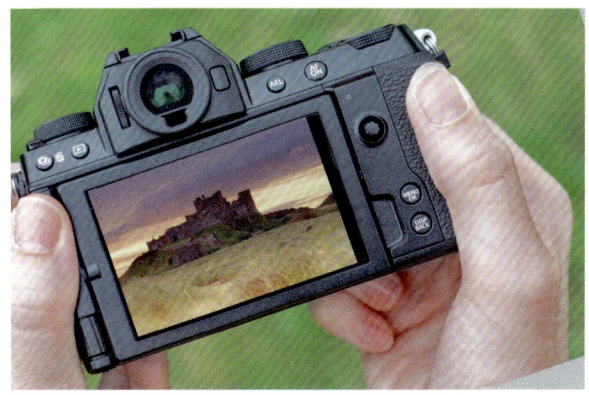

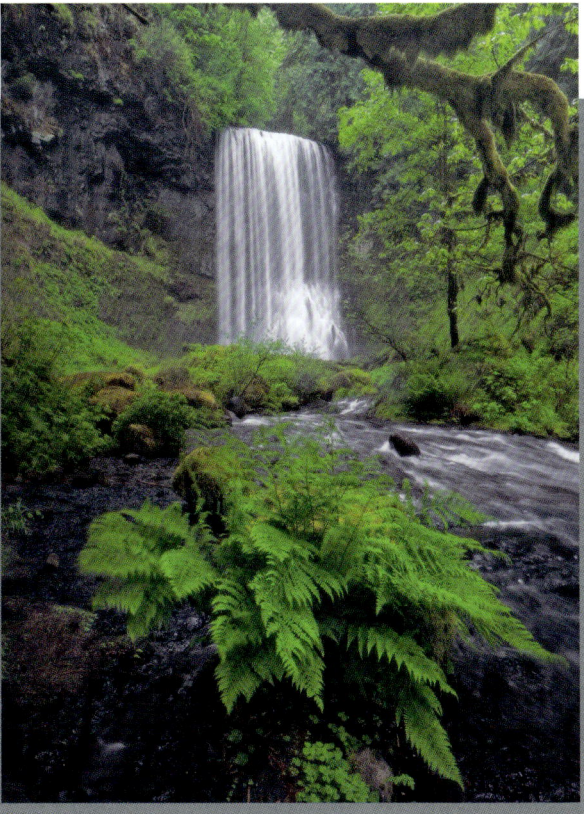

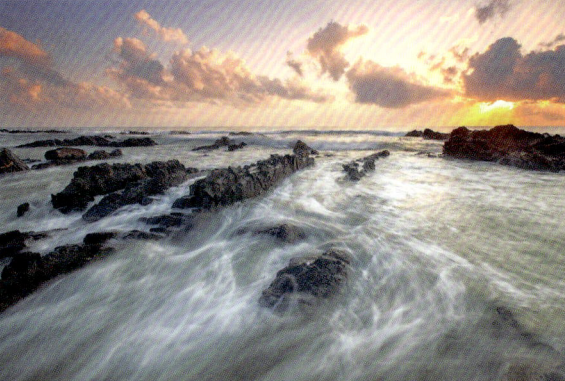

SHOOTING INSPIRATION

Use the motion blur technique to add visual interest and to provide contrast between static and dynamic elements in your scene.

ABOVE **Moving water crashing against jagged rocks is a classic combination that will always create impact.**

LEFT **Motion blur doesn't always need to take centre stage – here it provides a more restrained focal point.**

INJECT MOVEMENT

Module 1.6
Get abstract

Now that we've learned the basic rules, it's time to throw the rulebook away and embrace our inner anarchist. School's out, folks! Landscape photography can be a very conservative genre in which sharpness and detail are hugely important factors, meaning that camera shake is usually something to be avoided at all costs, but what happens when you exaggerate its effects by deliberately moving the camera while the shutter is open? You end up with a popular technique known as 'intentional camera movement' (ICM), a creative style more concerned with abstraction and impressionism than technical perfection.

ICM is a fun yet experimental approach that has the power to transform ordinary scenes into dynamic streaks of light and colour by 'spreading' a scene across your camera's sensor in the same way that an artist might brush his paint across the canvas. When used with skill, the results can have more in common with J. M. W. Turner and Claude Monet than landscape photography standard-bearers such as Ansel Adams and Edward Weston. The only downside is that it can be rather hit and miss and so a degree of patience and perseverance is required, as is the ability to visualize which scenes and subjects will work and which won't.

Your shutter speed needs to be slow enough to allow you to move the camera mid-exposure and this will typically fall between 1/30 second and 1 second. Any faster and there won't be enough time for you to capture enough blur; any slower and you risk losing any semblance of detail – although individual leaves, grasses and clouds will lose their definition, ICM works best when your subject is still vaguely recognizable. You can move the camera up and down, side to side or freestyle (I've actually seen photographers throw their cameras in the air!), though I would recommend you follow the lines of your landscape at first – left to right for seascapes and country scenes with strong horizontal lines, and up and down for subjects with strong vertical lines such as trees.

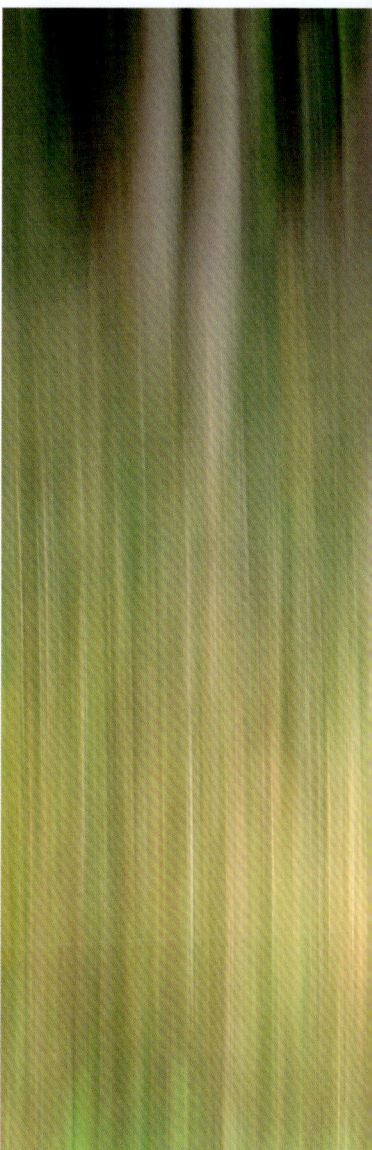

ABOVE Trees are the perfect ICM subject, as they remain recognizable even when blurred.

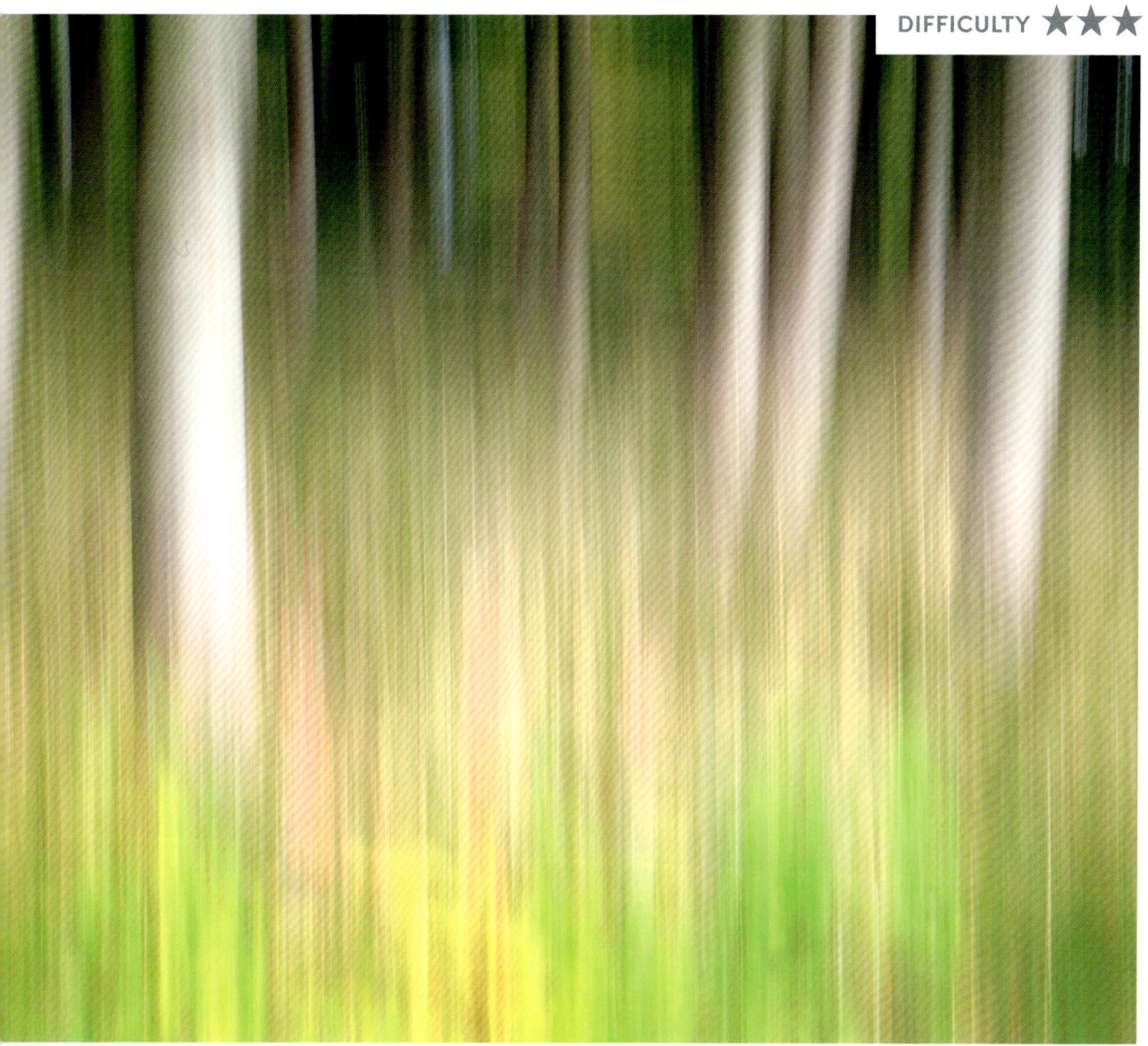

DIFFICULTY ★★★

RECOMMENDED SETTINGS

- Shooting mode: **Shutter-priority**
- Aperture: **Any**
- Shutter speed: **1/30sec to 1 second**
- ISO: **100**
- Focal length: **23mm**
- AF area: **Single-point AF**
- AF operation: **Single-shot AF**
- Drive mode: **Single-shot**
- Metering mode: **Evaluative/matrix**
- White balance: **Auto or daylight/cloudy**
- Picture style: **Landscape**

Camera settings

As the basis of ICM technique is a slow enough exposure, we are going to break with convention and select shutter-priority. This is a semi-automatic shooting mode that allows us to take control of shutter speed while the camera selects the corresponding aperture. Shutter-priority or time value is abbreviated to S or Tv and can be found on your camera's mode dial. Visually, aperture is largely irrelevant for ICM and will have only the slightest impact on the final result, so don't worry about trying to maximize depth of field – different rules apply here.

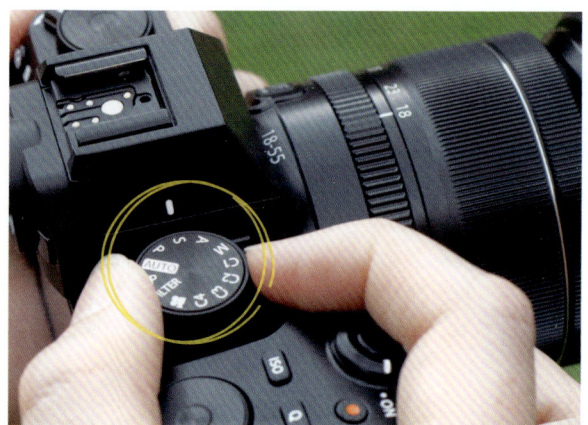

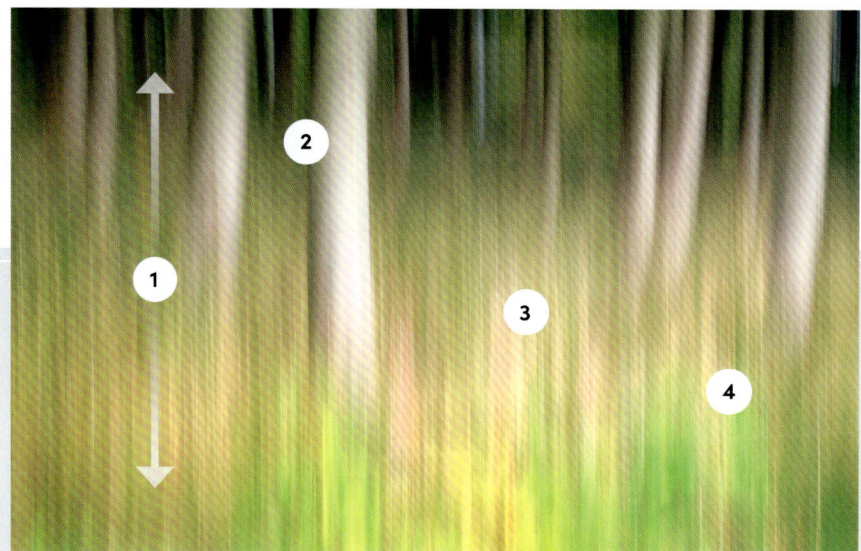

WHY THIS SHOT WORKS

1 A smooth up-and-down 'panning' action has resulted in an impressive ICM image with clean vertical lines that perfectly complement the straight lines in the natural environment.

2 The colours and contrasts provided by the grass and silver birch trees in the foreground and the darker woodland in the background give the image a greater sense of depth and interest.

3 Using a shutter speed between 1/30 second and 1 second gave the photographer enough time to smoothly pan the camera and capture just the right amount of blur and detail.

4 Location and/or time of day are essential to successful ICM images and dense woodlands such as this, and provide the perfect low-light conditions for long exposures.

The 'perfect' shutter speed will depend on your scene, subject and artistic vision, though I'd recommend you start at 1/2 second and experiment for the best results: faster shutter speeds will produce more subtle effects while slower shutter speeds will yield more abstract results. Unlike film cameras, digital cameras allow us to review our shots immediately and mistakes cost nothing, so change settings and move the camera at different speeds until you find an exposure and direction of movement that suits your subject.

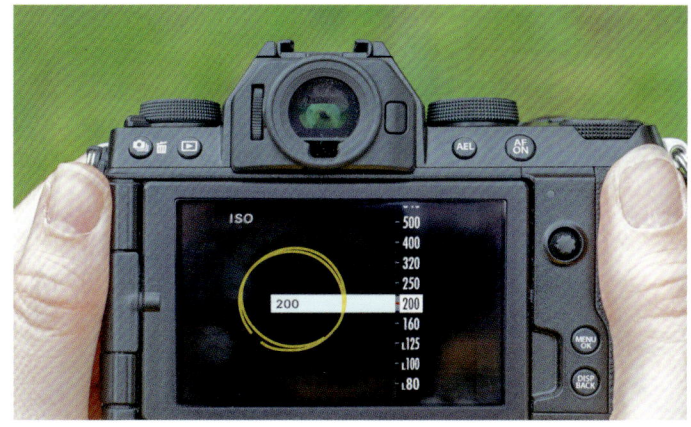

As ICM depends on long exposures, ISO should be set to your camera's base value so that the sensor is at its least sensitive to light. If this means that you can't achieve a slow enough shutter speed, wait until light levels drop sufficiently – shooting at dawn or dusk, waiting for an overcast day or shooting in sheltered woodland will all provide suitably ICM-friendly low-light conditions.

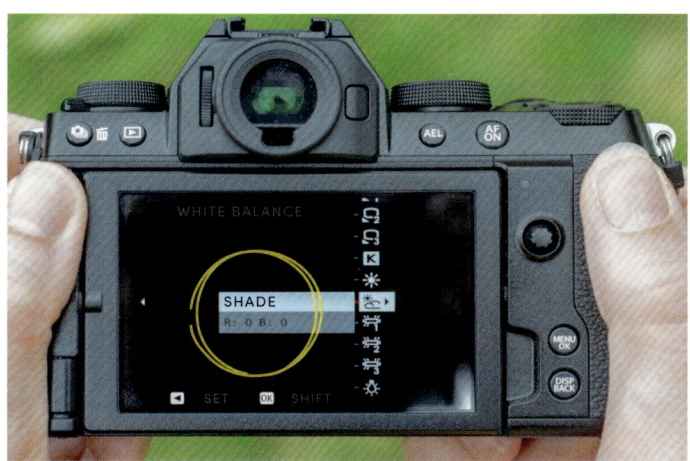

Other camera settings follow more traditional landscape conventions. As we are shooting in natural light, auto white balance will deliver consistently neutral colours, or you could select the daylight or cloudy presets if you prefer.

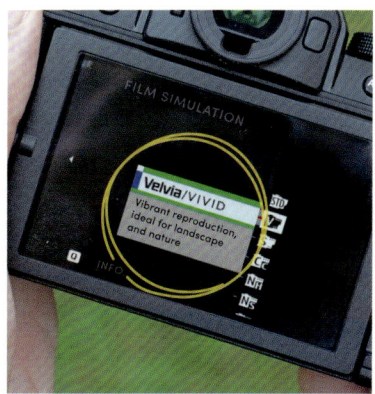

ICM images often benefit from punchy colours so select the Landscape preset from your camera's Picture Style menu to inject an extra degree of saturation.

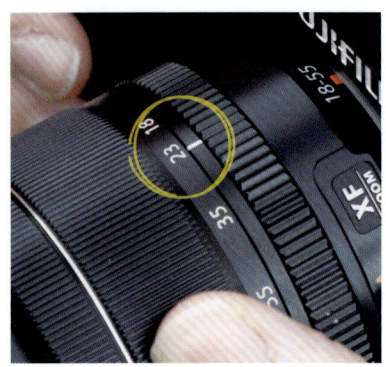

Lens settings

At wider focal lengths, vertical lines near the edges of the frame can appear to swell outwards – an optical imperfection known as 'barrel' distortion – and even though ICM is an inherently abstract technique, this is an effect we want to avoid, particularly if shooting popular subjects such as trees. To ensure distortion-free verticals, start with your kit lens at 23mm, as this will give you an effective focal length of around 35mm, and don't zoom out any wider. Also, with the subject still needing to be recognizable, autofocus (AF), single-point AF (AF area) and single-shot AF (AF operation) modes are still relevant.

Technique

Despite its impressionist nature, accurate focusing is still an important part of ICM. If you are shooting more traditional landscape subjects such as coastal views, mountains or rolling hills, use the same focusing method as before; if shooting trees, position your active AF point over the trunk nearest the camera, half-press the shutter to engage AF and switch to manual focus (MF) once focus has been found to lock it off. This means you can now forget about focusing and concentrate on moving, or 'panning', the camera.

Start by panning along a single plane, either up and down or side to side – there's plenty of time to go freestyle once you have mastered the technique. Tuck your elbows into your body and use your body rather than your arms to create the movement, rotating your hips or arching your back to ensure a smoother, more fluid action. It's good practice to start the pan a split-second before you press the shutter and continue moving until after the shutter closes. I can almost guarantee that your first few efforts won't be keepers – it often takes me at least half a dozen attempts before I get anything like a decent ICM image – but persevere and you will soon get the hang of it.

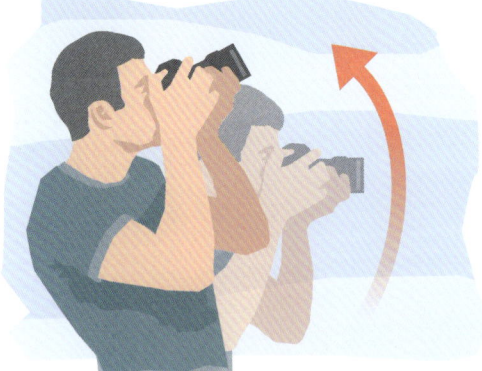

LEFT To achieve a fluid vertical pan, keep your elbows tucked in and arch your back rather than just move your arms.

TIP

ICM isn't restricted to just up-and-down or side-to-side actions – you could try shaking the camera, rotating it like a steering wheel and even holding it still for the majority of the exposure and only moving it a split-second before the shutter closes. Experimentation is the key to ICM success.

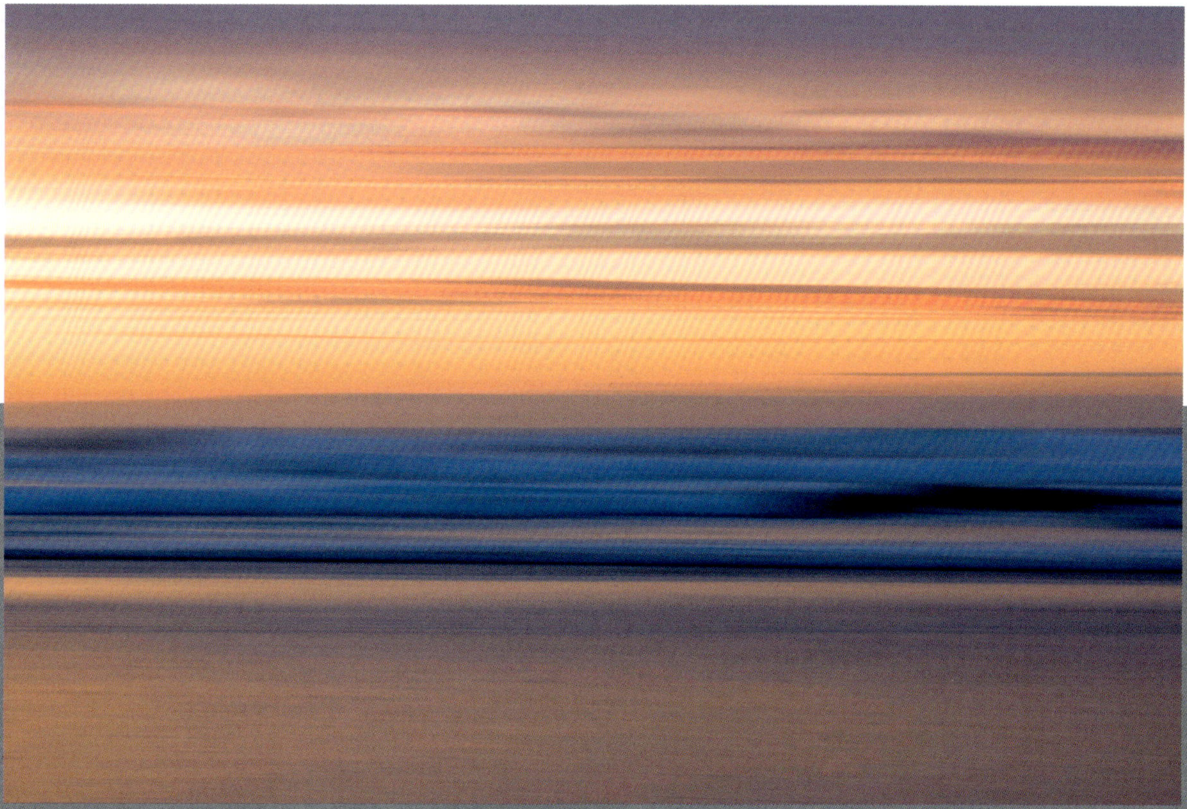

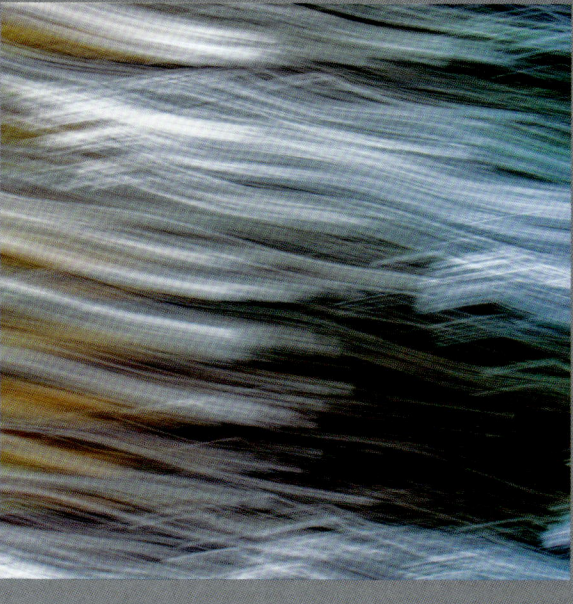

SHOOTING INSPIRATION

ICM is a surprisingly versatile technique that can be used to abstract even the most traditional of subjects – and can even create abstraction as a subject in itself.

ABOVE The strong horizontal lines of this sun-kissed seascape demanded a smooth left-to-right panning motion.

LEFT Even more abstract results can be achieved with jerkier pans, longer shutter speeds and less obvious subject matter.

GET ABSTRACT

Module 1.7
Use your illusion

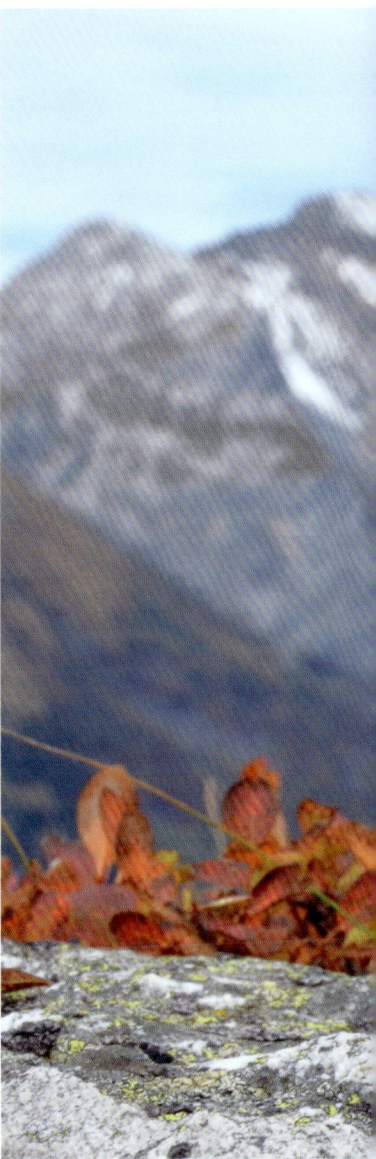

ABOVE **Forced perspective can trick the viewer into thinking they're looking at the real thing, if only for a second.**

Until now, the landscape has played the starring role, dazzling us with its ability to change appearance at the whim of the weather and time of day. But it can also play a supporting role and lend its realism to other more imaginative ideas. We've all seen snapshots of holidaymakers cupping the sun in the palm of their hands and tourists propping up the Leaning Tower of Pisa – it's almost compulsory when you visit the Italian city. These playful images use a simple optical illusion known as 'forced perspective' and here we are going to look at how we can use this technique to make the viewer look twice.

A few years ago, a then-unknown Swiss photographer by the name of Kim Leuenberger started posting images of toy cars in the landscape on her Instagram page (@kim.ou). These forced-perspective images – of an old VW camper van and Beetle in sand, snow and city streets – proved so popular that they started a craze. Kim's secret weapon was her ability to combine her subjects, locations and camera technique in such a seamless way that viewers were left guessing whether the toy car was real or not. And that is the genius of forced perspective – you can make objects appear larger or smaller, closer or further away, just by adopting a different way of 'seeing'.

For a heightened sense of realism, viewpoint is the most important compositional consideration. Imagine you are looking at the 'face' of a real camper van – at standing height, you would be able to see the windscreen, the headlights and possibly part of the roof depending on how tall you are. Now imagine you are looking at a toy camper van from the same standing height – it would look so much smaller and you would only be able to see the roof as you would be forced to look down. To transfer the real-world viewpoint to your forced perspective image, you would need to adopt a much lower 'eye-level' shooting position, which may mean laying on the ground or finding an elevated platform on which to position your toy car.

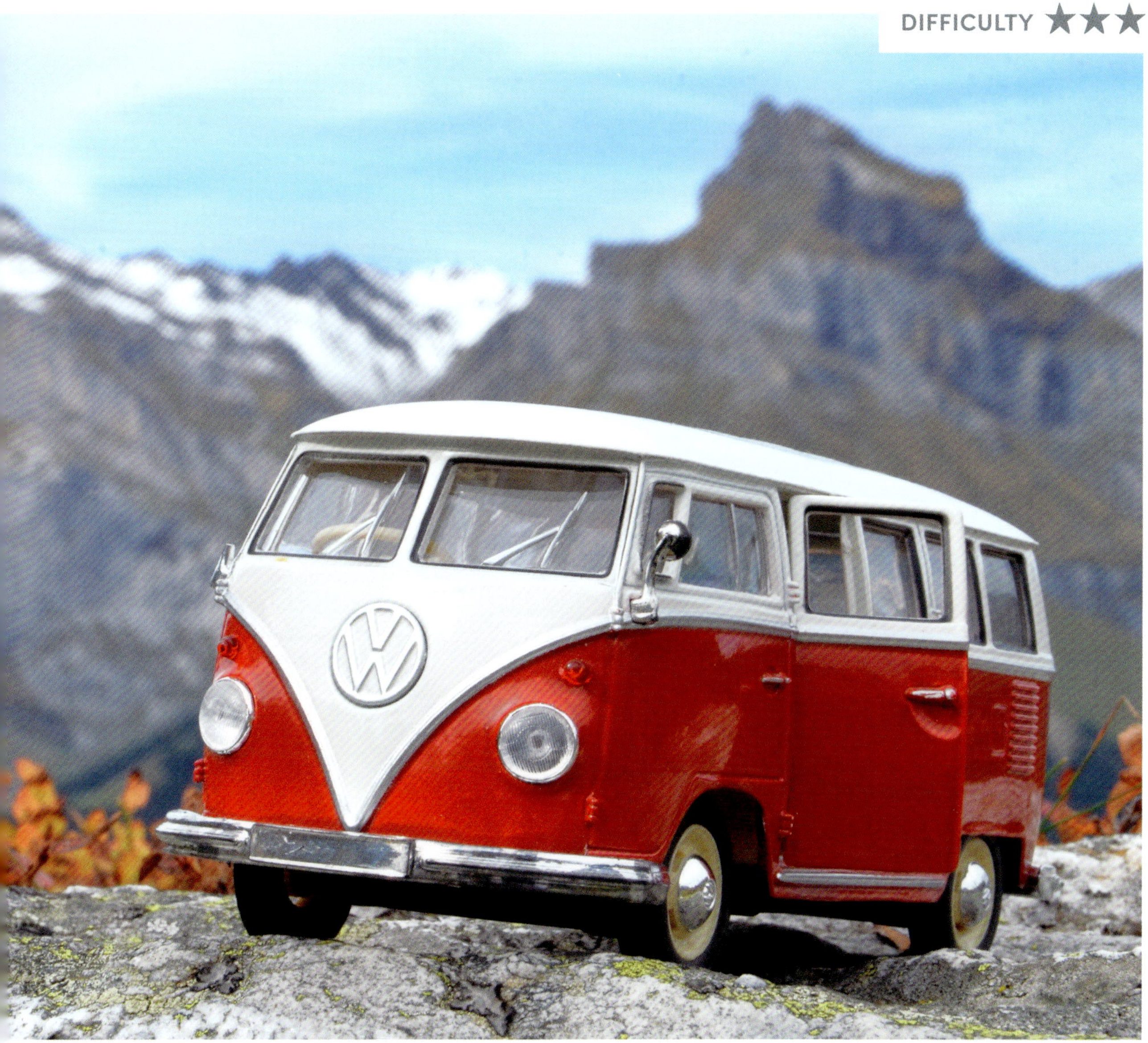

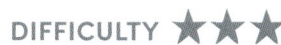

RECOMMENDED SETTINGS

- Shooting mode: **Aperture-priority**
- Aperture: **f/5.6**
- Shutter speed: **1/125sec** (if shooting handheld)
- ISO: **100**
- Focal length: **23mm**
- AF area: **Single-point AF**
- AF operation: **Single-shot AF**
- Drive mode: **Single-shot**
- Metering mode: **Evaluative/matrix**
- White balance: **Auto or daylight/cloudy**
- Picture style: **Landscape**

USE YOUR ILLUSION 45

Camera settings

The most effective forced perspective landscape images are those that fool the eye into thinking that objects near and far are of the same scale. This is often achieved by using a wide aperture and shallow depth of field to create a degree of separation between toy and background, focusing all attention on the subject while throwing the rest of the scene out of focus.

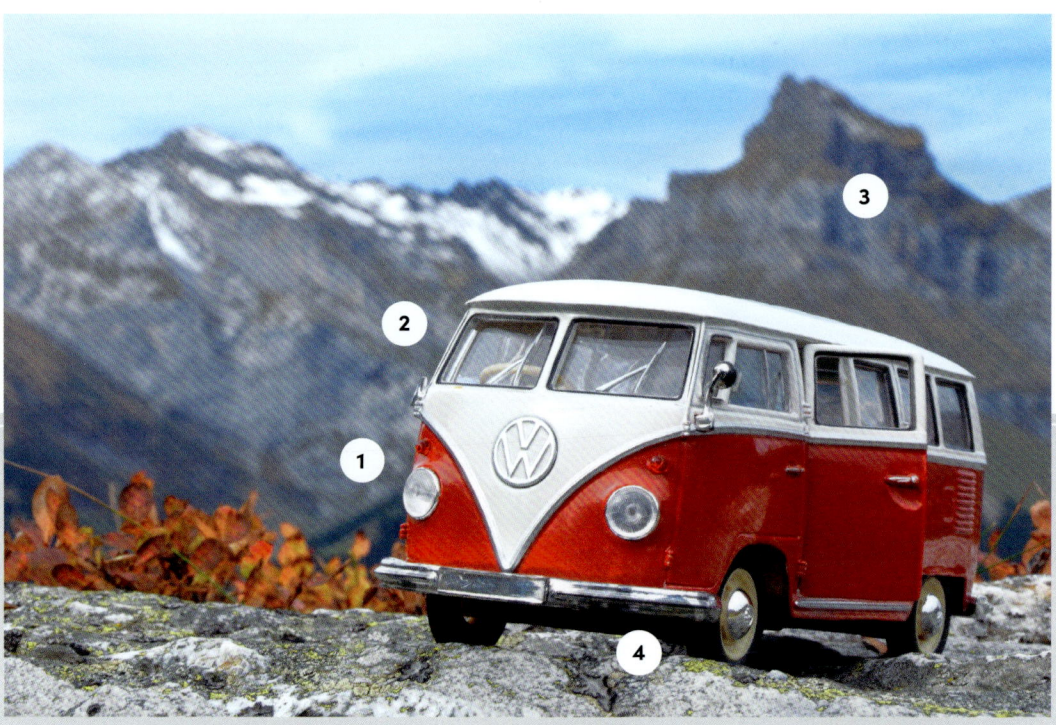

WHY THIS SHOT WORKS

1 This classic VW camper van feels right at home among the mountainous scenery. You can almost hear its engine chug away as it climbs the narrow, twisting roads. A sleek sports car or a less realistic toy would shatter the illusion.

2 The 'eye-level' viewpoint and angle of the van heightens the sense of realism, which is further enhanced by the open door – attention to detail is vitally important when the viewer's attention is directed solely at one subject.

3 The use of a wide aperture has limited the depth of field and created a degree of separation between the VW camper van in the foreground and the snow-capped mountains beyond.

4 The 'face' of the toy car is absolutely pin-sharp. Think of the windscreen and headlights as the 'eyes' of a portrait – this is where the viewer's attention is first directed, so accurate focusing is critical.

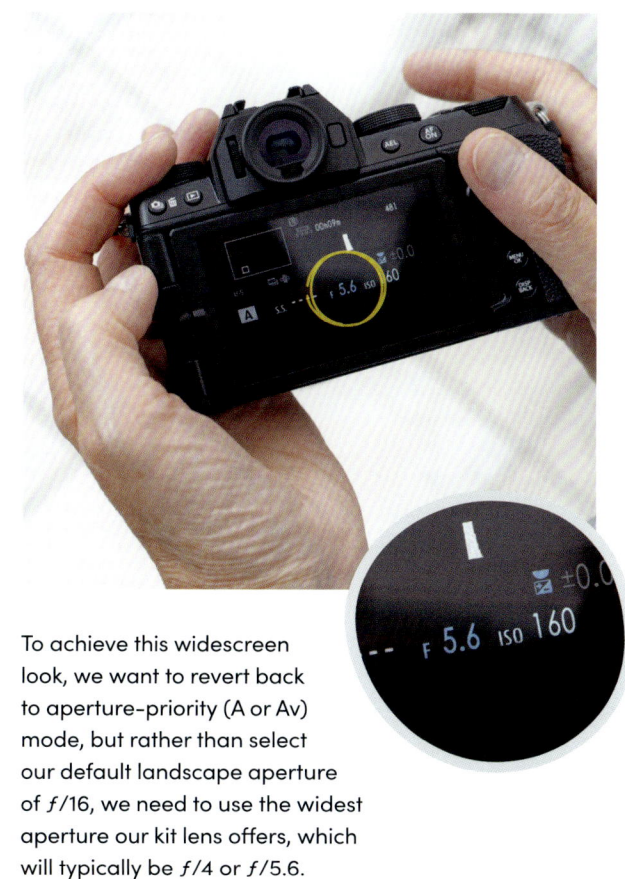
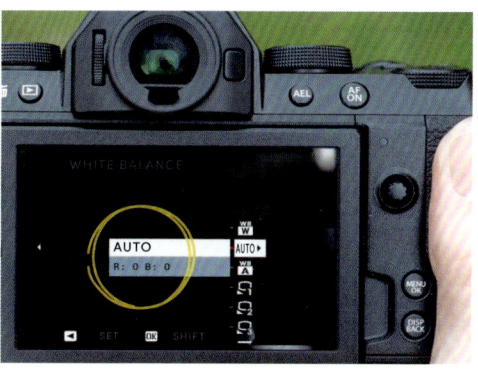

To achieve this widescreen look, we want to revert back to aperture-priority (A or Av) mode, but rather than select our default landscape aperture of *f*/16, we need to use the widest aperture our kit lens offers, which will typically be *f*/4 or *f*/5.6.

Set ISO to 100 (or whatever your camera's lowest native base value is) for the best possible image quality, leave white balance on auto (or daylight or cloudy) for neutral colours, and select the Landscape preset in the Picture Style menu for added saturation. Although the camera will be calculating shutter speeds, it is worth keeping an eye on this setting if you are shooting handheld (you don't need to worry about it if you are using a tripod). Aim to keep your exposures above 1/125 second – this is always my handholding limit whenever focusing is important – and raise ISO to 200 (or beyond) if a faster shutter speed is needed.

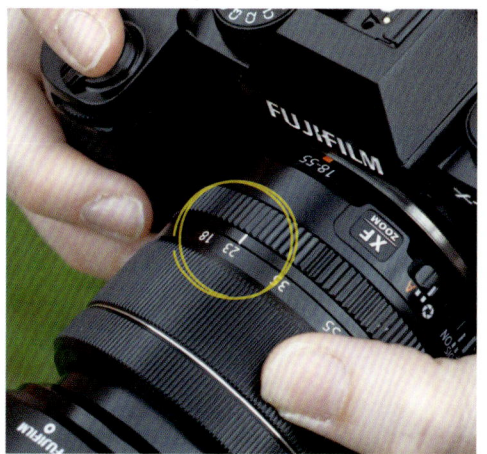

Lens settings

Curiously, when it comes to lens settings, forced perspective has much in common with ICM, particularly if our main subject is positioned anywhere near the edges of the frame. As we want our toy car to look as realistic as possible, we want to avoid any kind of optical distortion and so it is best to avoid wider focal lengths. Instead, start at 23mm, which will give you a subtle wide-angle field of view, and zoom in slightly to exclude unwanted detail if necessary. As always, set autofocus (AF), single-point AF (AF area) and single-shot AF (AF operation), and if shooting handheld switch image stabilization (IS) on as this will help you keep your camera super-steady (make sure IS is switched off if using a tripod).

Technique

With beaches, rocky paths and grassy fields being such popular settings for forced perspective images involving toy cars (or any kind of realistic models), laying on the ground for an eye-level view may be your only option. As not everyone wants to risk getting wet and/or dirty, it may be worth packing a ground sheet or bin bag, just in case – you may get a few curious looks from passers-by, but it may also save you from staining that favourite t-shirt. And as most tripods will only spread so low, you may need to improvise when it comes to camera support at ground level – kit bags, beanbags and even rolled-up jumpers could be used.

When framing up, consider the rules of composition we have discussed so far, in particular the rule of thirds and foreground interest. Position your toy car on a power point for balance and impact, and position other important visual elements, such as the horizon or distant mountains, on a vertical or horizontal grid line. If you look at Kim Leuenberger's images – the project is called 'Travelling Cars Adventures' and is well worth a few minutes of your time, if only for inspiration – she often positions stones, leaves and grass between her models and camera to create realistic out-of-focus foreground interest.

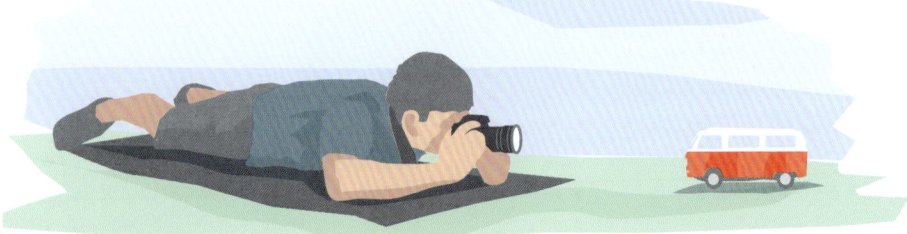

RIGHT **A simple binbag will save your clothes from getting wet or dirty when shooting close to the ground.**

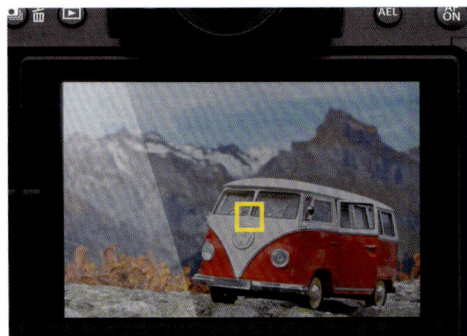

Our focusing technique differs for this technique due to the wide aperture we are shooting at. While small apertures such as $f/16$ create a large depth of field that spans from just in front of the camera to infinity, wide apertures such as $f/4$ and $f/5.6$ produce a much shallower depth of field, which means that accurate focusing is much more critical. Position your active AF point over the 'face' of your model and use Live View and the zoom/magnify button to ensure your subject is absolutely pin-sharp, angling your camera's rear LCD screen if shooting at an awkward angle.

TIP

Interesting angles and settings that could imply dynamic movement are a great way to create the illusion that your toy car is travelling through the scene. Look for rocky shorelines, road markings and fallen tree trunks, and remember that diagonal lead-in lines are the most effective at conveying a sense of depth.

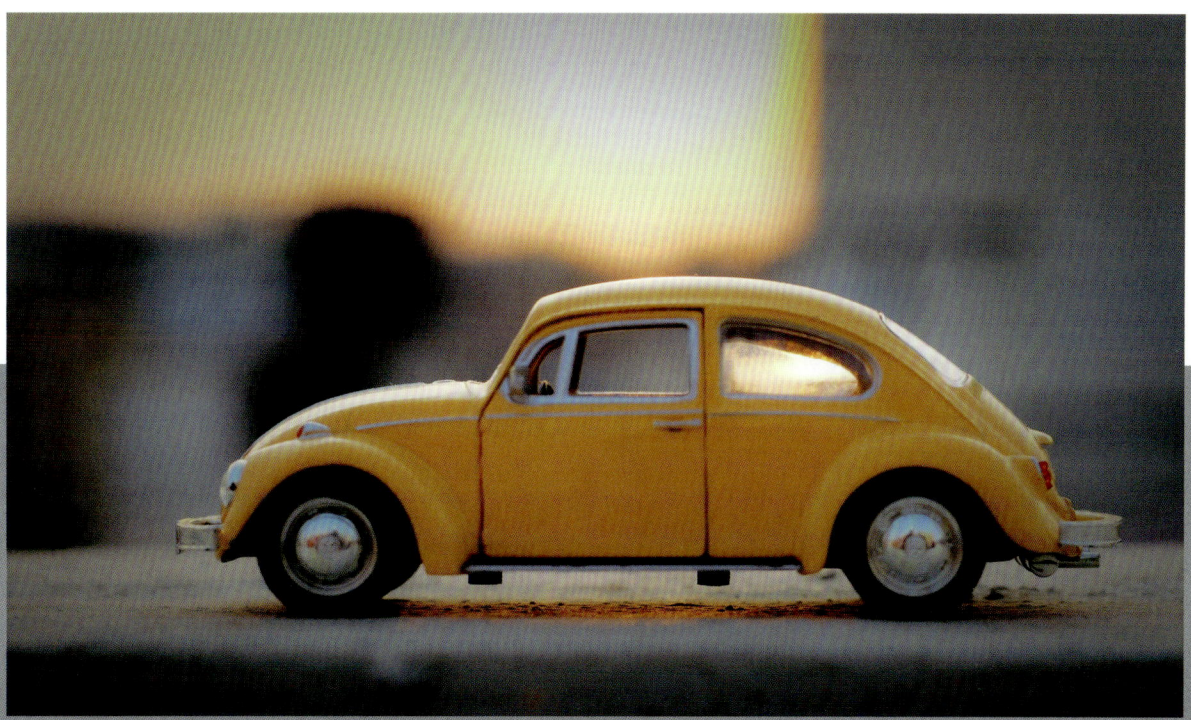

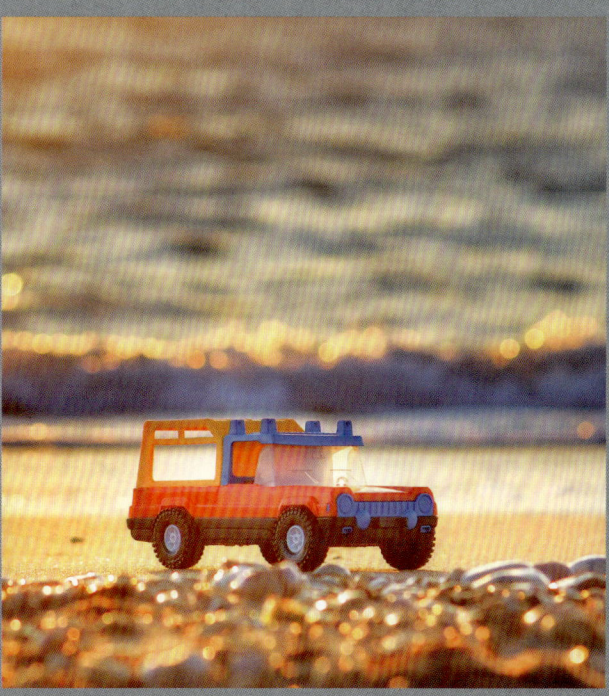

SHOOTING INSPIRATION

Whether in the city or on the beach, with the right props (which is a very adult way of saying toys), forced perspective can be used to create instant optical illusions.

ABOVE This static, side-on perspective suggests that this classic VW Beetle has been parked up while its owner watches the setting sun from out of shot.

LEFT A more dynamic, angled viewpoint creates greater visual energy, with the shallow depth of field helping the model to really stand out.

2 PORTRAITS

Module 2.1
Start with the face

The human face is unique in its diversity and expressiveness. Even before we learn to speak, we're able to communicate through facial gestures in ways that no other creature in the animal kingdom can. Our eyes in particular can convey so much – emotion, interest, surprise, concern – and allow us to communicate without ever saying a word. This is why eye contact is so important and why we instinctively look at the eyes first when viewing a portrait. Which, conveniently, is where we're going to start our adventures in portrait photography.

In my days as a magazine editor, whenever reader survey results were shared, portraits always finished a distant second in the popularity stakes. While landscape photography was perceived as accessible and solitary, portrait photography was seen as daunting and interactive (the horror!), yet I've always found it to be a hugely rewarding genre. Find a subject that you feel at ease with and it suddenly becomes a lot less scary. Of course, there's more to it than finding a willing model, so we're going to start with a simple composition you can shoot in the comfort of your own home using nothing more than window light.

Look around for an uncluttered background and a north- or south-facing window – a painted wall is perfect and the bigger the window the better. For the most diffused, flattering light, shoot on a bright but overcast day, and tuck any curtains or blinds out of the way to let in as much light as possible. Ask your subject to stand around 1m (3ft) from the window and the same distance from the background, and frame up just the head and shoulders, using the rule of thirds to position your subject's eyes on the upper horizontal grid line. Being close to the light source will add a catchlight – the window's reflection – to your model's eyes, bringing your portrait to life.

RIGHT Use a wide aperture to blur the background of your subject...

Aperture ƒ/22

Large depth of field = small aperture

Aperture ƒ/5.6

Narrow depth of field = wide aperture

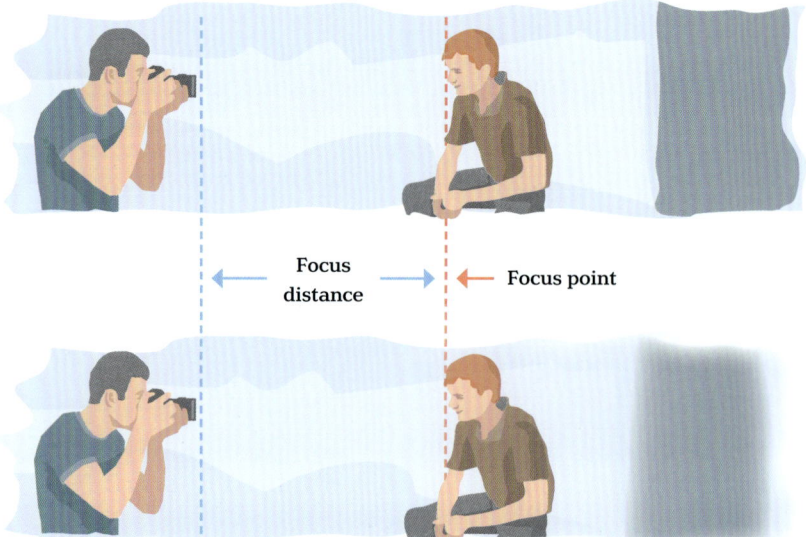

← Focus distance →   ← Focus point

DIFFICULTY ★ ★ ★

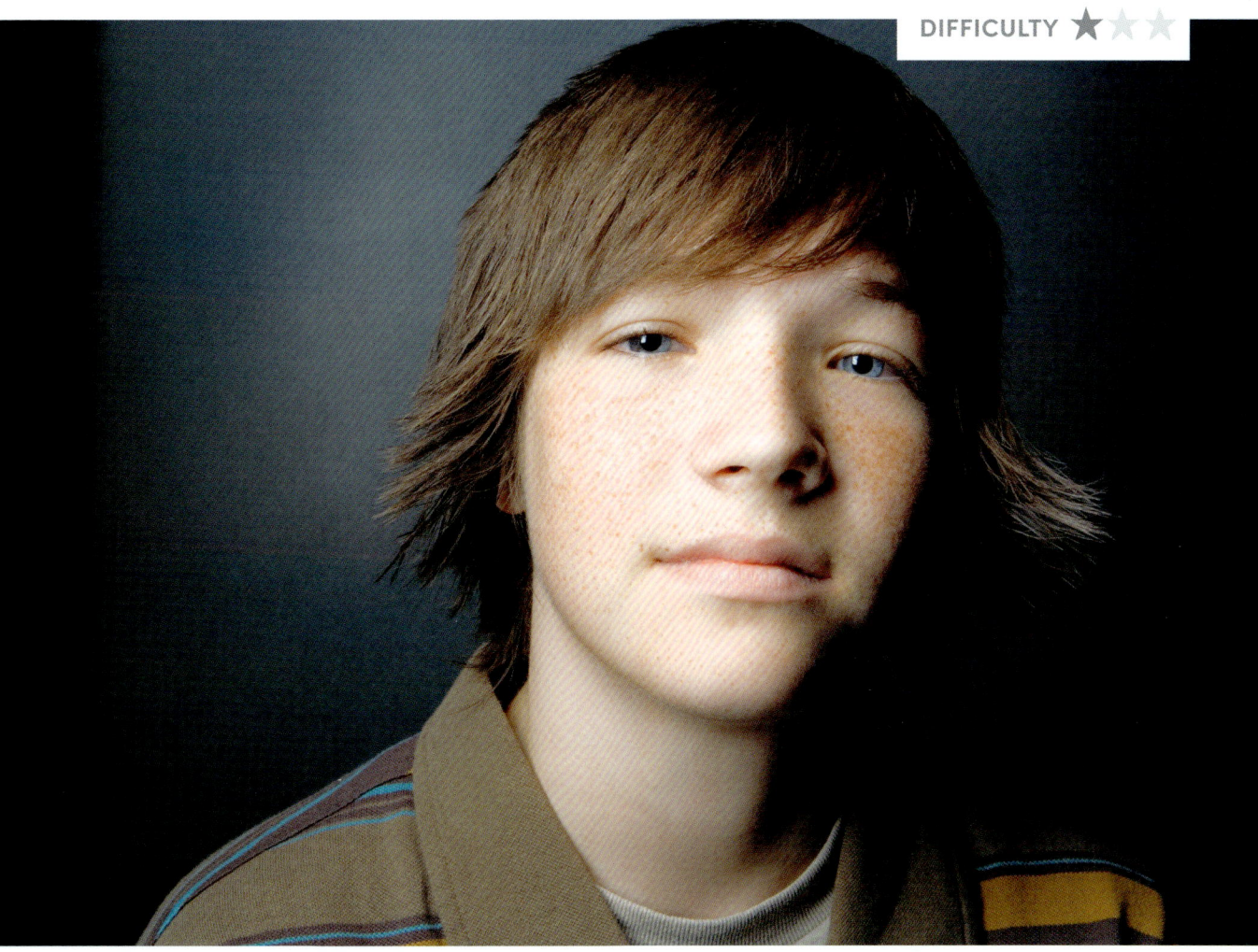

ABOVE **This simple head-and-shoulders portrait features strong eye contact, soft natural light and a blurred background.**

RECOMMENDED SETTINGS

- Shooting mode: **Aperture-priority**
- Aperture: **ƒ/5.6**
- Shutter speed: **1/125sec**
- ISO: **200 (or higher)**
- Focal length: **55mm**
- AF area: **Single-point AF**
- AF operation: **Single-shot AF**
- Drive mode: **Single-shot**
- Metering mode: **Evaluative/matrix**
- White balance: **Auto or daylight/cloudy**
- Picture style: **Portrait**

START WITH THE FACE 53

Camera settings

As with landscapes, depth of field is hugely important when shooting portraits, but how we deploy it is very different. Rather than using a small aperture to maximize front-to-back sharpness, here we want to use a large aperture to draw attention to the subject's eyes and throw the background out of focus. This will create a sense of separation between model and background and help them stand out. To achieve this, select aperture-priority mode and choose your kit lens' widest aperture, which is typically $f/5.6$. The further away from the background your model stands, the more out of focus the background will appear.

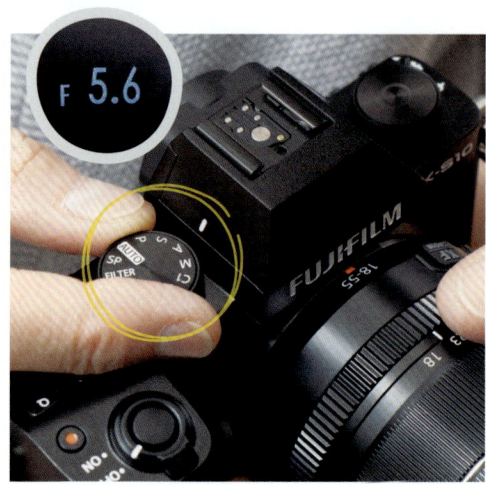

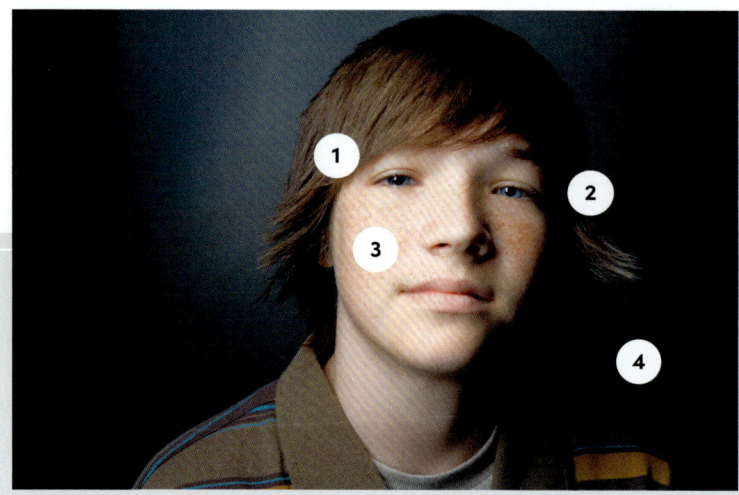

WHY THIS SHOT WORKS

1 The model's eyes are pin-sharp and perfectly positioned on the upper horizontal rule-of-thirds grid line. Plus, both eyes have catchlights – the window's reflection – which really makes them stand out.

2 Selecting a wide aperture and focusing on the model's eyes has created a nicely blurred and unobtrusive background, which creates a pleasing sense of depth and separation.

3 The photographer has metered for the brightest part of the subject's face i.e., the cheek nearest the window, creating dark shadows. This is called 'split lighting' and can be very dramatic.

4 Shooting at eye level immediately creates a natural connection between subject and viewer. Any lower and he appears too dominant, any higher and he looks too submissive.

Finding the 'perfect' exposure is always a balancing act and this is particularly true when shooting indoors using window light. Because we need to keep shutter speed above a certain level to ensure sharpness (see below), we also need to push our camera's sensitivity to balance the equation, which means setting an ISO of at least 200. You may even need to push it to 400 or 800, depending on the quality of light. While this may seem counterintuitive in terms of image quality, a little noise is infinitely more preferable to a blurred portrait.

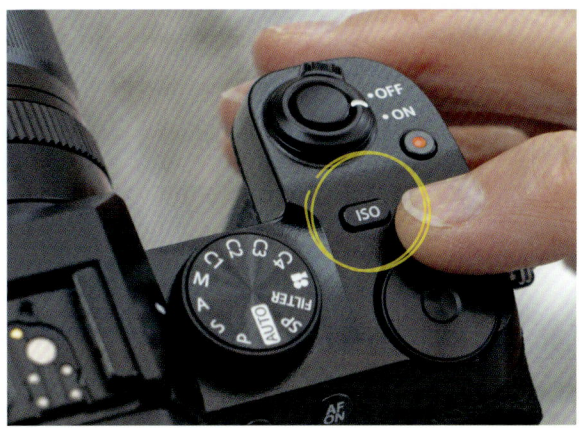

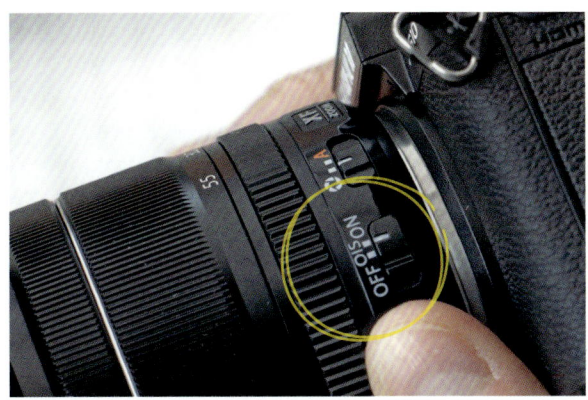

Whenever shooting handheld in low light – even though it may seem bright to the human eye – it's always best to aim for a shutter speed of 1/125 second or faster, as this will minimize the risk of camera shake. As we're shooting in aperture-priority mode and the camera will calculate the optimum shutter speed for you, you'll need to keep one eye on the settings while you work. This is also a good time to switch on your camera or lens' image stabilization (IS) system, as this will compensate for any movement caused by your hands and improve your chances of capturing a pin-sharp shot. There will either be an IS switch on your lens barrel or an option in the menu.

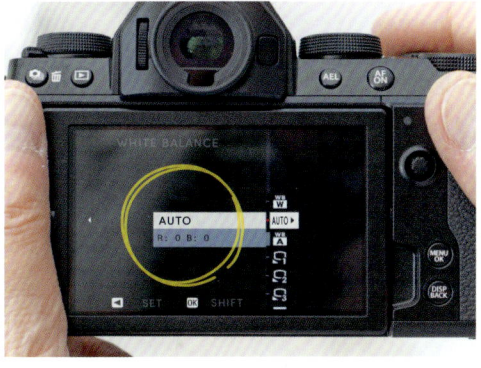

Auto white balance or the daylight or cloudy presets will ensure that the window light is perfectly neutral, but always make sure that all other internal light sources are switched off before you start shooting – mixed lighting is a whole other complication and not one we want to delve into here. For more flattering results, head to your camera's main menu, navigate your way to Picture Styles and select the Portrait option – this will subtly boost skin tones and saturation while smoothing skin texture.

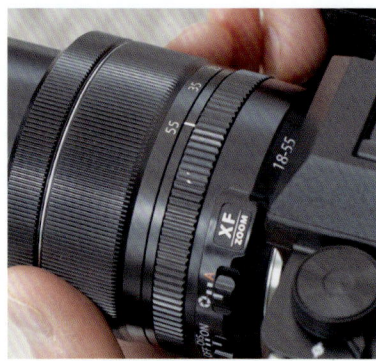
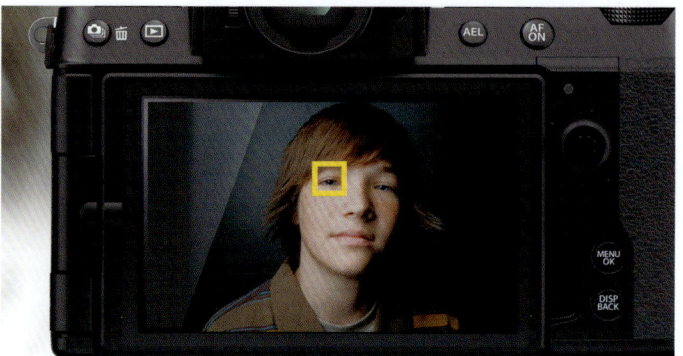

Lens settings

Longer focal lengths between 50mm and 85mm are usually preferred for head-and-shoulder portraits as the perspective is flattering. Also, they allow for a comfortable working distance between you and your model. So, zoom your kit lens in to its longest focal length, which will typically be 55mm (this will give a 35mm equivalent focal length of nearly 85mm on an APS-C camera). As focusing needs to be more accurate when shooting with wide apertures, owing to the shallow depth of field, switch your camera and/or lens to AF and select single-point AF (AF area) and single-shot AF (AF operation) modes.

Technique

Once you have composed your portrait, using the rule of thirds to position your subject in the frame, move the active AF point over one eye if the subject is standing straight on to the camera, or the eye nearest the camera if they are standing at a slight angle. Half-press the shutter button to find focus and fully press it to take a picture. Remember to focus and shoot in one smooth, fast action and gently squeeze rather than punch the shutter button so you don't tilt the camera. Lock your upper arms and elbows into your chest for extra stability.

Evaluative/matrix metering is perfect for all but the most complicated lighting scenarios and works by averaging out the shadows and highlights. However, if certain areas look too bright, use exposure compensation to darken the shot slightly and take a few test images to check the exposure. Ideally, you want to be metering for the brightest part of your model's face – the side nearest the window – to avoid blown highlights.

TIP

If the shadow side of your model's face is too dark, either move them away from the window slightly to reduce the contrast, diffuse the light source with a sheet of muslin, or use a large piece of white card to bounce light back into the shadows. You may need an assistant to help you with this. Even better, invest in a collapsible reflector, available from all good photo stores.

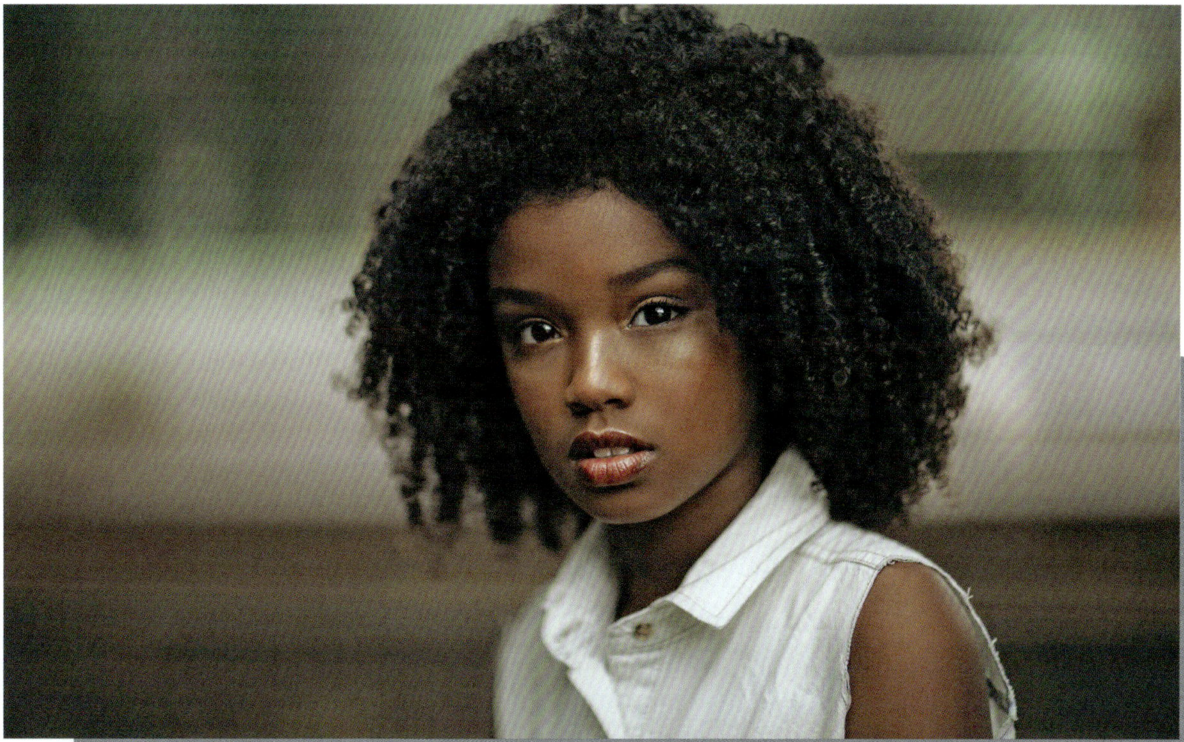

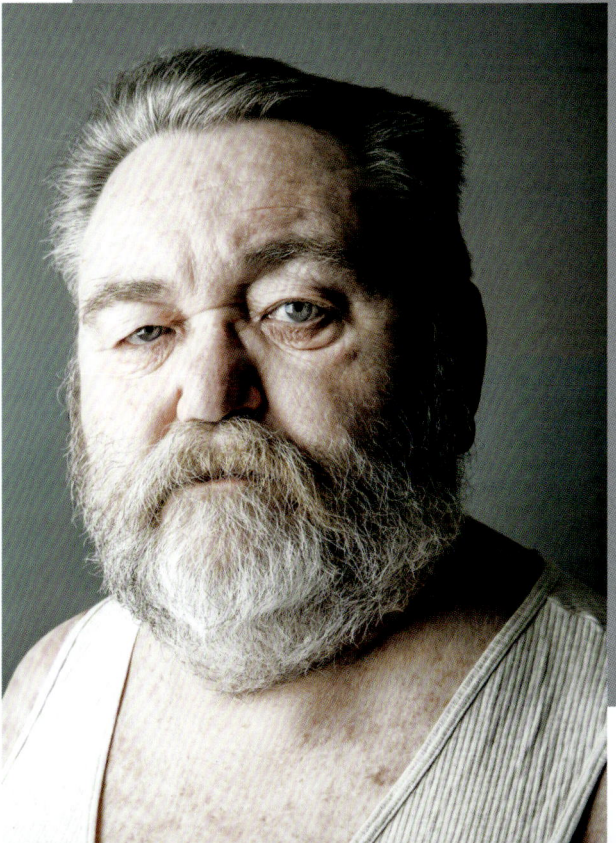

SHOOTING INSPIRATION

The basic head-and-shoulders portrait is a classic image that can be recreated in any number of different ways and locations.

ABOVE You don't have to take portraits indoors. Shoot outside on an overcast day and use a wide aperture to put the background out of focus.

LEFT The faces of older sitters can be full of interest and make great portrait subjects. Use slightly harsher light to really focus on the texture of the skin.

Module 2.2
Add context

Now that we understand the importance of eye contact and its ability to engage and communicate, we can start to zoom out and think about the bigger picture. Storytelling is a key part of portrait photography and is an often-overlooked pictorial element that can be the difference between an image that tells us who a person is and what they look like – think of a typically unflattering passport shot – and what a person is and what they are interested in. We can use our knowledge of a person's personality, profession and hobbies to place our subject in context and reveal something about them through the use of location, props and clothing.

Known as 'environmental' portraits, this type of image moves beyond the standard 'headshot' we looked at in the first module and introduces a number of other key skills. Planning is crucial – your choice of location should complement the subject in some way, helping them to relate and relax. A carpenter in his workshop, a gardener in her greenhouse, a shop owner behind the counter... you get the idea. Even if you are shooting close family or a friend you have known for years (which is a great way to practice), involve them and ask them where and how they want to be photographed. The more comfortable the subject, the more natural the pose and expression.

Explore the location and look for the light. As in the first module, we ideally want to be shooting indoors using natural light on a bright but overcast day so look for windows and doors a few metres (or around 10 feet) from where your subject will be positioned. Will they be standing, sitting or leaning? Most people feel less self-conscious when they have something to occupy their mind and hands so a relevant prop or task may help tell the story. And what will they be wearing? Work-stained overalls and hard hats will make more sense in an industrial context than a sharp suit and tie. Finally, as important as the location is, it should never detract from the subject so always keep one eye on the background and make sure there are no unsightly objects 'growing' out of people's heads.

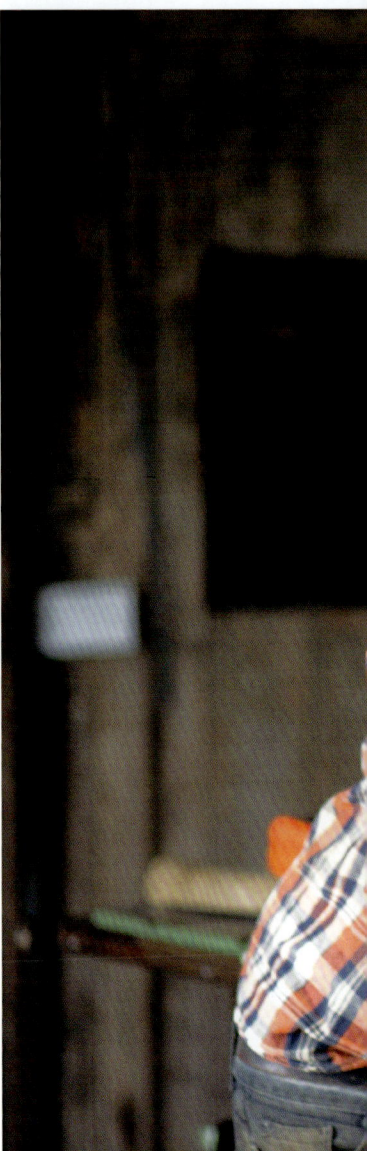

ABOVE **A quick scan around the frame reveals quite a lot about our portrait subject.**

DIFFICULTY ★★★

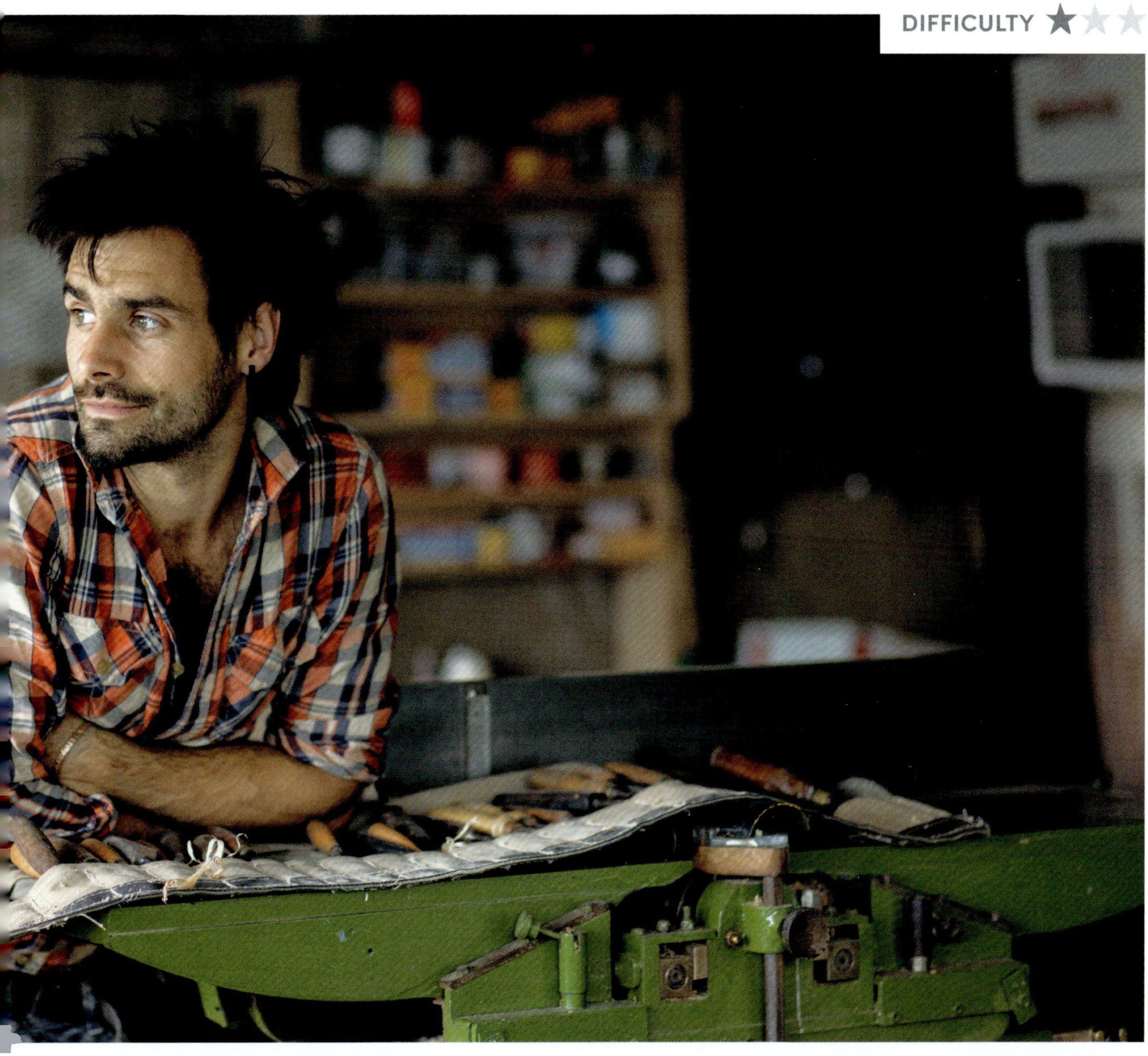

RECOMMENDED SETTINGS

- Shooting mode: **Aperture-priority**
- Aperture: **f/5.6**
- Shutter speed: **1/125sec**
- ISO: **400 (or higher)**
- Focal length: **35mm**
- AF area: **Single-point AF**
- AF operation: **Single-shot AF**
- Drive mode: **Single-shot**
- Metering mode: **Evaluative/matrix**
- White balance: **Auto or daylight/cloudy**
- Picture style: **Portrait**

ADD CONTEXT 59

Camera settings

While environmental portraits use locations for context and storytelling to reveal far more than just a subject's likeness, the sitter is still the star of the show and so we want them to stand out from the background. This typically means shooting 'wide open' – with your lens at its widest aperture – to create a shallow depth of field that will help blur objects in the distance. Again, we want to select aperture-priority mode and an aperture of ƒ/5.6 (or whatever your lens' widest aperture is) to achieve this. Although this potent combination requires precise focusing, it is a relatively simple technique for capturing a more three-dimensional sense of depth.

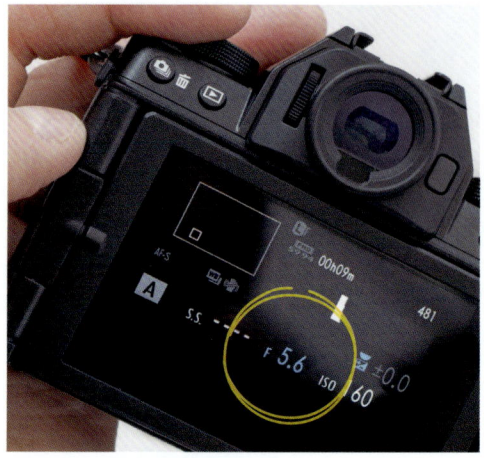

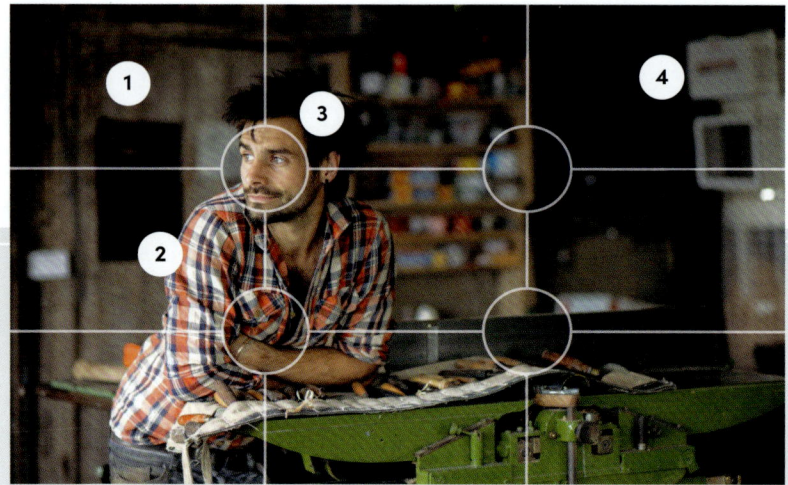

WHY THIS SHOT WORKS

1 The carpenter's workshop is the perfect location for an environmental portrait as it adds context and tells us far more about the subject than a standard head-and-shoulders portrait would.

2 The model's casual pose and wistful glance out of the frame suggest a relaxed character at ease with his surroundings. A comfortable subject is an expressive subject.

3 The subject's face has been positioned on a rule-of-thirds power point, creating a well-balanced environmental portrait with a clear focal point and plenty of negative space.

4 By using a wide aperture and focusing on the eye nearest the camera, the photographer has thrown the background out of focus, adding context without distracting the viewer.

Fear of high ISOs is a common phobia among less-experienced photographers, but it should simply be seen as another creative exposure tool that can be used to allow for faster or longer shutter speeds and smaller or wider apertures. Whereas in pre-digital days, a film with an ISO of 3200 would produce grain the size of golf balls, the latest generation of DSLRs and mirrorless cameras are so adept at controlling noise you could easily shoot at ISO 3200 and capture clean and perfectly usable results. So, start with an ISO of 400 and don't be afraid to push it to 800 or higher if light levels and shutter speed demand it.

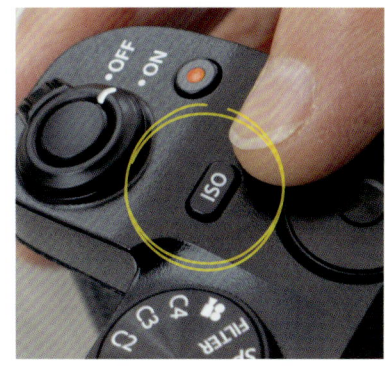

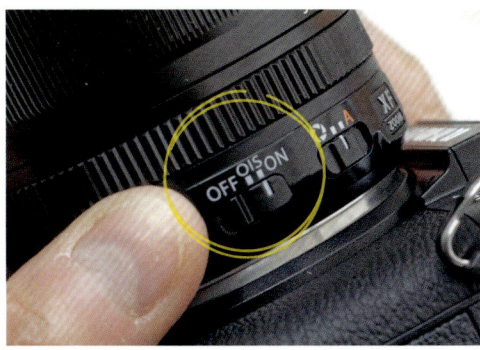

There's an age-old rule of thumb that suggests that shutter speed should always match or exceed focal length when shooting handheld. For instance, if shooting at 50mm, a shutter speed of 1/50 second or faster should be fast enough to capture sharp shots devoid of camera shake. Of course, with the advent of digital crop factors, this analogue-era rule isn't quite as simple as it used to be, so today I aim for a shutter speed that is at least double the focal length. This is why I always recommend 1/125 second as a minimum handholding exposure time. However, if your camera or lens features IS, this will allow you to shoot at slower shutter speeds such as 1/60 second and even 1/30 second. Confused? Don't be – it makes a lot more sense in practice.

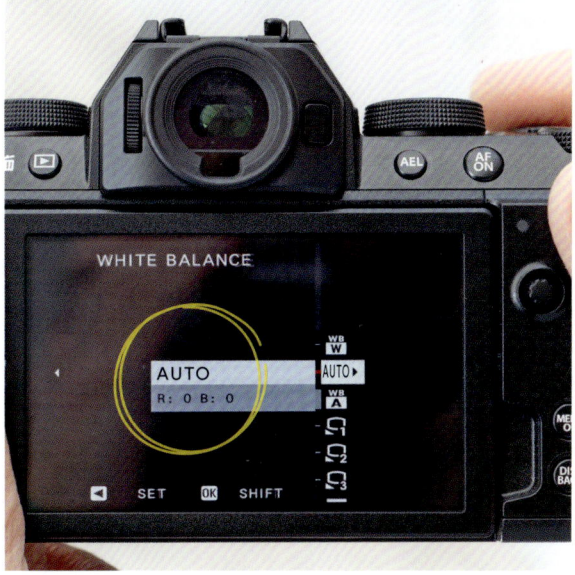

White balance and Picture Style settings can stay the same as before – as we are switching off all internal light sources and using natural light only, auto white balance (or daylight or cloudy presets) will produce neutral colours, while the Portrait preset will deliver more flattering pictures with brighter colours and more natural-looking skin. Also, consider composing and shooting using Live View instead of your camera's viewfinder as this moves the camera away from your face and allows for easier communication between you and your subject.

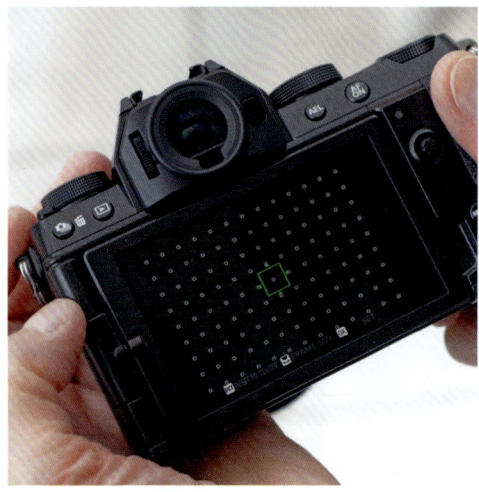

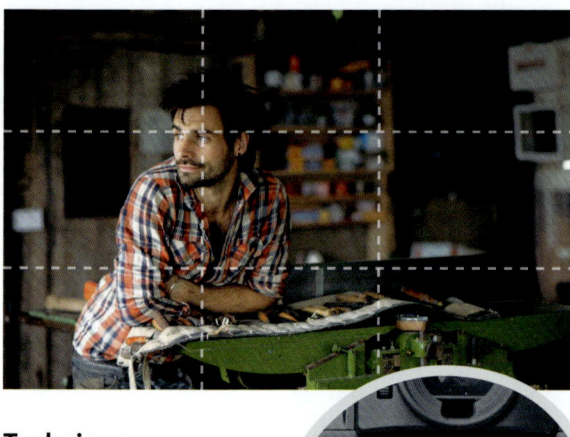

Lens settings

As we are widening the scope of our subject matter from head-and-shoulders to environmental, we also want to widen our perspective to allow us to include more visual information. A focal length of around 35mm will give us a wide enough field of view and a flattering, distortion-free image while also maintaining a comfortable working distance, which should always be an important consideration when working with people. This mid-range setting gives a 35mm equivalent focal length of 50mm, which is considered by many to be the definitive portrait 'lens'. With focusing being so critical, we need to take full control so again select single-point AF (AF area) and single-shot AF (AF operation).

Technique

With your subject occupying a much smaller area of the frame, we can use the rule of thirds to position the entire face rather than just the eyes. For greater balance and impact, try to use one of the upper power points – where the vertical and horizontal grid lines intersect – and think about your viewpoint. Portraits taken at eye level tend to look the most natural as this encourages an immediate connection, but don't think that your sitter always has to be looking directly at the camera – a more casual pose with the subject gazing wistfully out of the frame can often convey a more relaxed, less self-conscious vibe.

TIP

While holding your camera vertically – known as portrait format – might seem like the most obvious way to shoot a portrait, holding it horizontally – known as landscape format – will allow you to include more space around your subject. Shoot from the waist up and always focus on the eye closest to you.

As before, move the active AF point over your model's eyes (or the eye nearest the camera), gently half-press the shutter to find focus and fully press it to take a picture. As we are shooting in single-shot AF mode using a wide aperture, it is important that you repeat this process every time you press the shutter as even the smallest body or hand movement could shift the zone of sharpness slightly. For stability, tuck your elbows into your body and stand with your feet shoulder-width apart, mimicking the shape of a tripod.

If the window light is particularly harsh, you may find that the shadows falling on your subject's face are too dark and unflattering. If this is the case, you can reduce the contrast between shadows and highlights by moving the person away from the window slightly or bouncing light back into the shadows by using a sheet of white card or collapsible reflector. These simple light modifiers often feature several different reflective surfaces, such as white and silver or gold; while the metallic sides will warm up or cool down the light, the white side will always provide the softest, most natural effect.

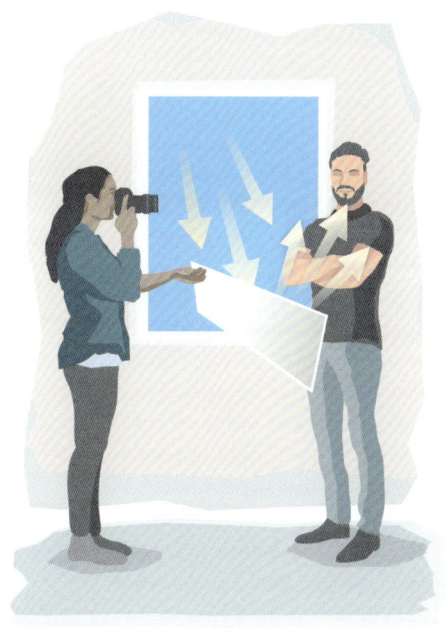

ABOVE **A simple sheet of white card can reflect light and illuminate any harsh areas of shadow.**

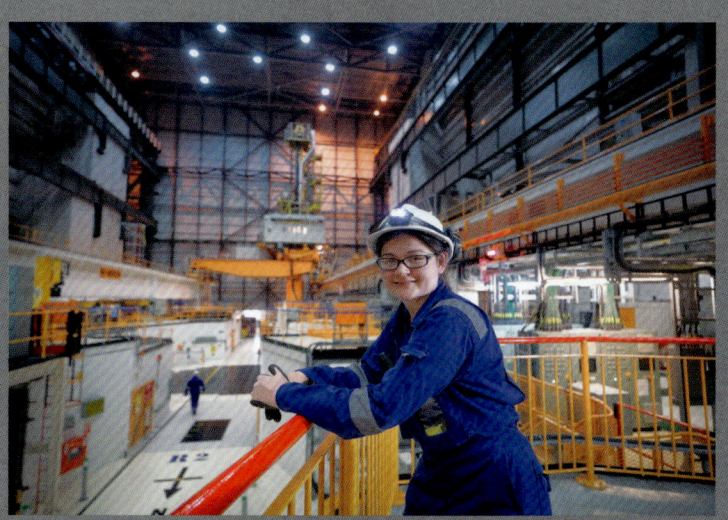

SHOOTING INSPIRATION

Environmental portraits rely on clothes, props and location to tell their stories, but the subject should always take centre stage.

LEFT **Overalls and hard hats are perfectly at home in industrial settings such as this, and the subject appears comfortable and relaxed.**

Module 2.3
Capture kids at play

Not all portrait styles benefit from being so orchestrated. While environmental portraits allow you to tell a story, the need for constant direction can often lead to a lack of spontaneity that can result in obviously posed images. If you want to capture more natural-looking photos, you will need to adopt a more free-flowing approach that is more in keeping with your subject's personality. Kids love to play and rarely sit still for long, but what they lack in patience they more than make up for in energy and enthusiasm, and they are typically much less self-conscious in front of a camera, making them fun yet challenging subjects to shoot.

'Lifestyle' photography is a portrait style that sits between posed and candid and allows you to capture magical moments instinctively and spontaneously, just as a sports photographer shoots the action. Rather than guide the subject and obsess over every little detail, your job is to suggest locations, activities, clothes and props that will capture their imagination and then step back and let them express themselves. Of course, you still need to plan lifestyle shoots to a certain extent – kids love their toys and games, and it is always a good idea to suggest more than one location. Gardens, parks and beaches are great open spaces where kids can run freely.

Midday sun is rarely flattering and can lead to harsh shadows and extreme contrasts so plan your lifestyle shoots for when the sun is low in the sky and the quality of light is softer and more even. For now, shoot with the sun to the side of your subject (we'll look at more dramatic lighting in the next module) and avoid gloomy and overcast days as the quality of light can look rather cold and unappealing. Spend time getting to know your subject so they feel comfortable around you and involve yourself in the games and activities – pull faces, make silly noises and become part of the 'gang'. Shoot at eye level for the most natural-looking portraits.

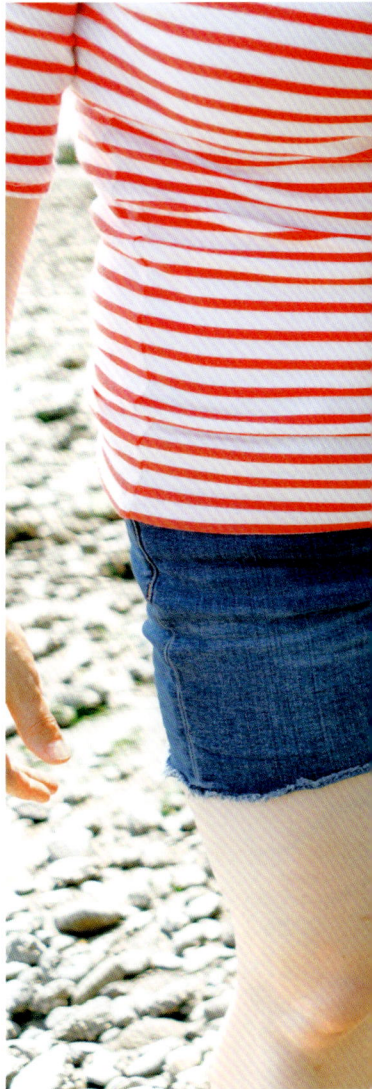

ABOVE **The more relaxed the shoot, the more the subject's personality will shine through.**

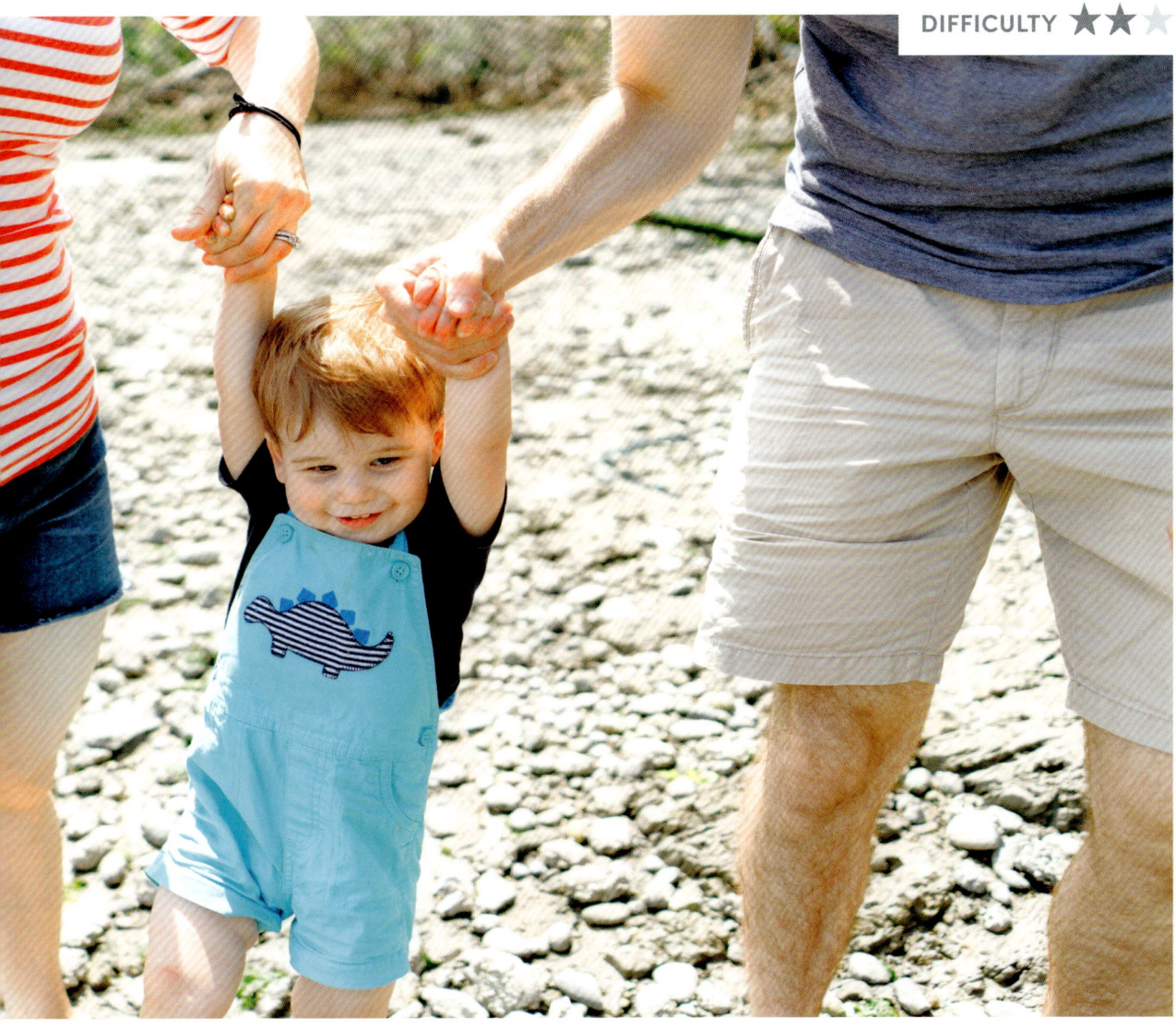

DIFFICULTY ★★☆

RECOMMENDED SETTINGS

- Shooting mode: **Shutter-priority**
- Aperture: **Any**
- Shutter speed: **1/250sec (or faster)**
- ISO: **200**
- Focal length: **35–55mm**
- AF area: **Single-point AF**
- AF operation: **Continuous AF**
- Drive mode: **Continuous**
- Metering mode: **Centre-weighted**
- White balance: **Cloudy/shade**
- Picture style: **Portrait**

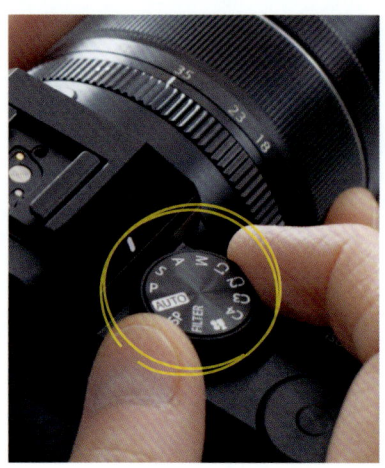

Camera settings

With a potentially moving subject to contend with, we want to concentrate on shutter speed rather than aperture when shooting lifestyle portraits. While an exposure of 1/125 second may be fast enough to freeze an adult's more measured movements, children tend to move quickly and unpredictably so we need to select a faster shutter speed that will allow us to capture unexpected moments without motion blur. Switch to shutter-priority mode (S or Tv) and select a shutter speed of at least 1/250 second – this may be overkill in many situations, but it will ensure that you don't miss a shot. This semi-automatic shooting mode will select aperture for you.

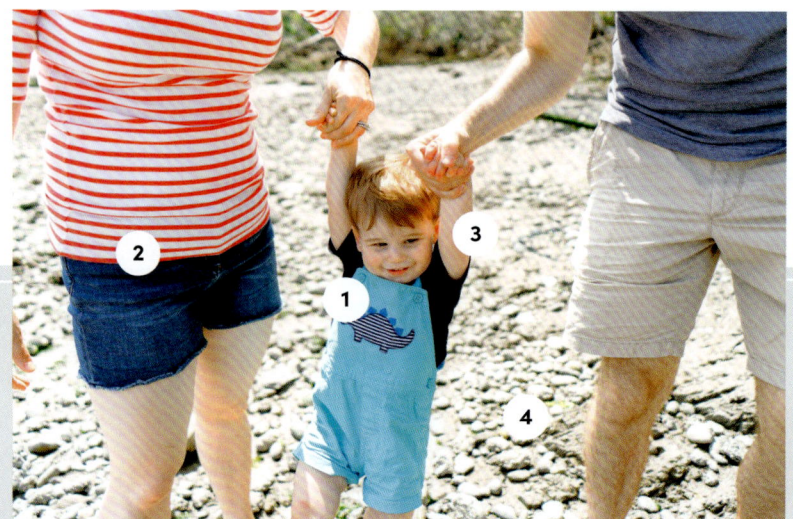

WHY THIS SHOT WORKS

1 The boy's cheeky grin suggests that he is relaxed and having fun, which is exactly what lifestyle portraits should be all about. We want natural-looking photos that capture a subject's personality.

2 The models' choice of clothes is simple yet colourful and adds an air of authenticity to the portrait. Also, the lack of brand names and logos won't date the shot so quickly.

3 The near-eye level viewpoint and central composition cleverly crops the parents out of the shot, using their bodies as human 'frames' to focus the viewer's attention on the child in the middle.

4 Beaches are perfect locations for lifestyle portraits as the subjects can run freely and enjoy themselves while you concentrate on capturing those special split-second moments.

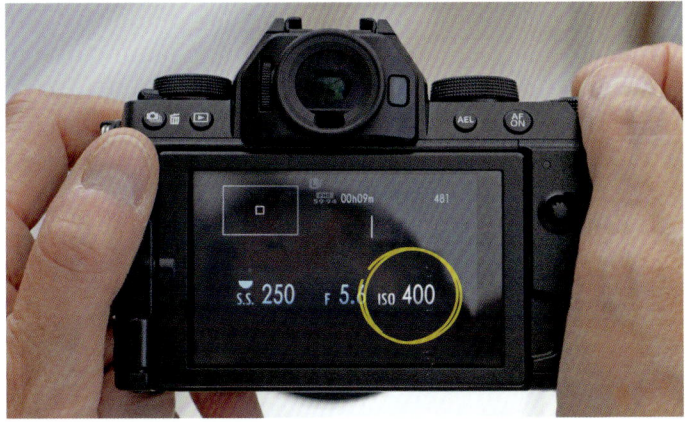

Ordinarily, we would want to select the lowest ISO possible to keep noise to a minimum, but as we are shooting in relatively low light (or shade on a sunny day) and using a faster shutter speed, we need to use ISO to balance the exposure. An ISO of 200 is a sensible starting point for spontaneous lifestyle portraits, though you may need to increase this to 400 or even 800 if light levels drop sufficiently. As in the previous module, don't overthink ISO – a brilliant photograph with a little noise is infinitely preferable to no photograph at all.

When shooting portraits of any kind, white balance will determine the accuracy of skin tones. Auto white balance is a safe option and many photographers leave their cameras in this mode permanently, but we can also use the presets to add a warm tinge to our photographs, making for more flattering, sun-kissed colours. If you are feeling brave, consider using the cloudy or shade presets to add a subtle glow – this will replace the cold blues of the daylight preset with warmer yellows and oranges. Take a moment to really look at your subject's skin and select the most appropriate preset.

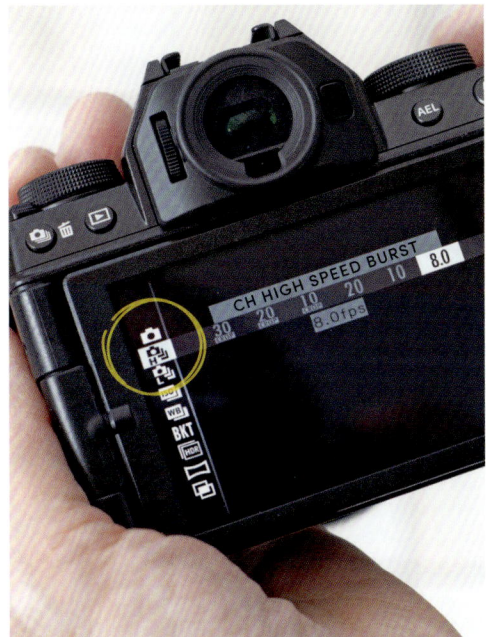

Lens settings

Here's where we get radical. So far, for every module, we have used single-point AF (AF area) and single-shot AF (AF operation) modes, giving us control over the active AF point and allowing us to take one picture at a time. This is a fail-safe combo for static subjects, but for energetic lifestyle portraits we need to shoot as many photos as possible to ensure we capture those special split-second moments, which requires a more dynamic approach.

Instead of single-shot, we are going to select continuous, or 'burst', shooting. This action-friendly drive mode takes a number of shots in quick succession for as long as the shutter button is held down, capturing a sequence of frames that will hopefully include the perfect shot. All cameras have a frames-per-second (fps) rate, with entry-level models typically featuring a burst rate of around 7–8fps.

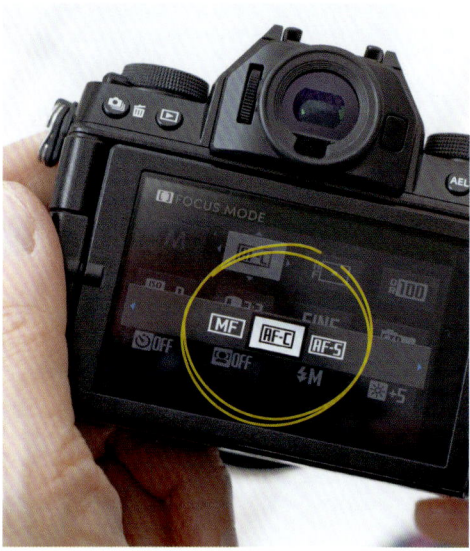
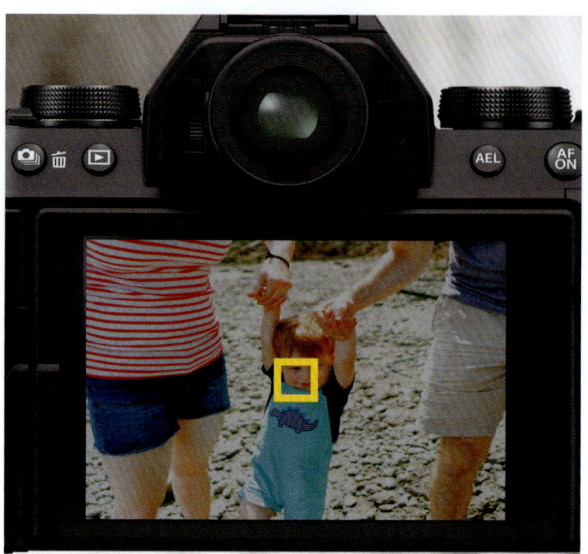

Next, we want to switch the AF operation from single-shot AF to continuous AF, often abbreviated to AF-C or Ai Servo. This mode will lock focus on a moving subject and continually focus and refocus for as long as you keep the shutter button half-pressed. This is a focusing technique that takes practice and isn't always foolproof – accuracy often depends on the size, speed and direction of your subject and the technical prowess of your camera – but it will dramatically increase your chances of capturing sharp shots of kids at play.

Technique

Continuous AF still allows you to position a single AF point so think about where you want your subject to appear in the frame. The rule of thirds is an obvious framing device to employ here and positioning your AF point off-centre will help create more interesting compositions. That said, capturing emotion and 'the moment' are more important than technical perfection so if central compositions allow you to focus more attention on the subject, as in our main example, don't obsess over the rules – they exist to be broken.

TIP

Involve your subjects by sharing your images with them every so often and asking for their feedback. The more input they feel they have, the more likely they are to engage with the shoot, which will help you find the perfect balance between spontaneity and guidance.

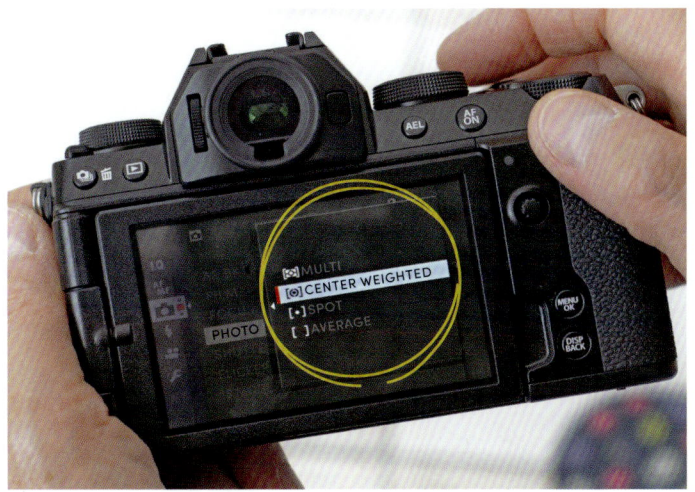

If composing centrally, I'd recommend you select centre-weighted metering. This mode takes 60–80% of its exposure reading from the central portion of the frame and is ideal for outdoor portraits with darker or lighter backgrounds that could potentially prevent the subject from being correctly exposed. You can also use centre-weighted metering for off-centre subjects, though you will need to position your subject in the centre of the frame and half-press the shutter to take the exposure reading, and then recompose with the shutter still half-pressed to take the photo.

Shoot in short bursts of five or six frames at a time and check your exposures at regular intervals. If your subject is too light or dark, use exposure compensation to adjust the brightness. And don't expect every shot to be pin-sharp and perfectly framed – using burst mode and continuous AF together can be a hit-and-miss approach, but get it right and you will be rewarded with a unique photograph of a never-to-be-repeated special moment.

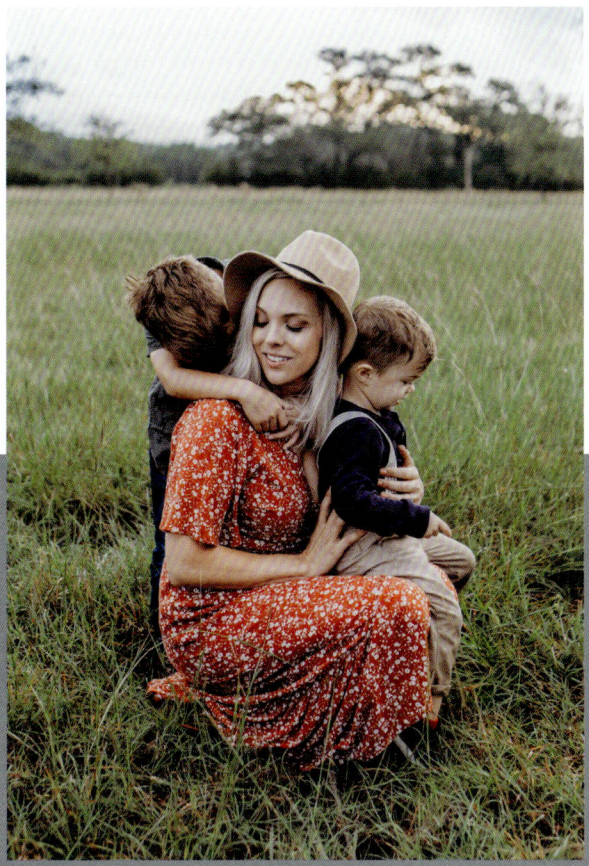

SHOOTING INSPIRATION

Involving the parents in a lifestyle portrait shoot can encourage younger subjects to express themselves more naturally.

LEFT **Mum** provides a familiar leaning post for these camera-shy children.

CAPTURE KIDS AT PLAY 69

Module 2.4
Create emotion with light

From simple head-and-shoulder compositions to more involved environmental and lifestyle images, all styles of portrait photography can benefit from one magical ingredient: emotion. This intangible quality can help engage the viewer and provoke a reaction, perhaps via a cheeky smile, colourful clothing or clenched fist. It can even be conveyed by dramatic light, and one lighting technique that can deliver emotion in spades is backlighting. Also known as *contre-jour* **(French for 'against daylight') and rim lighting, this dramatic effect creates striking portraits that lift the subject from the background and inject a sense of romance and mystery.**

As its name suggests, backlighting involves illuminating a subject from behind, with the model positioned directly between you and the light source. This creative technique produces a glowing 'halo' of light around the subject as well as extreme contrasts between them and the background. It also means that the model's face will be in shadow, which stops them from squinting and often allows for more natural facial expressions. It isn't the simplest form of lighting and requires practice, but get it right and you will be amazed by how evocative the effect can be.

Soft, warm light is the most flattering and so shooting during the golden hours – the hours around sunrise and sunset, when the sun is low in the sky (see page 19) – is the best time of day for backlighting. Shooting at midday will mean the sun is higher in the sky and you will have to adopt a low viewpoint and look up at your subject, which isn't advisable. Your subject should 'eclipse' the sun, leaving only small amounts of 'spill' light around them. You may find that this causes lens flare and haze, but this can often enhance the 'dreaminess' of a portrait. The slightest shift in viewpoint can dramatically change the backlighting effect so always experiment with different angles.

RIGHT **Backlighting can really lift a portrait, giving it a natural warmth and radiance.**

RECOMMENDED SETTINGS

- Shooting mode: **Aperture-priority**
- Aperture: **f/5.6**
- Shutter speed: **1/125sec**
- ISO: **100**
- Focal length: **35-55mm**
- AF area: **Single-point AF**
- AF operation: **Single-shot AF**
- Drive mode: **Single-shot**
- Metering mode: **Spot**
- White balance: **Cloudy/shade**
- Picture style: **Portrait**

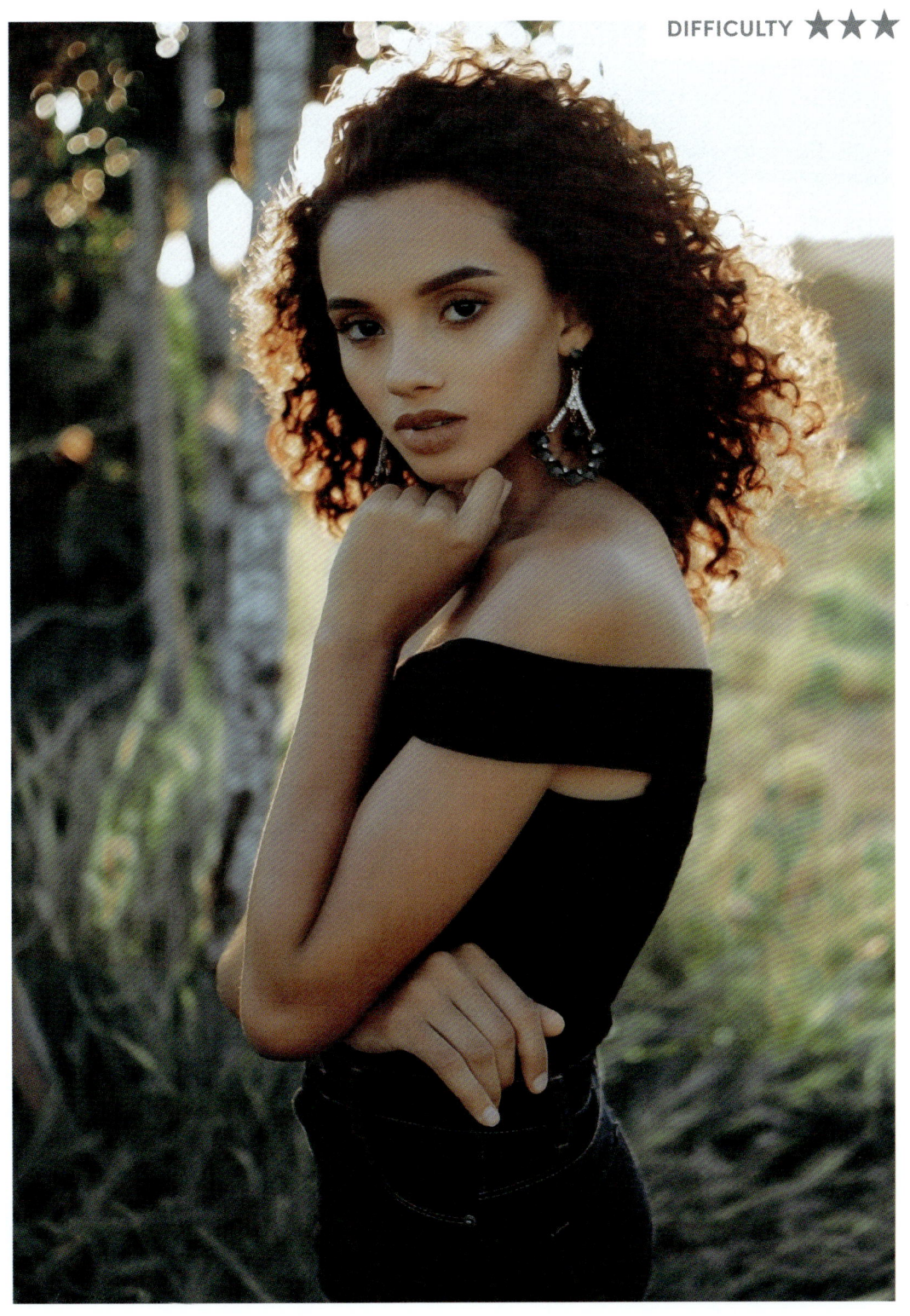

Camera settings

The biggest change-up for this technique is the way in which we determine exposure. So far, we have mostly used evaluative/matrix metering, which calculates an average exposure reading by measuring light from across the whole frame. This default mode is fine for low-contrast scenes and subjects, but it can be fooled by extreme brightness around smaller, darker areas, resulting in these parts being underexposed. When only a small area of the frame needs to be correctly exposed, such as the subject's face when shooting backlit portraits, we need a more precise method and so we are going to select spot metering for the first time.

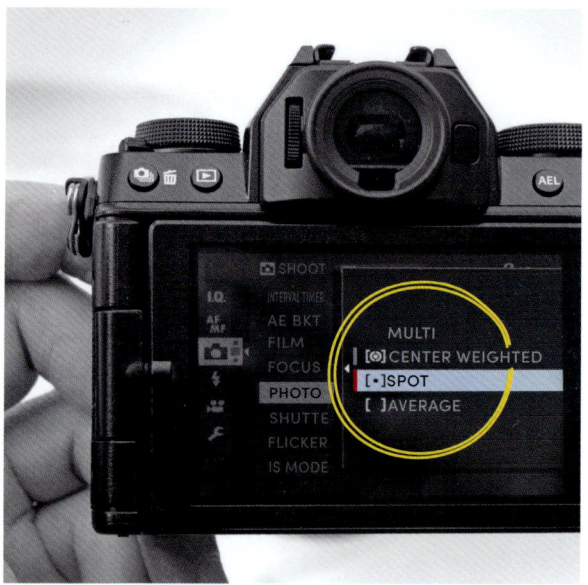

WHY THIS SHOT WORKS

1. Shooting into the light with the model 'eclipsing' the sun has produced a characteristic golden halo around the model's hair, with more subtle rim lighting along her left arm.

2. By using spot metering to meter for the face only, the model is perfectly exposed while the brighter sky behind her is overexposed. This is typical of backlit portraits shot outdoors using natural light only.

3. The sun is low in the sky, allowing the photographer to adopt a natural eye-level viewpoint, and the quality of light is warm and attractive, which flatters the model.

4. Shooting wide open and focusing on the model's eyes has created a strong focal point and sense of depth, with the landscape beyond falling nicely out of focus.

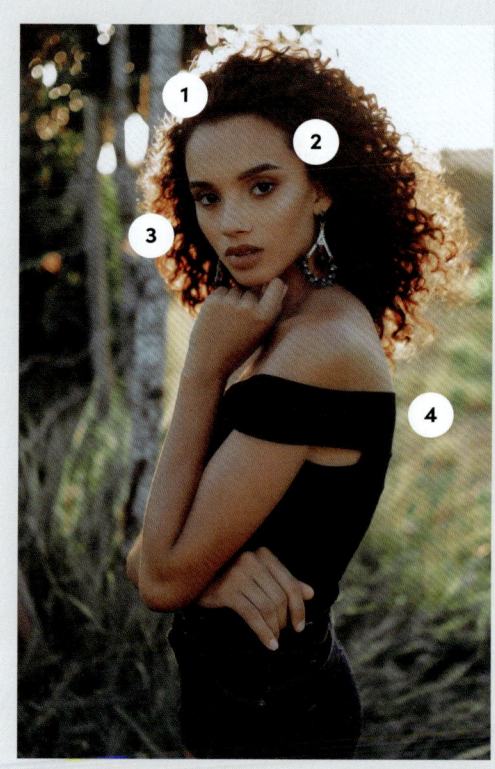

Spot metering measures light from just 1–2% of the frame – typically the 'spot' around your chosen AF point – and ignores the rest of the frame entirely. Changing metering modes differs from model to model and you will either need to use a dedicated button on your camera's top plate or dive into the menu and find the metering option. Unsurprisingly, spot metering mode is usually symbolized by a small 'spot' icon.

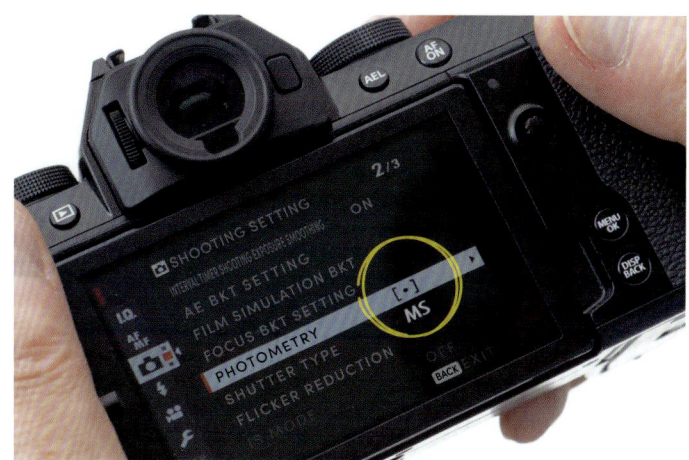

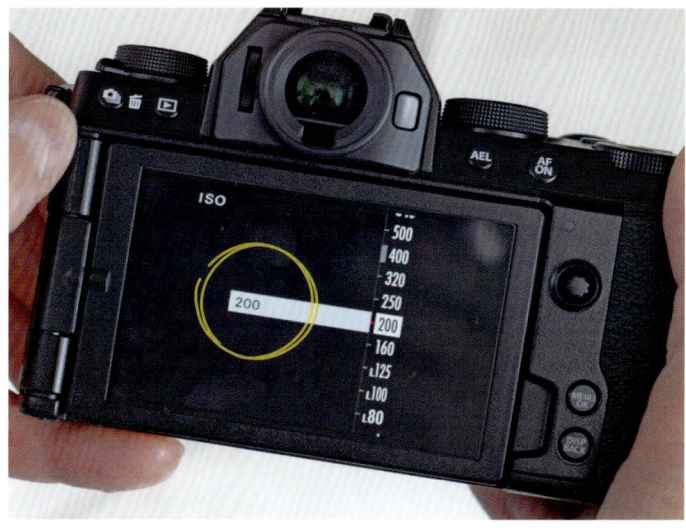

Elsewhere, we want to stick to the same tried-and-tested settings we used for our head-and-shoulders and environmental portraits, using a large aperture to draw attention to the subject's face and eyes while blurring the background. Switch back to aperture-priority mode (A or Av) and select the widest aperture your kit lens allows. As is always the case when shooting portraits handheld, we should be aiming for a shutter speed of at least 1/125 second so start at ISO 100 and increase the value to 200 or 400 if needed.

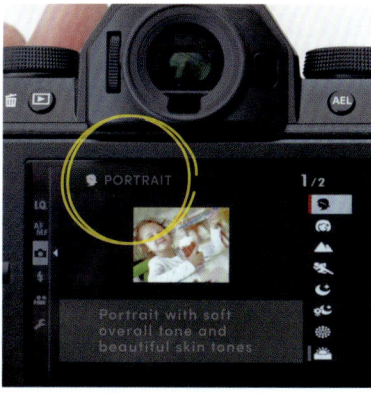

Although we are shooting into the sun, our subject's face will be in shadow so we can select either the cloudy or shade white balance preset to ensure skin tones are vibrant and true to life. For Picture Style, stick to the Portrait preset for more flattering skin tones and texture.

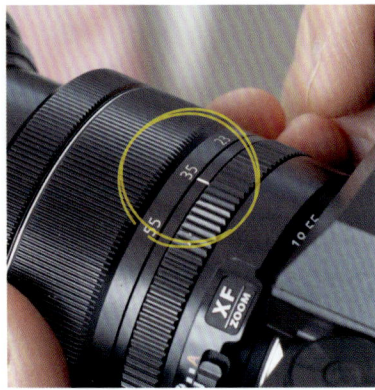

Lens settings

After the drastic changes to our focusing technique in the previous module, for *contre-jour* portraits we want to revert back to the single-shot AF (AF operation)/single-shot (drive mode) combo as it provides us with the control and accuracy we need when working with wide apertures and a shallow depth of field. If shooting a head-and-shoulders portrait, zoom in to your lens' longest focal length of 55mm, and if shooting waist-height or full-length portraits, choose a focal length of 35–55mm for a slightly wider yet still distortion-free perspective.

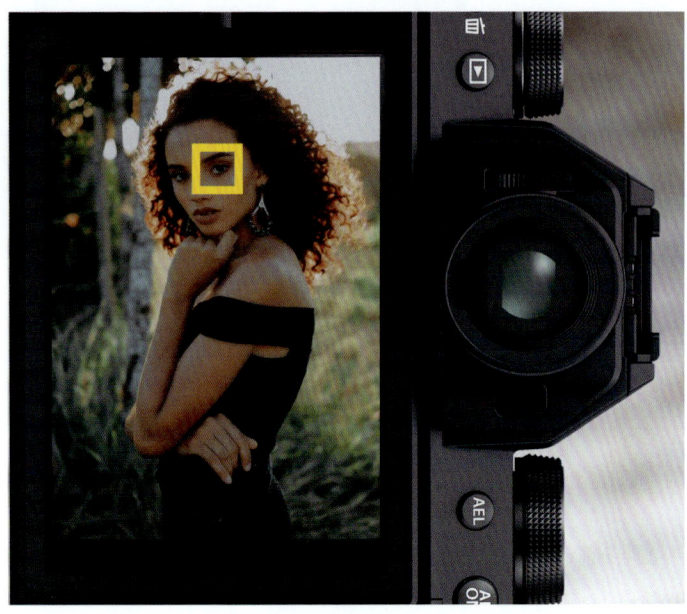

Technique

The secret to success when using spot metering is knowing where to meter for and why. Thankfully, in our case this is relatively simple as we only want the face to be correctly exposed so we can position the single AF point over one of the model's eyes (or whichever is nearest the camera) and half-press the shutter button. This will not only engage AF, it will also prompt the camera into taking an exposure reading from this very specific area. If your model occupies only a small part of the frame, and the rest of the scene is bright, the lightest areas of the background will almost certainly overexpose, but don't worry – this is all part of the technique's dramatic charm.

TIP

Semi-automatic modes, such as aperture-priority, still allow us a degree of manual control over exposure and we can always use exposure compensation to lighten or darken a scene – or in our case, areas of a scene. And if necessary, we can use a reflector to bounce light back into the shadows to give natural light a helping hand.

AF can struggle to find focus when shooting into the light so either attach your lens hood or, if you don't have one to hand, hold your free hand over the top of the lens to block a degree of light while your camera focuses. You will know when your lens is struggling as it will 'hunt' as it tries to lock onto an area of contrast, which is why scenes flooded with low, or with very little light, can prove challenging.

To compose, use the rule of thirds to help position either your subject's eyes, face or body, depending on how much of the frame they occupy. As always, it's a question of finding a visual balance and by now you should be fairly adept at making sense of potentially complex scenes and including only what adds to a picture's impact. Do anything enough times and at some point, it will invariably become instinctive.

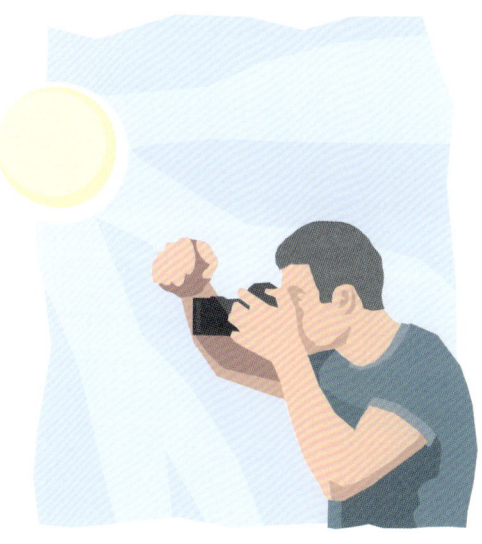

ABOVE **Hold your free hand over the top of the lens to block light while your camera focuses.**

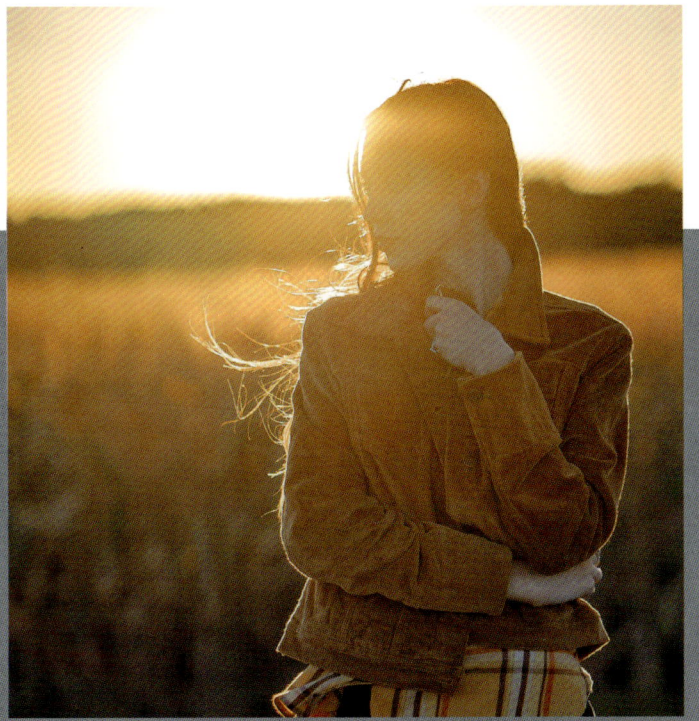

SHOOTING INSPIRATION

Backlighting requires precise metering, but once you've mastered the basics, you can start to experiment for more artistic effects.

LEFT **Your subject doesn't always need to fully eclipse the sun – lens flare and 'spill' can be just as evocative.**

CREATE EMOTION WITH LIGHT 75

Module 2.5
Focus on pets

Let's turn our attention to portraits of the furrier kind. In many ways, cats and dogs are a lot like children – they are full of personality but have limited attention spans and can be challenging to photograph. Plus, they are impossibly cute and we love them unconditionally, even when they leave us special 'presents' every morning (I'm speaking from personal experience here). We have already looked at three very different portrait techniques that we can use to photograph both static and moving subjects, and we can use and adapt these same techniques to photograph furry critters at home. Just let your pet's personality dictate the style you opt for.

Working with animals requires patience and understanding. Pets will feel calmer and more comfortable in their home environment and this is where their unique personalities will shine through. Every dog and cat has a happy place where they like to snooze – maybe a sofa, bed or owner's lap – and a tired pet is a more amenable portrait sitter. Also, the calmer you are, the more relaxed the pet will be – dogs in particular are emotional sponges and will sense any stress or anxiety. Move slowly, spend time with the owner to encourage the pet to accept you, and familiarize them with the sound of your camera's shutter with a few 'clicks' before you start taking pictures. This is where our head-and-shoulders and environmental portrait skills come into play – the subject may be smaller and hairier, but our end goal is the same.

Of course, not all subjects will be as obliging and puppies and kittens in particular can be more unpredictable. Maybe they have a favourite toy they like to chase and chew on, or a scratching post they like to attack. This is where our lifestyle portrait approach comes into its own, as it allows us to focus continually and shoot in bursts, increasing our chances of capturing the perfect photo. As we need fast shutter speeds to freeze the action, this approach is best deployed in a safe outdoor space. Whichever technique you adopt, always shoot at a pet's eye level, even if this means laying on the ground, as this immediately places the viewer in the animal's world.

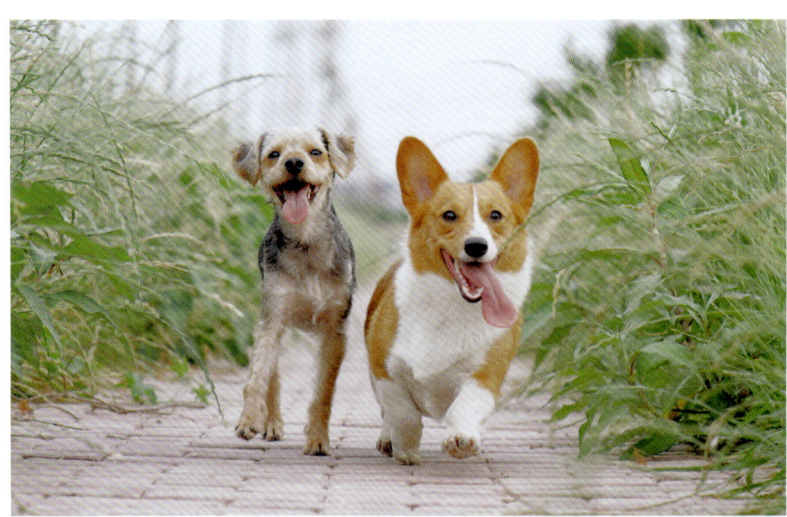

ABOVE & OPPOSITE **Tongues will wag!** Younger pets tend to be more active and less controllable, while older pets are typically more sedentary and obliging.

DIFFICULTY ★★☆

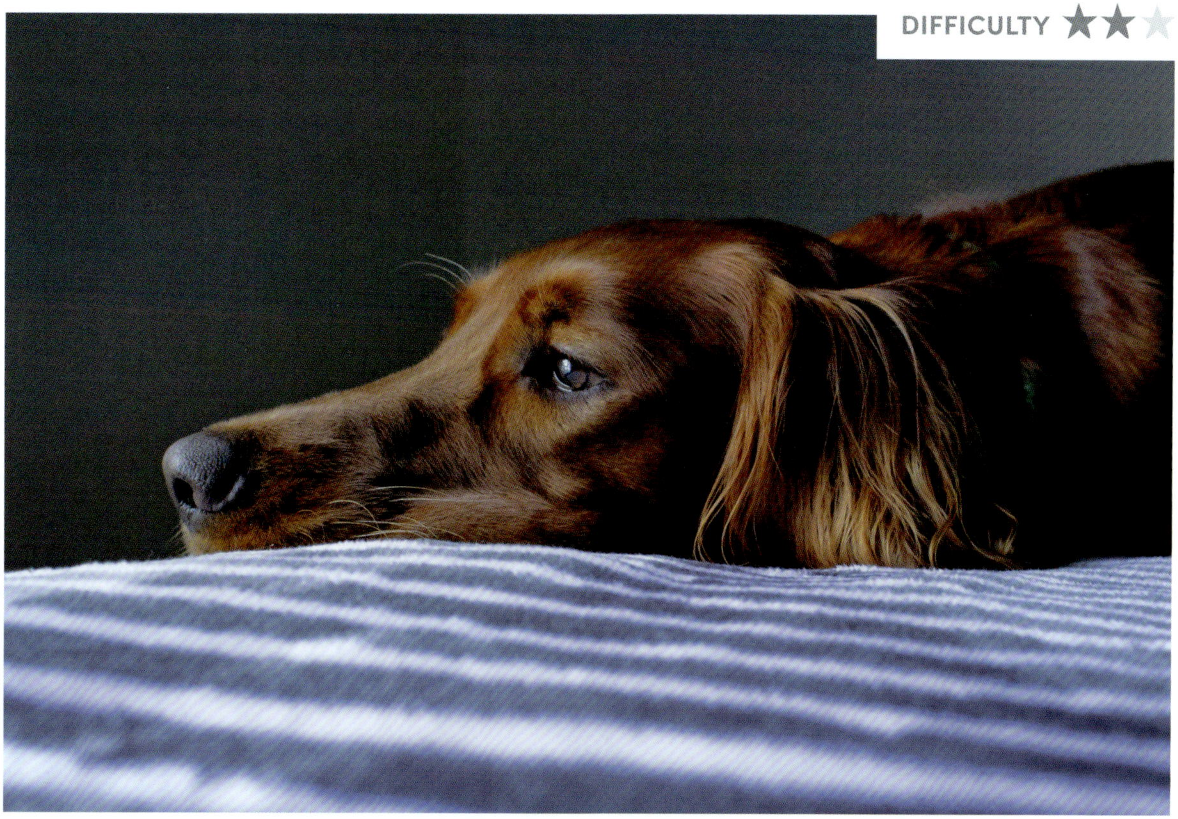

RECOMMENDED SETTINGS - PETS AT REST

- Shooting mode: **Aperture-priority**
- Aperture: **ƒ/5.6**
- Shutter speed: **1/125sec**
- ISO: **200 (or higher)**
- Focal length: **55mm**
- AF area: **Single-point AF**
- AF operation: **Single-shot AF**
- Drive mode: **Single-shot**
- Metering mode: **Evaluative/matrix, centre-weighted or spot**
- White balance: **Auto or daylight/cloudy**
- Picture style: **Portrait**

RECOMMENDED SETTINGS - PETS AT PLAY

- Shooting mode: **Shutter-priority**
- Aperture: **Any**
- Shutter speed: **1/500sec (or faster)**
- ISO: **100 (or higher)**
- Focal length: **55mm**
- AF area: **Single-point AF**
- AF operation: **Continuous AF**
- Drive mode: **Continuous**
- Metering mode: **Evaluative/matrix or centre-weighted**
- White balance: **Auto or daylight/cloudy**
- Picture style: **Portrait**

FOCUS ON PETS 77

Camera settings

If taking the static 'pets at rest' approach, which is a sensible place to start, the settings are much the same as they are for standard head-and-shoulders and environmental portraits. We want to use a large aperture to draw attention to the subject and blur the background – and, in our example, the foreground – to create depth and separation, so switch to aperture-priority (A or Av) and shoot wide open. As we are shooting indoors using natural light, start with an ISO of 200 and increase this to 400 or 800 if needed to achieve a fast shutter speed of at least 1/125 second, and switch image stabilization on to counteract any camera shake.

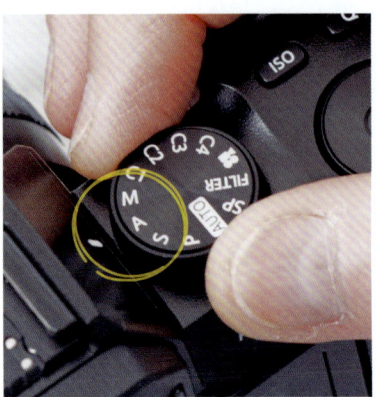

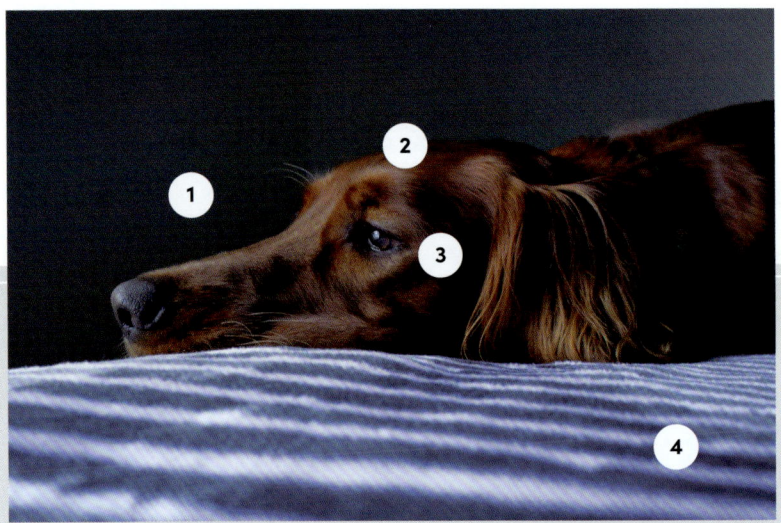

WHY THIS SHOT WORKS

1 And the prize for the most chilled-out dog goes to... this one! The more relaxed the subject and photographer, the more natural the expression. This dog's look of tired resignation is one we can all associate with at times.

2 Window light can be soft, even and incredibly flattering. Just look at the subtle highlights, shadows and textures around this dog's ears, eyebrows and nose. Gorgeous.

3 The dog's eye is very much the point of focus and the catchlight – the window's reflection in the eye – adds an extra sparkle that really brings this lovely portrait to life.

4 By shooting wide open at the dog's eye level, the photographer has been able to include some interesting foreground detail, which has been nicely blurred so it doesn't detract.

If opting for the more dynamic 'pets at play' approach, which is significantly more challenging and requires a lot more practise, we need to take a leaf out of the lifestyle photography handbook and focus on speed rather than aperture. This means switching to shutter-priority (S or Tv) and selecting a shutter speed of 1/500 second or faster – as with lifestyle shots of people, this may be overkill in some instances, but if your pet decides to have a crazy five minutes, you will be able to freeze those split-second moments. Set an ISO of 100 and increase it if the exposure warning flashes – this is to tell you that the camera's sensor needs to be more sensitive to light to allow for faster shutter speeds.

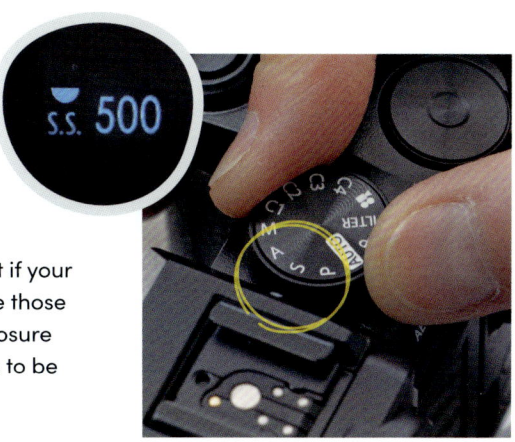

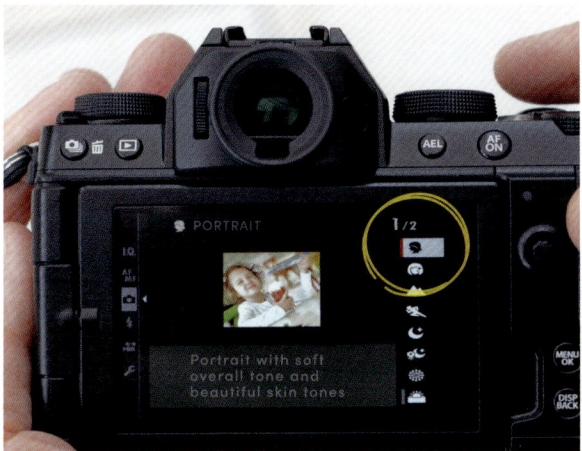

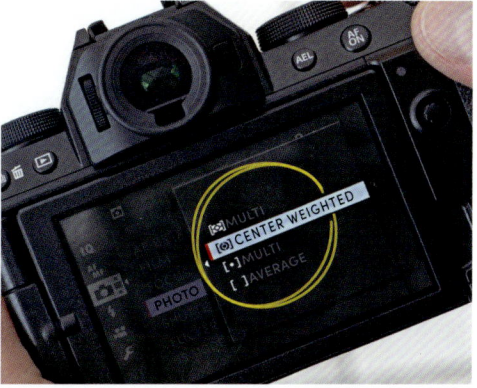

Whether shooting indoors or out, so long as you are using natural light only – and I wouldn't recommend using flash with pets as it can spook them – you can leave the white balance in auto or select either the daylight or cloudy preset. Leave Picture Style set to Portrait, but if your camera allows, increase sharpness – by default, this preset is designed to smooth textures, which can be flattering for human skin but not so much for animals with particularly fine hair. How you customize a Picture Style preset differs from model to model, so check your camera manual for details.

Which metering mode you choose will depend on location and intensity of light. If shooting indoors in soft, even light with low contrast, evaluative/matrix should be your default mode; if shooting in stronger, more directional light with greater contrast, switch to centre-weighted and compose, meter and recompose if framing off-centre; if shooting *contre-jour* with extreme contrast, spot will give the most accurate exposures.

Lens settings

Zoom your kit lens in to its longest focal length for a short telephoto of roughly 85mm (35mm equivalent) on an APS-C camera. This will not only provide you with a natural, distortion-free perspective, it will also increase the distance between you and your subject. Cats and dogs are easily distracted and so the further away you shoot from, the better your chances of capturing genuinely candid moments that show your pet's true personality. For static shots, select single-shot AF (AF operation) and single-shot (drive mode); for lifestyle shots, select continuous AF (AF operation) and continuous (drive mode).

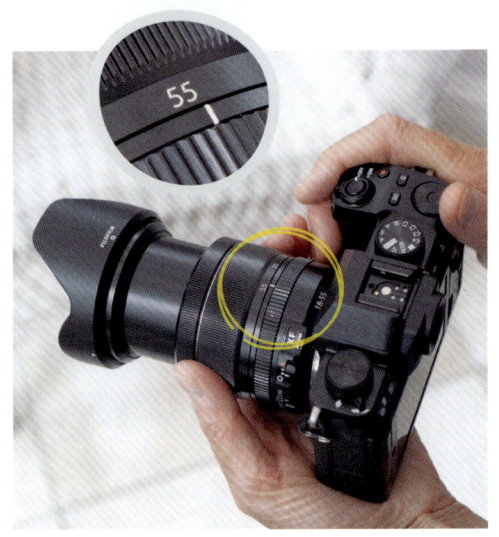

Technique

Shooting static pet portraits is no different to shooting static people portraits so the same rules apply. Find a well-lit space free from clutter, choose your moment (remember, tired pets are amenable pets) and use the rule of thirds to position your subject in the frame. Focus on the eye nearest the camera and fully squeeze the shutter in one smooth action. Some cameras have a silent shutter mode, which could help minimize distractions. If laying prone, use a rolled-up jumper or even your non-picture-taking arm to support your camera for extra stability.

TIP

If you need inspiration for your pet portraits, take a look at the work of Elke Vogelsang (elkevogelsang.com). Elke is a professional pet photographer and her images of cats and dogs (and the occasional horse) are hilarious, ingenious and super-cute in equal measures.

If using continuous AF and shooting, you will need to follow your subject's movements with your camera and shoot in short bursts. Continuous AF will constantly focus and refocus, allowing you to concentrate on and respond to your pet's antics. Some cameras feature more than one burst mode, typically continuous low (CL) and continuous high (CH). The only difference is the number of frames your camera will capture per second and CH is always advisable when photographing an unpredictable subject.

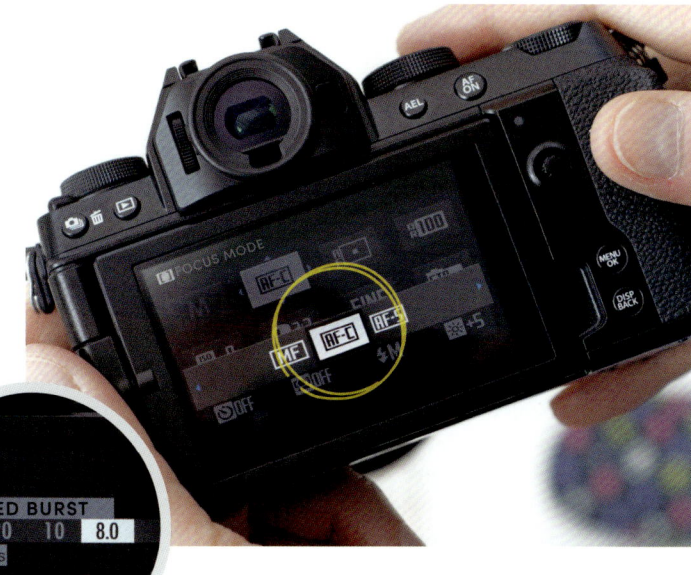

It's worth noting that darker fur absorbs light while lighter fur reflects it, so you may need to use exposure compensation to deliberately over- or underexpose your pet portraits slightly to extract more detail from fur.

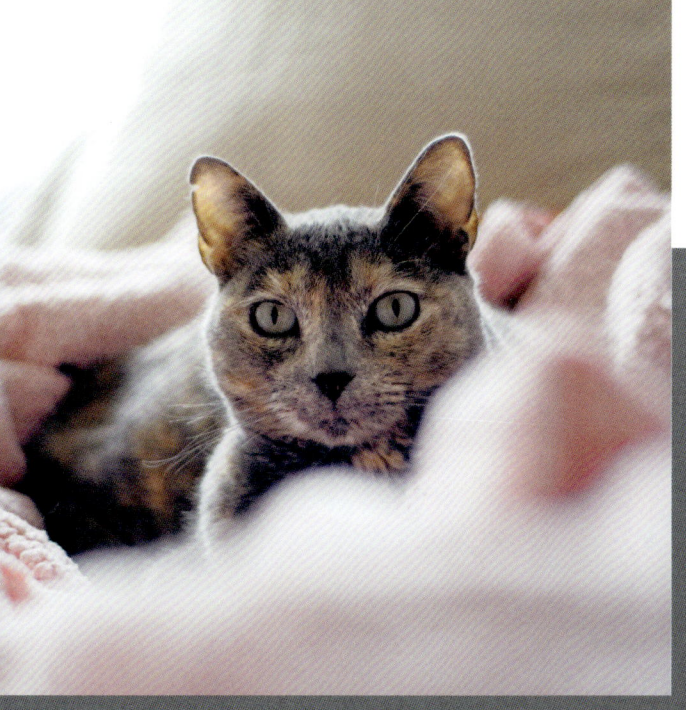

SHOOTING INSPIRATION

Duvets, blankets and jumpers are particular favourites (in my house, at least), so position a 'bed' near a source of natural light.

LEFT Cute animal portraits can be enhanced with emotive backlighting.

Module 2.6
Take a closer look at hands

Eyes may be the window to the soul, but hands can be just as revealing. We rub our palms together with excitement, clench our fists with anger and 'steeple' our fingers when we are confident; we convey sincerity, annoyance, affection and frustration, all with subtle, unconscious gestures. Those of us who 'talk' with our hands are seen as warm and welcoming while those of us who are less animated are perceived as cold and calculated. It's no wonder then that hands are the second most expressive part of the human body and the perfect subject for a portrait of a very different kind.

A portrait is defined as a likeness, but there's no rule that says that likeness has to include a face. A close look at a person's hands will reveal a fascinating miniature landscape full of contours and creases, and we can use these details to create a character study that says just as much about the sitter as a traditional head-and-shoulders portrait. All you need is a willing subject and soft, diffused light, whether outdoors in shade or indoors near a window. To portray a sense of character, think about the kind of mood you want to evoke. If your model is anxious, they may clasp their hands together; if they are relaxed, they may rest their hands on top of each other.

Once you have found the perfect hand, there are various techniques we can use to enhance our portrait. The first is to use side lighting and experiment with angles – even the subtlest change of position can dramatically alter how shadows and highlights play out across the skin. The second and by far my favourite is to shoot in black and white – replacing colour with tone removes any potential distractions and forces the viewer to focus on textures and contrasts. This is a classic technique we will revisit at various points in this book. The third is to use ISO more creatively to complement the subject's character – for instance, high ISOs generate more noise, which can be used to mimic film grain for a gritty 'documentary' look when photographing older, more grizzled hands.

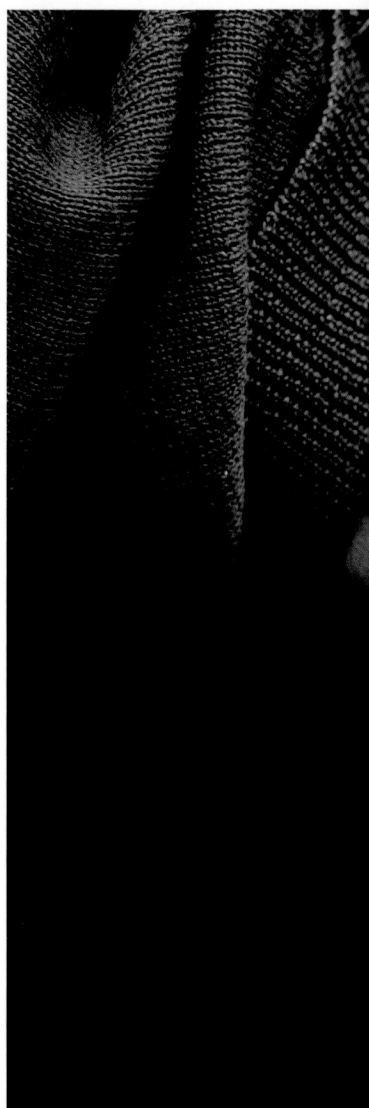

ABOVE **Shooting in black and white reveals the wrinkles and creases in these well-worn hands.**

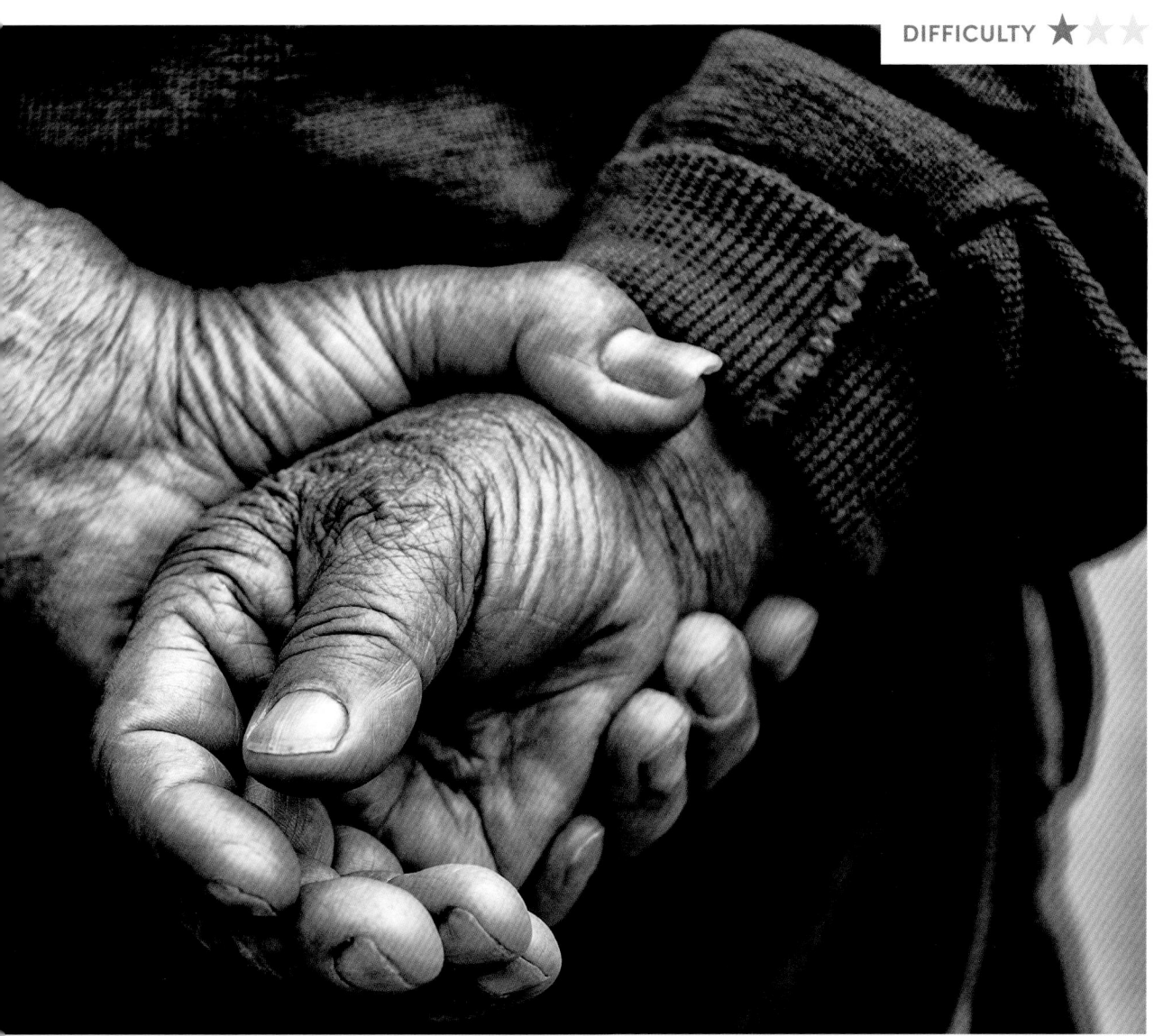

DIFFICULTY ★★★

RECOMMENDED SETTINGS

- Shooting mode: **Aperture-priority**
- Aperture: **f/5.6**
- Shutter speed: **1/125sec**
- ISO: **100 for smooth skin; up to 3200 for wrinkled skin**
- Focal length: **55mm**
- AF area: **Single-point AF**
- AF operation: **Single-shot AF**
- Drive mode: **Single-shot**
- Metering mode: **Evaluative/matrix**
- White balance: **Auto or daylight/cloudy**
- Picture style: **Monochrome**

Camera settings

With no eyes to fix the viewer's gaze, and no surrounding environment for context, we have to be more creative in how we add interest and intrigue. In this instance, the hands are the 'face' of our portrait, but not all of the face needs to be in sharp focus – in essence, we get to choose where the 'eyes' will be and what we want the viewer to look at – and so we can pick out the most interesting areas by shooting wide open and using a shallow depth of field. As with all of our static portrait projects, switch to aperture-priority and select your lens' widest aperture.

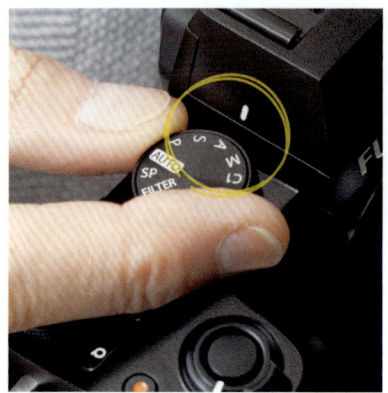

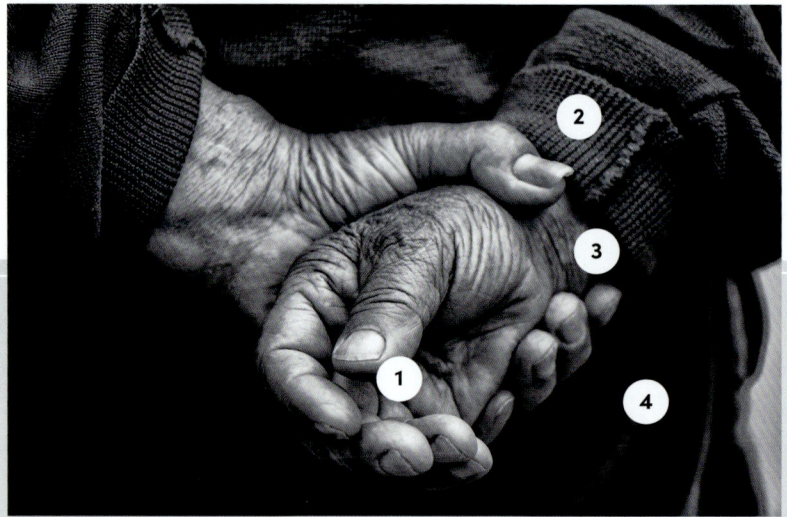

WHY THIS SHOT WORKS

1 By using a wide aperture to generate a shallow depth of field, and focusing on the fingernail nearest the camera, the photographer has picked out a clear focal point while subtly blurring the rest of the hands.

2 Positioning the clasped hands in the centre of the frame creates a sense of immediacy and power, with our attention quickly drawn to the thumb and right hand.

3 Shooting in black and white has transformed this simple hand portrait into a fascinating study of textures, tones and contrasts. Just look at those fingernails!

4 Hand gestures can be unconscious but revealing of a person's character or mood – clasped hands could suggest authority, confidence, superiority or fearlessness.

Although shutter speed will be determined by the camera's metering system, we still need to ensure that it doesn't drop below 1/125 second to avoid camera shake. Shooting wide open will help by letting more light in, as will selecting a higher ISO than is strictly necessary. Impossibly smooth newborn skin will benefit from a low ISO and minimum noise, in which case stick to ISO 100, but wrinkled skin suits the grainy look of old analogue cameras, in which case push ISO to (but not beyond) 3200. My favourite black-and-white film is Kodak T-Max P3200, and although ISO 3200 on a DSLR will look very different to the grain produced by T-Max – grain is an integral part of a film's structure whereas noise is simply a digital signal – the extra 'fuzziness' can still be very evocative.

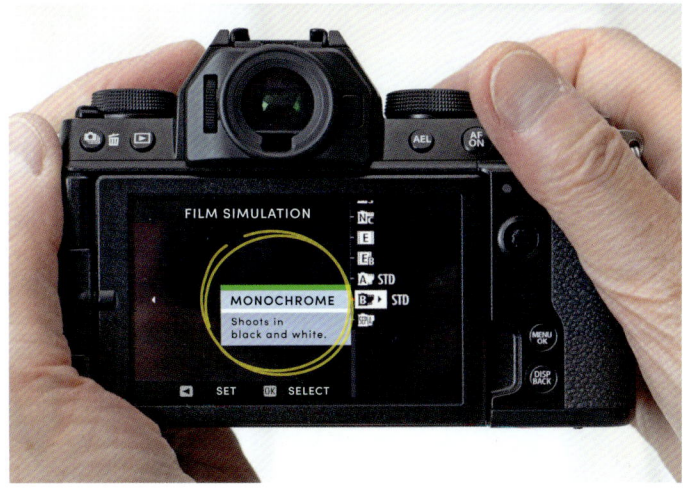

To go mono, scroll through your camera's picture style menu and select the Monochrome preset. Not only will this option convert your JPEGs to black and white in camera, it will also show you a real-time view of the world in various shades of grey via your camera's Live View (or electronic viewfinder if shooting with a mirrorless camera). To emphasize textures even more, customize the preset by diving into the Monochrome settings and pushing the Contrast slider as far as it will go – although this process will differ from model to model and you may need to consult the manual for specifics, being able to customize presets is a powerful way to 'edit' images.

Lens settings

Despite their inherent limitations in terms of focal length, aperture and image quality, kit lenses are remarkably adept at close-up photography. Many feature a minimum focusing distance of around 25cm (10in) – a measurement taken from the sensor plane rather than the end of the lens – which means that when fully zoomed in to 55mm you can comfortably fill the frame with subjects as small as 8cm (3in) in width. Not only does this make for impactful pictures, it also further minimizes the apparent depth of field for more artistic blur. For accuracy when focusing, select single-point AF (AF area) and single-shot AF (AF operation) modes.

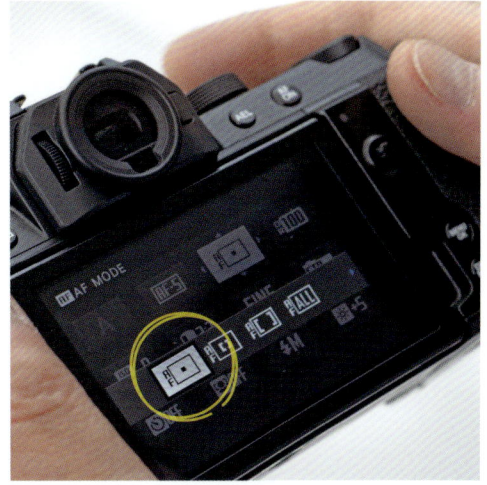

Technique

The biggest challenge whenever shooting wide open, particularly when you are relatively close to the subject you are photographing, is focusing. Even at $f/5.6$, which is not an especially 'fast' aperture compared to some 50mm prime (fixed focal length) lenses out there – which open as wide as $f/1$ and even $f/0.95$ – your plane of focus may only be a few millimetres wide. This means that both your camera and subject need to be perfectly still while you focus and shoot. A tripod will eliminate any camera movement, but you will still need to ask your hand model to remain as still as possible. Carefully position the AF point over the nail, knuckle or wrinkle you want to be sharp, then focus and shoot in one quick but smooth action for greater accuracy.

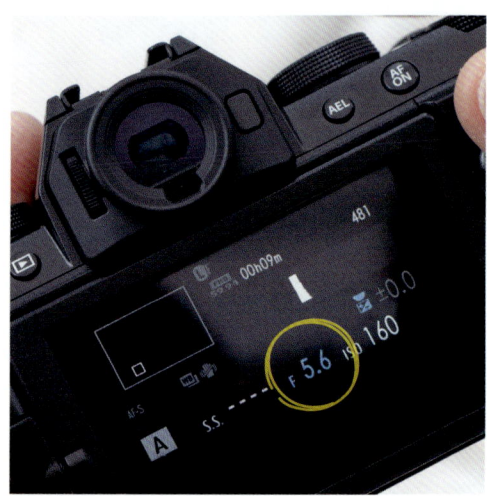

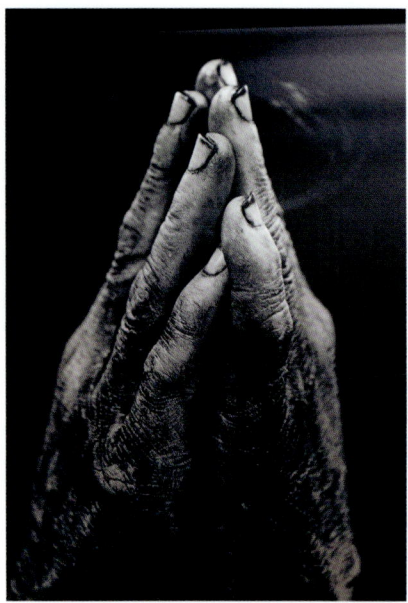

The rule of thirds is a versatile compositional device (see page 8), but it is not a one-size-fits-all solution and won't always produce the most compelling shots. Hand portraits are one instance in which central compositions can be the most effective. When filling most of the frame with a single subject, placing the focal point in the middle of the scene guarantees that it will grab the viewer's attention quickly and efficiently. Simplicity is, after all, the essence of all good design. Look for graphic vertical lines and experiment with camera orientation – clasped hands may suit the landscape format while fingers pointed into a steeple shape may fit the portrait format more snuggly.

LEFT **Consider the general shape of your subject's hands and their position and choose a camera orientation to match.**

TIP

For images with even greater contrast, try using a standard desk lamp positioned to the side of the hand or hands. Shooting in Monochrome mode will override any unwanted colour casts caused by the artificial light source, and you can direct the light more easily to emphasize textures and shadows.

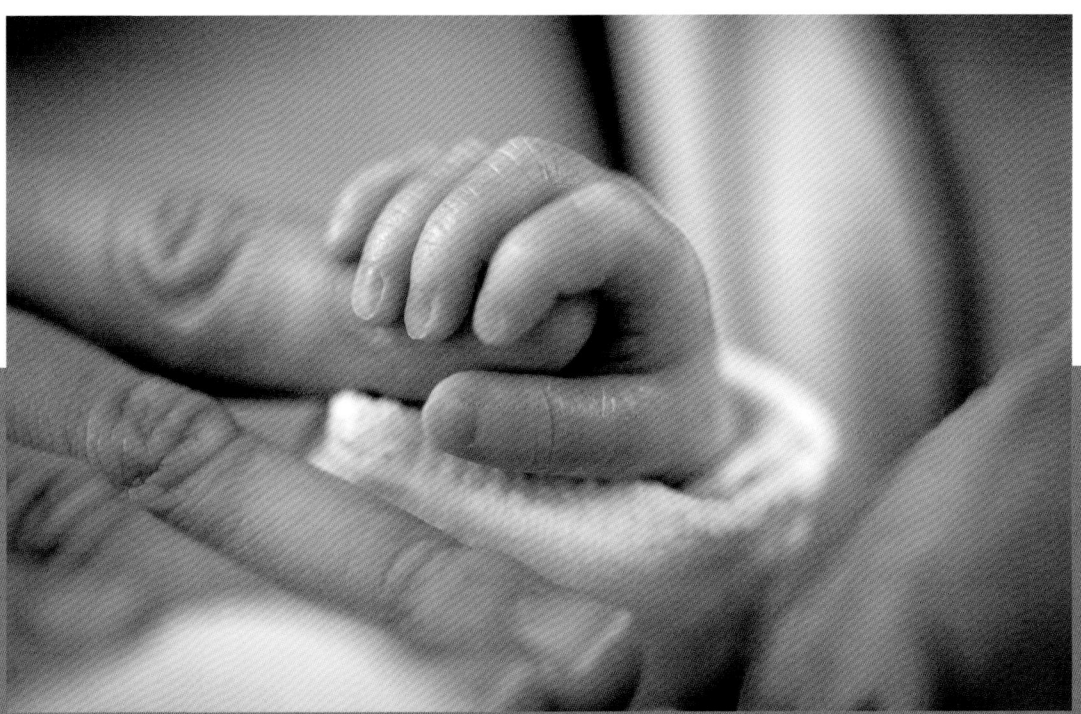

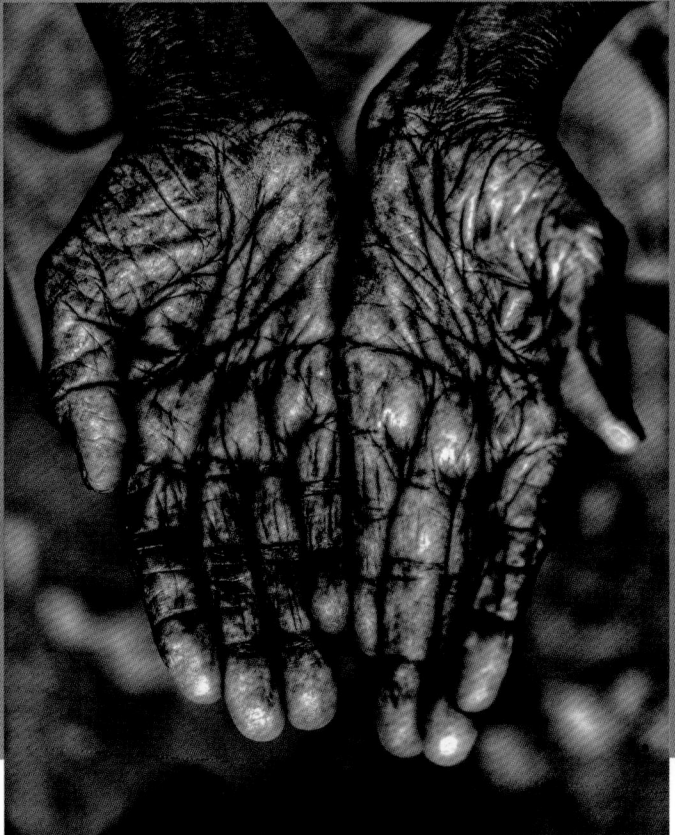

SHOOTING INSPIRATION

Young or old, smooth or wrinkled, hands are fascinating subjects that reveal almost as much about a person as their face does. Take a closer look at your own for starters.

ABOVE Subtle black-and-white tones create a gentle contrast between newborn and adult hands.

LEFT From one extreme to another – the lines on these weather-worn hands read like roads on a map. Look for older subjects whose hands tell interesting stories.

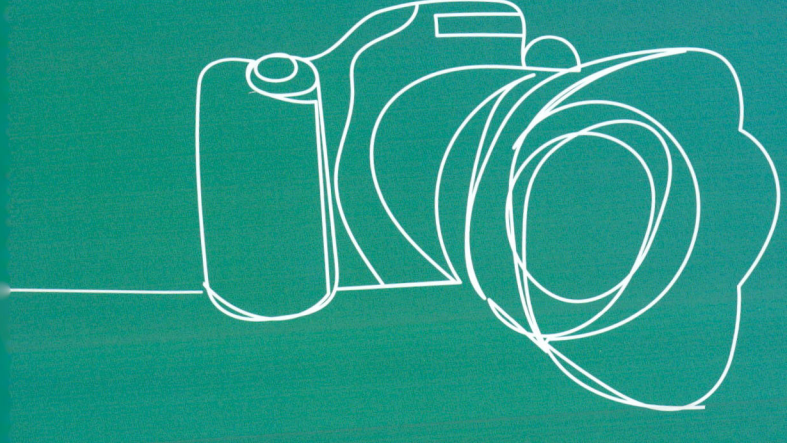

3 NATURE

Module 3.1
Focus on flowers

Flowers are captivating subjects. With their intricate designs, kaleidoscopic colours and evocative fragrances, these joyful symbols of life have been inspiring artists and poets for millennia. And while it's tempting to think that you have to travel to far-flung corners of the world to find the most exotic species, your garden or local park are home to enough fascinating flora to fill several portfolios of amazing natural world images. Studying a flower up close is the best way to unlock its hidden beauty, so for our first creative project we're going to zoom right in.

Kit lenses are surprisingly adept at close-up photography. Most feature a minimum focusing distance of 25cm (10in), which is measured from the camera's sensor (or film) plane, represented by a small symbol on top of the camera that looks like a circle with a line running through it. Depending on the size of your camera and lens, this means that you can position your lens' front element as close as 10cm (4in) from your subject and still achieve focus. When shooting larger flowers such as chrysanthemums, gerberas and, in our case, a dahlia, you can easily fill most or all of the frame for more artistic compositions without the need for specialist equipment.

Soft, diffused light is ideal for such delicate subjects with so much texture and detail, so wait for a bright but overcast day and don't worry if your only option is to shoot in a shaded area – I strongly recommend you use a tripod for this project and so shutter speed shouldn't be a primary concern. What is important is that your flower remains relatively still while you work, as even the smallest movements will be magnified at such close proximity, so use a reflector or sheet of card to buffer any wind if necessary. Compose using the rule of thirds (see page 8), positioning the centre of the flower – your subject's 'eye' – on a horizontal grid line to create a visual balance.

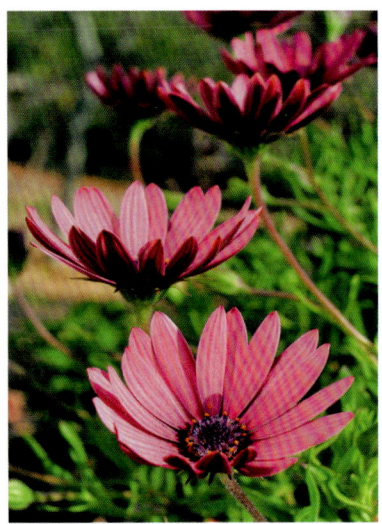

Aperture: ƒ/22

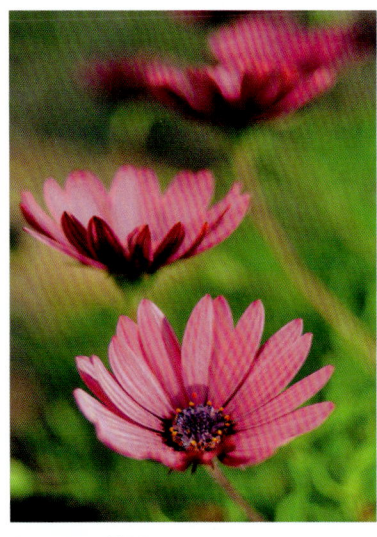

Aperture: ƒ/5.6

LEFT **Experiment with your aperture setting to find the perfect depth of field.**

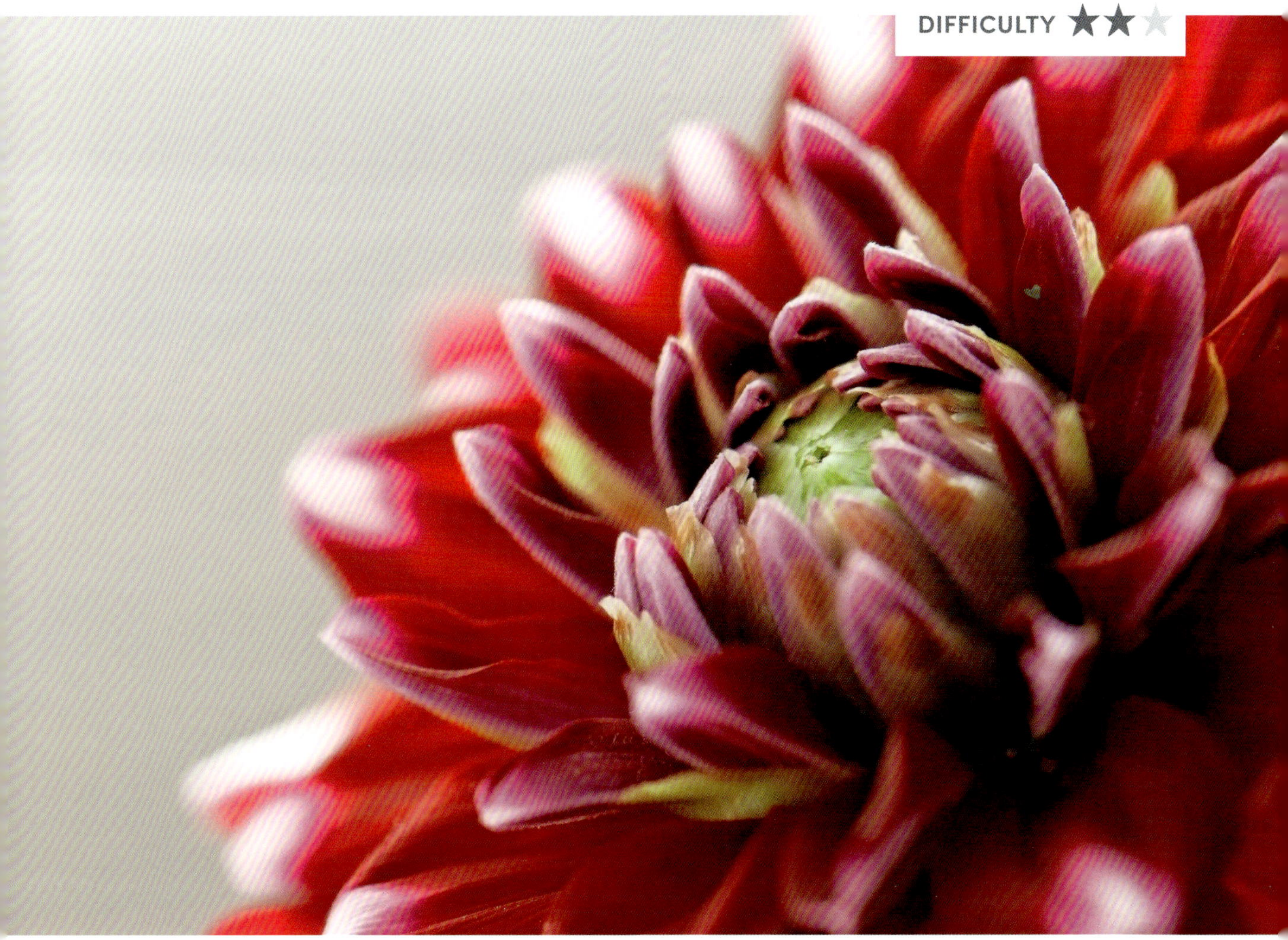

DIFFICULTY ★★☆

ABOVE **Large flowers such as dahlias are colourful, intricate and easy to fill the frame with.**

RECOMMENDED SETTINGS

- Shooting mode: **Aperture-priority**
- Aperture: **f/5.6**
- Shutter speed: **Will vary**
- ISO: **100**
- Focal length: **55mm**
- AF area: **N/A**
- AF operation: **Manual**
- Drive mode: **Single-shot or self-timer**
- Metering mode: **Evaluative/matrix**
- White balance: **Auto or daylight/cloudy**
- Picture style: **Vivid or Landscape**

Camera settings

Because our lens' front element is just a few centimetres away from our subject, depth of field is already going to be fairly shallow. By adding a large aperture to the mix, we can minimize the zone of sharpness even further, throwing not just the background out of focus, but large areas of the flower itself. This potent combination can be used to create more expressive images that blend sharpness and blur to accentuate scale and depth. Select aperture-priority mode, set an aperture of ƒ/5.6 and scan the backdrop for any potentially distracting elements – natural greens and browns are fine, but brightly coloured garden tools or kids' toys should be removed.

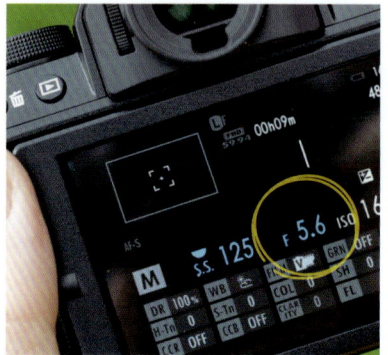

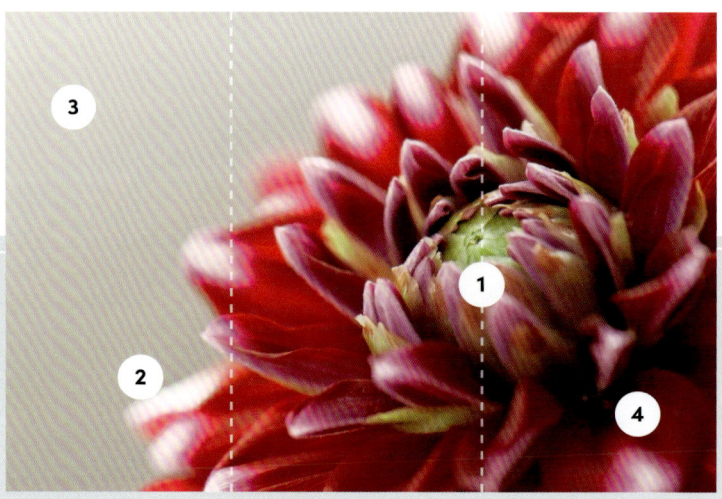

WHY THIS SHOT WORKS

1 The centre of the flower – the subject's 'eye' – is perfectly sharp and carefully positioned on a horizontal rule-of-thirds grid line. This creates the illusion of the 'eye' looking into the frame.

2 The combination of a close focusing distance and wide aperture has created a very shallow depth of field that has blurred not only the background but also large areas of the flower itself, creating a more artistic close-up.

3 The background is a natural – and neutral – colour that works to highlight and boost the flower's rich red-purple tones. Consider using a coloured sheet of card if you can't find a suitably uncluttered backdrop.

4 Shooting from an oblique, side-on angle adds an interesting three-dimensional quality to what could have been a rather flat composition had the shot been taken from directly above the flower.

Using a tripod for this project serves two purposes: it allows us to set the lowest ISO for the best image quality without having to worry about shutter speed; and it forces us to slow down and spend more time fine-tuning our composition. This is never more important than when shooting close-up photography, when even a fraction of a millimetre will have a significant impact on what goes where in the frame. Use Live View and tilt your camera's LCD upwards to make this process more intuitive and comfortable. Shutter speeds will vary depending on how much natural light is available, but it's best practice to trigger the shutter without touching the camera, so use a remote shutter release or your camera's self-timer.

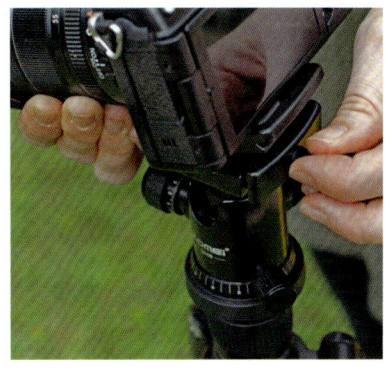

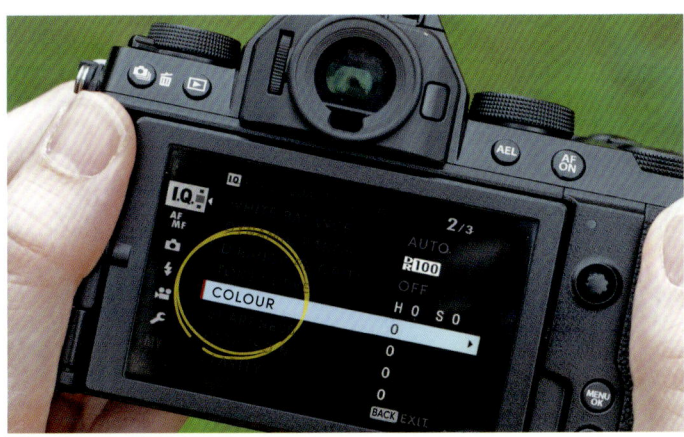

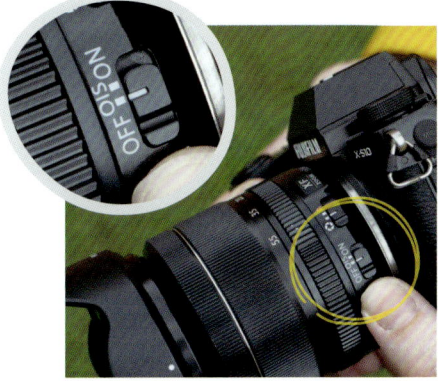

As we're shooting outdoors in overcast conditions, either the daylight or cloudy white balance preset will result in neutral colours. Which you choose will depend on how overcast the weather is, and how shady the area you are working in is (auto is also a safe bet in natural light if you'd rather let your camera do the heavy lifting). With such a dazzling array of colours at our disposal, we can also give Mother Nature a helping hand by selecting a 'Vivid' Picture Style, which will boost contrast, brightness, saturation and sharpness (or you could select the Landscape preset and increase saturation). Not all camera brands use the same preset names and some are even customizable – just resist the urge to overcook certain effects.

It's tempting to leave any image stabilization (IS) technology switched on regardless of what and how you're shooting, the assumption being that sharper is always better. Usually you'd be spot on, but when using a tripod, it's important that you turn any IS off – as IS is designed to detect and reduce vibrations in the lens, if it can't find any, the internal IS mechanism will actually create its own. Just to confuse the issue, it's worth noting that some newer lenses feature a 'tripod detection' IS mode, in which case there's no need to switch it off.

FOCUS ON FLOWERS 93

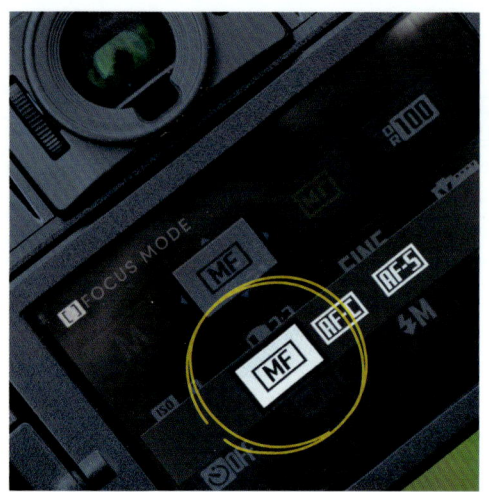

Lens settings

We want to fill as much of the frame with our flower as possible while still being able to obtain sharp focus. To achieve this, we need to zoom our kit lens in to its longest focal length, which not only narrows our field of view and gets us closer but also provides us with a comfortable working distance between the lens' front element and the petal nearest the lens. As focusing is so critical, we're also going to switch to manual focus mode for the first time. Flick the AF/MF switch on your lens barrel to MF and select the single-shot drive mode if using a remote shutter release.

Technique

Slowly rotate your lens' focusing ring to bring your desired focal point into sharp focus. Before the advent of digital cameras and rear LCD screens, you'd have needed either a double-jointed neck or a specialist device called a 'right-angled viewfinder' to compose when shooting near to the ground. Today, we can simply activate Live View, tilt the LCD and use the zoom/magnify buttons to check focus, which is incredibly useful when depth of field is so shallow. You'll actually be able to see the plane of focus move forwards and backwards as you turn the focusing ring.

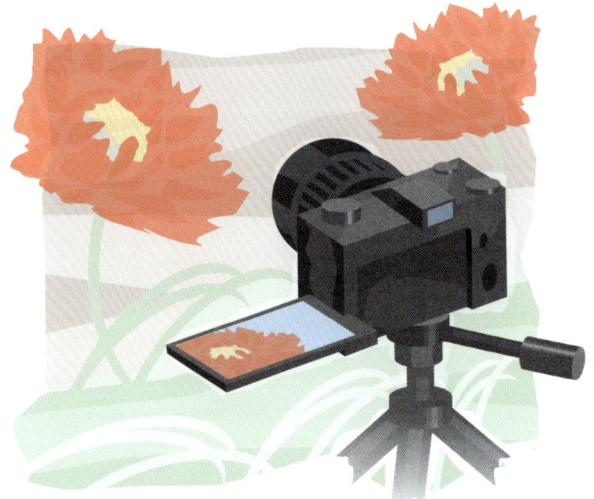

ABOVE **If your camera has a flip-out screen, you can use Live View to easily see what you're shooting.**

TIP

Once you've composed your floral close-up, use Live View's zoom/magnify button to inspect your subject's petals. If you spot any obvious imperfections – dirt, debris or dead insects, for instance – use a pair of tweezers to carefully remove them. All good floral/close-up photographers carry an old pair of tweezers for this exact job.

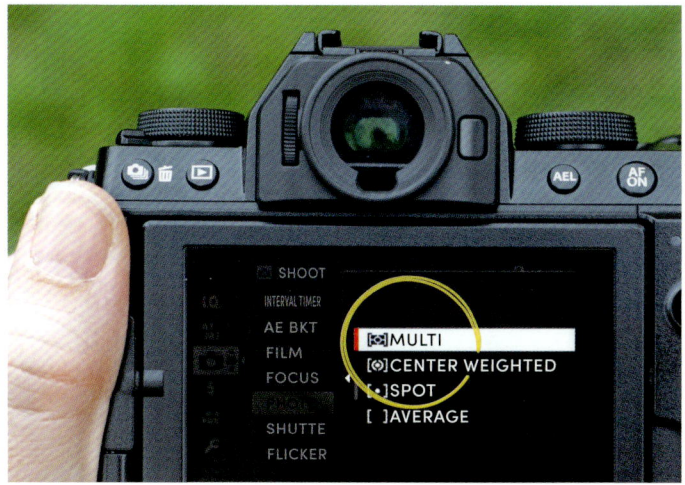

One of the reasons why overcast conditions are preferred to direct sunlight when dealing with such delicate subjects is because it reduces contrast levels, producing a softer, more evenly spread quality of light. As a result, evaluative/matrix metering will produce a perfectly exposed image, albeit one that may appear rather flat. If this is the case, use exposure compensation to lighten the exposure slightly, brightening colours and creating more pleasing true-to-life results.

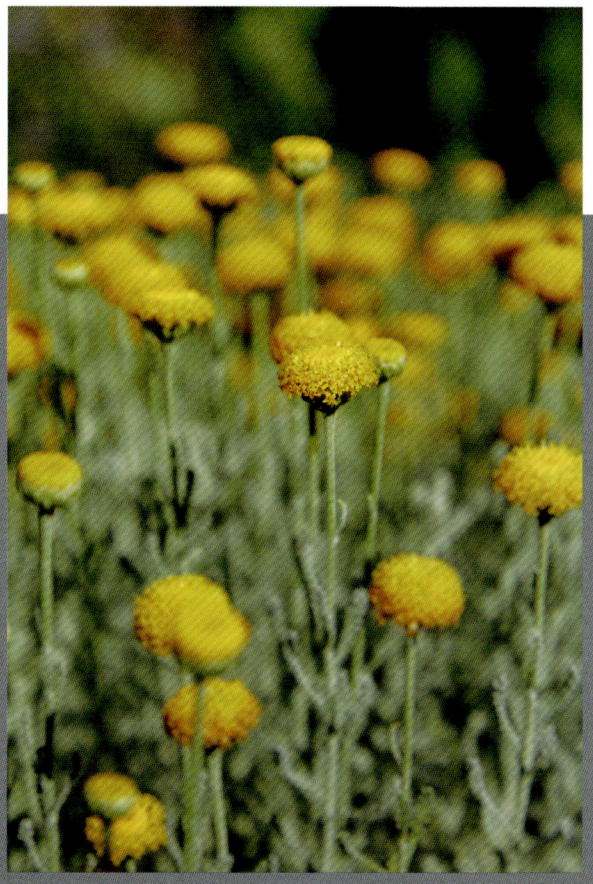

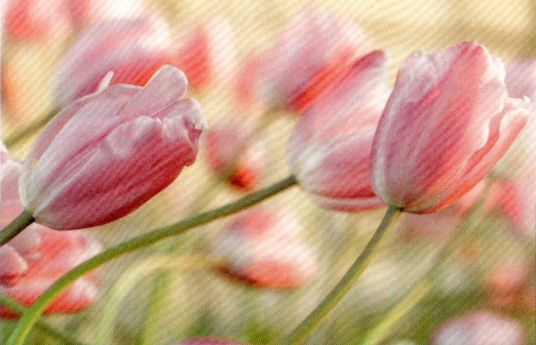

SHOOTING INSPIRATION

Flowers are a great subject and offer a huge range of shooting options:

ABOVE These vibrant pink tulips really leap out of the sandy backdrop.

LEFT Shoot with a wide aperture and pick one flower head to focus on.

FOCUS ON FLOWERS 95

Module 3.2
Get low for grass

The natural world is a weird and wonderful place where even the most mundane subjects can take on new meaning when viewed from unfamiliar angles. How many times have you walked past a lawn and thought nothing of it? Blades of grass, maybe a few leaves, perhaps even a bug or three... all rather humdrum. This is because we typically view the natural world from eye level – our eye level – but what happens when we adopt an insect's eye view? Suddenly, that uniform carpet of green becomes a tangled jungle of towering skyscrapers, each with their own unique shapes and contortions.

By laying on our stomachs and searching for new perspectives, we can transform seemingly ordinary subjects into intriguing images. This often means getting cold, wet and muddy, though there are various accessories we can use and adapt to make life more comfortable – bin bags and ground sheets for staying dry, gardener's knee pads for protecting ourselves on rocky ground. We can also add drama to our low-level natural world images by shooting just after dawn, when every blade of grass glistens with dew, and by pointing our cameras into the low sun to turn those dewdrops into magical orbs of spectral light.

The visual qualities of an image's out-of-focus areas are described by the Japanese word *bokeh*. Literally meaning 'blur', this word has become something of a buzz term recently, with the effect often described as 'dreamy' or 'swirly'. *Bokeh* can be 'good' or 'bad' (although this is subjective) and its form is determined by the shape and number of the blades that make up your lens' aperture. Also, the wider the aperture, the longer the focal length and the closer the subject, the more pronounced the *bokeh*. The effect can be accentuated when shooting into the light – in our example, the blurred dewdrops have magnified and reflected the sun's rays.

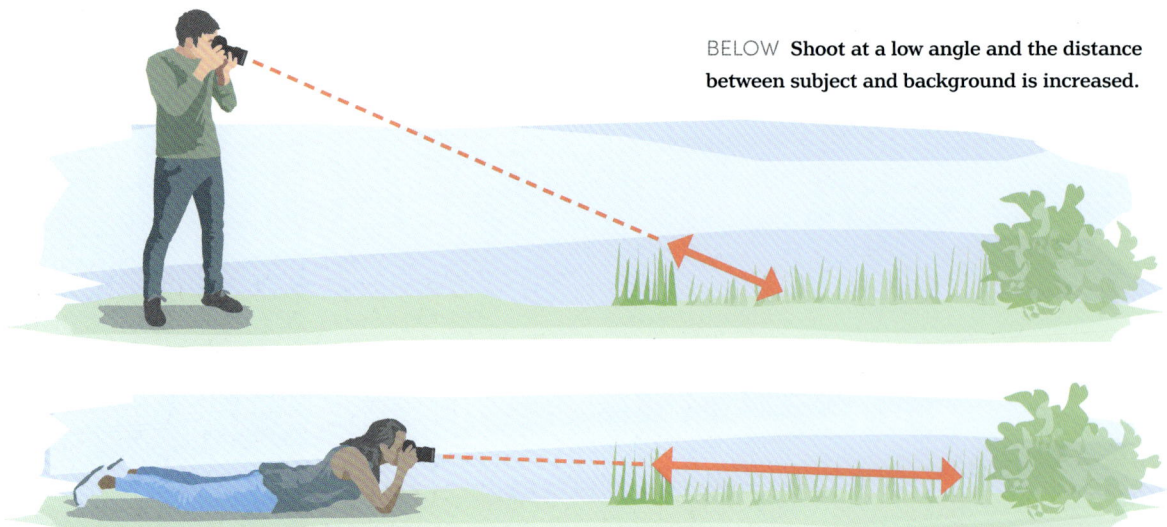

BELOW Shoot at a low angle and the distance between subject and background is increased.

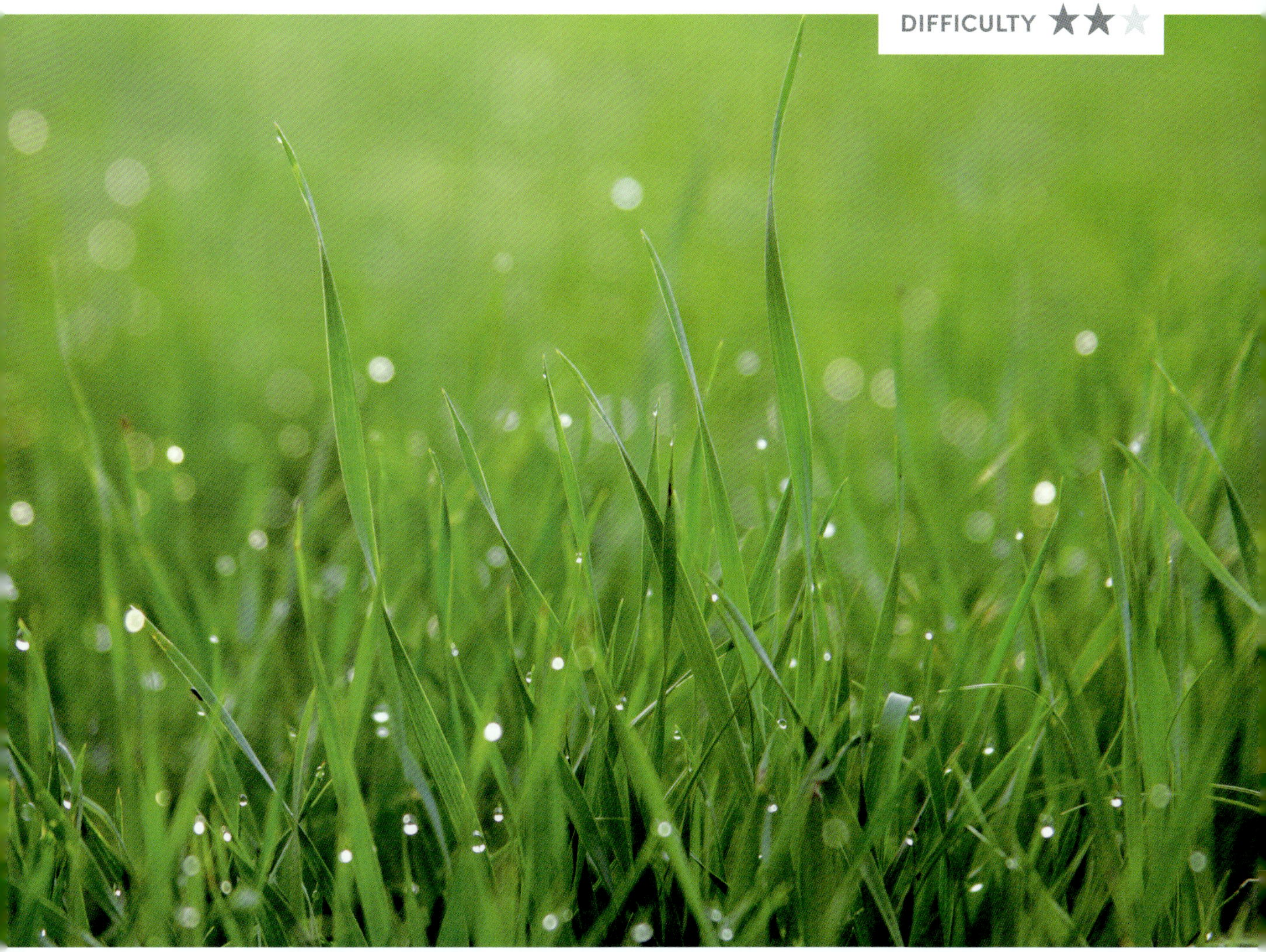

DIFFICULTY ★★★

ABOVE **View the natural world from an insect's perspective and even mundane subjects, such as grass, become intricate latticeworks of greenery.**

RECOMMENDED SETTINGS

- Shooting mode: **Aperture-priority**
- Aperture: **f/5.6**
- Shutter speed: **1/125sec (still); 1/250sec (windy)**
- ISO: **100**
- Focal length: **55mm**
- AF area: **N/A**
- AF operation: **Manual**
- Drive mode: **Single-shot**
- Metering mode: **Evaluative/matrix**
- White balance: **Auto or daylight/cloudy**
- Picture style: **Vivid or Landscape**

GET LOW FOR GRASS

Camera settings

Having filled the frame with colourful flowers in the previous module, you should be well versed in the art of close-up photography and the settings needed to create more impressionistic depictions of the natural world. We want to generate a very shallow plane of focus, with only the few blades of grass sitting along a small strip of lawn to be in sharp focus, while everything in front of and behind quickly falls out of focus, not only creating a sense of depth but also a clear and obvious focal point to draw the viewer's attention. Again, the best settings for this are aperture-priority mode and your lens' widest aperture.

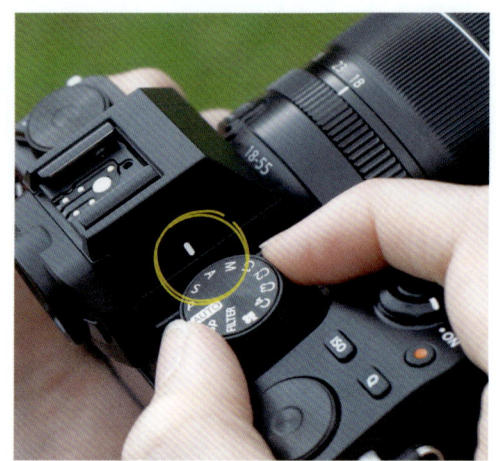

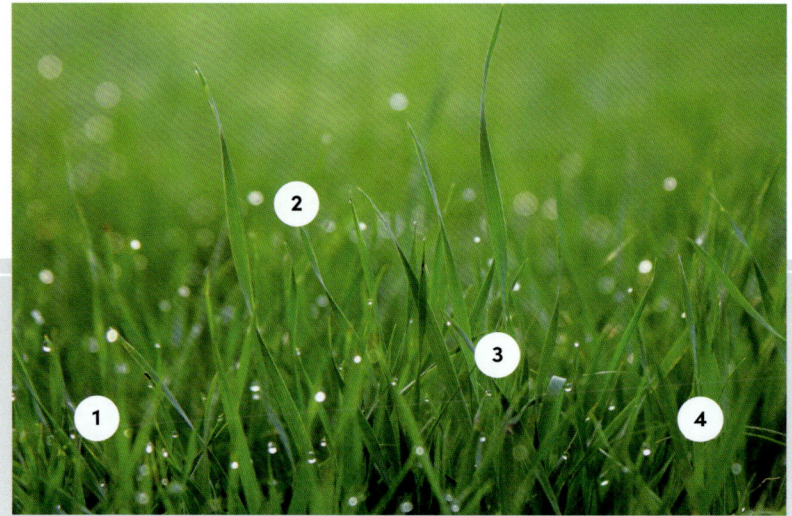

WHY THIS SHOT WORKS

1 By lying prone and adopting a worm's eye view, the photographer has transformed an ordinary patch of grass into a fascinating tangle of writhing skyscrapers.

2 Those spectral *bokeh* highlights really bring this image to life. This was achieved by shooting into the light just after dawn, when the sun is low in the sky and the grass is glistening with dew.

3 The plane of focus is incredibly shallow, with only a few blades of grass picked out as focal points and the rest falling out of focus to create a sense of depth.

4 The colour palette may be limited to just green, but there are more than enough vibrant tones, highlights and shadows here to create a visually appealing natural-world close-up.

Of course, there's more to aperture than just depth of field – the smallest *f*/number will also let in the most amount of light for the fastest shutter speed possible. This is important when laying prone as you will need to improvise when it comes to camera support (see below). On a still day when the grass is perfectly static, aim for a shutter speed of 1/125 second as this will be fast enough to eliminate any unwanted motion blur; on blustery days, aim for a shutter speed of at least 1/250 second and wait for a lull in the wind. For ISO, start at 100 and only increase this setting if the shutter speed falls below the recommended levels.

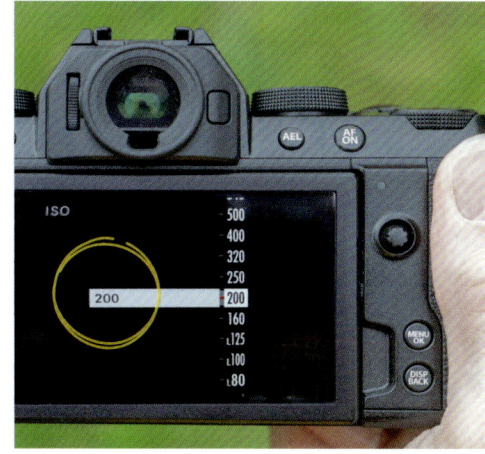

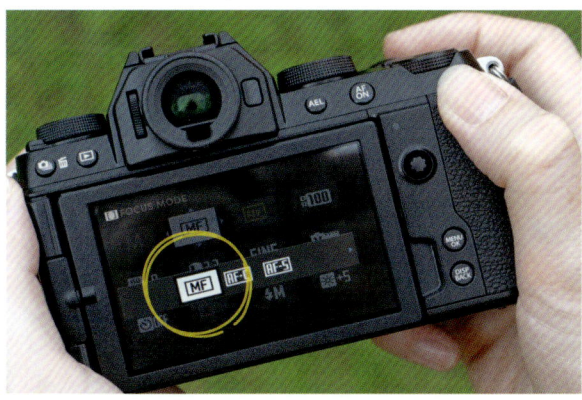

Close-up photography and limited depth of field go hand in hand and often the zone of sharpness can be no more than a few millimetres. This makes focusing more challenging than when shooting portraits, for instance, and why focusing manually is a more precise method than using autofocus. Live View not only allows us to see what the camera sees in real time, it also allows us to zoom into a live image to see how sharp – or otherwise – our intended focal point is. Use this intuitive feature rather than your camera's viewfinder to focus and compose, using the 3x3 grid overlay to balance your scene without cricking your neck.

Lens settings

The more restricted the field of view, the more pronounced the shallow depth-of-field effect will be, so zoom your kit lens all the way in for the most amount of foreground and background blur. With a 35mm equivalent focal length of almost 85mm, this short telephoto will 'compress' your scene slightly, an optical illusion that appears to pull the foreground closer to you (the opposite appears to happen with wide-angle focal lengths). Take full control of the focusing process by leaving the AF/MF switch set to MF and the drive mode set to single-shot. Switch image stabilization on if leaning on your elbows and switch it off if using a beanbag – see overleaf.

Technique

While some tripods allow you to invert the centre column and 'hang' the camera from the bottom of the tripod head, I have always found this to be a rather awkward method as you have to change the settings upside down, which can be frustratingly unintuitive. Instead, I'd recommend you use either a beanbag or lean on your elbows to keep your camera steady. Beanbags are widely available from specialist suppliers and can be filled with lentils or rice for a firm yet malleable base; you could even make your own or improvise with a rolled-up jumper. If you don't have a beanbag to hand, lay flat and prop yourself up with both elbows, creating a rigid triangle with your forearms, hands and camera. Resist the urge to hold your breath – instead, gently breath out when pressing the shutter to minimize movement.

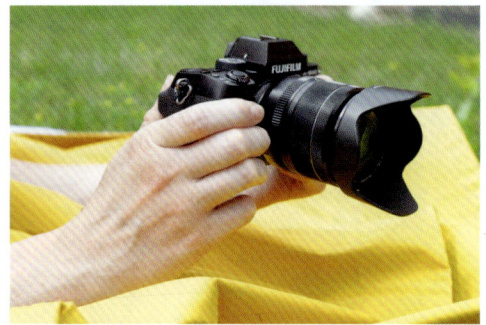

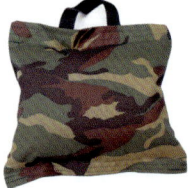

ABOVE **Beanbags are a more convenient camera support when shooting at ground level.**

Focusing follows the same technique as in the previous module, slowly rotating your lens' focusing ring to bring your intended focal point into sharp focus. However, when handholding, adjusting the focusing ring isn't always practical and so there is another method we can use to fine-tune sharpness, which is particularly useful when the subject is prone to movement. Known as the 'rocking' technique (a name I definitely didn't just make up), once we have focused as accurately as possible using Live View, we can very gently rock the camera back and forth to shift the plane of focus by a few millimetres.

Our grass close-up is like a miniature landscape in that it can be roughly divided into three horizontal zones: foreground, midground and background. The sharp grass sits in the foreground zone, the most attractive *bokeh* 'orbs' sit in the midground zone, and the most blurred grass, which almost morphs into one large green 'belt', sits in the background zone. Meanwhile, the two most prominent blades of grass are positioned on vertical rule-of-thirds grid lines (see page 8), which tells us that compositionally this image isn't as freeform as it might first appear. Use Live View's 3x3 grid overlay to help balance your scene, using zones to create greater depth.

TIP

Dew only forms when a cool, clear evening follows a warm, clear day, so if these conditions aren't forthcoming, use a spray bottle – the kind you can find at any garden or DIY store – and 'mist' water onto the grass you want to photograph. This will recreate the 'dew' look and give you glistening highlights.

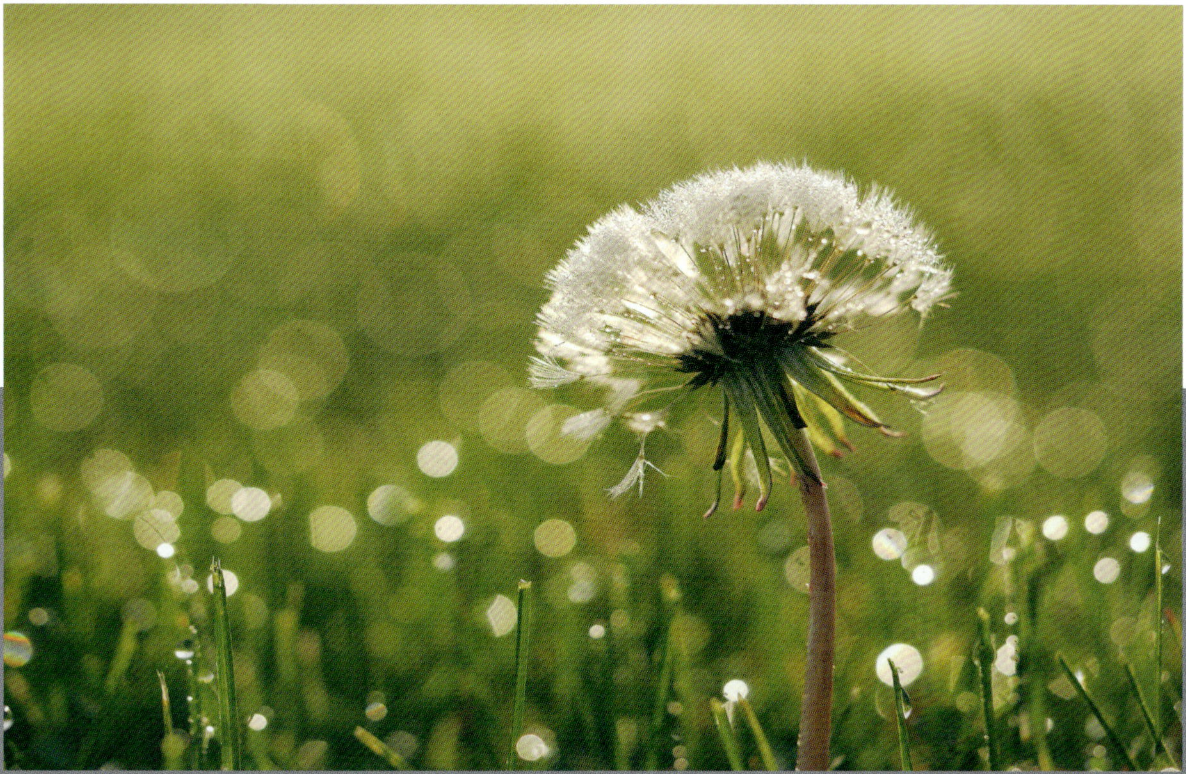

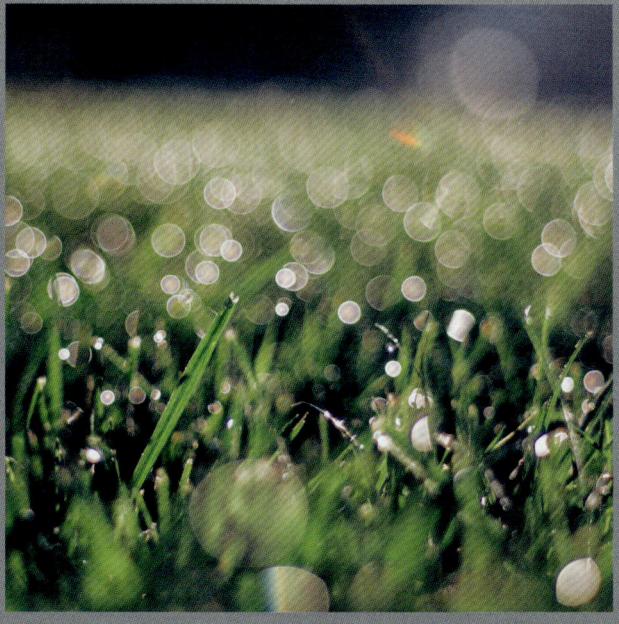

SHOOTING INSPIRATION

Grass may not be the most obvious subject for artistic exploration, but combine it with floral subjects, dramatic lighting and early morning dew, and you'll be pleasantly surprised.

ABOVE Dandelions are very common and their seedheads (or 'clocks') make particularly attractive garden subjects.

LEFT Use a wide aperture and shoot into the light to transform drops of dew into glowing *bokeh* 'orbs'.

Module 3.3
Reveal a leaf's patterns

Leaves are like maps – look at them closely enough and you will see an intricate latticework of major and minor roads, criss-crossing their way across the epidermis. If it has been raining, you may also find the occasional pond or reservoir. During spring and summer, when the natural world is at its most ostentatious, these micro maps are lush and vibrant; when autumn arrives and the light starts to fade, the colour palette shifts from garish greens to golden oranges and yellows; the dark days of winter see a leaf's veins turn to skeletal highways, delicate to the touch yet fascinating to the eye.

Whatever the season, hold a leaf up to the light and you will see a uniquely patterned subject perfect for close-up photography. Although a relatively simple technique, this project will encourage you to take a closer look at the minutiae of the natural world and will reward you with absorbingly abstract images of instantly recognizable subjects. Start by collecting a few suitable specimens – we either want perfect leaves free from damage and decay or decomposed leaves with their shape and detail still intact. Be careful when handling your specimens as they are easily damaged, and look for leaves that can be laid flat as this will help when focusing.

At its simplest, this project involves you (or an assistant) holding a leaf up to the light and shooting away, with the backlighting illuminating the intricate details and bringing the subject to life. However, this approach has its limitations as you can only hold one or two leaves in front of the camera, particularly if you are working solo. For more elaborate compositions, you can arrange your leaves into a visually appealing 'collage' and then sandwich them between two panes of glass – the non-reflective kind you find in picture frames is perfect. Just dry the leaves first as any moisture will stick to the glass, and make sure the glass is clean and free from fingerprints.

RIGHT **Find the perfect specimen for images packed with intricate details.**

RECOMMENDED SETTINGS

- Shooting mode: **Aperture-priority**
- Aperture: **f/5.6**
- Shutter speed: **1/250sec**
- ISO: **100**
- Focal length: **55mm**
- AF area: **Single-point AF**
- AF operation: **Single-shot AF**
- Drive mode: **Continuous**
- Metering mode: **Evaluative/matrix**
- White balance: **Auto or daylight/cloudy**
- Picture style: **Vivid or Landscape**

DIFFICULTY ★★☆

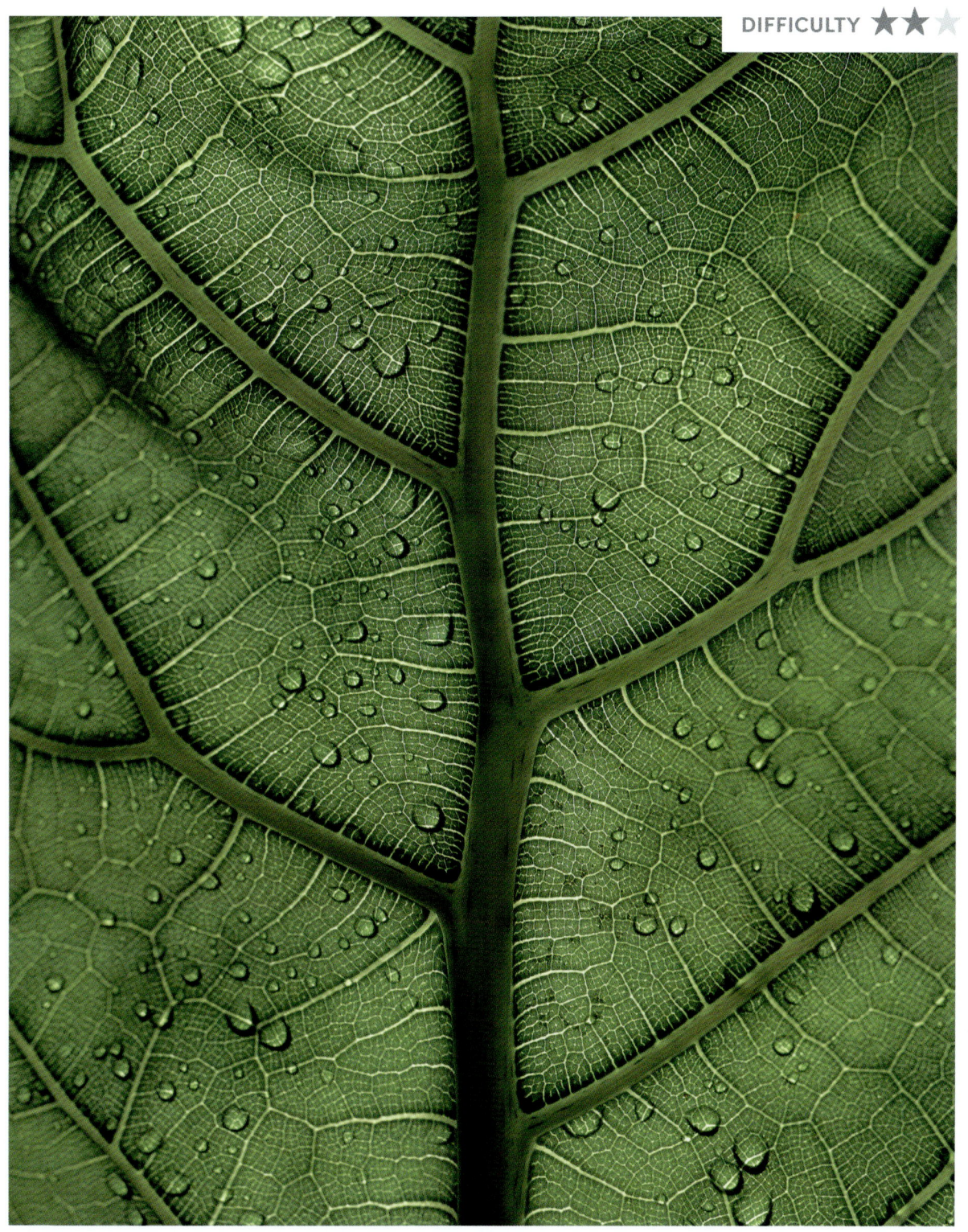

REVEAL A LEAF'S PATTERNS 103

Camera settings

While still in the world of close-up photography, we are moving from real-world images with strong focal points and blurred backgrounds to abstract images of flat subjects with no obvious focal points or sense of depth. This means that although our camera settings stay the same, the reasons why we use these settings change slightly. For instance, although aperture is still an important consideration, because we are shooting perpendicular to a flat surface, depth of field is not – instead we simply want to use aperture to let in as much light as possible. So, leave the mode dial turned to aperture-priority and again select your lens' widest aperture.

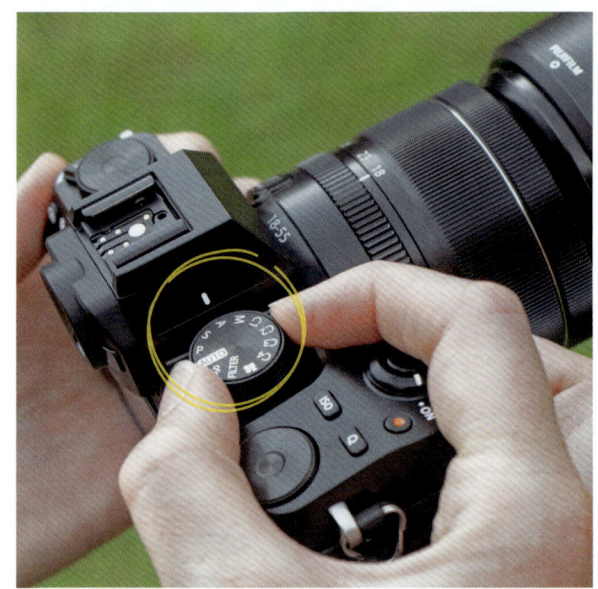

WHY THIS SHOT WORKS

1. The leaf's veins look like roads running across a map, with the central midrib creating a strong vertical line from which the smaller veins emanate from, like the branches of a tree.

2. The backlighting highlights every intricate line, pattern and texture – fascinating details that you only see when taking a much closer look at the natural world.

3. This particularly fresh and vibrant specimen completely fills the frame, giving us an eye-catching yet abstract close-up of an instantly recognizable subject.

4. The water droplets add an extra layer of interest, which magnify the patterns below – you could easily add your own using a spray bottle and a fine 'mist' of water.

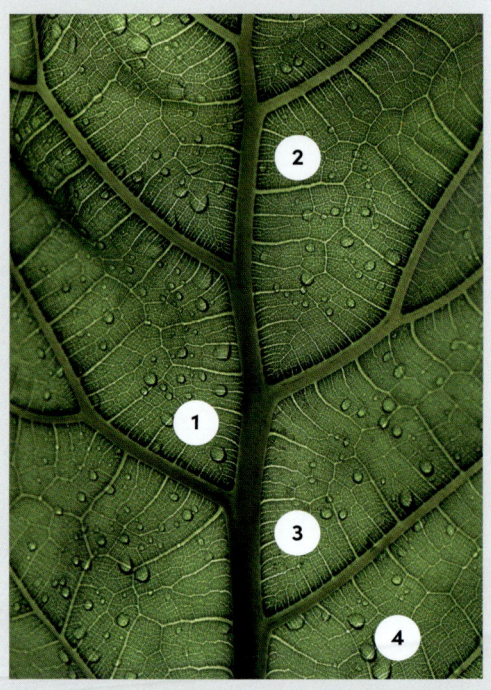

We are effectively replacing depth with detail in this project, and we need to use both shutter speed and ISO to ensure even the smallest veins and textures are sharp as razors. Exposure times simply need to be fast enough to allow us to handhold our cameras without worrying about motion blur. As always, the slowest shutter speed I would recommend is 1/125 second, although faster is better in this instance and so 1/250 second would be preferable. I would also recommend shooting outdoors on a sunny day, which means that ISO shouldn't have to creep up beyond 100 to achieve a fast enough exposure.

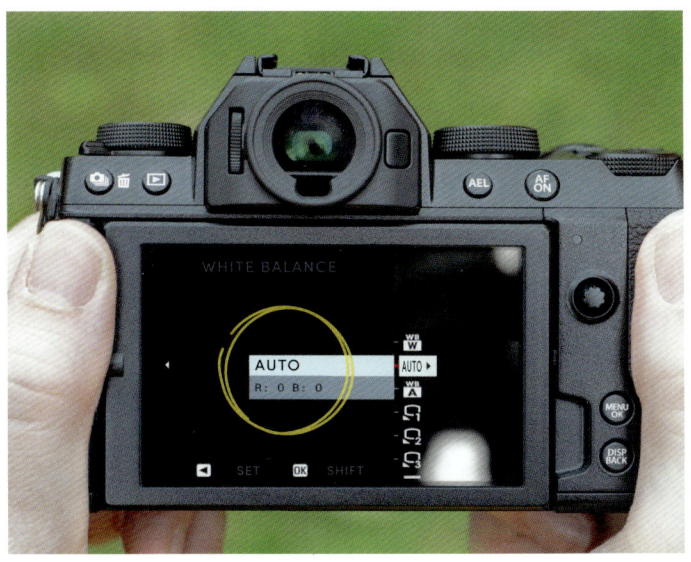

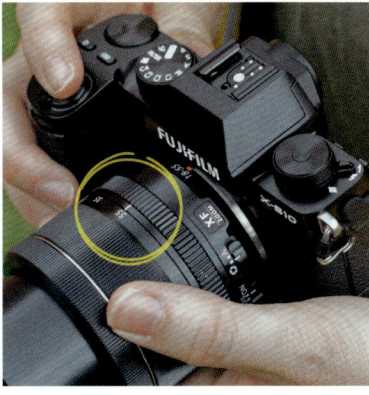

As well as crisp detail, we want the colours to be vibrant and punchy, particularly when shooting autumn leaves, and again we can use either a standard 'Vivid' picture style or a customized preset with saturation increased. Select either the daylight or cloudy white balance preset (or leave WB on auto) and switch image stabilization (IS) on if your camera utilizes this technology. While not a fix-all solution in every situation, IS is always a benefit when shooting static subjects handheld, particularly when critical sharpness is key and/or light levels are low. As we are no longer laying prone, we can compose and focus using either our camera's viewfinder or Live View.

Lens settings

Leaf close-ups are most effective when you fill the frame, so zoom all the way in and take advantage of your kit lens' minimum focusing distance (remember, this is measured from the sensor plane rather than the end of the lens itself). This gives us a short telephoto focal length (in 35mm equivalent terms) that will give us distortion-free images. Flick the AF/MF switch back to AF, but change the drive mode to continuous – this will allow us to shoot in short bursts, increasing our chances of capturing that one perfectly pin-sharp frame.

Technique

If shooting a single leaf, make sure you get close enough to completely fill the frame and look for graphic lines and shapes that can be used to inform composition. Guidelines such as the rule of thirds are less effective when shooting flat, abstract subjects due to the lack of depth and the absence of an obvious focal point; instead, we want to seek out natural patterns and symmetries, using strong vertical and diagonal lines to give our images a sense of structure and direction. In our example, the leaf's main vein – known as the midrib (remember that for your next pub quiz) – runs through the centre of the frame, with smaller veins emanating sideways and upwards like the branches of a tree. The small droplets of water add interest to the leaf's surface texture.

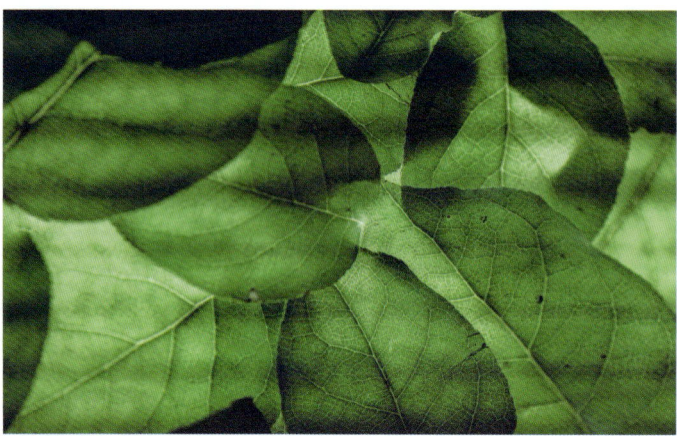

If shooting several leaves together, carefully arrange them to create repetitive, overlapping patterns that still allow the light to penetrate their translucent 'skins' and highlight the various shapes, colours and details. You could even overlap darker leaves around the edge of the frame to create a natural 'vignette' and position one particularly shapely specimen in the centre. There is no right or wrong here so just experiment, have fun and indulge your inner botanical artist – the more you shoot, the more you can review and refine your arrangement until you are 100% happy with it.

Ask your assistant to hold the leaf 'sandwich' at head height and shoot over their shoulder towards the light, making sure there are no distractions, such as trees or buildings, between you and the sun. Use the AF point to focus on an area of contrast and shoot in short bursts – as both you and your assistant are handholding, this will help to negate any movement. Just as you would when shooting portraits, tuck your elbows into your stomach and stand with your feet shoulder-width apart for stability. Hold your camera perpendicular to the glass as even the slightest change in angle could result in parts of the subject falling out of focus – unless, of course, this is the desired effect.

TIP

You don't always need natural light to create abstract leaf close-ups – you could arrange your specimens on an old lightbox or LED panel. This gives you a constant light source that you can use indoors without the need for an extra pair of hands.

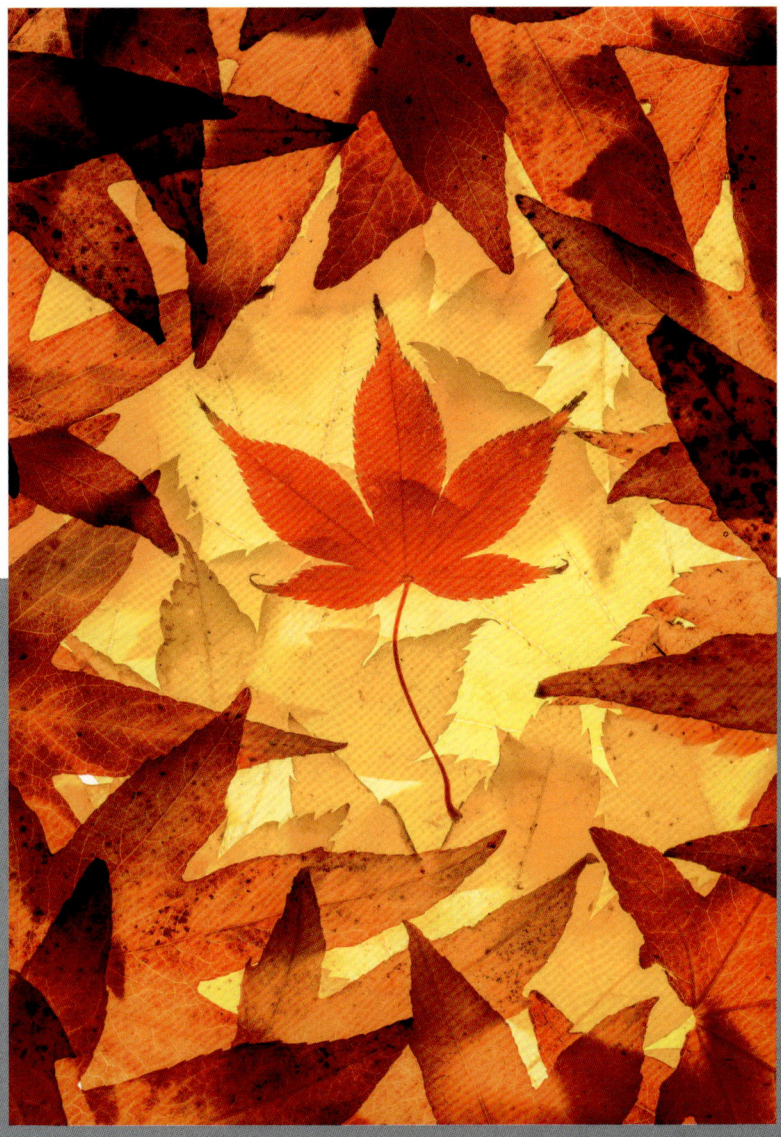

SHOOTING INSPIRATION

Leaves change colour and appearance as the seasons ebb and flow, so take advantage of nature's ever-shifting tonal palettes.

ABOVE Use the varying shades of autumn to create attractive tonal contrasts and highlight a central – and carefully chosen – subject.

REVEAL A LEAF'S PATTERNS

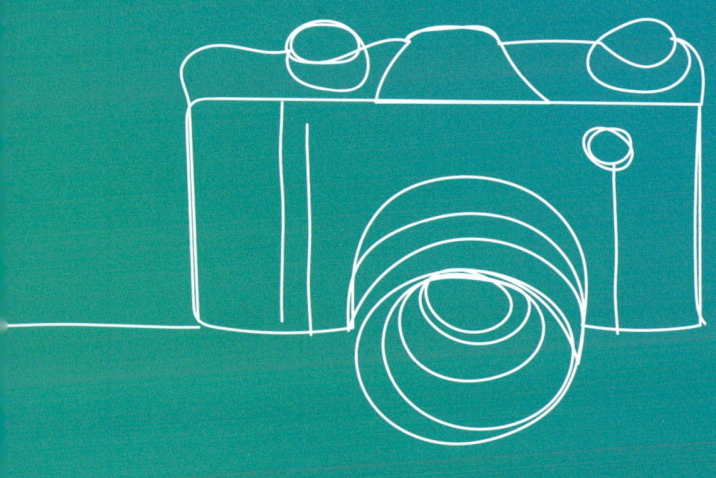

4 MOVEMENT

Module 4.1
Capture traffic trails

Traffic trails are the perfect after-dark starter project. While the human eye has a refresh rate of between 30 and 60 frames per second (fps) and sees the world as a continuous feed of updated screenshots, cameras 'see' for as long as the shutter remains open. The faster the exposure, the more 'frozen in time' any moving subjects will appear; the slower the exposure, the more 'transient' moving subjects become, to the extent that even the bright lights of a speeding car will register as blurred streaks if the shutter is left open long enough.

As the sun sets and ambient light levels drop, artificial light becomes more pronounced, so modern cities and busy motorways just after dusk are particularly effective locations. Trails themselves are rarely strong enough on their own to make an interesting composition, so static elements such as buildings and signs will provide a stark yet dynamic contrast to the blurred streaks of colour. How these streaks lead the eye through the frame is also important, and curved roads and/or elevated viewpoints are easy ways to add interest to your traffic trail images.

Sunset offers the perfect balance between ambient and artificial light – and allows for longer exposures – so arrive on location an hour or so before twilight and be ready to shoot just as the sun dips beneath the horizon. On cloudy evenings this will guarantee a warm, luminous glow to the sky, while on cloud-free evenings you'll be rewarded with a rich blue sky. Once the fading ambient light disappears completely, it's time to pack up, even if your window of opportunity was just a few minutes. Finally, don't forget your tripod – although the technique for traffic trails is relatively simple, it relies entirely on your camera being absolutely still during the long exposures.

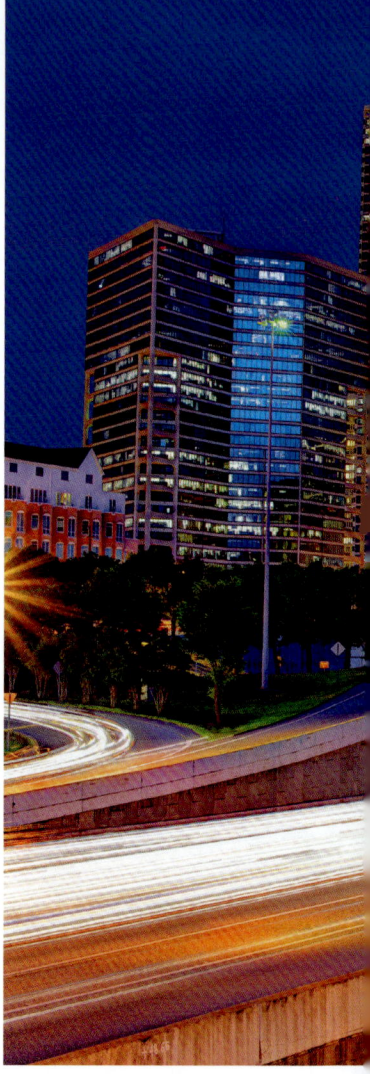

ABOVE **The dynamic streaks of light weave in and out of the cityscape's unmoving structures.**

LEFT **A sturdy tripod is essential when shooting traffic trails and other long-exposure techniques.**

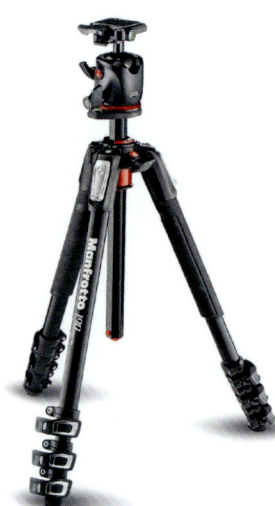

DIFFICULTY ★★★

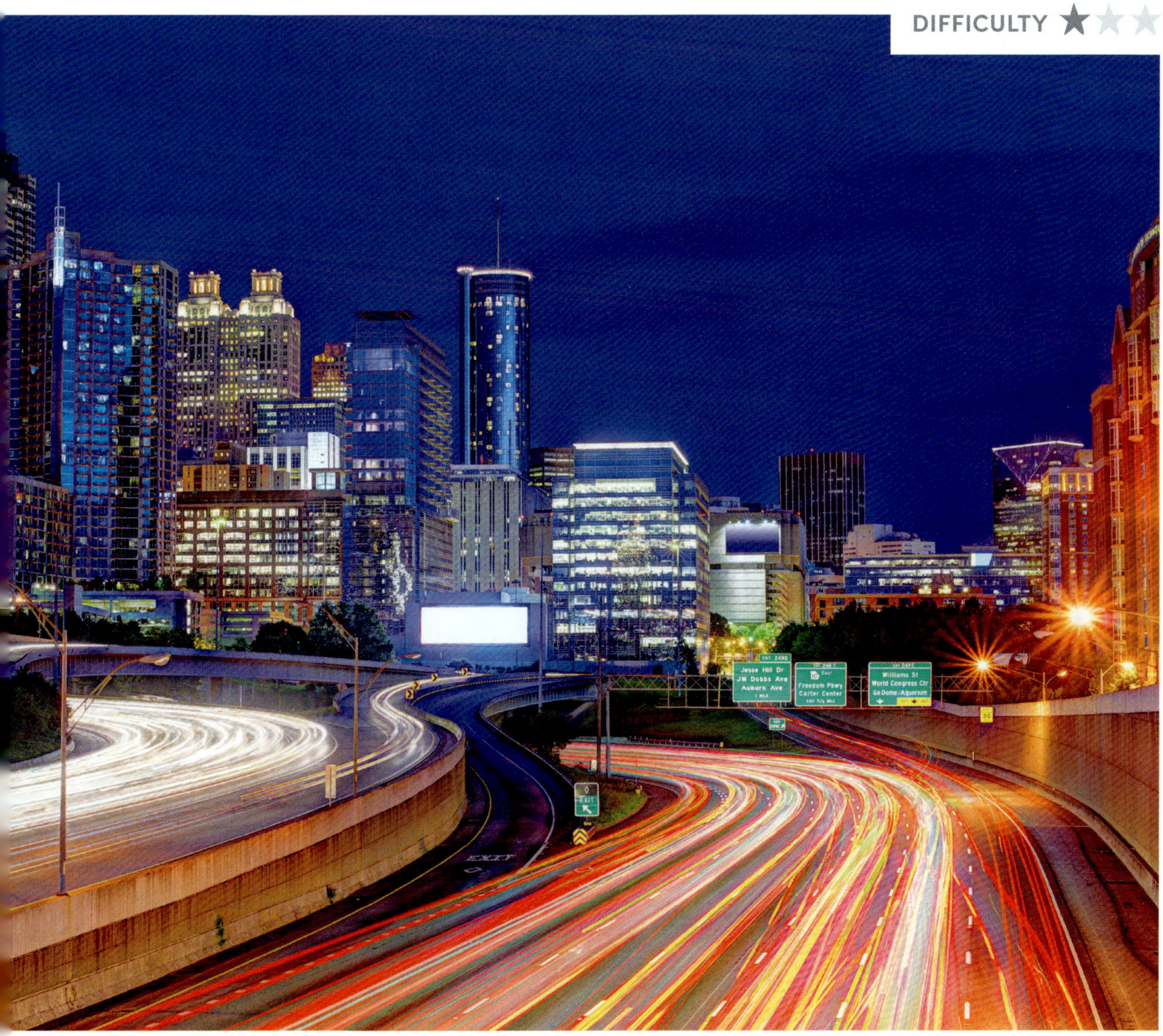

RECOMMENDED SETTINGS

- Shooting mode: **Manual**
- Aperture: **f/11**
- Shutter speed: **10–30 seconds**
- ISO: **100**
- Focal length: **18–55mm**
- AF area: **N/A**
- AF operation: **Manual**
- Drive mode: **Single-shot (remote shutter release) or self-timer**
- Metering mode: **Evaluative/matrix**
- White balance: **Tungsten or incandescent**
- Picture style: **Landscape**

CAPTURE TRAFFIC TRAILS 111

Camera settings

When shooting traditional landscapes, aperture and depth of field are usually our primary concern. However, when shooting traffic trails in the landscape, shutter speed takes precedence. This is because we need to allow the light source – in our case, the headlights of moving cars – enough time to move through the frame while also recording enough ambient light to add scenic interest.

Switch to manual mode (M) to take complete control of exposure and start with a shutter speed of 10 seconds. Once you start shooting, you may need to increase (up to 30 seconds) or decrease (down to 1/2 second) exposure time according to the subjects' speed, how far away they are, the direction in which they're travelling and your focal length (and how zoomed in or out you are).

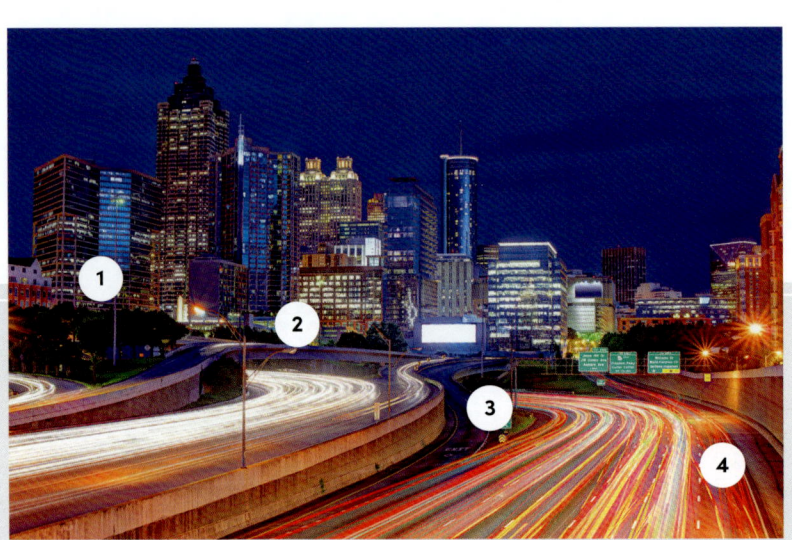

WHY THIS SHOT WORKS

① Bustling modern cities guarantee endless streams of traffic, even at twilight, resulting in bright and continuous trails that elegantly bend and flow as the roads dip under and over each other.

② Despite being a long-exposure image, the traditional rules of landscape photography have been applied, with the traffic trails occupying the bottom third of the frame and the cityscape the top two thirds.

③ The natural light and artificial light have been well balanced, with the richly coloured, near-featureless blue sky providing the perfect backdrop to the futuristic skyscrapers.

④ A mid-range aperture and low ISO, together with the camera firmly attached to a sturdy tripod, has ensured plenty of front-to-back detail and minimal noise. The perfect traffic trail image.

Because the camera is in a 'locked-off' shooting position, we can set the lowest ISO possible, which will usually be 100. This not only provides the best image quality and least amount of noise – the scourge of all low-light photographers – but also works in tandem with aperture to achieve longer shutter speeds, allowing us to get creative with light in ways that simply wouldn't be possible during the day without the use of special filters.

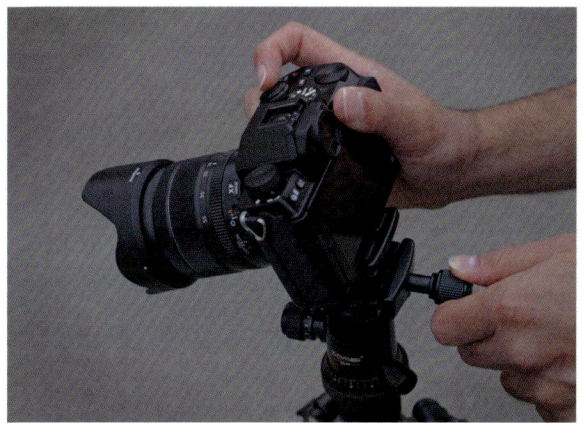

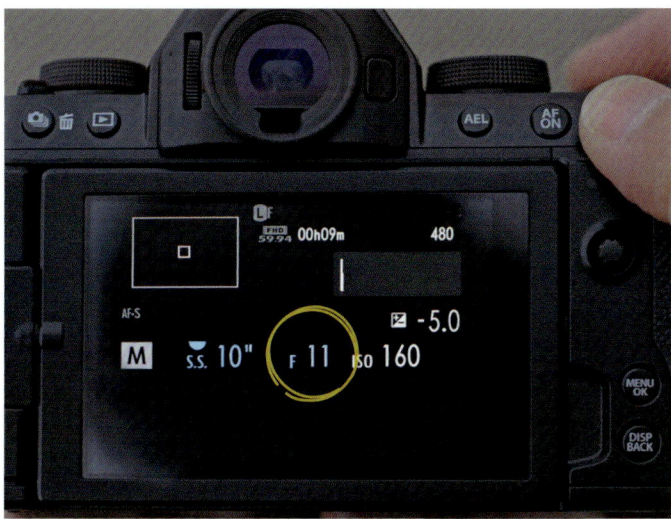

Start with a mid-range aperture of ƒ/11. Every lens has a 'sweet spot' – the point at which it performs at its sharpest – and this is typically 2–3 stops up from its widest aperture, so if you've got an ƒ/4-5.6 kit lens, this will be between ƒ/8 and ƒ/11 depending on focal length. If your traffic trails are too bright, close down to ƒ/16, and if your traffic trails are too dark, open up to ƒ/8. Just remember that aperture directly affects depth of field so it's best to not stray any wider than ƒ/8.

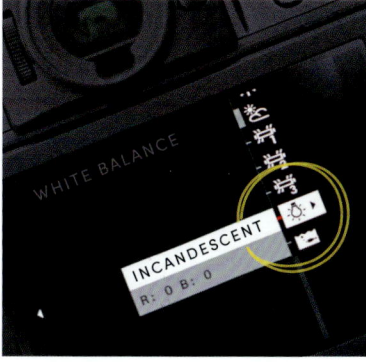

The mix of ambient and artificial lighting – from both the cars and buildings if shooting in the city – could result in some 'interesting' colour casts if white balance (WB) is left on auto, so this is definitely an instance where we need to dive in and select a more appropriate preset. Sodium lights are commonly used to light streets and industrial areas and these give off a strong yellow-orange glow so a tungsten or incandescent WB will produce more true-to-life results.

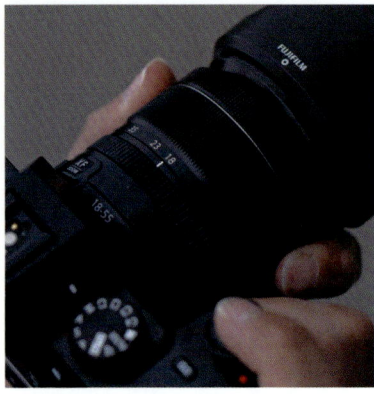

Lens settings

The usual landscape rules of composition apply here – rule of thirds, power points, lead-in lines etc (see page 20) – so select a focal length that allows you to create a visually balanced composition that includes only the absolute essentials. However, it's worth noting that the wider the focal length the thinner the traffic trails and vice versa. Focusing will be challenging in low light so switch to the manual focus mode (MF) and use Live View and the zoom/magnify buttons to help you focus a third of the way into the scene. Select the single-shot drive mode if using a remote shutter release.

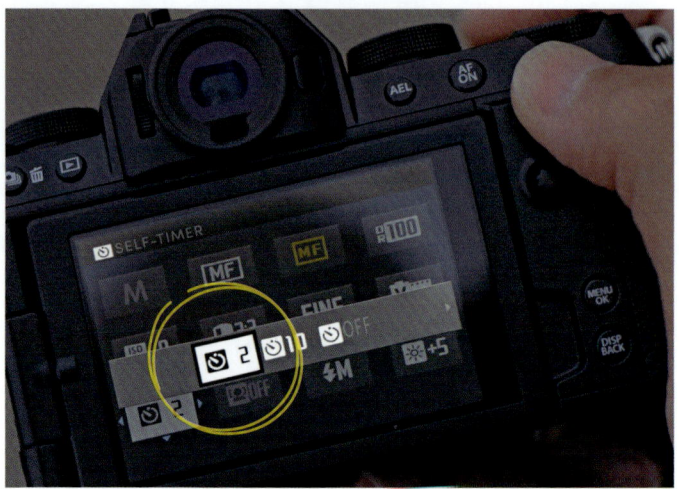

Technique

This is definitely a remote shutter release kind of technique. While your camera's self-timer mode will suffice, you'll need to predict where traffic will be in 2 or 10 seconds, which isn't always easy. A remote shutter release, on the other hand, will allow you to time the start of your exposures far more accurately. As ambient light levels will change while you shoot (artificial light levels will remain constant), you'll need to keep taking test shots and assessing the results on the rear screen, changing the aperture to adjust exposure if necessary.

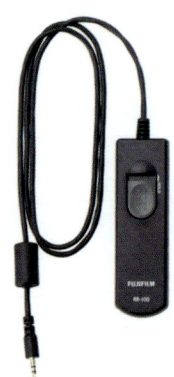

ABOVE **A remote shutter release will allow for more accurately timed exposures.**

TIP

Take a head torch so you can safely pack up your equipment and find your way back in the dark, particularly if shooting traffic trails in more remote areas away from bright artificial lights. Also, pack waterproofs for both you and your camera – while many cameras and lenses are 'weather sealed', they're not actually fully waterproof.

Shooting in urban areas and around traffic requires a much greater awareness of your surroundings than when shooting rural landscapes in glorious solitude. Position your tripod away from pedestrians and make sure that any spare equipment is safely secured. Also be aware that passing traffic can cause bridges to vibrate, which could potentially result in blurred traffic trails. To avoid this, position yourself above a bridge support or time your shots when traffic is moving towards but not directly beneath you.

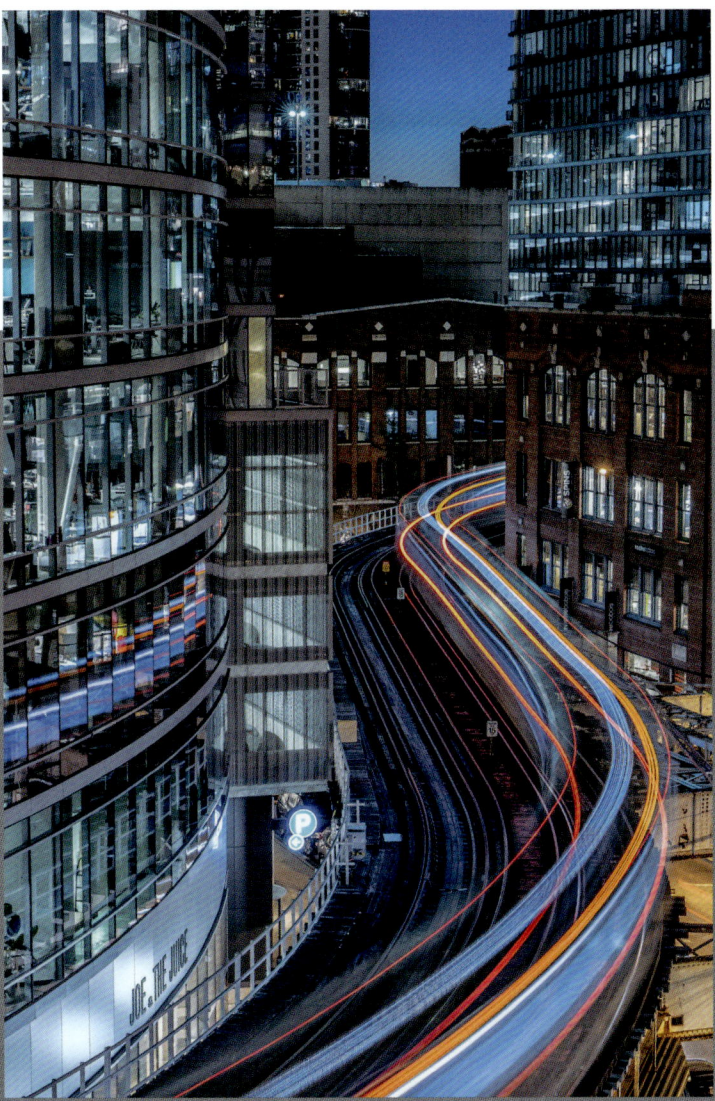

SHOOTING INSPIRATION

Look for high vantage points and curving lines – particularly those that interact with static structural elements – to add interest to your traffic trails.

LEFT Cars aren't the only moving subjects that create streaks of light – trains are also highly effective for this technique.

Module 4.2
Travel at warp speed

Shooting traffic trails is a fun and intuitive way to understand how cameras see and record light. So long as the camera is perfectly still, the subject is moving and the balance of ambient and artificial light is just right, you are almost guaranteed great shots. But it is also a technique that is ripe for experimentation. Years ago, while stuck in traffic at some ungodly hour, I had the idea to shoot traffic trails from my slowly moving car. Crudely balancing my DSLR on the dashboard (don't worry, my wife was driving), I fired off a few 2-second exposures. Although we were travelling at no more than 20mph (30kph), the results were spectacular and my obsession with 'warp speed' exposures was born.

The vibrations of the car caused the camera to move mid-exposure, which in turn caused the light trails created by traffic travelling in the opposite direction to vibrate also. Gone were the smooth lines of our static traffic trails and in their place were futuristic 'hyperspace' streams of light that looked like something from a sci-fi movie. The various road signs, oncoming and overtaking cars, and even smeared rain on the windscreen all seemed to add to the overall effect. I love 'imperfect' photography and this spontaneous discovery pressed all the right buttons.

Busy motorways, junctions and city centres are perfect places to shoot hyperspace images, though even a road with just a few passing cars on it will produce interesting enough light streams while you practise the technique. To add context, you could sit in the back and frame up with the dashboard and windscreen within the shot, and for smoother trails you could even squeeze a tripod into the footwell – just remember to use rubber tripod feet and not metal spikes to avoid damaging the car's upholstery. And don't think that this technique is for cars only – I've seen it deployed on subway trains and moving walkways to equally mesmerizing effect.

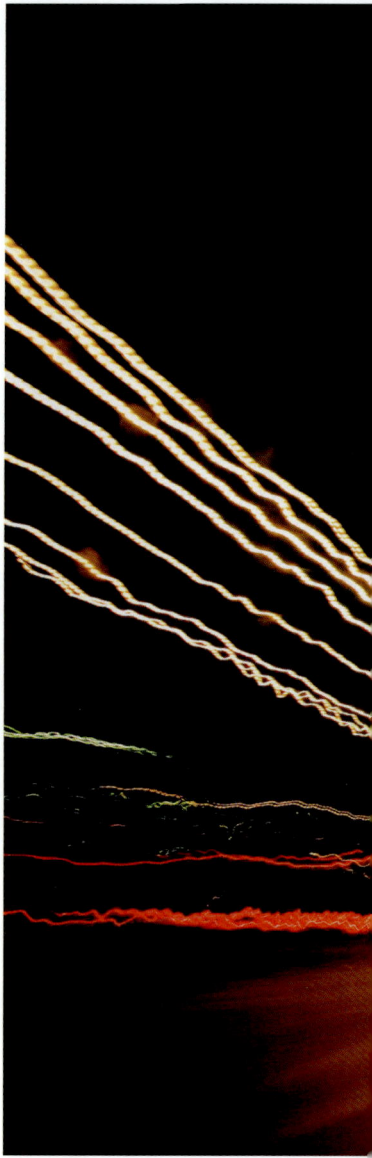

ABOVE **No tripods were used in the making of this photo!** This is a fun technique to try next time you're stuck in slow-moving traffic.

DIFFICULTY ★★★

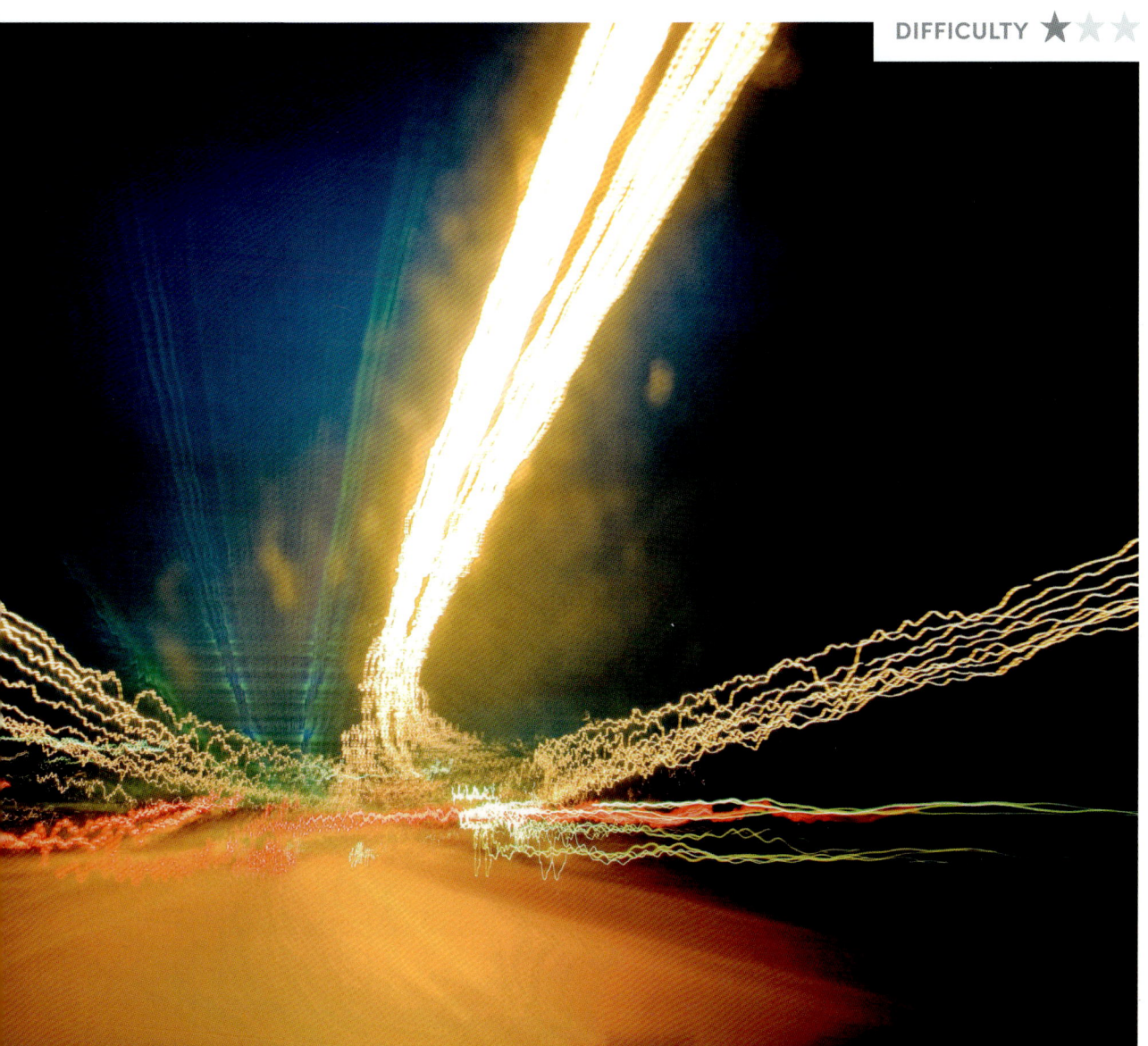

RECOMMENDED SETTINGS

- Shooting mode: **Manual**
- Aperture: **f/16**
- Shutter speed: **2–5 seconds**
- ISO: **100**
- Focal length: **18mm**
- AF area: **N/A**
- AF operation: **Manual**
- Drive mode: **Single-shot**
- Metering mode: **Evaluative/matrix**
- White balance: **Tungsten or incandescent**
- Picture style: **Landscape**

TRAVEL AT WARP SPEED

Camera settings

Although our hyperspace images appear dramatically different to the classic traffic trails we created in the previous module, many of the camera settings remain the same. Shutter speed is still our primary concern and we still want to take complete control of exposure so leave your camera set to manual mode (M) and start with a shutter speed between 2 and 5 seconds.

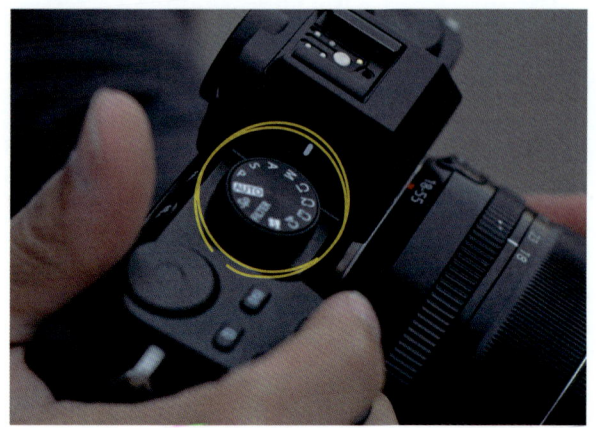

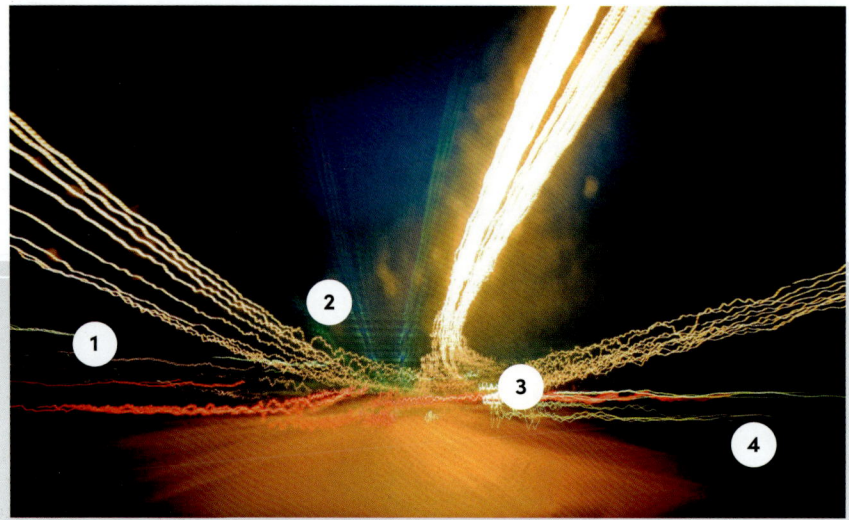

WHY THIS SHOT WORKS

1 The vibrating streaks of light create the illusion of speed, or flying through space, a futuristic sci-fi effect created by hand-holding the camera while shooting a long exposure from a moving vehicle.

2 The car's headlights illuminate the immediate foreground with a warm glow that contrasts with the dazzling glare of the streaks of light, anchoring the shot with a vague semblance of the road.

3 The road's vanishing point – the point at which parallel lines appear to converge – has been positioned on the lower horizontal rule-of-thirds grid line, filling the rest of the frame with dramatic streaks of light.

4 An aperture of $f/16$ has ensured sharp light trails, a shutter speed between 2–5 seconds has captured a mixture of white and red light streaks, while an ISO of 100 has minimized noise.

Faster car speeds and smoother roads will result in cleaner, more linear streaks while slower car speeds and bumpier roads will produce wavy streaks that resemble the fluctuating lines on a heart monitor. An exposure time of 2 seconds may be enough if hurtling along a motorway at 70mph (110kph), while 5 seconds may be needed if trundling along at 20mph (30kph). Experiment to find the perfect balance between car speed and shutter speed.

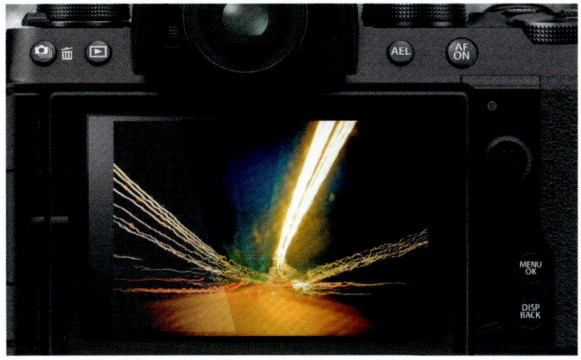

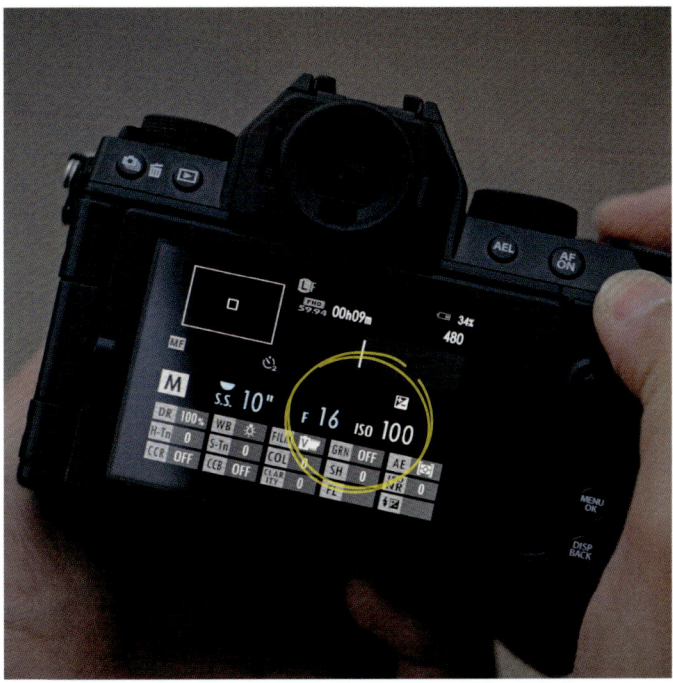

Leave ISO set to 100 and dial in an aperture of ƒ/16. Although the camera is moving along with the car, we still want the streaks of light to be clearly defined, no matter how much they waver, and this narrow aperture setting will not only provide us with enough depth of field to capture this front-to-back clarity, it will also ensure the best possible image quality (remember that diffraction can cause a loss of sharpness at a lens' smallest aperture).

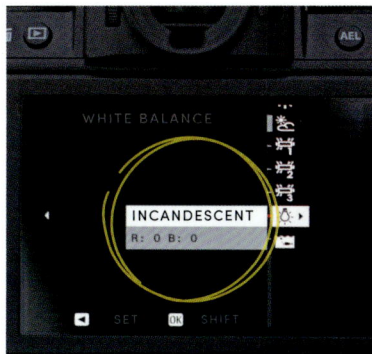

Activate Live View and select the 3x3 Grid Display option as this will help you compose your hyperspace images, particularly when the camera is balanced on the dashboard and held at arm's reach, and position the horizon on the lower horizontal rule-of-thirds grid line. Leave white balance set to tungsten or incandescent to ensure that unwanted colour casts produced by any sodium street lights are neutralized.

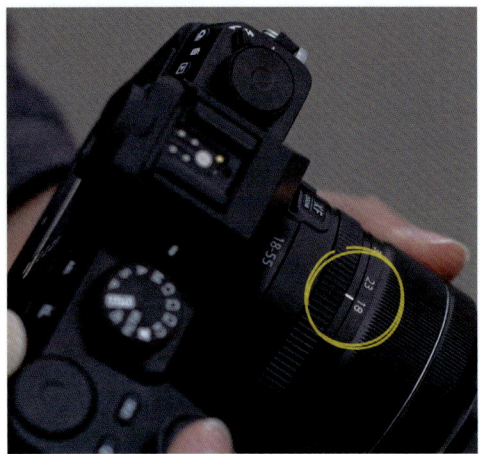

Technique
Find a road with street lights, neon signs and, of course, lots of traffic. Position your camera as close to the front windscreen as possible to minimize flare, using your lens hood to protect the lens' front element, and take a test shot. A 2-second exposure will feel like an eternity when you are waiting for the shutter to close and you will feel the camera shake in your hands, even though it is resting on the dashboard, but rest assured that motion blur is a key part of this technique and every bump in the road will only enhance the shaky warp-speed look.

Lens settings
Zoom all the way out to 18mm and leave the AF/MF switch set to MF. A wide-angle focal length – in our case a 35mm equivalent focal length of around 27mm – will subtly exaggerate the perspective of our warp-speed effect, with thinner streaks in the distance appearing to grow much larger as they get closer to the car, while focusing manually means we don't have to rely on autofocus in a tricky low-light situation (AF will always struggle when it can't 'see' its intended target). Instead, we can use the distance scale printed on the lens' focusing ring to focus roughly 5 metres (16 feet) ahead of the car. Select single-shot drive mode so that you are only taking one photo at a time, and switch off any image stabilization on your lens and/or camera.

Review your first image on the rear LCD screen and press the magnify button to zoom in and check sharpness and exposure. If the light trails are too bright, nudge shutter speed down towards the 2-second mark; if the light trails are too dark, push shutter speed up towards 5 seconds (and beyond if necessary). If driving on a busy road with two-way traffic, you will quickly amass a veritable bagful of hyperspace images, with red light trails created by overtaking cars and white light trails created by oncoming traffic, all anchored with the warm glow of your own headlights in the immediate foreground.

TIP
If you want to add yet another layer of interest to your hyperspace images, venture out when it is raining heavily. This may seem counterintuitive, but the constant streaks of water across the windscreen will further blur the light trails and add abstract, spectral highlights.

Whereas classic traffic trails are best shot at sunset, this technique doesn't rely on ambient light to work its magic. Instead, it needs only artificial light to 'paint' its colours across the frame and you can experiment long after the sun has disappeared beneath the horizon. My first experiments were conducted in the dead of night and if anything, the pitch-black darkness added to the atmosphere. In space, no one can hear you take photographs...

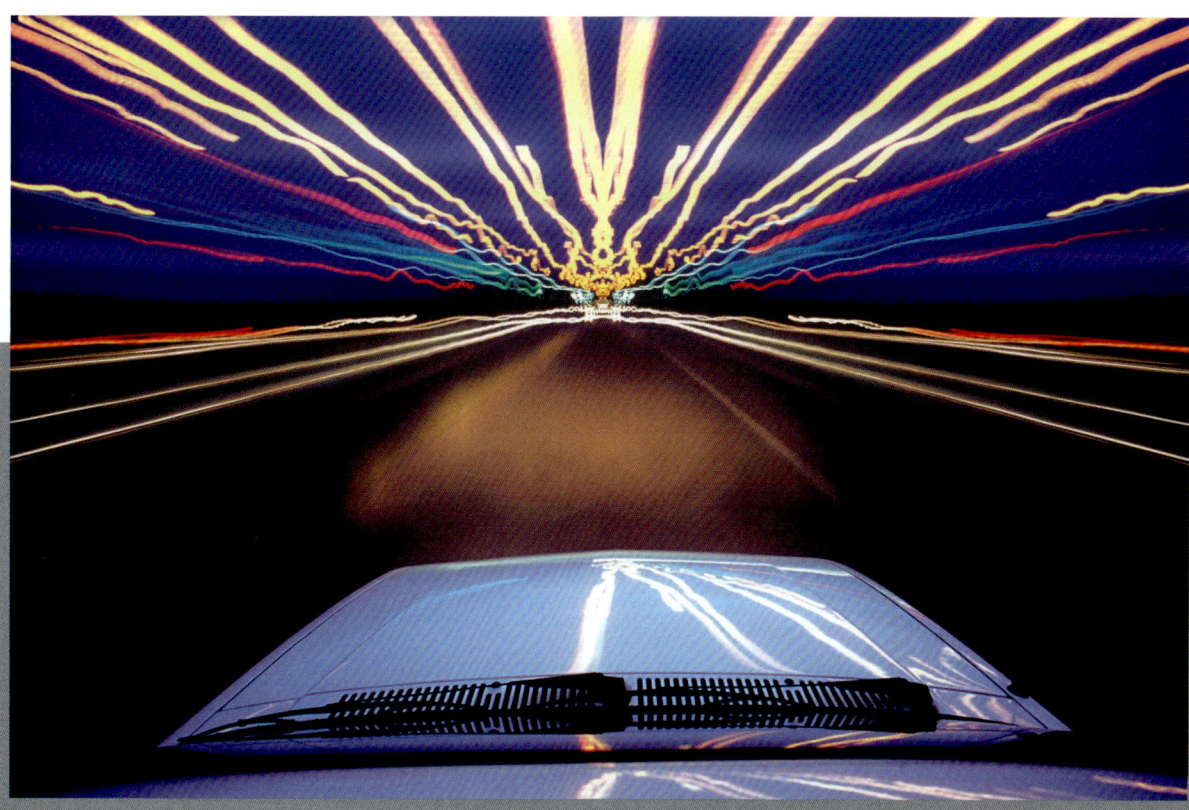

SHOOTING INSPIRATION

Adding static elements to your 'warp speed' light trails can provide a stark contrast to the blurred streaks, creating a greater sense of speed.

ABOVE Including parts of the car, such as the bonnet, dashboard and windscreen, adds context to an otherwise abstract image.

Module 4.3
Suggest speed with blur

Sometimes a small amount of blur can create a more dramatic sense of movement. Just as we added an extra creative layer to our landscapes by using slower shutter speeds to inject subtle dynamism (see page 32), we can apply the same principle to our action images, the difference this time is that the blurred element will be moving through the frame and not just fluttering in the wind. We can also experiment with this technique during the day, which means that rather than transforming car headlights into abstract streaks of light, our blurred subject will be instantly recognizable, conveying an exhilarating sense of speed in an otherwise static scene.

You may be wondering how we generate 'slow' shutter speeds during the bright daylight hours. Well, we don't necessarily need an exposure time of several seconds to capture movement because the faster your subject is moving, the faster your shutter speed can be, so 1/125 second might be 'slow' enough to blur a high-speed train, 1/30 second might blur a speeding car and 1/8 second might blur a cyclist at full pelt. Plus, shutter speeds can be even faster as you zoom in and/or get closer to the moving subject as it will have less distance to travel across the frame. The visual effect that distance has on blur is the same as when looking out of the side window of a fast-moving car – objects in the foreground fly by while objects in the distance barely move.

While the contrast between static landscape and blurred subject creates the visual energy, we can enhance the sense of movement by using some of the compositional guidelines we explored in the landscape chapter (see pages 8–31). Start with lead-in lines – roads and railways are perfect as they tell you exactly where your subject will move to and from and can be used to guide the viewer's eye through the frame. Use the rule of thirds to position your horizon (see page 8) – assuming your photo features one – and a power point to position your subject. Look for diagonal compositions and low viewpoints – images in which your subject travels corner to corner rather than top to bottom or side to side are always going to be more dynamic.

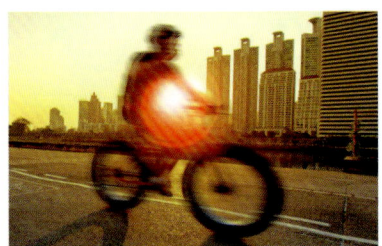

Bike: 1/8 second

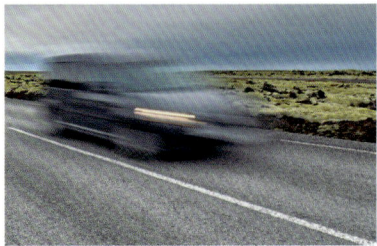

Car: 1/30 second

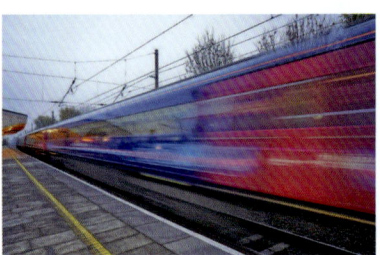

Train: 1/125 second

ABOVE **Depending on how fast your subject is moving, even relatively fast shutter speeds can capture a sense of speed.**

DIFFICULTY ★★☆

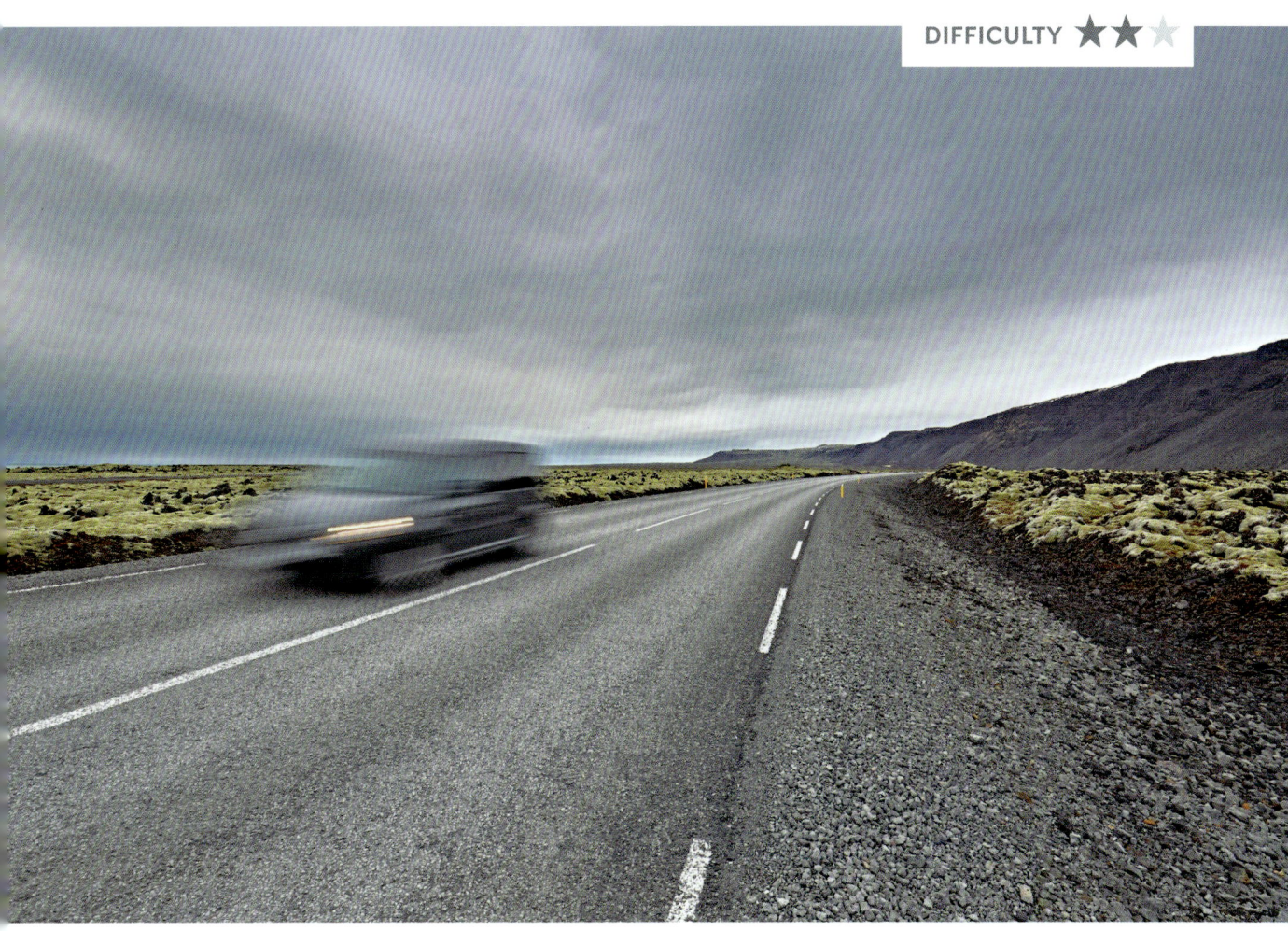

ABOVE **Look for lead-in lines such as roads and railways, as these will tell the viewer where the subject is moving from and to.**

RECOMMENDED SETTINGS

- Shooting mode: **Aperture-priority**
- Aperture: **f/16**
- Shutter speed: **1/125sec–1/8sec**
- ISO: **100 (or 'L')**
- Focal length: **18mm**
- AF area: **Single-point AF**
- AF operation: **Single-shot AF**
- Drive mode: **Continuous**
- Metering mode: **Evaluative/matrix**
- White balance: **Auto or daylight/cloudy**
- Picture style: **Landscape**

SUGGEST SPEED WITH BLUR 123

Camera settings

As important as shutter speed is in capturing just the right amount of motion blur, aperture and ISO play crucial roles when we want to add a sense of movement to our pictures. Not only do these reciprocal exposure settings allow us to control depth of field and sensor sensitivity, they also allow us to limit the amount of light that enters our lens and stretch exposure times. Shooting in aperture-priority means we can control aperture while adjusting shutter speed in ways that ensure we don't overexpose the landscape part of our photograph.

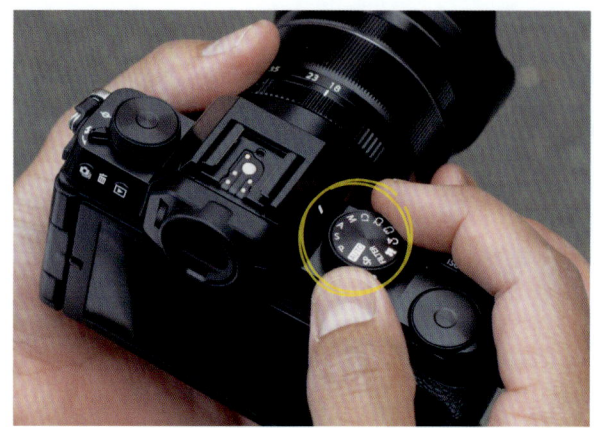

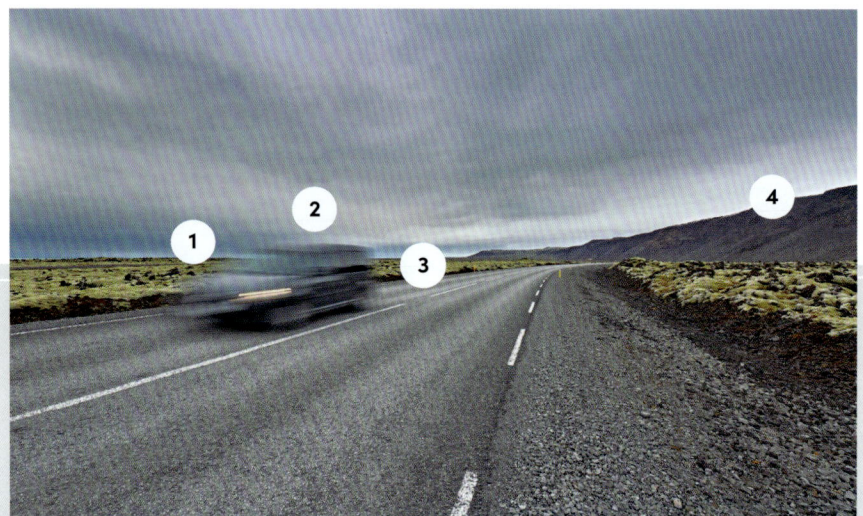

WHY THIS SHOT WORKS

1 The blurred car speeding out of the frame provides an eye-catching focal point that contrasts perfectly with the distant fields and mountains. You can almost hear the whirr of the engine as it whizzes by.

2 The photographer has captured just the right amount of motion blur, with the moving subject instantly identifiable as a car but not so ghostly that it disappears completely.

3 The car is travelling along a diagonal to the bottom-left of the frame, creating a dynamic composition with the road acting as a lead-in line, taking the viewer's eye into the landscape beyond.

4 Even without the car, this would still be a striking landscape image, albeit one lacking an obvious focal point. It provides the perfect 'static' counterpoint to the speeding car.

While the focal point will be the moving subject, the static elements will provide the context so it's important that we capture front-to-back sharpness, just as we would when shooting any other traditional scenic image. An aperture of ƒ/16 – our default setting when shooting landscapes – will provide plenty of depth of field, which will also prove more forgiving when it comes to focusing (see below). You can always close down to ƒ/22 if you need to force a slower shutter speed – just remember that diffraction affects sharpness at your lens' smallest aperture.

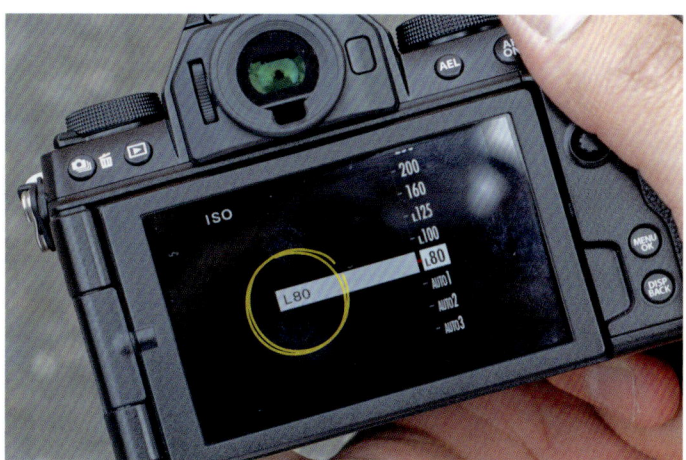

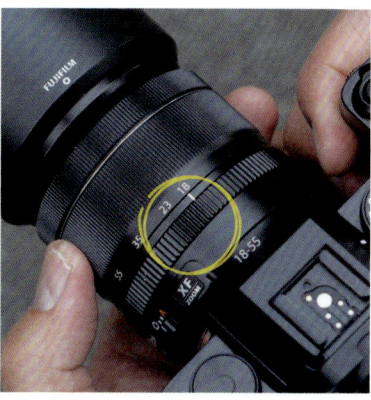

ISO can stay at 100 for now, as this is the least light-sensitive value, but don't forget that you can select ISOs above and below your camera's native range by using its 'extended' menu. Most DSLRs and mirrorless models feature a special 'low' setting (often abbreviated to 'L'), which takes ISO as low as 80 or, in some instances, even 50. Extended ISOs use digital processing rather than the sensor to create 'equivalent' values, which don't strictly reduce your camera's sensitivity to light, but they are a useful option when aiming for slower shutter speeds.

The 'perfect' shutter speed will be relative to how fast your subject is moving and how close you are to it and will take a little trial and error to get right. Shooting in aperture-priority mode means that the camera will select this setting for you, but if the motion blur effect is more or less pronounced than intended, use aperture and ISO – or shoot at a different time of day – to shorten or lengthen your shutter speed.

Lens settings

For the most part, we can approach this project as if we were shooting a traditional landscape. Zoom out to 18mm to include as much of your static element as possible, and zoom in slightly if you need to exclude any untidy areas. Flick the AF/MF switch back to AF and the AF operation to single-shot AF, but – and here is the twist – change the drive mode to continuous. This rapid-fire setting shoots bursts of consecutive images for as long as the shutter button is pressed, making it easier to capture the perfect shot of a moving subject in exactly the right part of the frame.

Technique

Start by attaching your camera to a tripod. Chances are shutter speeds will be slower than the recommended 1/125 second minimum for handholding so a stable camera is an absolute must. Even if shutter speeds do reach the 1/125 second threshold, I'd still recommend using a tripod as not only will this slow you down and encourage you to take a more measured approach to composition, it will also help you focus your attention on the moving subject and the timing of your exposures.

In addition to aperture, ISO and time of day, we can also use exposure compensation to not only brighten or darken our scene, but also to extend or reduce shutter speed. In aperture-priority mode, this 'override' option gives us the ability to change the shutter speed while aperture remains constant; an exposure compensation of +1 halves the exposure time while -1 doubles it. Note, however, that many cameras don't reset this setting back to zero when switched off, so you may need to do this manually next time you use it.

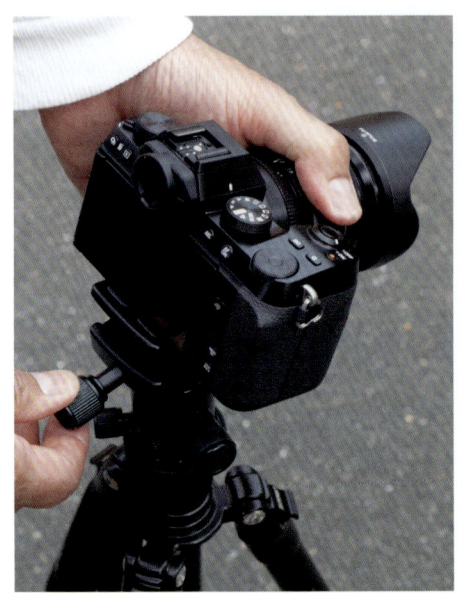

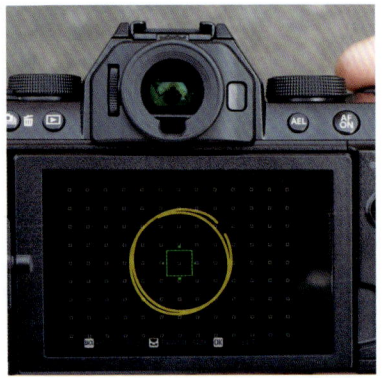

Place your AF point over the area of road or railway track where you want your blurred subject to appear, half-press the shutter button to engage AF, and flick the AF/MF switch back to MF to 'lock off' focus. This is a simple technique known as pre-focusing and means that your camera won't try to continually refocus every time you squeeze the trigger. Activate Live View to take your eye away from the viewfinder and use a remote shutter release to trigger the shutter. Because timing is so crucial and we need to react in an instant, your camera's self-timer mode won't work in this instance.

TIP

If the idea of carrying a large, heavy tripod with you at all times doesn't appeal, consider investing in a mini/travel tripod. These pocket-sized camera supports are lighter, cheaper and much more portable, making them ideal for long-exposure photography on the fly. I've had a Manfrotto PIXI EVO stashed in my kit bag for years and it's been used far more than my 'proper' tripod.

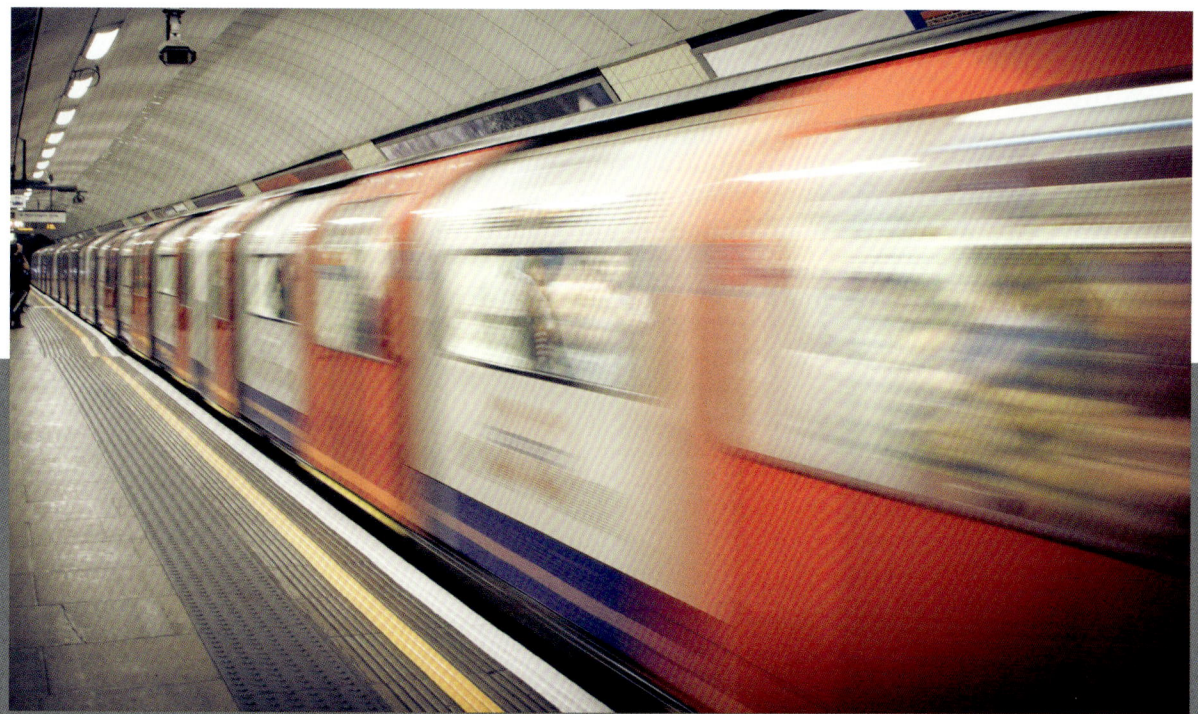

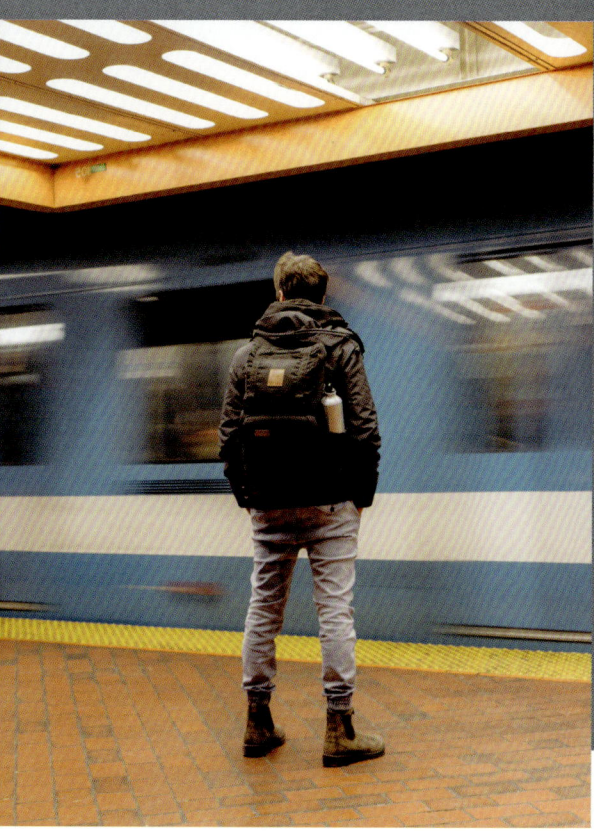

SHOOTING INSPIRATION

This is a versatile technique that can be deployed indoors and out – just be careful when using a tripod, as they are not always safe and practical in busy areas.

ABOVE Diagonal lines can emphasize perspective and depth, while also adding an extra layer of dynamism to a composition.

LEFT Including a human element not only adds a sense of scale, it also helps tell a story and makes your images more personal.

Module 4.4
Follow a moving subject

What if you want your fast-moving subject to be perfectly sharp and the background a streak of high-energy blur? You will need to 'pan' your camera. Panning is an advanced technique that marries slow shutter speeds with horizontal camera motion to create images that scream 'Action!' It may seem rather intimidating at first, and it admittedly requires a lot of practise and even a little physical exertion, but get it right and the results can be truly spectacular. Panning is often described as the ultimate trial-and-error technique, yet with the right settings and approach, you can quickly improve your hit rate.

The secret to successful panning is finding the perfect shutter speed relative to your subject and, just as in the previous module, this will be determined by two key factors, the first of which is how fast your subject is moving. For instance, a panning shot of a car travelling at 30mph (50kph) will require a faster shutter speed than a panning shot of a cyclist travelling at 15mph (25kph). The second factor is how close you are to your subject – a car moving just a few metres (about 10 feet) away will require a faster shutter speed than a car driving 20m (65ft) away. Remember the car window analogy – objects appear to move faster the closer they are.

Consistent technique is also crucial. Whatever the subject and its speed, you want to start tracking it in your viewfinder or via Live View as soon as it appears and continue to follow it until it has sped past you, keeping your subject in the same part of the frame and only firing the shutter at the optimal moment. Your panning motion should be smooth and, ideally, you want to capture the front or side of your subject rather than its rear view as images of cars or bikes moving towards or parallel to the viewer will be more impactful than images in which the subject is travelling away. Finally, avoid shooting against cloudless blue skies – while your subject will be sharp, your backdrop will become a blur of colour, and so background 'details' will help to convey a sense of movement.

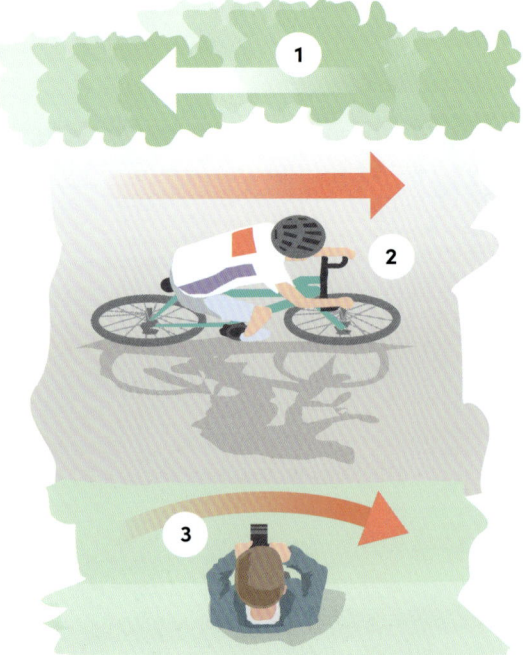

1. The background will blur as the camera pans across it.

2. The subject will remain sharp as it moves at the same speed as the pan.

3. The panning motion must be smooth and consistent.

DIFFICULTY ★★★

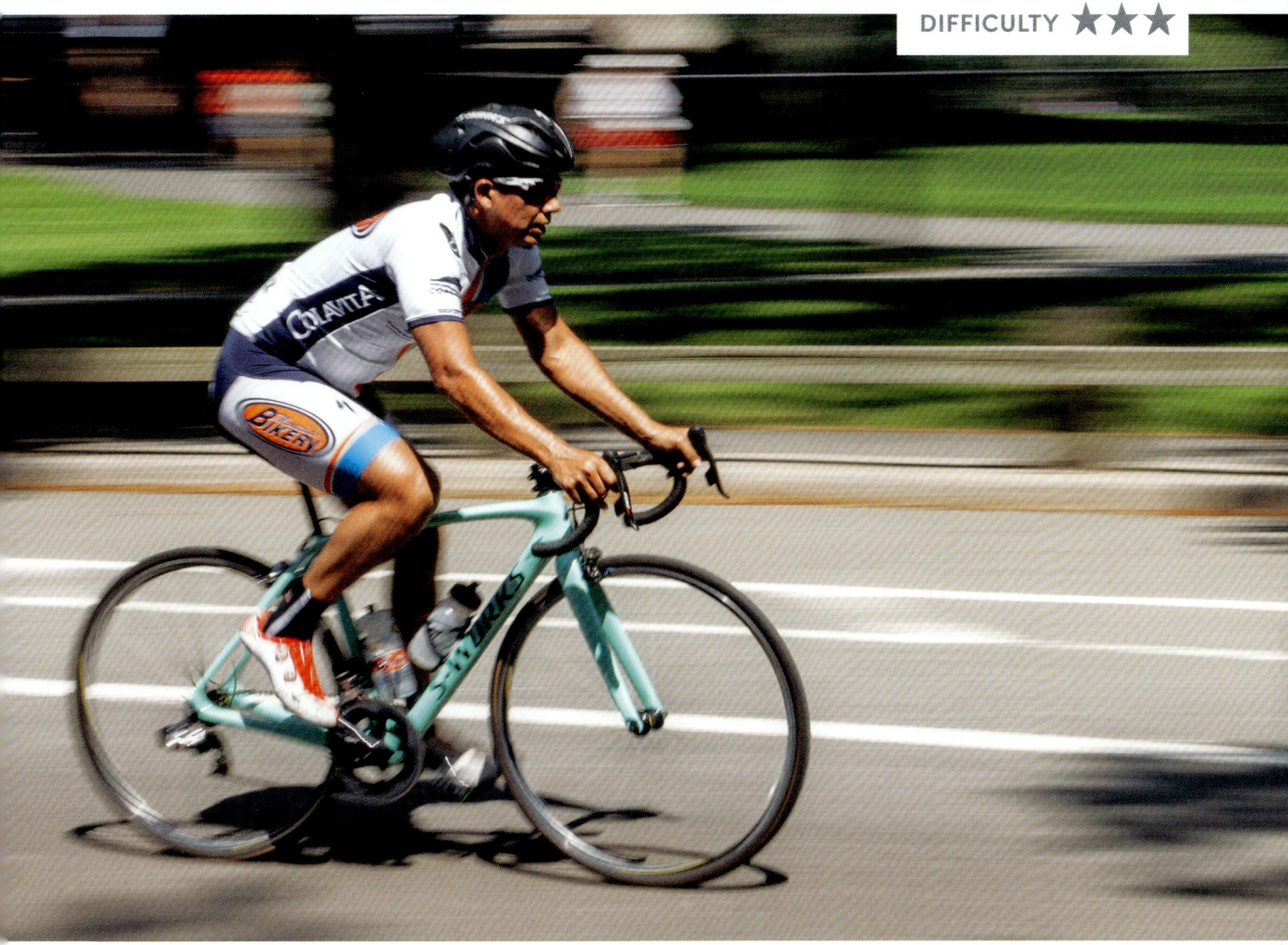

ABOVE **Cyclists, joggers and cars all make great subjects to practice on – and don't worry too much about your backgrounds being 'clean'.**

RECOMMENDED SETTINGS

- Shooting mode: **Shutter-priority**
- Aperture: **Any**
- Shutter speed: **1/30sec**
- ISO: **100**
- Focal length: **18–55mm**
- AF area: **Zone AF**
- AF operation: **Continuous AF**
- Drive mode: **Continuous**
- Metering mode: **Evaluative/matrix**
- White balance: **Auto or daylight/cloudy**
- Picture style: **Landscape**

Camera settings

While similar to the 'static' motion blur technique (see page 32) in so far as speed and distance are important factors, the landscape element is entirely missing here and so aperture becomes irrelevant. Instead, we want to focus solely on shutter speed. Turning your mode dial to shutter-priority (S or Tv) will allow us to control exposure time while letting the camera worry about f-stops.

Although you will need to adjust the shutter speed according to velocity and distance, an exposure of 1/30 second is a sensible starting point. If your subject appears frozen in time, use a slightly slower shutter speed of, say, 1/15 second; if your subject appears too blurred, use a slightly faster shutter speed of, say, 1/60 second.

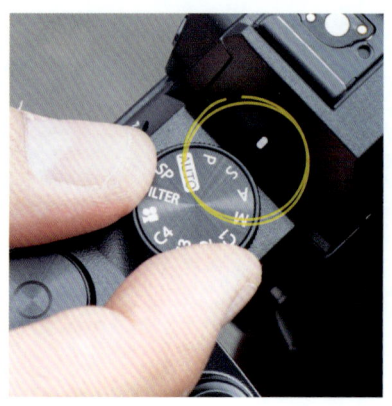

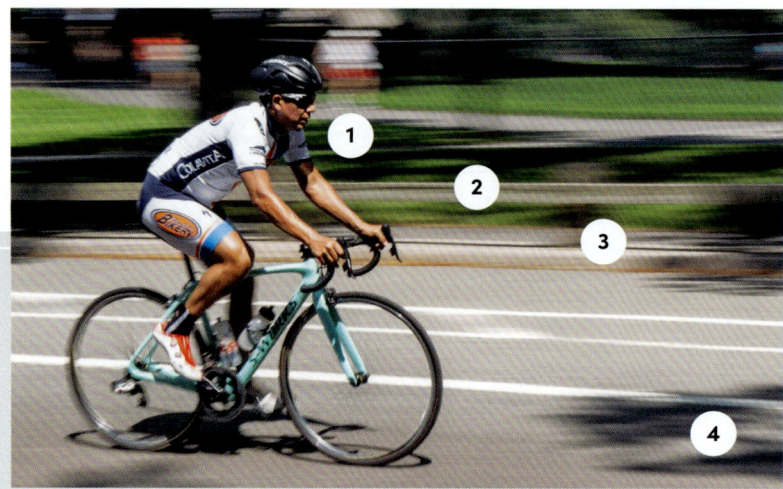

WHY THIS SHOT WORKS

1 The cyclist's head, arms and upper torso are the sharpest parts of the shot, while his legs and feet show traces of motion blur and the bike's tyres have blurred smooth. This all screams 'Speed!'

2 A smooth panning motion has turned the background into a blurred wash of colour and streaky lines, adding to the sense that this bike is travelling at some velocity.

3 There is plenty of active space in front of the cyclist for him to move into, enhancing the illusion of speed and forward momentum, with only a small amount of dead space behind him.

4 By shooting short bursts in continuous shooting mode, the photographer was able to capture a sequence of images from which he could choose the perfect frame.

As we are using 'slow' shutter speeds during daylight hours (I keep using quotation marks because so much photographic terminology is relative), we want to leave ISO at 100. This is not only the least light-sensitive value, it is also the cleanest in terms of noise, providing us with the best possible image quality.

As always, use exposure compensation to lighten or darken your images, making sure that the brightest highlights don't burn out to pure white – in shutter-priority mode, shutter speed and ISO will remain constant while your camera will adjust the aperture to balance the exposure triangle.

Like abstract ICM images (see page 38), panning shots often benefit from saturated colours that grab the viewer's eye so leave the Picture Style set to the Landscape preset and white balance set to daylight or cloudy according to conditions. This will ensure that any blurred streaks of green grass, grey tarmac or vibrant city scenes are consistently neutral and realistic while your subject packs a visual punch.

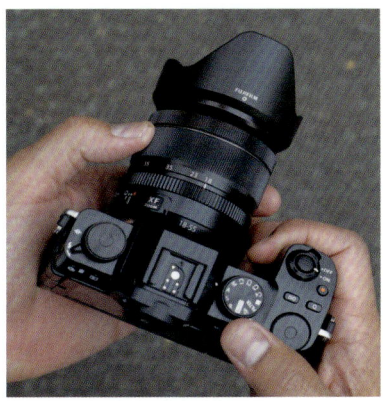

Lens settings

How large your subject appears in the frame will determine how visible the panning effect is – too big and the subject will eclipse the blur; too small and the blur won't be visible enough. So, while there is no one-size-fits-all focal length for this technique, wide angles between 18mm and 23mm will work well with nearby subjects while short telephotos between 40mm and 55mm will get you closer to more distant subjects (remember that a digital camera's crop factor effectively multiplies a lens' stated focal length).

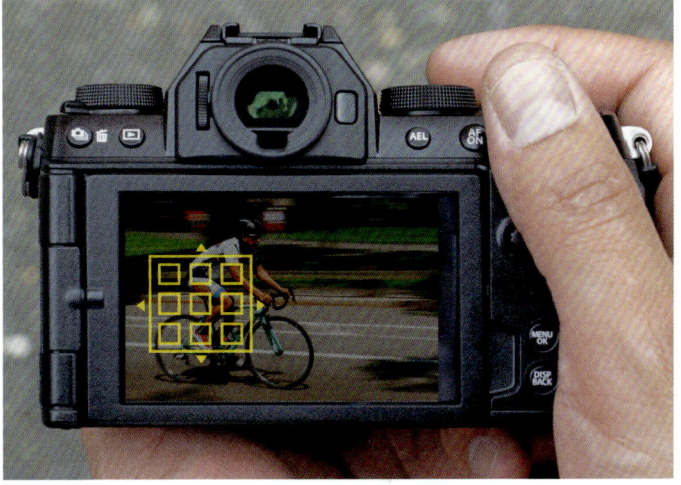

Leave the AF/MF switch set to AF, change the AF operation to continuous AF (AF-C or Ai Servo, depending on camera make and model) and the drive mode to continuous. As the distance between you and the subject will be constantly changing, we need the camera to continually adjust its focus to keep the subject sharp throughout the panning motion. Also, change your camera's AF area to zone AF – this mode activates a group of AF points and is more accurate than single AF points when shooting fast-moving subjects – and select the zone nearest the left vertical rule-of-thirds grid line to aid composition.

Technique

First, check your stance – feet should be shoulder-width apart, elbows tucked into your body and left hand supporting the lens barrel. Position yourself so that you are perpendicular to your subject's path and pivot with your hips rather than your arms and shoulders, keeping your camera firmly braced directly in front of you at all times. This is a physically demanding technique and I strongly recommend you practise this pivot motion a few times as moving the camera while rotating your body will feel quite alien to begin with.

Next, pivot to face the approaching subject, start following it in your viewfinder and half-press the shutter to engage continuous AF, positioning the AF group over the largest part of your subject. The longer your pan, the smoother your movement and the sharper your results will be. Anticipate the moment early by fully pressing the shutter when the subject starts to fill the desired amount of the frame and only release it when the subject has sped past and is moving away from you, continuing to pivot smoothly throughout the entire pan. Continuous shooting means that your camera will rattle off between three and ten frames per second, depending on make and model.

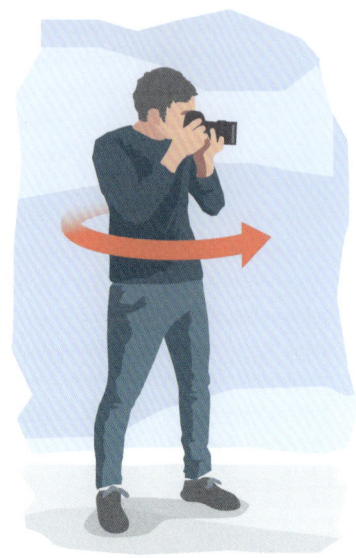

ABOVE **Adopt the correct stance to capture smooth panning shots.**

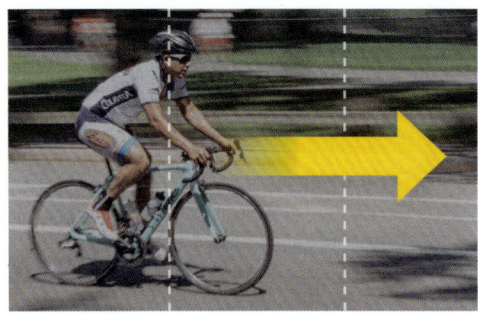

Positioning our AF zone on the left side of the frame gives our subject plenty of space to move into, enhancing the illusion of speed and forward momentum. This empty area in front of the subject is known as 'active space', while the area behind it is known as 'dead space' – a ratio of roughly two-thirds active space and one-third dead space creates the perfect compositional balance. Too much dead space makes the subject look as though it is about to drive into a wall and is best avoided.

TIP

Panning is a bit like a sweaty gym workout in that repetition is the only way to improve your technique. Before you brave a racing event, practise on someone who can run, cycle or drive at the same speed and in the same direction again and again... hundreds of times. Even the professionals do this – it is the only way to learn.

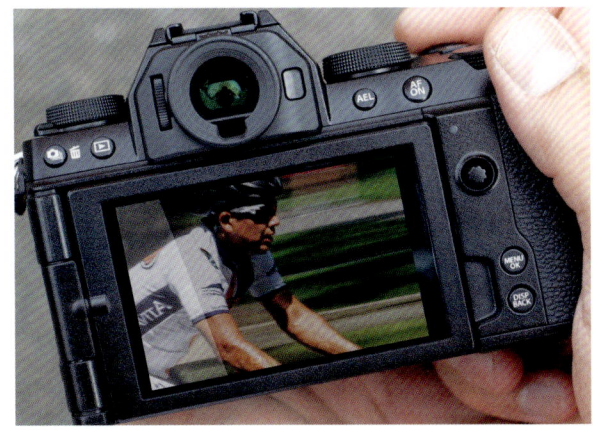

Review your panning images at regular intervals to check focus and blur. A small degree of motion blur around the edges of our subject is perfectly acceptable and can even add to the sense of speed, but the subject should always be the sharpest part of the image. Just to iterate and reassure, this is an advanced camera technique that takes time and practice to perfect, and even a hit rate of one in twenty should be considered an achievement.

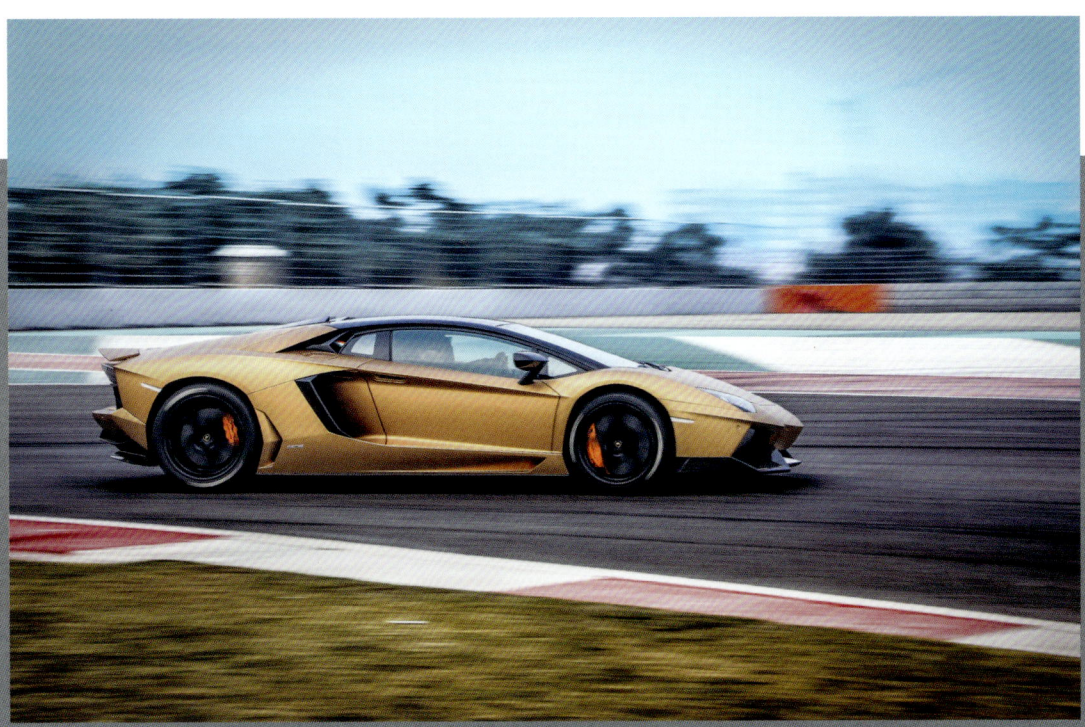

SHOOTING INSPIRATION

Once you've perfected your panning technique, take your skills to the next level by attending a track day at a local racing circuit.

ABOVE To improve your hit rate, position yourself at or near to a corner, where even the fastest cars and bikes have to slow down.

Module 4.5
Go slow with flash

Flash is a subject that bamboozles and intimidates in equal measures – and it's true that you could write entire books on the subject – but there is one remarkably simple technique you can try that will add a dynamic sense of movement to your action shots in no time. Known as slow-sync flash, this low-light technique combines slow shutter speeds with a burst of flash, freezing the subject in the foreground, even if it is moving, while exposing – and blurring, if shooting handheld – the ambient light in the background. The sense of energy created by the effect is popular with music and wedding photographers. It's also the perfect technique for using alongside panning, due to the slower shutter speeds involved.

All entry-level DSLRs and mirrorless cameras feature a pop-up flash. Most 'serious' photographers will wince at the thought of using this on-body artificial light source, as it can produce harsh and very unflattering light when used without modification. However, with just one quick menu tweak, we can turn it into a fun and creative tool. The basics of flash are, well, very basic. Pop-up flash has a duration of around 1/1000 second, so if you are using a shutter speed of, say, 1/15 second, the flash part of the equation will comprise only a fraction of the total exposure. The flash can be fired at the start of the ambient exposure – known as front- or first-curtain sync – or at the end – known as rear- or second-curtain sync (the curtain is simply the shutter that opens and closes to let light in).

Which curtain you choose will determine how any ambient movement registers: with front-curtain sync, any motion blur will appear in front of the subject; with rear-curtain sync, any motion blur will appear behind the subject. For this reason, rear-curtain flash is recommended for action photography when speed and forward momentum are the key ingredients. We also need to consider the flash-to-subject distance, as pop-up units have a limited range of just 1–3m: any closer and your subject will be too bright; any further and your subject will be too dark. All other creative considerations follow the panning advice given in the previous module.

RIGHT **Pop-up flash is fired in between the front curtain opening and the rear curtain closing.**

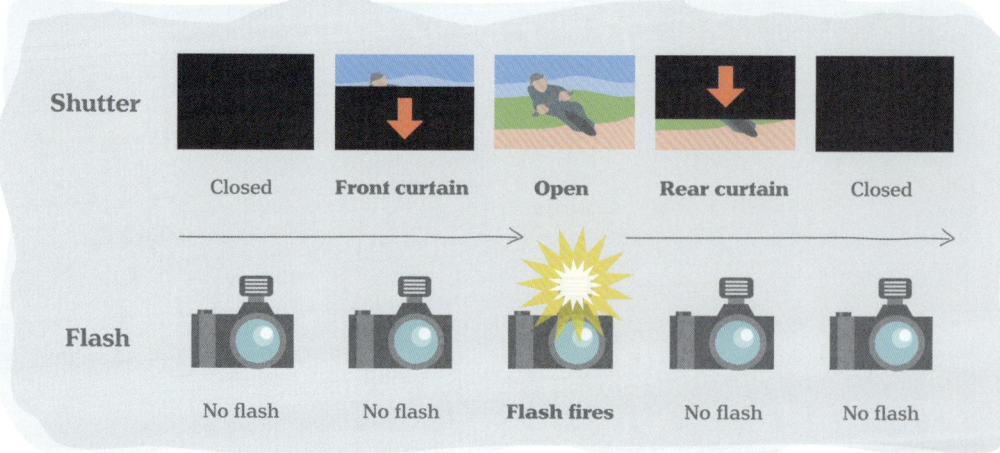

134 MOVEMENT

DIFFICULTY ★★★

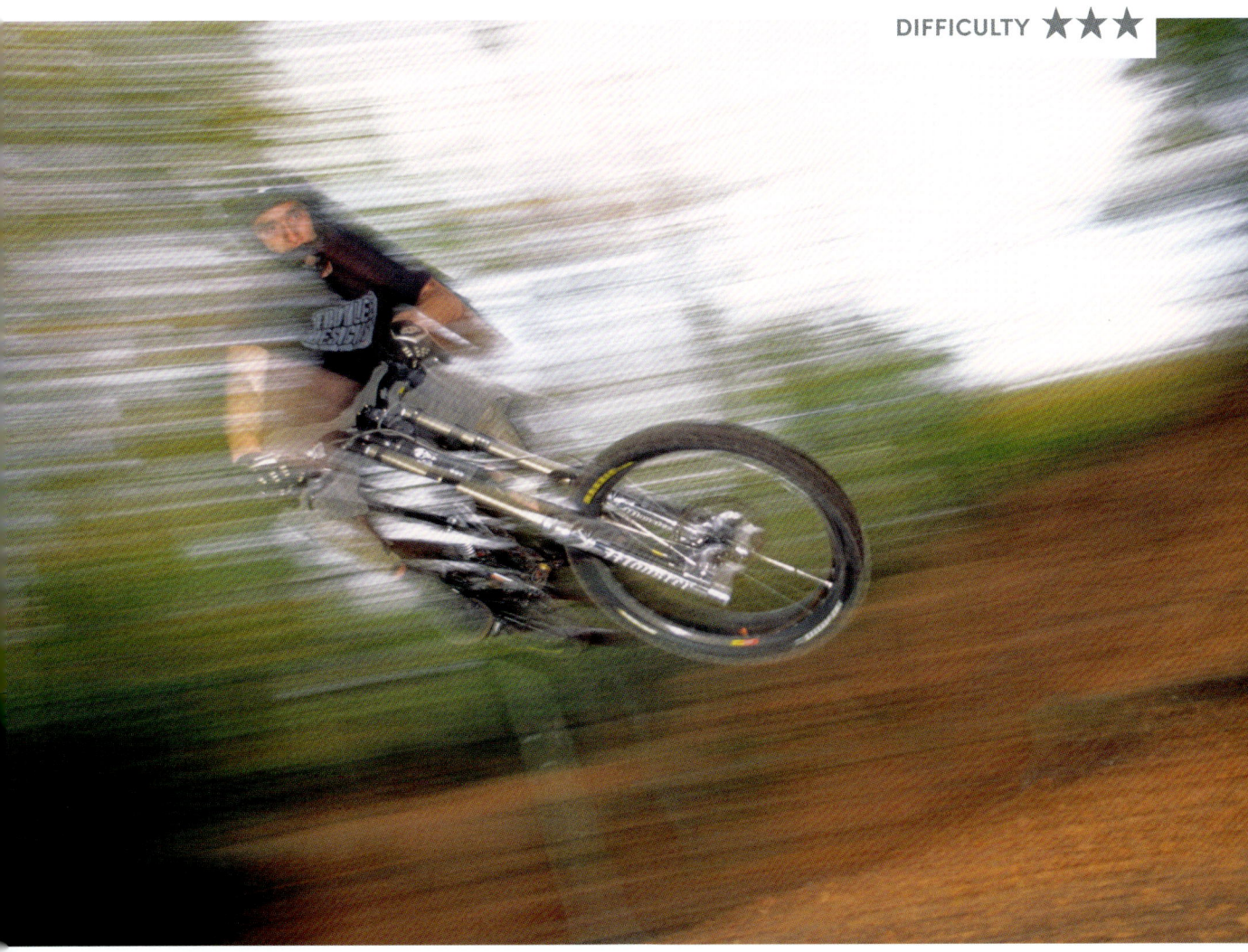

ABOVE **Combine slow-sync flash with the panning technique for high-energy images that scream 'action'.**

RECOMMENDED SETTINGS

- Shooting mode: **Shutter-priority**
- Aperture: **Any**
- Shutter speed: **1/2sec**
- ISO: **100**
- Focal length: **18–23mm**
- AF area: **Zone AF (panning); single-point AF (twisting)**
- AF operation: **Continuous AF (panning); single-shot AF (twisting)**
- Drive mode: **Continuous (panning); single-shot (twisting)**
- Metering mode: **Evaluative/matrix**
- White balance: **Auto or daylight/cloudy**
- Picture style: **Landscape**

GO SLOW WITH FLASH 135

Camera settings

Although flash is the magic ingredient here, shutter speed still determines how much ambient light is recorded so leave your mode dial set to shutter-priority (S or Tv). Start with a default shutter speed of 1/2 second – the longer the exposure, the more pronounced the motion-blur effect so keep this in mind when practising your technique.

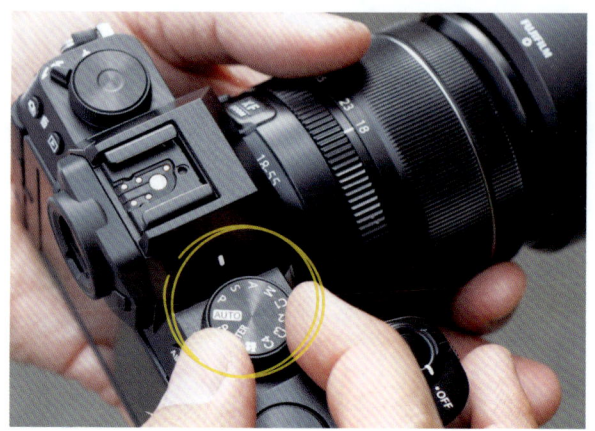

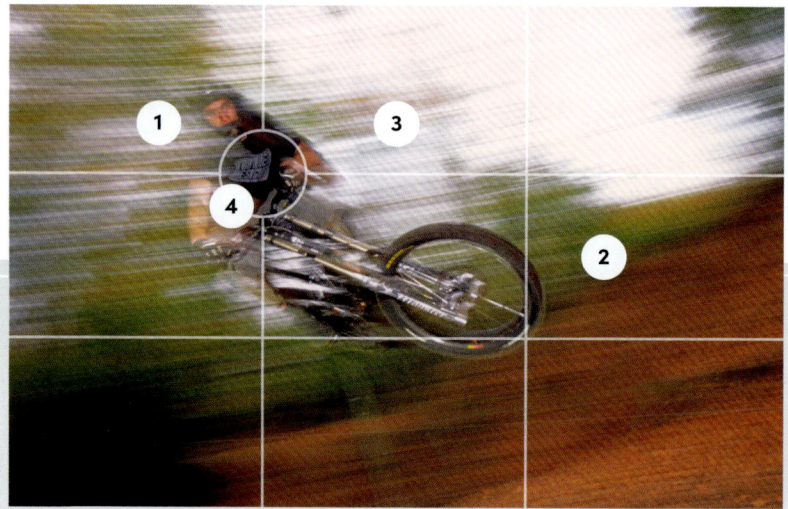

WHY THIS SHOT WORKS

1 The speeding cyclist is within range of the camera's flash and fills the perfect amount of space in the frame, with the burst of flash freezing the rider and his bike amid a sea of background motion blur.

2 Head for the woods! Low-light locations are perfect for slow-sync flash techniques as the lack of ambient light allows for slower shutter speeds and more pronounced motion blur effects.

3 Although blurred and abstracted, the clearly defined panning 'lines' in the background suggest a smooth action, perfect for keeping the subject in the same place in the frame throughout the pan.

4 The cyclist is positioned on the top-left power point, with plenty of active space to the right of the frame for him to move into. Plus, the diagonal angle of the bike suggests top-left to bottom-right movement.

If shooting outdoors during the day, an ISO of 100 will help to keep shutter speeds long enough; if shooting indoors in low light, you may need to push ISO to 400 or even 800 to balance the exposure (you may find that an aperture warning starts to flash on your camera's LCD panel – this is your camera telling you to increase ISO). Remember that this setting will depend entirely on light levels and shutter speed and, as always, a little noise is preferable to no image at all.

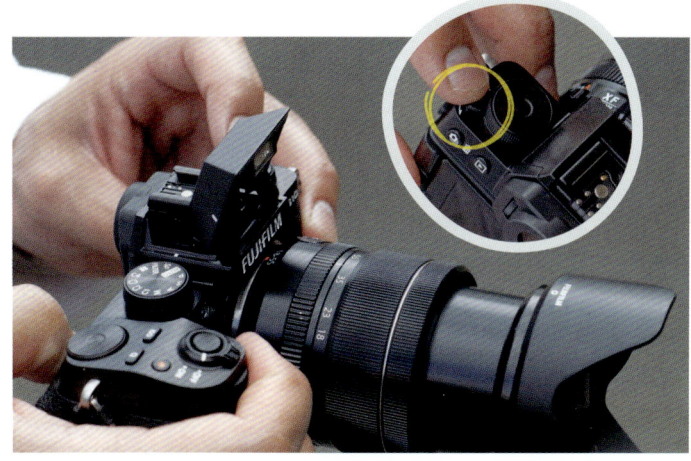

When shooting in semi-automatic modes, we will need to activate the pop-up flash manually, typically via a button on the front of the camera body indicated with a lightning bolt symbol. Press this button and the flash unit will pop open.

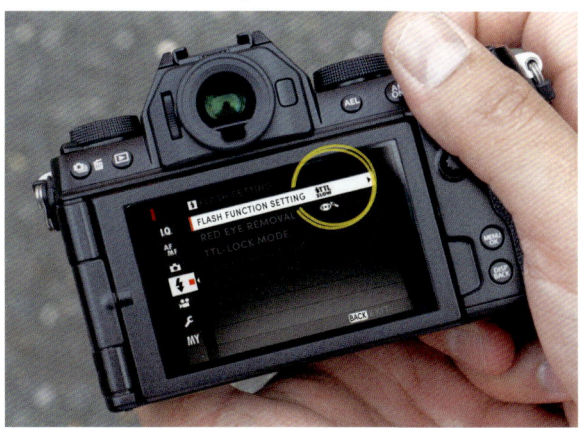

Now for the magical 'one quick menu tweak' we mentioned earlier… to select rear- or second-curtain sync, scroll through your camera's main menu and select the 'flash control' option (the exact wording will differ from model to model). Within this menu, look for a 'built-in flash settings' option and select the 'shutter sync' setting. Here, you can activate your curtain of choice.

Just as we use exposure compensation to lighten or darken our images when working with ambient light, we can use flash-exposure compensation to lighten or darken our subjects without affecting the ambient light by increasing or decreasing the flash power. So, if your subject is closer or further away than your pop-up flash's limited 1–3m (3–9ft) range, adjust the power by a stop or two either way. How you access flash-exposure compensation varies from camera to camera, so you may need to dip into the manual for specifics. It is also worth noting that exposure compensation and flash-exposure compensation work independently and have no effect on the other.

Lens settings

When coupling slow-sync flash with panning, we still want the panning effect to be visible and so we still want the subject to occupy just the right amount of the frame i.e., not too much and not too little. As your subject will invariably be close to you, a wide-angle focal length of between 18mm and 23mm will allow you to capture full-height images of joggers and cyclists (these are safe and predictable 'starter' subjects to practise on – you don't want to be 1m (3ft) away from a speeding train!).

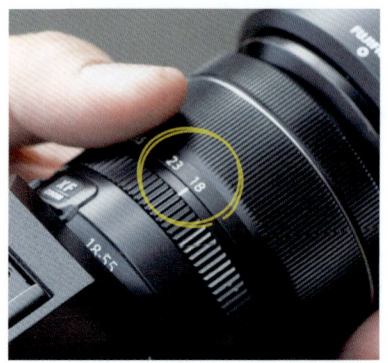

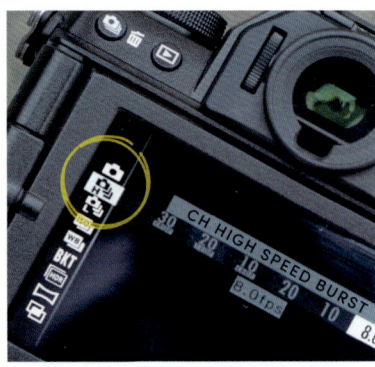

If panning, all other lens settings can stay the same, with AF operation set to continuous AF, drive mode set to continuous and AF area set to zone AF. So long as there is enough ambient light, the camera will continually focus and refocus while rattling off a sequence of images, thus improving your chances of capturing that one perfect frame.

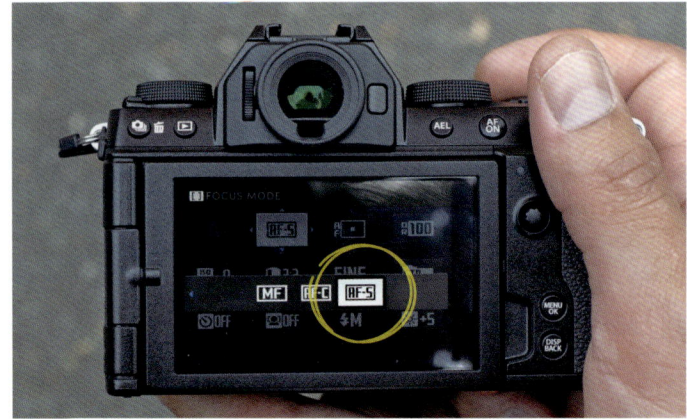

If twisting the camera rather than panning it (see opposite), I'd recommend you change AF operation to single-shot AF, drive mode to single-shot and AF area to single-point AF. Slow-sync flash is a super-creative technique that allows for endless experimentation – and not all motion blur has to be linear.

TIP

If you want to get really experimental with slow-sync flash, try zooming in or out during the exposure rather than twisting the camera. This is a technique known as 'zoom burst' and creates blur that appears to radiate outwards or inwards from the centre of the frame.

Technique

If you have been practising your panning technique, you are already one step ahead when it comes to using slow-sync flash for action shots because a smooth pan is crucial to keeping the subject in the same place in the frame for the duration of the exposure. As before, start by adopting a solid yet comfortable stance, with your feet apart and elbows tucked in, and with space in which to pivot. With your subject moving across the frame rather than towards you, track it in your viewfinder, engage AF and squeeze the shutter when it enters the area of the frame you want it to appear in. Continue to smoothly track the subject and only release the shutter when the flash starts to fire.

Alternatively, you could try twisting your camera instead. This is a creative way to add motion blur to static subjects and works by freezing anything that falls within the flash's range, and blurring any background detail that falls beyond it. Because the camera is being rotated around a central point, the ambient light trails create 'radial' motion blur – a dramatic spinning effect that users of Photoshop will no doubt be familiar with. In this instance, position your active AF point over the most prominent subject nearest the camera, engage AF, press the shutter and quickly spin the camera. As with panning, this technique will take a few attempts to perfect, but the results will be unique and can turn a simple walk in the woods into a fun 'camera twist' challenge.

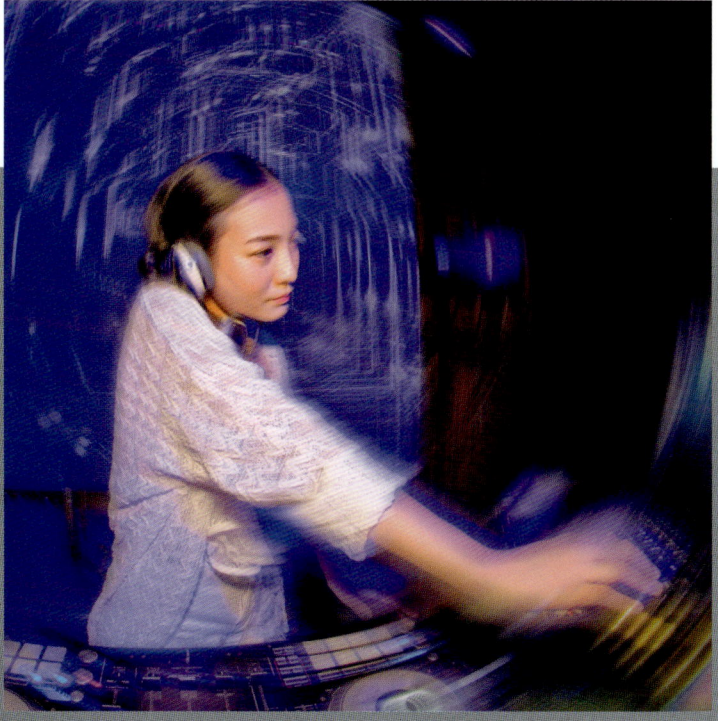

SHOOTING INSPIRATION

So long as the subject remains in the same place in the frame while the camera is moved, you can experiment with panning, twisting and even zooming mid-exposure.

LEFT Rotating the camera – essentially a circular panning technique – creates 'radial' motion blur.

Module 4.6
Paint with light

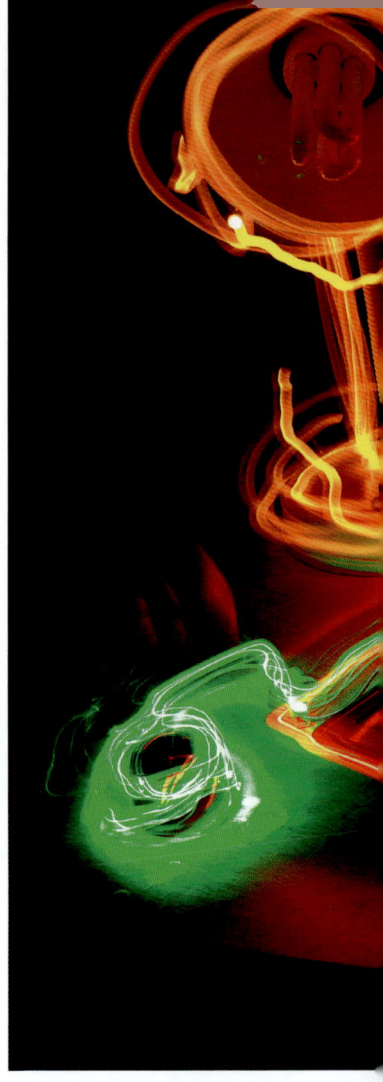

The word 'photograph' literally means 'drawing with light'. It was coined by British scientist Sir John Herschel in 1839 when he combined the Greek words *phos*, meaning 'light', and *graphê*, meaning 'drawing'. Creative types such as Pablo Picasso took this literal definition to heart, 'painting' with a small electric torch in a darkened room to produce some of his most iconic photographs, or 'light drawings' as they have since become known as. With a little DIY ingenuity, we can very easily replicate this artistic technique, using nothing more than a camera, tripod and light source.

As we have already discovered in this chapter, any subject that moves across the frame while the shutter is open will blur to some degree. 'Drawing' with a torch is no different – so long as the location is dark enough and the shutter speed is slow enough, the torch's movement will register as a continuous light trail across the camera's sensor, allowing you to combine the basics of long-exposure photography with your own artistic inclinations. You can paint freehand, like Picasso, and draw pictures and write words, or you can 'outline' household objects and give them a novel twist. Even better, you can practise and experiment in the comfort of your own home.

A small pen torch with a single bulb, a single LED light or even a mobile phone's 'flashlight' mode can be used for this technique. To achieve a black background, you will also need to shoot in a very dark space – while a small amount of light will inevitably 'spill' onto any objects within close proximity, the darker the backdrop, the more the light trails will stand out. You may also want to wear dark clothes and gloves to reduce the risk of your body and hands appearing in the shot. Like so many long-exposure techniques, painting with light requires a lot of practise and persistence, but unlike Picasso, we can review our artworks immediately and make any necessary adjustments without needing to run off to the darkroom.

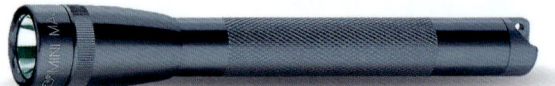

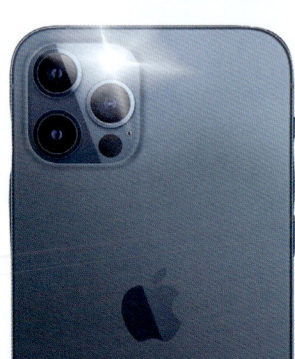

ABOVE & LEFT **A Maglite torch is the perfect light source for this technique, although a mobile phone light can be just as effective.**

140 MOVEMENT

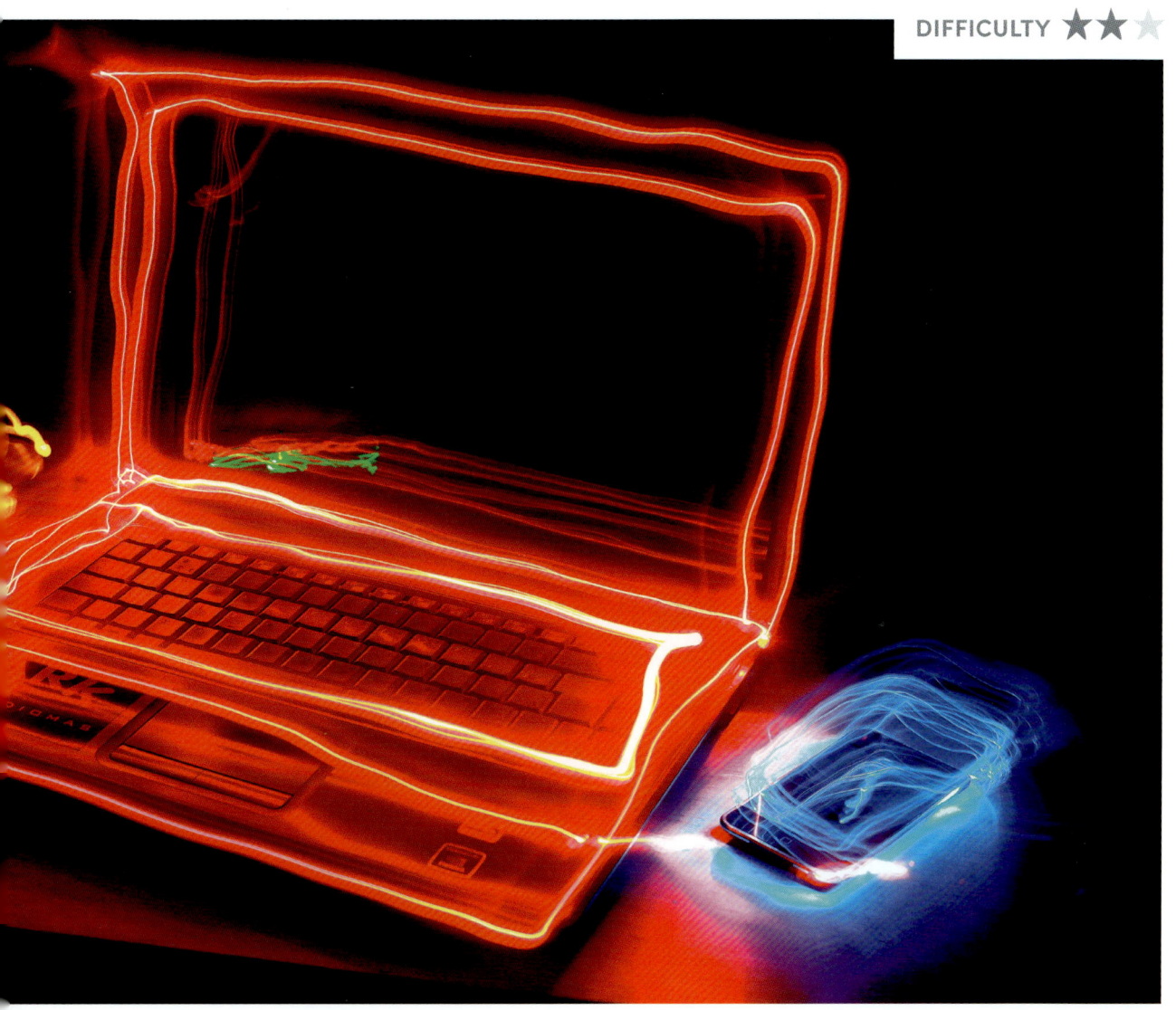

ABOVE 'Paint' around household objects such as laptops, lamps and phones to refine your technique.

RECOMMENDED SETTINGS

- Shooting mode: **Manual**
- Aperture: **f/16**
- Shutter speed: **30 seconds**
- ISO: **100**
- Focal length: **35mm**
- AF area: **Single-point AF**
- AF operation: **Single-shot AF**
- Drive mode: **Self-timer**
- Metering mode: **Evaluative/matrix**
- White balance: **Any**
- Picture style: **Standard**

DIFFICULTY ★★☆

Camera settings

Painting with light is a technique that demands full control of the three exposure variables, so turn the mode dial to manual (M) and select a shutter speed of 30 seconds. This is typically the longest speed DSLRs and mirrorless cameras allow and will give us plenty of time to create random patterns, write words and draw around objects. If you are 'painting' around a small subject, you may only need a shutter speed of 5–10 seconds, but it's best to try a few practice runs first before adjusting this setting.

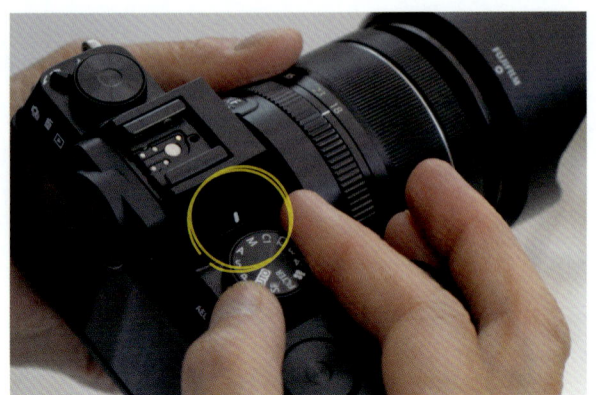

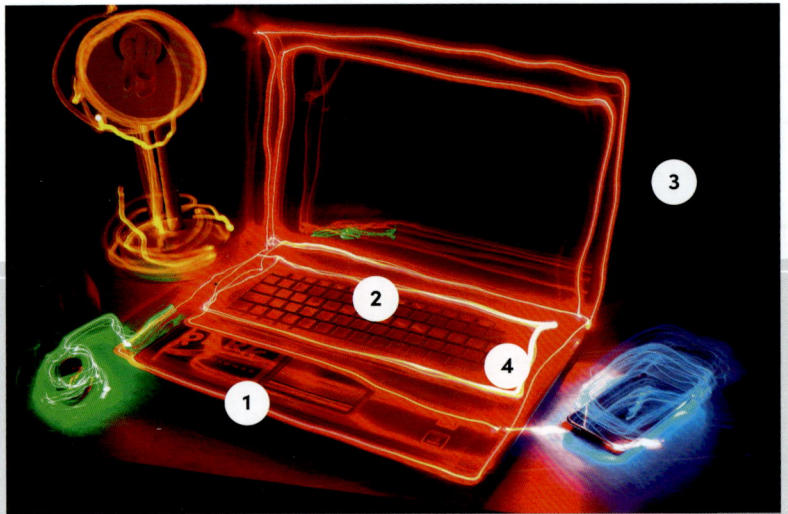

WHY THIS SHOT WORKS

1 The laptop, light and phone have been very precisely outlined with a smooth and controlled painting motion, with just enough light spilling from the torch to illuminate the props.

2 The exposure is perfectly balanced, with a shutter speed long enough for complete light trails, an aperture narrow enough to capture front-to-back sharpness and an ISO that gives just the right amount of brightness.

3 The background is clean and dark, which ensures that the light trails really 'pop' and the spill is a subtle but not distracting glow. If your backdrop isn't dark enough, move your subject further away from it.

4 The subjects fill the frame nicely, with just enough space around them for the light trails to work their magic. Centralized compositions can work well with this technique.

The best aperture for this technique is f/16, particularly if shooting close up and filling the frame with smaller objects. This is because we want the light trails and any objects to be pin-sharp from front to back – any wider and any parts of the subject nearer or further away from the point of focus will fall out of focus; any narrower and there is a risk that diffraction will affect the sharpness across the entire frame. If writing words or drawing patterns freehand from a distance, a mid-range aperture of f/8 or f/11 will provide a large enough depth of field.

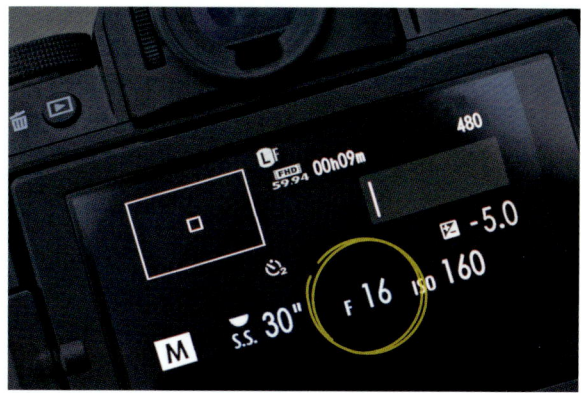

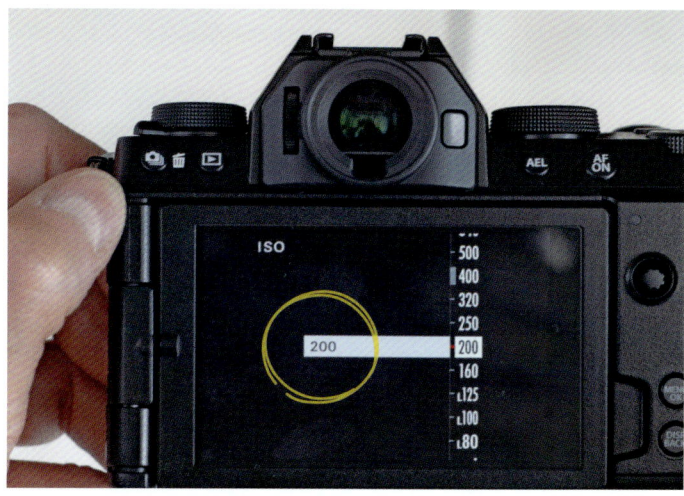

While aperture should remain constant and shutter speed need only be adjusted to accommodate the duration of your light-painting exploits, ISO is the variable that will create a balanced exposure. Too low and your subject will appear too dark; too high and your light trail will be too bright and your black background will lighten. Start at ISO 200 and drop to ISO 100 if your trails and subject need to be a touch darker, and raise ISO to 400 if they need to be a touch brighter. Just don't stray beyond ISO 800 as this will start to introduce noise.

So far in this book, we have used white balance to produce images with neutral colours, giving us an accurate representation of the scene we are photographing. Here, we can throw away the rulebook and have some fun, using this setting to determine how warm or cool our light trails appear. For instance, while the incandescent or tungsten preset will make a traditional household bulb appear white, the light from an LED bulb will appear as a cooler blue. Experiment with your camera's white balance presets to find a colour cast that appeals.

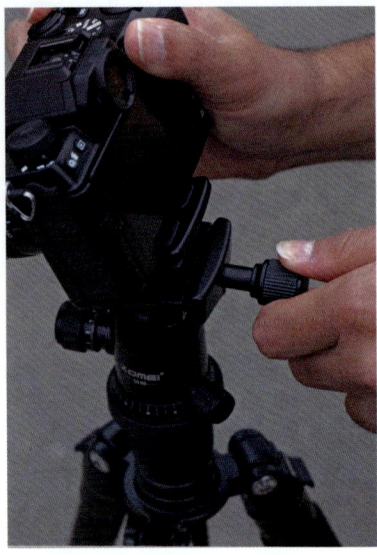
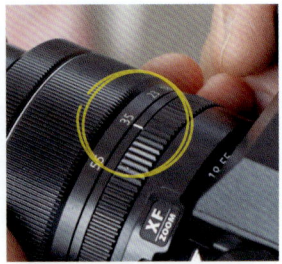
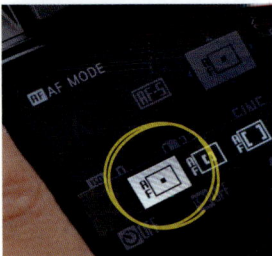

Technique

Turn on the room lights so it is bright enough to use autofocus; attach your camera to a tripod and compose your shot. Position the active AF point over the middle of your subject and half-press the shutter to engage AF. Once AF has locked on, use Live View to zoom in and check sharpness and flick the AF/MF switch to MF to lock it off. You can now turn the house lights back off. At this point – so long as you don't knock the tripod, focusing ring or subject – your image will stay sharp and your camera won't try to refocus every time you press the shutter.

Once you trigger the self-timer, get into position and keep the movement and speed of the torch as smooth and consistent as possible, with your hand behind or to the side of your subject, so the camera can see the light at all times. Aim for complete light trails that don't randomly stop halfway around your object or word – if you find that you can't complete your 'painting' in time, either move the torch faster or extend the shutter speed. If you need to push beyond the 30-second limit, you will need to turn the mode dial to bulb (B) and use a remote shutter release to start and stop the exposure.

Lens settings

Compositionally, we want a distortion-free view with just enough space around the subject for the light trails so a mid-range focal length of 35mm is perfect, as this gives us a 35mm equivalent focal length of just over 50mm. With the AF/MF switch still set to AF, flick the AF area back to single-point AF and the AF operation back to single-shot AF, and change the drive mode to self-timer – with your camera firmly rooted to a sturdy tripod, this will give you enough time to get into position before the shutter opens. If your camera has more than one self-timer option, select the longest direction, typically 10 seconds, so you don't have to rush.

TIP

Start small and use a light source proportionate to the size of your subject. A pen-sized torch with a bare bulb is perfect for props that require fine, precise outlines such as toy figures, electrical devices and light bulbs, while a larger outdoor torch is perfect for writing words and drawing patterns from a distance.

If you are feeling brave, you can create multiple light trails by turning the torch off at the end of one 'brush stroke', repositioning it and turning it back on to start another. You could even experiment with coloured gels held over the moving bulb to create kaleidoscopic effects. I should warn you – painting with light is brilliant fun and hugely addictive, and you will be channelling your inner Picasso in no time!

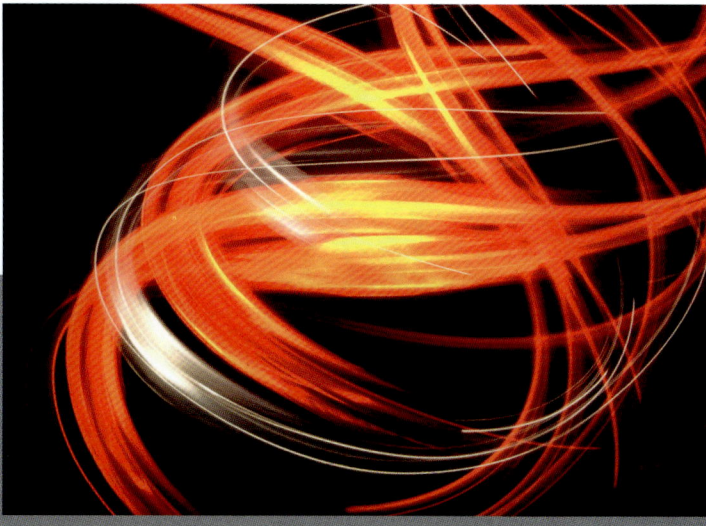

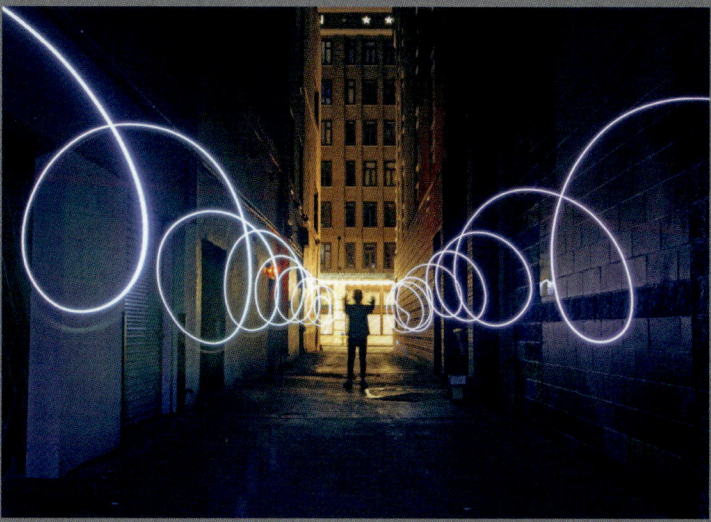

SHOOTING INSPIRATION

Create abstract masterpieces at home or take to the streets and use the urban environment as a backdrop to your light-painting artworks.

ABOVE LEFT **A coloured gel was wrapped around a bare bulb to make these flowing, freehand streaks of light.**

LEFT **You'll need a large outdoor torch to make luminous patterns on location, but the results can be stunning.**

PAINT WITH LIGHT 145

Module 4.7
Make a physiogram

If, like me, you were lucky enough to have a Spirograph set as a child, you will know all about the simple pleasures of spinning small gearwheels around plastic rings to create ornate geometric patterns. Great fun! Well, these same geometric patterns can be recreated via the medium of light painting, thanks to a studious type of imagery known as physiograms (I say studious because physiography is the study of natural patterns). The main difference is that the pen is replaced by a torch and the paper is replaced by a digital sensor – and there's not a plastic cog in sight.

The basic premise of a physiogram is simplicity itself: you swing a torch attached to string and tethered to a fixed point and keep the camera's shutter open long enough to capture the torch's beam as it rotates in ever-decreasing circles. While invisible to the naked eye, the camera's sensor will record the torch's entire journey in one long stream of light, resulting in abstract images that are as magical as they are unpredictable. We can use the same pen torch or LED light that we used in the previous module, and the same dark space. The only other props you needs are string (a metre/3 feet or so will suffice), sticky tape and an A4 sheet of white paper.

Start by tying one end of the string to the non-bulb end of your torch and taping the other end to the ceiling or a solid light fitting – the torch should hang around a metre (3 feet) above the floor so measure accordingly. Draw a large black 'X' on the paper and place this directly beneath the dangling torch – this is so your camera's autofocus has a clear area of contrast to lock onto. If your camera features a flip-out LCD screen that rotates 180 degrees, take advantage of this, as this will enable you to view your results without having to move the camera every time an exposure ends.

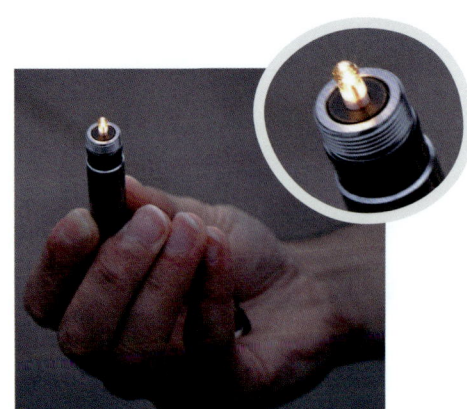

ABOVE **Spirograph, anyone?** This technique creates intricate light patterns.

LEFT **Remove your torch's bulb cover to capture a thinner, more defined light trail.**

DIFFICULTY ★★☆

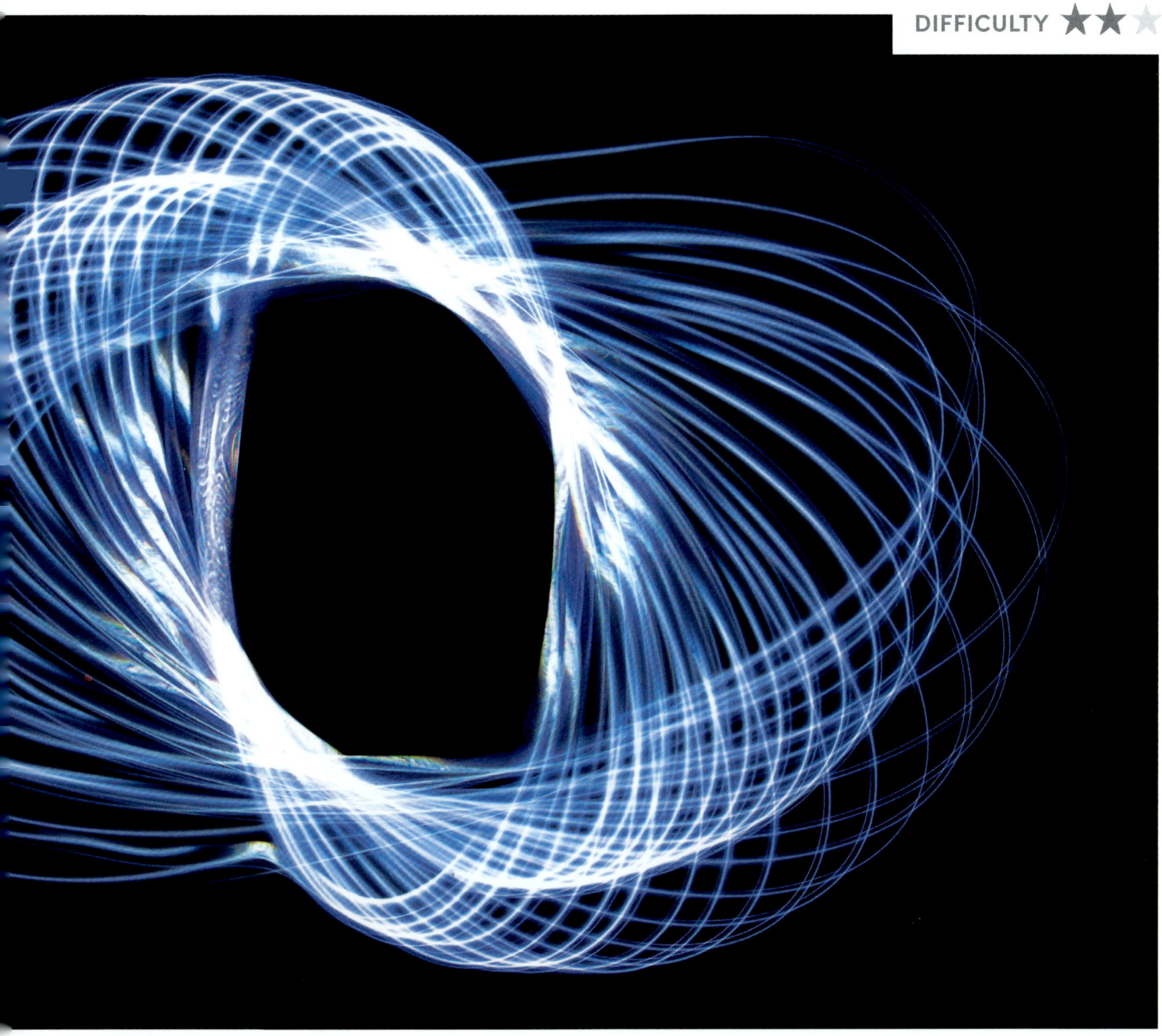

RECOMMENDED SETTINGS

- Shooting mode: **Manual**
- Aperture: **ƒ/16**
- Shutter speed: **15–30 seconds**
- ISO: **100**
- Focal length: **18mm**
- AF area: **Single-point AF**
- AF operation: **Single-shot AF**
- Drive mode: **Self-timer**
- Metering mode: **Evaluative/matrix**
- White balance: **Tungsten or fluorescent**
- Picture style: **Standard**

MAKE A PHYSIOGRAM 147

Camera settings

As we want the ceiling to be pure black to make our physiograms really stand out, we want to work in manual (M) mode again (the camera will expose the ceiling as a midtone grey if we shoot in a semi-automatic mode). The longer the shutter speed, the more intricate the patterns, so start at 15 seconds and increase the exposure time to 30 seconds if you want your light trails to include more rotations. If you own a remote cable release, you could even switch to bulb (B) mode and push the exposure to 60 seconds and beyond.

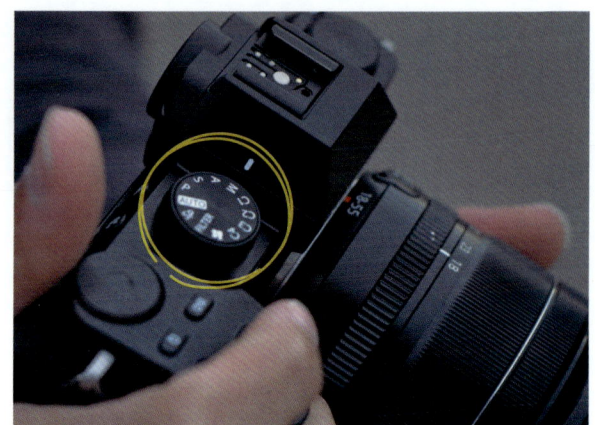

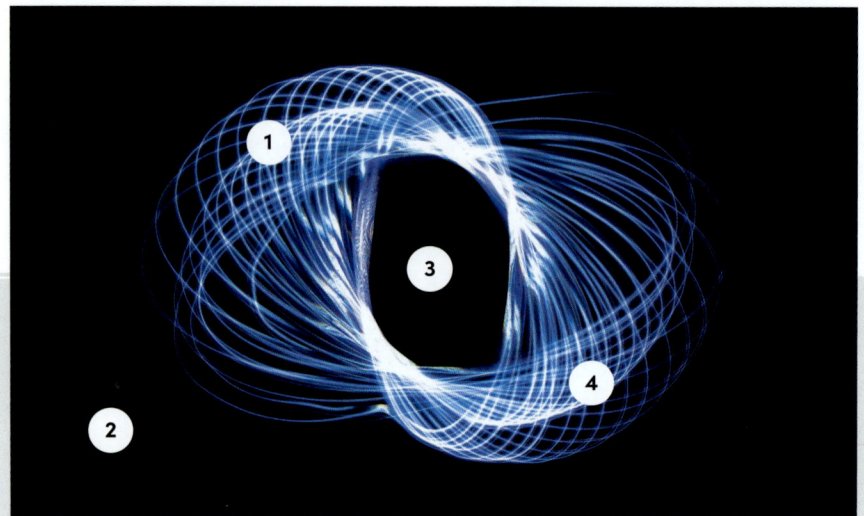

WHY THIS SHOT WORKS

1 A lengthy 30-second exposure has captured the entire journey of the torch bulb, creating a magical light pattern that ebbs and flows as the torch swings in ever-decreasing circles.

2 By taking control of exposure and shooting in manual mode, the ceiling has been rendered pure black, providing maximum contrast between background and physiogram.

4 A wide focal length and a practised swing has created the perfect composition, with the physiogram perfectly central in the frame and just enough negative space around it.

3 A large depth of field and careful focusing has ensured that the light trail is perfectly sharp throughout, even when the distance from the camera changes as it swings and rotates.

The distance between the camera and torch will change by a few millimetres as the latter swings and rotates and so we need to generate a relatively large depth of field to ensure the light trail stays sharp at all times. An aperture of $f/16$ is as narrow as we want to go – any smaller and the clarity of the light trails will actually soften, despite the depth of field being larger, due to the effects of diffraction. Set ISO to 100 and leave it there – ISO and aperture are the fixed exposure 'variables' in this equation.

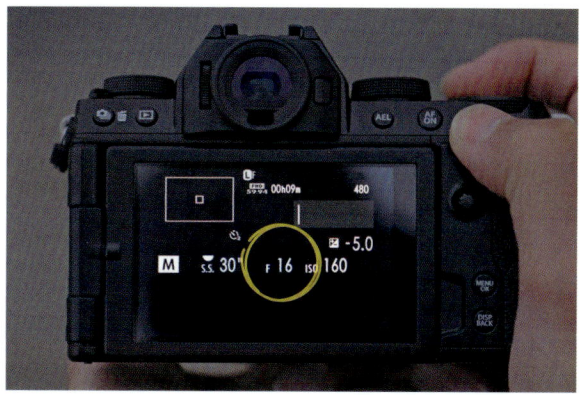

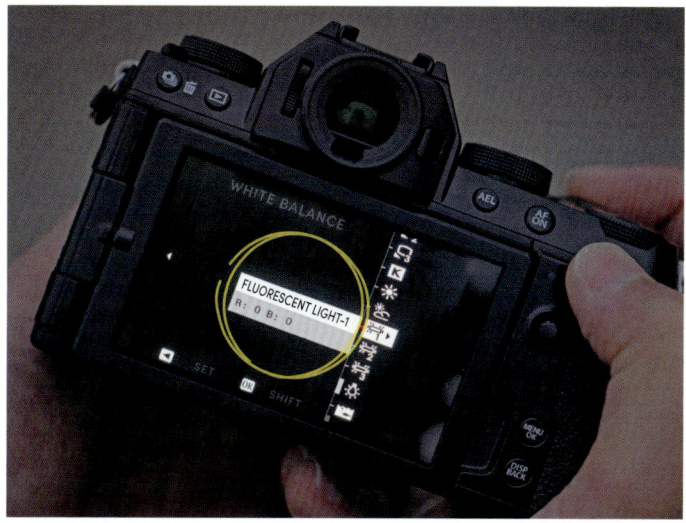

The colour temperature of torchlight varies according to the type of bulb used: incandescent bulbs are around 2700K while LEDs vary between 3800–4700K depending on whether they are neutral or warm white. So, for an accurate white balance, you will need to choose either the tungsten or fluorescent preset, or create a custom setting for your specific torch. Alternatively, you could experiment with colour casts, just as we did in the previous module. After all, rules are made to be broken and painting with light should be fun.

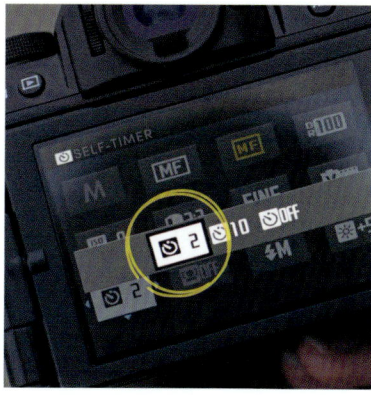

Lens settings

The wider the focal length the better for this technique, as we want to create the biggest canvas possible on which to paint our physiograms, so zoom all the way out to 18mm. Next, flick the AF/MF switch back to AF, set the AF operation to single-shot AF, drive mode to self-timer (or single-shot if using a remote shutter release) and AF area to single-point AF. The 2-second self-timer option will give you plenty of time to set the torch swinging and step out of the frame.

Technique

The camera needs to be focused on the torch's bulb, although this would be rather awkward with it resting on the floor. Instead, hold your camera next to the torch's bulb and point it straight down at the large 'X' you drew on an A4 sheet of white paper. Position the AF point in the centre of the frame, half-press the shutter button to achieve focus, then flick the AF/MF switch to MF to lock it off (it's a good idea to place your left thumb over this switch while squeezing the shutter with your right index finger, as this prevents you from accidentally moving the manual-focusing ring).

Now place the camera on the 'X', facing upwards, turn the room lights off and start the torch swinging. It will take a few seconds for centrifugal force to kick in and the torch to settle into a smooth motion, which is where the 2-second self-timer comes into its own – not only will it allow for any camera shake to dissipate, it will also trigger the shutter just as the torch's rotations even out. However, be careful not to swing the torch so hard that it disappears out of the frame. If in doubt, use Live View to judge the width of the swing and practise a few times before turning the lights off.

This is very much a trial-and-error kind of technique and you almost certainly won't achieve the perfect physiogram first time. While aperture and ISO must remain constant, the variables you can use to refine your patterns in addition to shutter speed include the type of torch you use, the force with which you push it and the length of string you dangle it from.

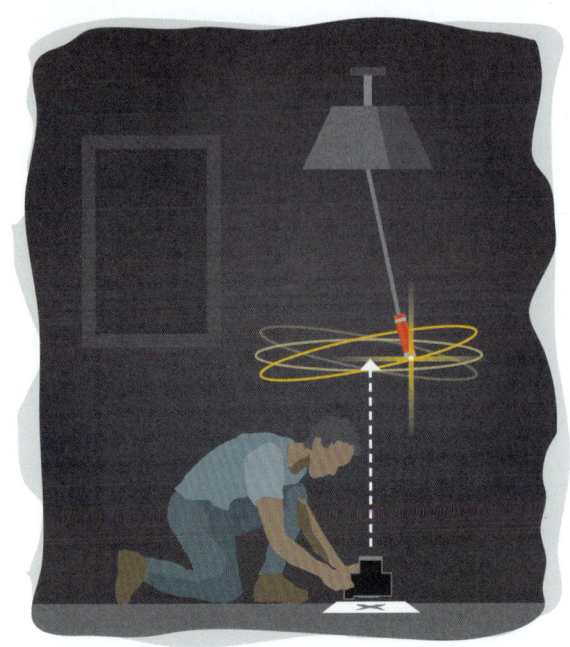

ABOVE **Position your camera directly below the dangling torch and, if possible, use Live View to fine-tune your composition.**

TIP

You can create multiple physiograms in a single frame by covering the lens mid-exposure, swinging the torch in a different direction and uncovering the lens again. You will need a longer exposure time for this technique, so turn the mode dial to bulb (B), use a remote shutter release and experiment.

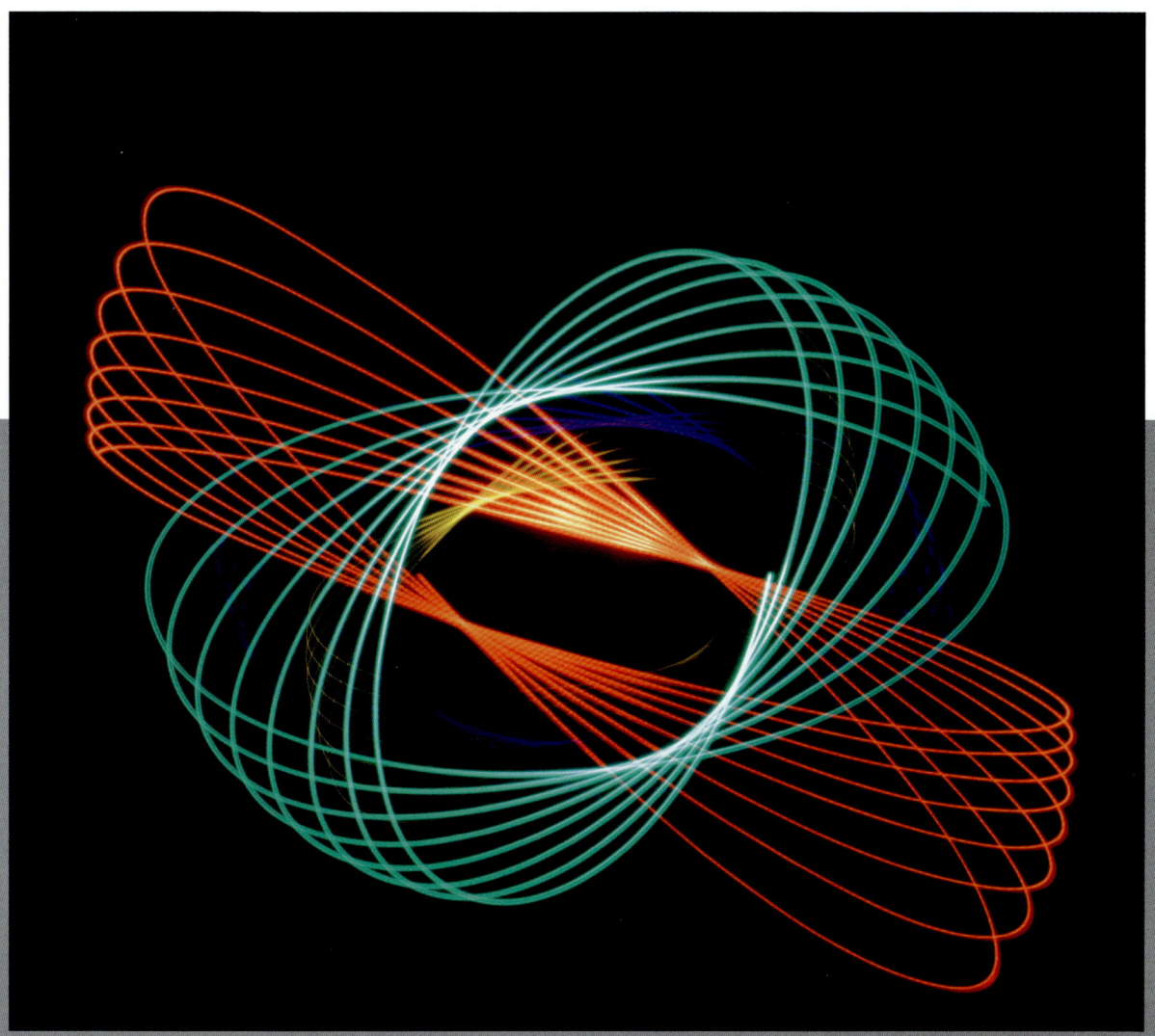

SHOOTING INSPIRATION

There are many ways in which you can develop the basic physiogram technique, from coloured gels to multiple patterns and beyond.

ABOVE Overlapping multiple physiograms in the same frame, each with a different colour, creates an attractive kaleidoscopic effect.

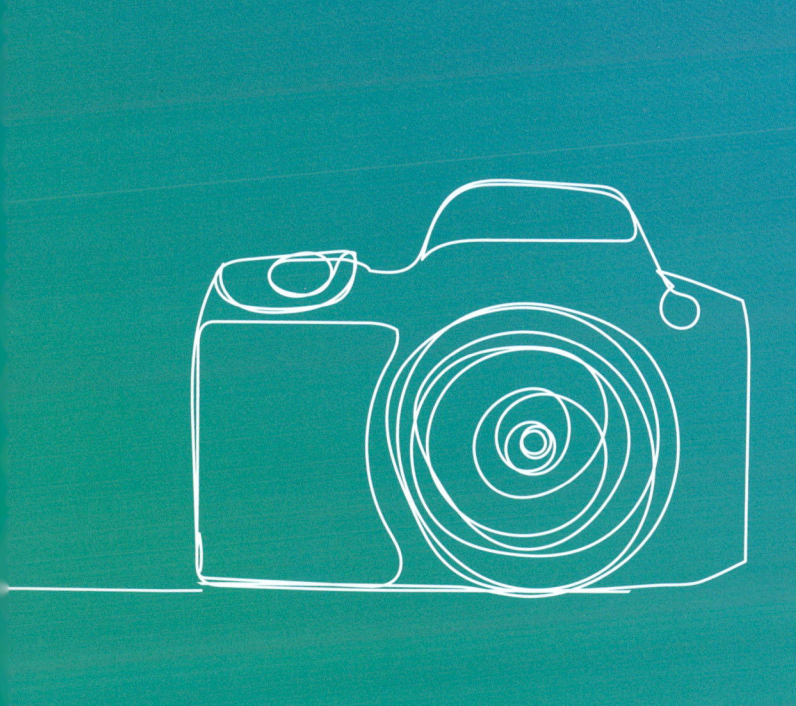

5 STILL LIFE

Module 5.1
Make a retro classic

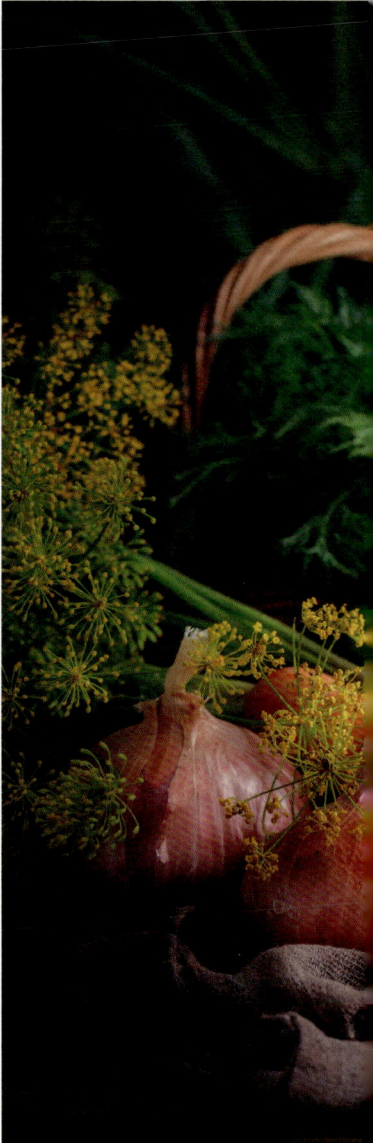

Our obsession with still life predates photography by centuries. Since the late 1500s, artists have been studying and painting inanimate objects, with flowers, food and game being particular favourites. In the 20th century, the likes of Edward Weston, Imogen Cunningham and Irving Penn reintroduced the genre as a photographic staple, imbuing it with a modern sensibility – check out Weston's peppers series for a classic example – while once again proving that careful consideration of subject matter, composition and lighting could turn everyday items into objects of beauty and intrigue.

Still life is a deceptively simple subject that requires patience and precision. With complete control over every aspect of the picture-taking process, the emphasis is on the photographer to set the stage and arrange objects in a visually pleasing way, using shape, colour and texture to add interest. Choose objects according to a theme and select a background that complements this – a plain white background suggests cleanliness and modernity; a dark metallic background could indicate industry and endeavour; a rustic hessian sack might signify agriculture and the countryside.

Start simple, work slowly and meticulously, and build in layers. Place your still life 'stage' near a window to create natural side lighting and dramatic shadows, and position the largest or most important objects first, as these will provide you with a fixed point around which you can arrange other objects. For more natural compositions, think about the number of larger objects you include – the rule of odds suggests that the human eye finds interest and comfort in odd numbers and that our gaze will naturally be drawn to objects in the middle of a group.

ABOVE **Brightly coloured and carefully arranged vegetables make for a classic still life study.**

154 STILL LIFE

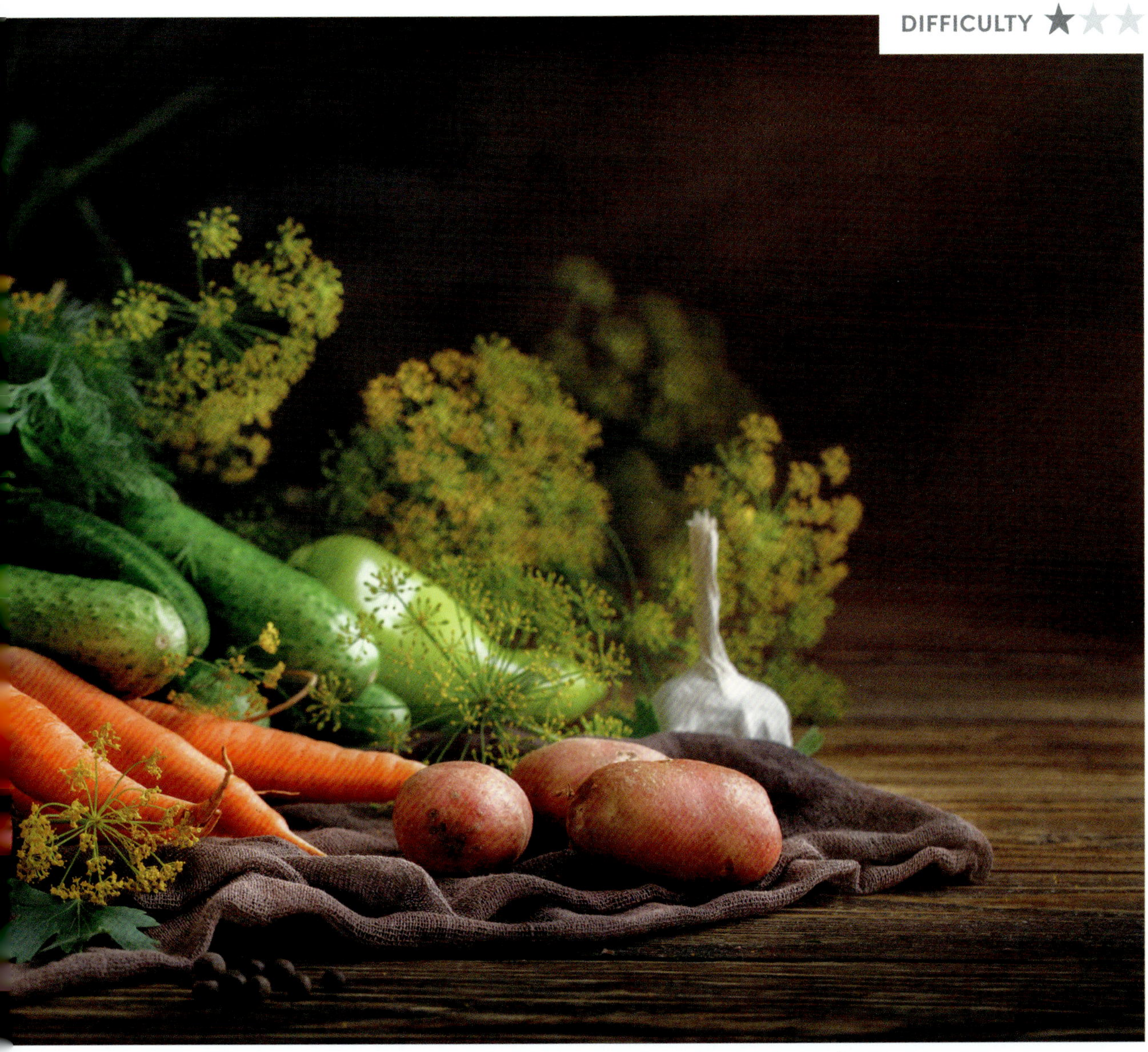

DIFFICULTY ★ ★ ★

RECOMMENDED SETTINGS

- Shooting mode: **Aperture-priority**
- Aperture: **f/5.6–f/8**
- Shutter speed: **Will vary**
- ISO: **100**
- Focal length: **35–50mm**
- AF area: **N/A**
- AF operation: **Manual**
- Drive mode: **Single-shot or self-timer**
- Metering mode: **Evaluative/matrix**
- White balance: **Auto or daylight/cloudy**
- Picture style: **Neutral or Vivid**

MAKE A RETRO CLASSIC 155

Camera settings

Still life should never be rushed so always use a tripod. This will not only encourage you to slow down and pay more attention to the finer details of your composition and viewpoint, it will also allow you to concentrate solely on aperture, control of which is crucial to creating images with a clearly defined yet almost subliminal focal point – or points, if multiple objects are positioned on the same focal plane – and a sense of depth and separation.

Turn the mode dial to aperture-priority (A or Av) and select your kit lens' widest aperture, which will typically be $f/4$–5.6. This will give you a shallow depth of field so time and attention must be paid to accurate focusing – see below. Depth of field is an often-overlooked aspect of composition, yet plays a critical part in how every pictorial element is rendered in the frame, so don't be afraid to experiment with aperture once you've finished arranging your objects – for instance, $f/8$ will increase the zone of sharpness and could allow you to include key details that may otherwise have been blurred to some degree at $f/5.6$.

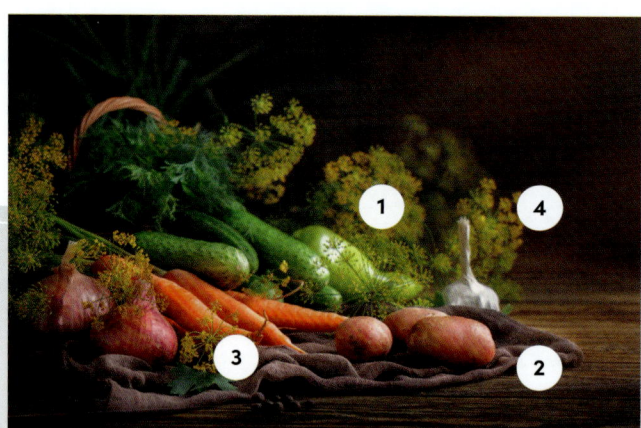

WHY THIS SHOT WORKS

1 The use of a wide aperture and careful focusing ensure that the vegetables positioned along the focal plane are sharp and draw our attention, while the vegetables further away are blurred and create a sense of depth.

2 The rustic wooden table surface and brown background create the perfect 'stage' for the countryside-themed objects, with the darker, colour palette allowing the brighter vegetables to 'pop'.

3 The rule of odds has been stealthily deployed to add greater visual interest. Three carrots, three potatoes, three main groups of vegetables in the foreground... three is indeed the magic number.

4 Soft, diffused natural light has been used to gently illuminate the vegetables and create just enough shadow and drama, imbuing the scene with a warm and welcoming end-of-the-day feel.

Remember also that the greater the distance between subject and background, the more out of focus the background will appear, so consider this when positioning your setup. A continuous backdrop that starts in front of your arrangement and finishes behind it and out of the frame – known as an infinity curve – is a great way to create a seamless still life 'stage'. Simple infinity curves can be made with large sheets of card or fabric.

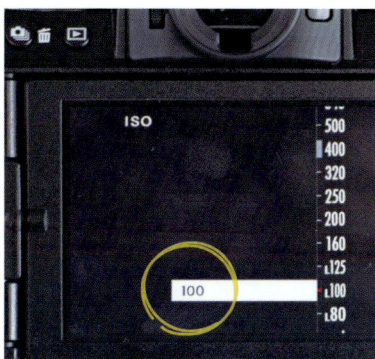

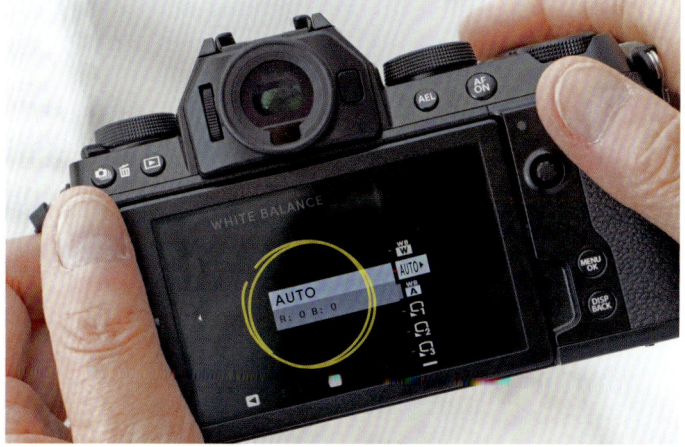

Image quality is all-important when shooting still life and so, as is almost always the case when working with a tripod, ISO should be set to 100. Although this low setting, together with the fact that we are using window light only, means that shutter speeds could be relatively slow, this isn't something we need to worry about – shooting in aperture-priority means that the camera will take care of exposure times while the tripod will take care of any potential camera shake.

As we're working indoors using nothing but natural light, the auto white balance preset will produce reliably neutral colours, however always check that all other light sources are switched off before you start shooting. If you would rather take a more hands-on approach, select either the daylight or cloudy preset according to the weather and the quality of light reaching your subject.

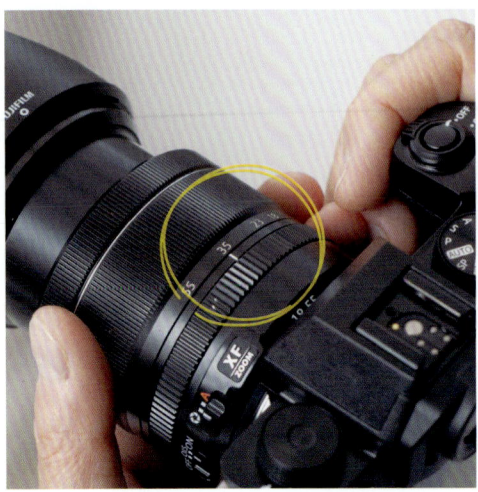

Lens settings

With the emphasis of still life photography being on accurate representation, we don't want to run the risk of introducing image distortion by using unnecessarily wide focal lengths. Instead, we want to use a standard focal length between 35–50mm – this versatile range provides a natural, compression-free perspective that is the 35mm equivalent of around 53–75mm. Move your tripod back rather than zoom your lens wider if you need to squeeze more into the frame. We also want to take full control of focusing so flick your lens' AF/MF switch to manual and select the single-shot drive mode if using a remote shutter release.

Technique

When you are 100% happy with your still life arrangement and have carefully assessed it through the viewfinder, using the rule of odds to create a natural sense of visual balance and paying particular attention to the edges of the frame for any unwanted distractions, activate Live View and use the zoom/magnify buttons to zoom into the part of the scene you want to be absolutely pin-sharp. Slowly and deliberately turn your lens' focusing ring until focus is exactly where you want it to be. As depth of field will be so shallow, this may take a few attempts to get right.

If you don't have a remote shutter release, select your camera's self-timer mode – the 2-second option is fine – and gently squeeze the shutter to start the countdown. If your test shot appears too light or dark, use exposure compensation to manually override the camera's selected shutter speed – start by dialling in +1 to brighten the shot and -1 to darken it. Also, if shadows appear too deep and 'blocky' in places, position a reflector or a sheet of white card directly opposite the window to bounce light back into the scene and lighten the shadows without completely removing them.

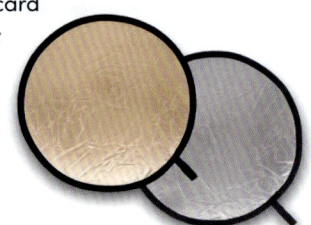

ABOVE

Reflectors often feature gold and silver sides for adding warmth and increasing contrast.

TIP

Space is an important part of any composition, so resist the urge to completely fill the frame with your still life arrangement. Negative space – the empty area around your subject – can actually draw attention to the positive space – the area that your subject occupies – while providing the eye with somewhere to rest and finish its visual journey.

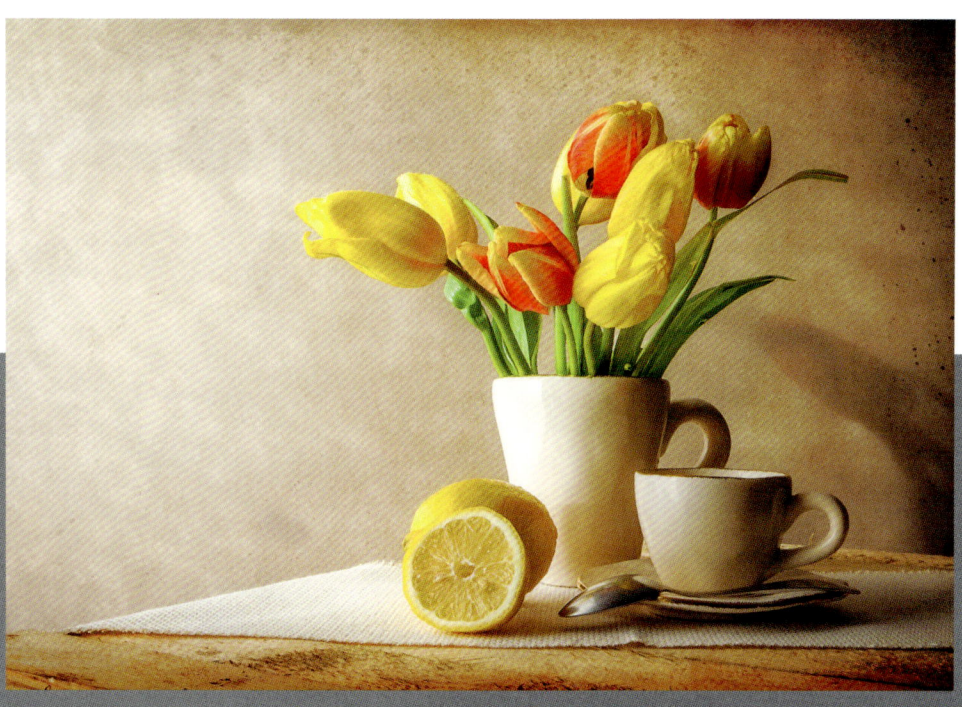

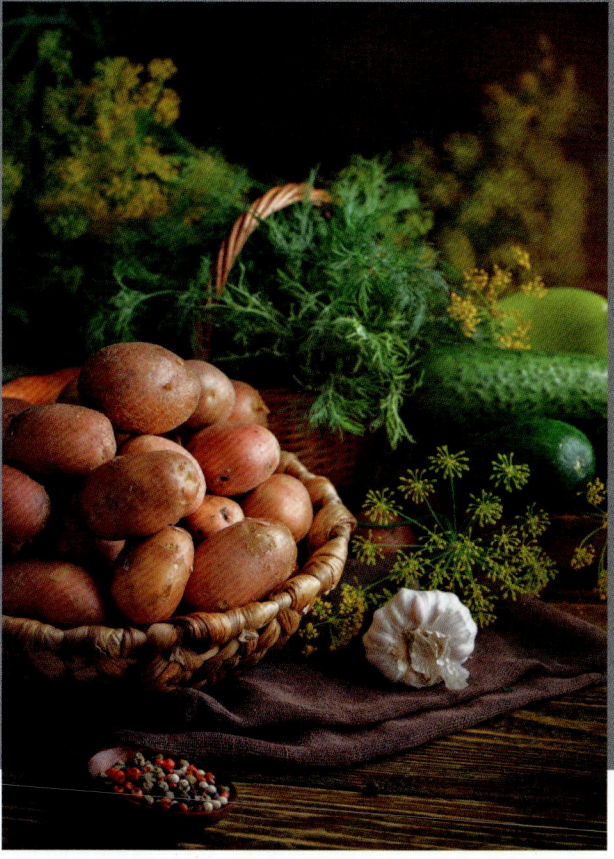

SHOOTING INSPIRATION

Still life is a form of static storytelling, so think about the narrative you want to convey and what kinds of objects you will need to develop it.

ABOVE Use colour to set the mood – warm yellows and oranges will make the viewer feel cheerful and energetic.

LEFT Wicker baskets and tablecloths are ideal props for containing objects and reinforcing the agricultural theme.

Module 5.2
Reinvent household objects

Despite its classical leanings, still life is just as relevant today as it was in the 1500s, and it still offers a unique lens through which to re-evaluate and reinterpret the aesthetic values of inanimate objects. And if there is one overriding reason to explore this fascinating genre, this is it: it encourages, if not forces, you to look at and think very differently about everyday items that you are intimately familiar with; not about their practical functions and qualities, but about their visual and material qualities. To illustrate the point, we are going to embrace a kind of still life mindfulness and take a much closer look at the humblest of kitchen utensils.

Open your kitchen drawer and pick a suitably mundane-looking fork. While this module is concerned with form rather than function, our aim is to transform something entirely average into something elegant and appealing. Imagine the object you are now holding in your hand is no longer a fork but a tactile entity comprising textures, contours and weight. Close your eyes, clear your mind and run your fingers across its surfaces. How does it feel? Smooth perhaps, or surprisingly heavy. Open your eyes and hold this tactile entity up to a window. How do its various surfaces react when you gently turn it one way or another?

What is it that interests you most about this entity? Once you can answer this question succinctly, isolating a distinct aspect or characteristic that captures your imagination, you can start to build a striking still life image around your vision. With the entity still in your hand, think about how close you will need to get, which viewpoint and direction of light will best highlight the features you want to draw attention to, how it might interact with other objects, and what kind of background will best complement or contrast with your entity's aesthetic qualities.

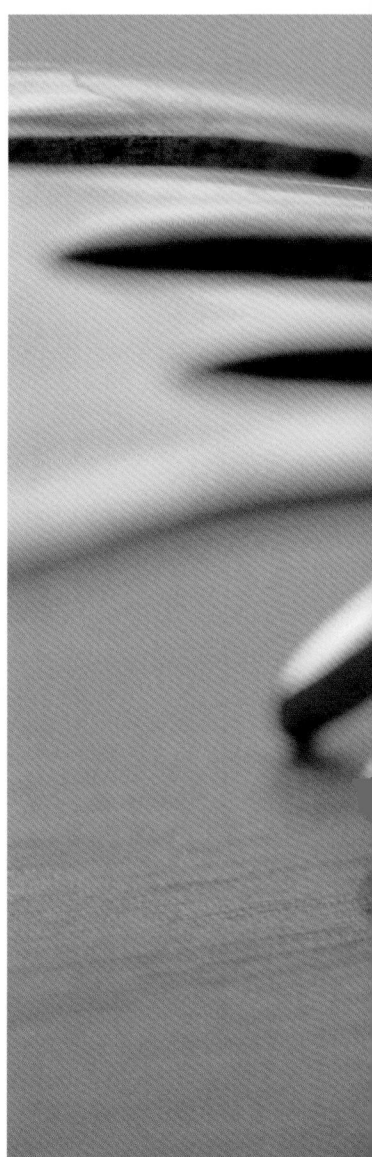

ABOVE **Even the most unremarkable household objects can be crafted into still life art.**

DIFFICULTY ★ ★ ★

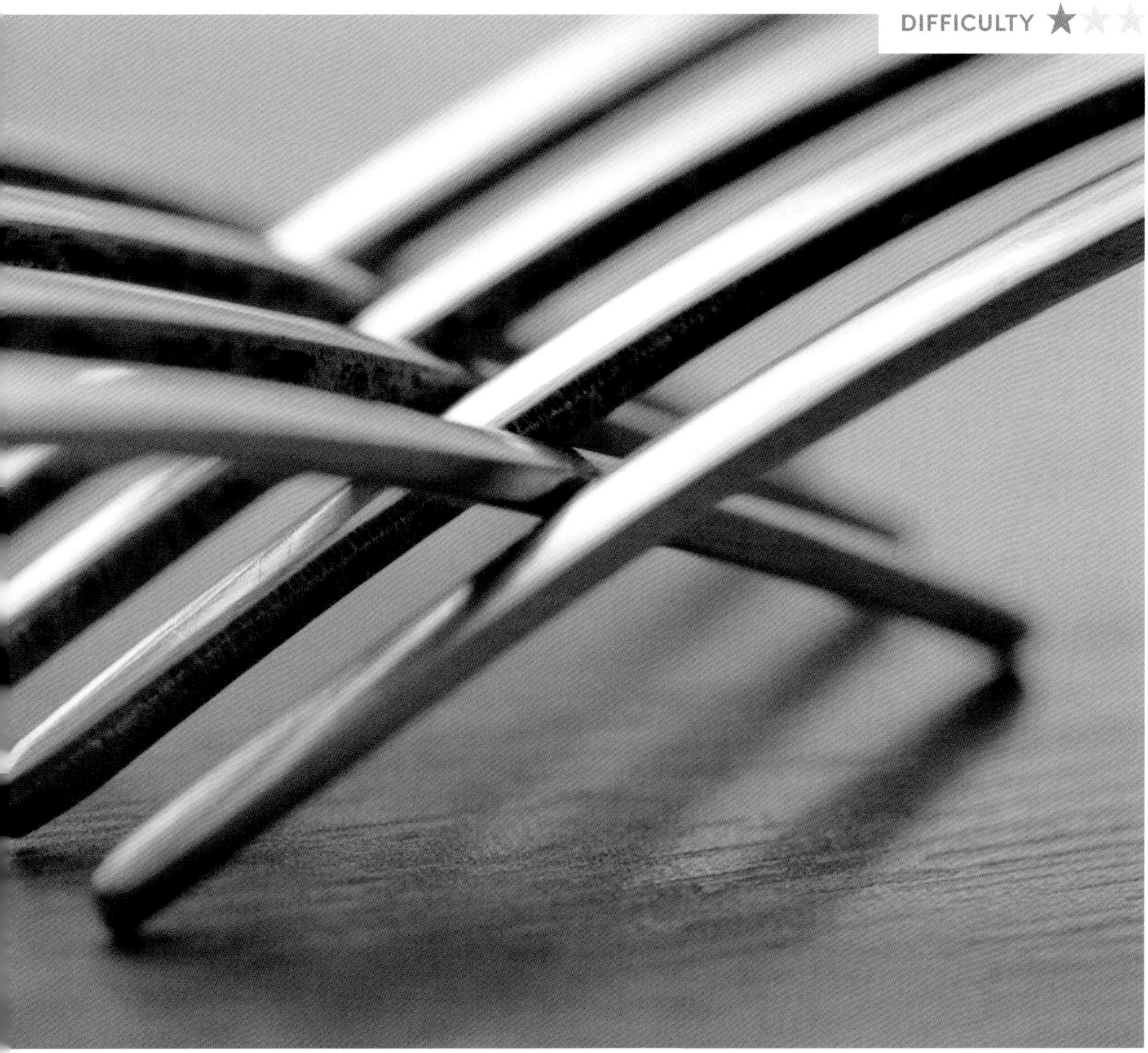

RECOMMENDED SETTINGS

- Shooting mode: **Aperture-priority**
- Aperture: **f/5.6**
- Shutter speed: **Will vary**
- ISO: **100**
- Focal length: **55mm**

- AF area: **N/A**
- AF operation: **Manual**
- Drive mode: **Single-shot or self-timer**
- Metering mode: **Evaluative/matrix**

- White balance: **Auto or daylight/cloudy**
- Picture style: **Monochrome**

REINVENT HOUSEHOLD OBJECTS 161

Camera settings

There's no denying that this module is all about the art of seeing, looking closer and reimagining, but once you form a vision in your mind's eye, you then need to bring that vision to life in the real world. The most important camera setting here is aperture, as this will control depth of field and how much of your subject is pin-sharp and how much – and how quickly – the rest of the scene falls out of focus. Leave the mode dial set to aperture-priority (A or Av) for complete control of aperture without having to worry about shutter speed.

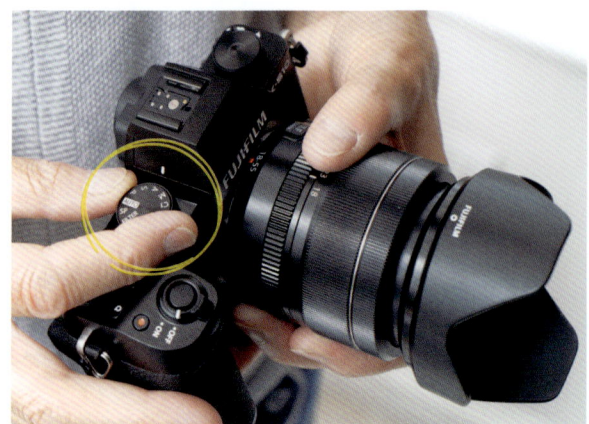

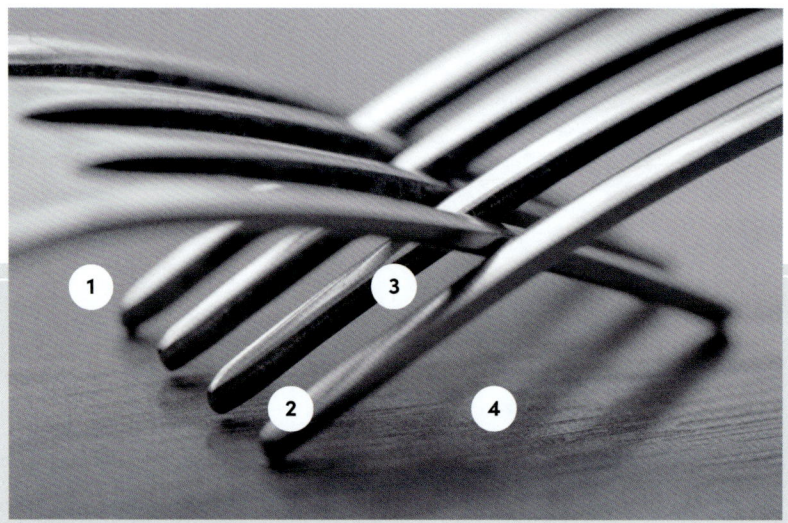

WHY THIS SHOT WORKS

1 When is a fork not a fork? When it's a neatly arranged tangle of metallic surfaces, abstracted with a tight crop and a shallow depth of field that renders only a single prong sharp.

2 This image is all about shape and contrast, and the black-and-white treatment highlights the hard edges, metallic qualities and tonal variations of these seemingly unremarkable objects.

3 The prongs of the fork create a strong 'X' shape in the centre of the frame, with diagonal lines running from or to all four corners. It's a simple minimalist composition but incredibly effective.

4 The slightly textured 'stage' offers a subtle contrast to the fork's shiny smoothness, with the narrow zone of sharpness highlighting only a small slither of the tactile surface.

A shallow depth of field will allow us to adopt a more creative, interpretative approach to our kitchen utensil, perhaps highlighting subtle details, shapes and textures within a narrow zone of sharpness, while abstracting the subject as a whole. In our main example, only one of the eight intertwined fork prongs is in focus, which is where the eye naturally gravitates to before it explores the blurred outer regions of the frame. Start at your lens' widest aperture and only step down to ƒ/8 and beyond if the narrow zone of sharpness proves too shallow.

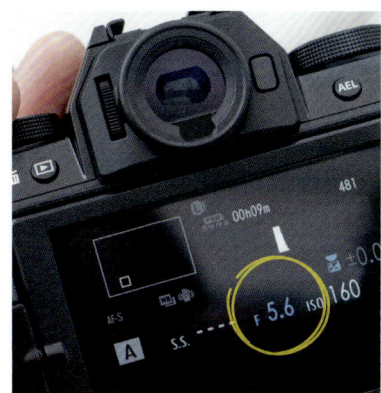

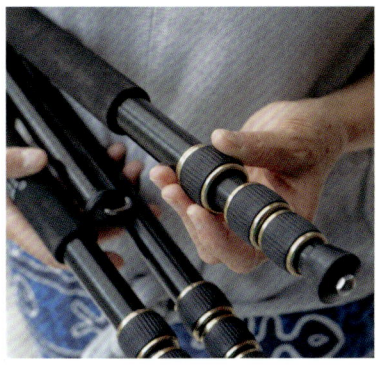

ISO can stay at 100. Still life is the ultimate rainy day challenge and even the most overcast skies will provide enough light to illuminate the small space that your subject will occupy, the only downside being that shutter speeds will be too slow to handhold. However, as your camera will be firmly rooted to a tripod, this won't be a problem. A decent tripod will last you a lifetime so look after it (don't dunk it in the sea and forget to wash the legs afterwards, as I once did – salt water is highly corrosive and it didn't end well for my three-legged friend).

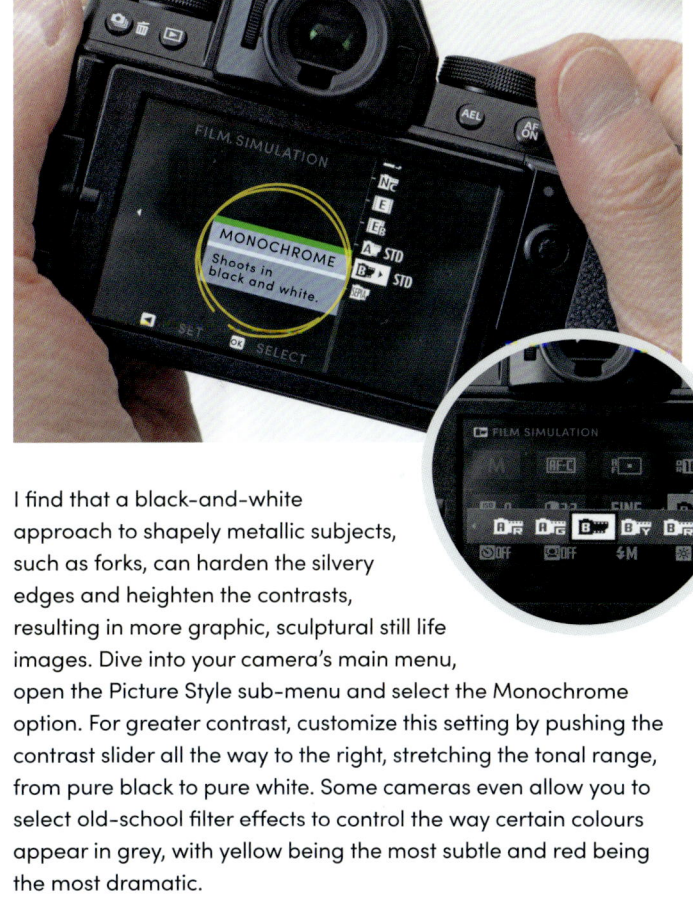

I find that a black-and-white approach to shapely metallic subjects, such as forks, can harden the silvery edges and heighten the contrasts, resulting in more graphic, sculptural still life images. Dive into your camera's main menu, open the Picture Style sub-menu and select the Monochrome option. For greater contrast, customize this setting by pushing the contrast slider all the way to the right, stretching the tonal range, from pure black to pure white. Some cameras even allow you to select old-school filter effects to control the way certain colours appear in grey, with yellow being the most subtle and red being the most dramatic.

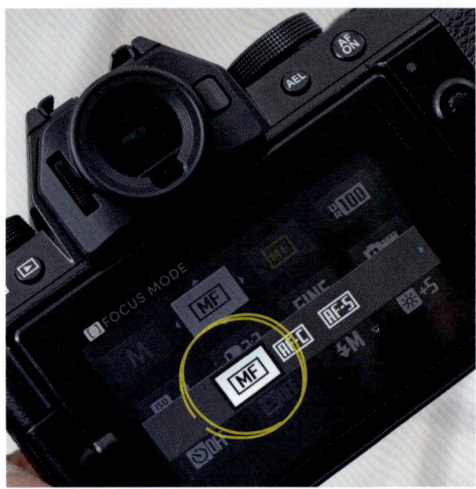

Technique

Still life is more controllable indoors, so find a suitable space near a window, attach your camera to a tripod (for more on tripod technique, see page 30) and create your 'stage'. This should complement but not detract from your subject, so for items such as shiny forks, think stainless steel chopping boards and other metallic surfaces. Add a DIY infinity curve (see previous module) if your viewpoint is low and horizontal enough. Finding the perfect still life composition takes time and patience, so don't expect to nail it first time – work by making micro adjustments to subject and camera position, using Live View to preview and fine-tune the arrangement.

Accurate focusing becomes all-important when working with such a shallow depth of field, as the narrow zone of sharpness means that only a tiny slither of your fork will be clearly defined at any one time – and this slither is effectively your focal point, the area where your viewer's eye will be directed first. As before, zoom in using Live View and very slowly turn the focusing ring until your intended focal point becomes pin-sharp. As simple as this process is in theory, it requires a delicate touch – when zoomed in, even the smallest nudge of the focusing ring will appear to move the zone of sharpness a considerable distance forward or backwards.

Lens settings

Exploring a subject through a camera's viewfinder is a very different experience to looking at it with the naked eye, as the four edges of the frame instinctively 'blinker' our vision, heightening our awareness of lines, shapes and tones. The closer we get, the more abstracted the subject becomes, so start by zooming all the way in for a short-telephoto perspective, and leave all other lens settings as they were in the previous module, with the AF/MF switch left on MF and the drive mode set to self-timer if you don't have a remote shutter release to hand.

TIP

Think cutlery is a boring household necessity with zero sex appeal? Think again. Although Bob Carlos Clarke was better known for his provocative portraits, his most endearing images – in my humble opinion, at least – are those of intertwined forks and spoons. Get Googling.

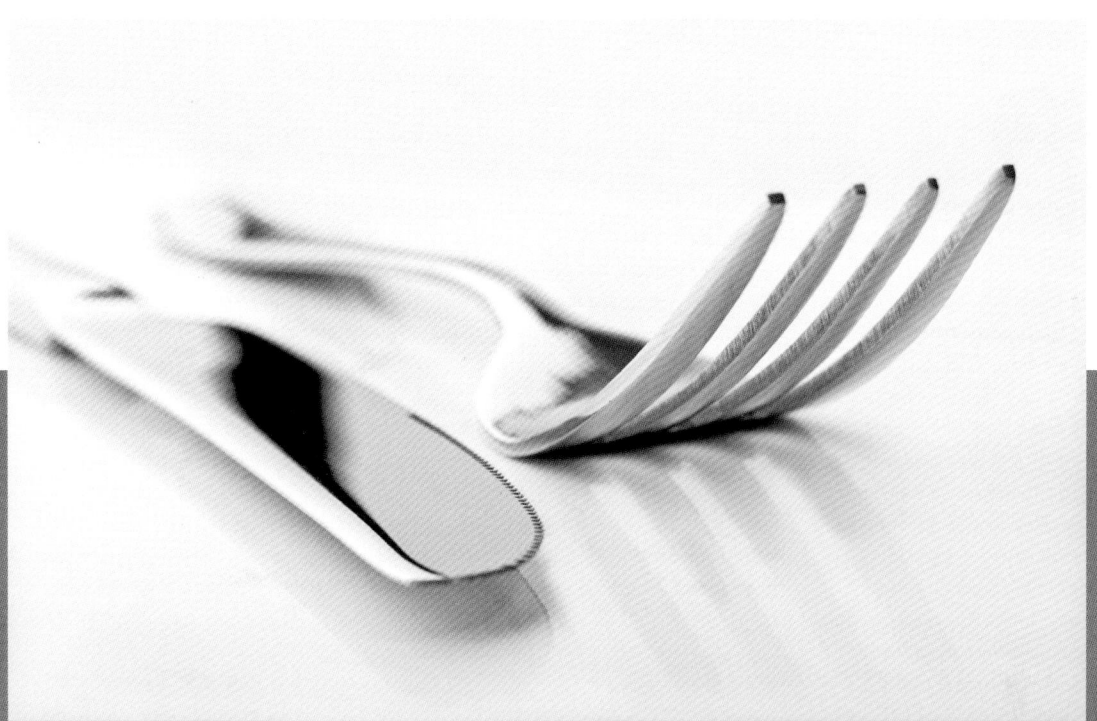

SHOOTING INSPIRATION

Cutlery may appear to be fiercely functional at first glance, but adopt a more mindful approach and you'll soon start to appreciate its tactile and aesthetic qualities.

ABOVE The various shapes and tones reflected in the cutlery's metallic surfaces add depth and three-dimensionality.

LEFT Use directional light and graphic shadows to duplicate, distort and elongate your subjects' shapes.

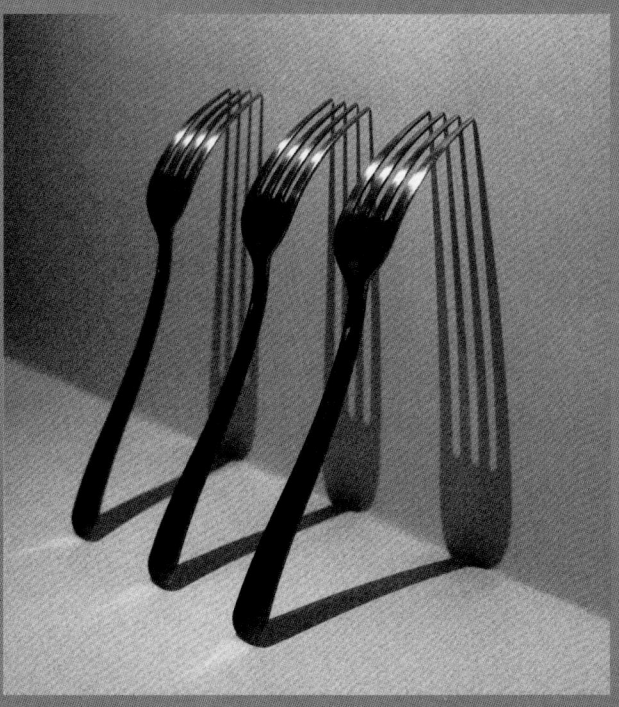

REINVENT HOUSEHOLD OBJECTS

Module 5.3
Sell your products

Product photography is the great invisible – it's everywhere we look and it is used to sell everything from haute-couture fashion and luxury cars to garden furniture and loft insulation. And yet, we rarely stop to appreciate the actual image, so bedazzled are we by the garment or device that will, no doubt, vastly improve our lives. Which, it has to be said, is the whole point. After all, the perceived value of a product is subconsciously conveyed by its visual presentation. But not all product photography needs to look (or cost) a million dollars – if you simply want to sell an old pair of shoes on eBay, a budget DIY approach can provide the perfect solution.

The purpose of any product photograph, particularly when selling online only, is to show a potential customer what the item looks like in the absence of being able to hold and touch it. The easiest way to achieve this is by placing your products against a white background, as this creates a distraction-free view that makes your items 'pop'. This is the most basic type of product image but also the most commonly used. To create a simple setup, all you need is a small table, white infinity curve, reflector, tripod, tape and window light. The results are unlikely to win you any awards for artistic merit, but they may tempt a customer to part with their cash.

Position your table against a wall, with a window to one side of your 'studio' (direct sunlight is rarely flattering). For your infinity curve, tape a sheet of thick white paper to the front of your table and bend it over and above the table to create a smooth vertical 'sweep'. Tape the top of the paper to the wall to keep the curve in place. I've found that white 5mm foam board makes for the perfect tabletop reflector, as it is light, rigid and cheap, so invest in a few A3 sheets and keep them to hand. This will help you to bounce light back into areas of shadow on the non-window side of your setup, making for more evenly lit product shots that show maximum detail.

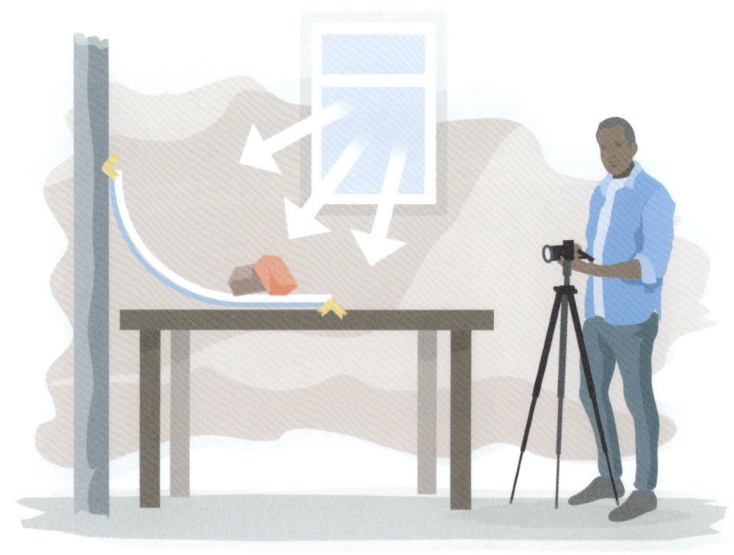

ABOVE **Tape a curved sheet of white card to a wall to create an infinity curve on your tabletop studio – and avoid direct sunlight for more attractive side lighting.**

DIFFICULTY ★☆☆

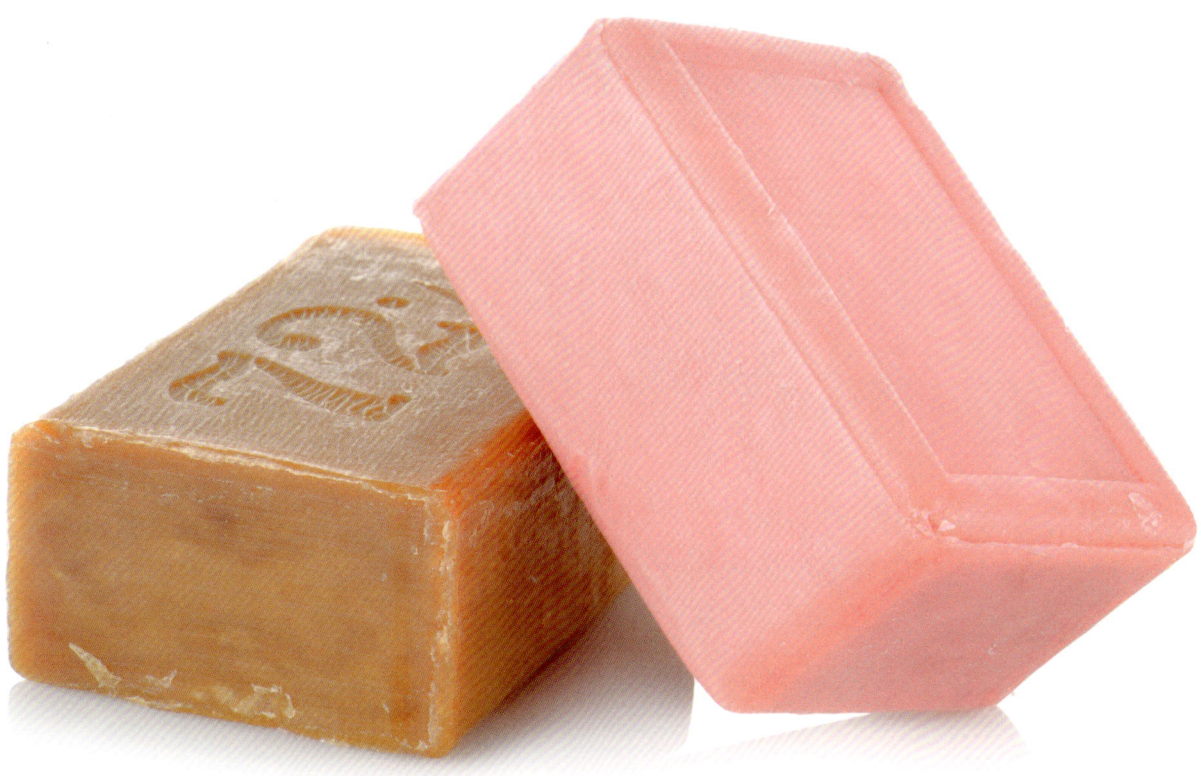

ABOVE **This is exactly the type of clean product shot you'd expect to see on a retailer's website.**

RECOMMENDED SETTINGS

- Shooting mode: **Aperture-priority**
- Aperture: ƒ**/16**
- Shutter speed: **Will vary**
- ISO: **100**
- Focal length: **55mm**
- AF area: **Single-point AF**
- AF operation: **Single-shot AF**
- Drive mode: **Self-timer or single-shot**
- Metering mode: **Centre-weighted**
- White balance: **Auto or daylight/cloudy**
- Picture style: **Standard**

SELL YOUR PRODUCTS

Camera settings

As we are selling a product rather than our photography skills, it is important that we capture a realistic depiction of the item in question, with every part of it in focus. Whereas in the previous module we used a wide aperture to create a shallow depth of field for a more artistic approach, for this challenge we want to use a narrow aperture to create a large depth of field for a more representational approach. Although shooting in manual is an option, working in aperture-priority means you have one less setting to worry about.

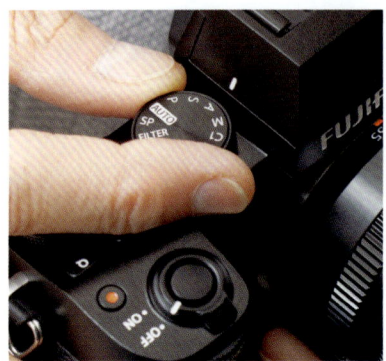

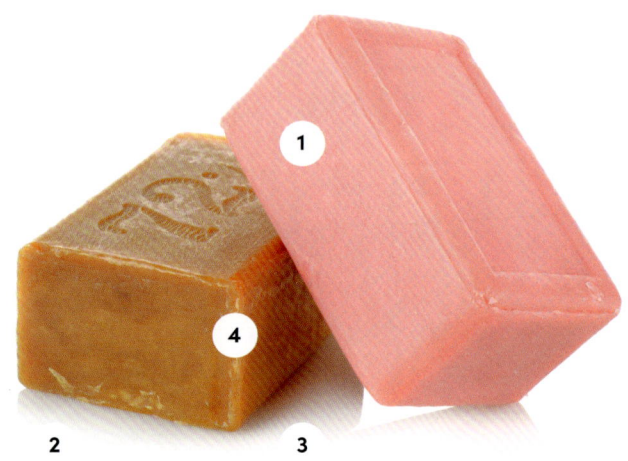

WHY THIS SHOT WORKS

1 These colourful bars of soap 'pop' against the plain white background, giving potential customers a distraction-free view of the product. You can almost smell the soapy fragrance!

2 With no creases or scuffs, the white infinity curve is effectively invisible, providing the perfect background to any number of modestly sized subjects. Always replace your curve as soon as it gets dirty.

3 The photographer has placed a sheet of clear plastic beneath the bars of soap, which has added subtle reflections to an otherwise standard product shot for a more three-dimensional feel.

4 The soft, even illumination from carefully controlled window light complements the subjects' indulgent nature. Overcast days provide the most flattering light, but direct sunlight can be diffused if needed.

The temptation when needing a large depth of field is to select your lens' narrowest aperture, which is likely to be ƒ/22, but as we learned in the landscape chapter (see page 11), it is best to shoot at an aperture of ƒ/16 or ƒ/18 owing to the effects of diffraction. Even though we will be focusing on a subject relatively close to the lens, assuming the product is no larger than a pair of shoes, this will still give us plenty of depth of field, ensuring that even the smallest details are perfectly sharp.

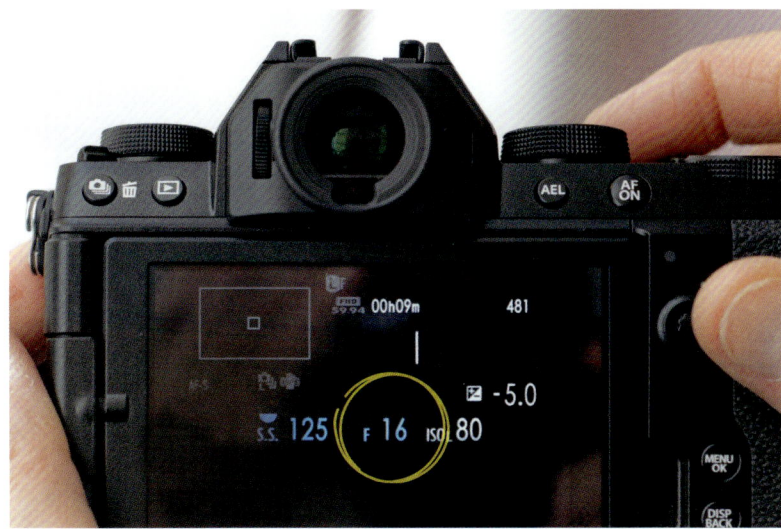

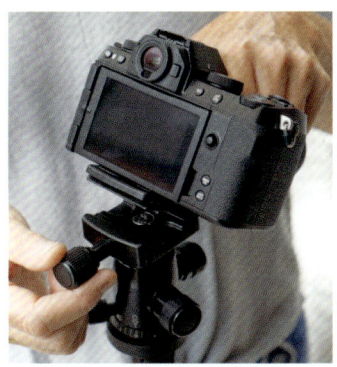

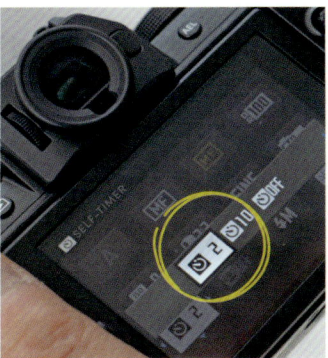

Still life and tripods go hand in glove as we are working with static subjects, lengthy exposures and carefully considered compositions. In turn, this allows for large ƒ/numbers and low ISOs. Keep ISO set to 100 and don't worry about shutter speeds – depending on the size of the window and quality of light, exposure times will vary from around 1/15 second to several seconds, but so long as we trigger the shutter using the camera's self-timer or a remote release to avoid camera shake, shutter speed is irrelevant.

All DSLRs and mirrorless cameras feature a 'standard' picture style that delivers an optimal amount of saturation, contrast and sharpness to add just enough punch without altering reality. Select this preset for 'straight' product shots and remember that you can customize individual settings for greater control, though I'd recommend you do this only after you have taken and reviewed a few images, and with restraint. For instance, you may want to add a touch more saturation, in which case only push the saturation slider in single increments at a time.

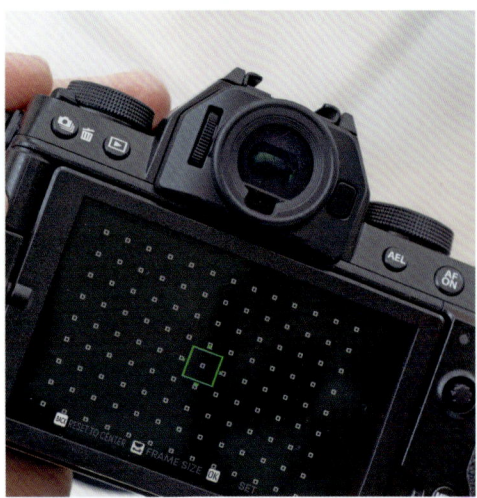

Technique

Before positioning your table and taping the infinity curve to the wall, consider the distance between your studio and the light source. The closer the window, the softer the light and the less defined the shadows; the further away the window, the more even the light and the more defined the shadows. The type of product will determine which is more preferable – fragrant soaps with pastel colours may benefit from softer light while hi-tech gadgets with vibrant colours may benefit from harder shadows. Overcast light is best, but if direct sunlight is your only option, you may also want to diffuse the light using cloth or paper to tone down harsh shadows and noticeable reflections.

Place your product at the foot of the curve, just in front of where the paper starts to sweep upwards, and make sure that any labels or important details are straight and centred. With all eyes on one single item, attention to detail is crucial. Compose centrally, with enough white space around the product to act as a frame, and position the AF point directly over the item's 'face' i.e., the most prominent label, logo or button. For an evenly lit image, use a sheet of foam board to bounce light back into darker areas, adjusting its angle and distance according to the subject's size and shape, and the direction and intensity of light. Just make sure it doesn't appear in the shot!

Lens settings

This is very much a what you see is what you get style of still life and product shots should be distortion-free and true to life, so zoom your lens in to 55mm and leave it there. If you need to adjust the subject's size in the frame, move your tripod instead. With little to no artistic interpretation needed, we can push the AF/MF switch back to AF and let the camera do the heavy lifting. Set the AF area to single-point AF, AF operation to single-shot AF and drive mode to self-timer (or single-shot if using a remote shutter release). If your camera features multiple self-timer options, select either the 5- or 10-second delay time to eliminate any trace of camera shake.

TIP

Once you've mastered the basics, experiment with coloured infinity curves to add an extra dimension to your product images. Use a lighter shade of the subject's colour to harmonize with it or a colour on the opposite side of the colour wheel to contrast with it.

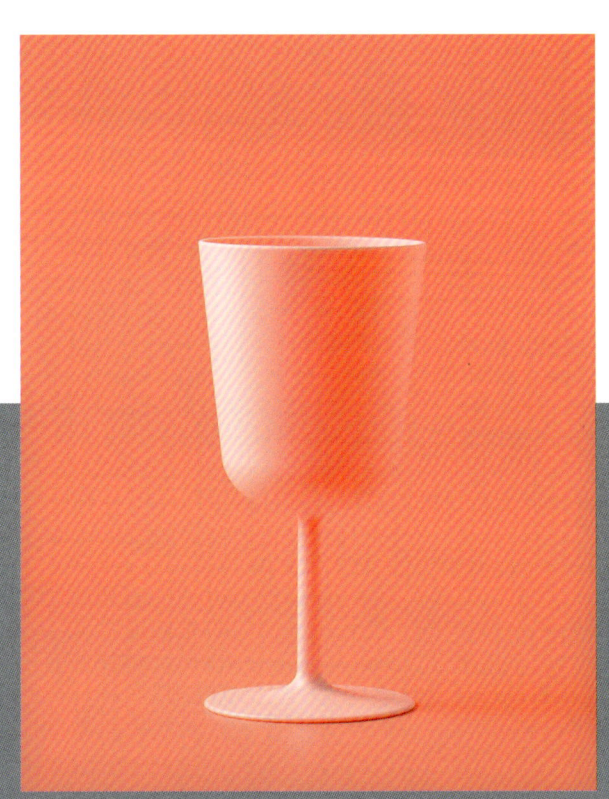
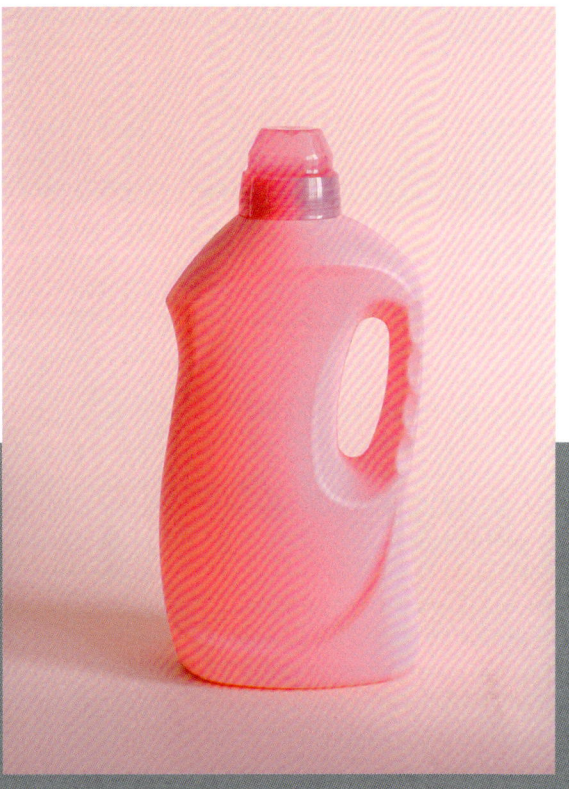
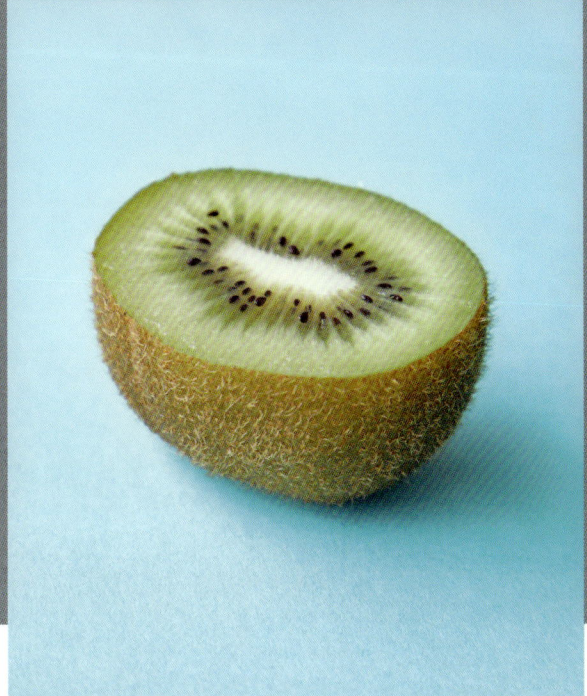

SHOOTING INSPIRATION

Creative use of colour can attract the eye and reinforce a brand message while offering a more playful alternative to the stark white product shot.

ABOVE **Monochromatic** colour schemes – those that use a single hue's tones, tints and shades – create a visual cohesion that is easy on the eye.

LEFT **Analogous** colour schemes – those that use colours next to each other on the colour wheel – often suit organic subjects.

SELL YOUR PRODUCTS

Module 5.4
Cook up a tasty dish

Fuelled by the rise of social media and our insatiable appetite for turning even the most mundane aspects of our private lives into photo ops, food photography – or foodography, if you live in the blogging world – has become so popular that it now has its own annual competition (Food Photographer of the Year). You only have to look at the number of cookery shows and celebrity chefs on TV – not to mention the abundance of food-related hashtags on Instagram – to see how obsessed we are. If you consider yourself a 'foodie' and enjoy spending time in the kitchen rustling up tasty dishes, this module was prepared just for you.

Foodography shares similarities with product photography and the simple 'studio' setup we created in the previous module can be repurposed here. Other than the food itself, light is the most important ingredient and soft, diffused light is the most effective way to bring your dish to life. A large window or patio door covered with cloth or tracing paper to tame direct sunlight will work perfectly, as will white foam board to 'fill' any overly dark shadows. If you want to add contrast, you may also want to pick up a sheet of black foam board – used in the same way as a reflector, this will absorb light and darken the shadows, a technique known as 'flagging'.

Read any food blog and you'll quickly find reference to 'the story'. This term refers to the overall theme of your image, from the ingredients and the way in which they are presented to the crockery, cutlery and accoutrements that you choose to include in the frame. Like classic still life, you build your food scenes, starting with the 'hero' of the story – the main dish and focal point – and filling the empty space with props that relate to the food such as sauces, herbs and utensils. Use a background surface or material that is sympathetic to your food – wood and hessian fabric is ideal for rustic dishes, while cleaner, smoother textures will complement modern cuisine.

RIGHT **Choose a theme for your food still life and build your scene around the main dish.**

RECOMMENDED SETTINGS

- Shooting mode: **Aperture-priority**
- Aperture: **f/5.6**
- Shutter speed: **Will vary**
- ISO: **100**
- Focal length: **55mm**
- AF area: **Single-point AF**
- AF operation: **Single-shot AF**
- Drive mode: **Self-timer or single-shot**
- Metering mode: **Evaluative/matrix**
- White balance: **Auto or cloudy/shade**
- Picture style: **Standard**

DIFFICULTY ★★☆

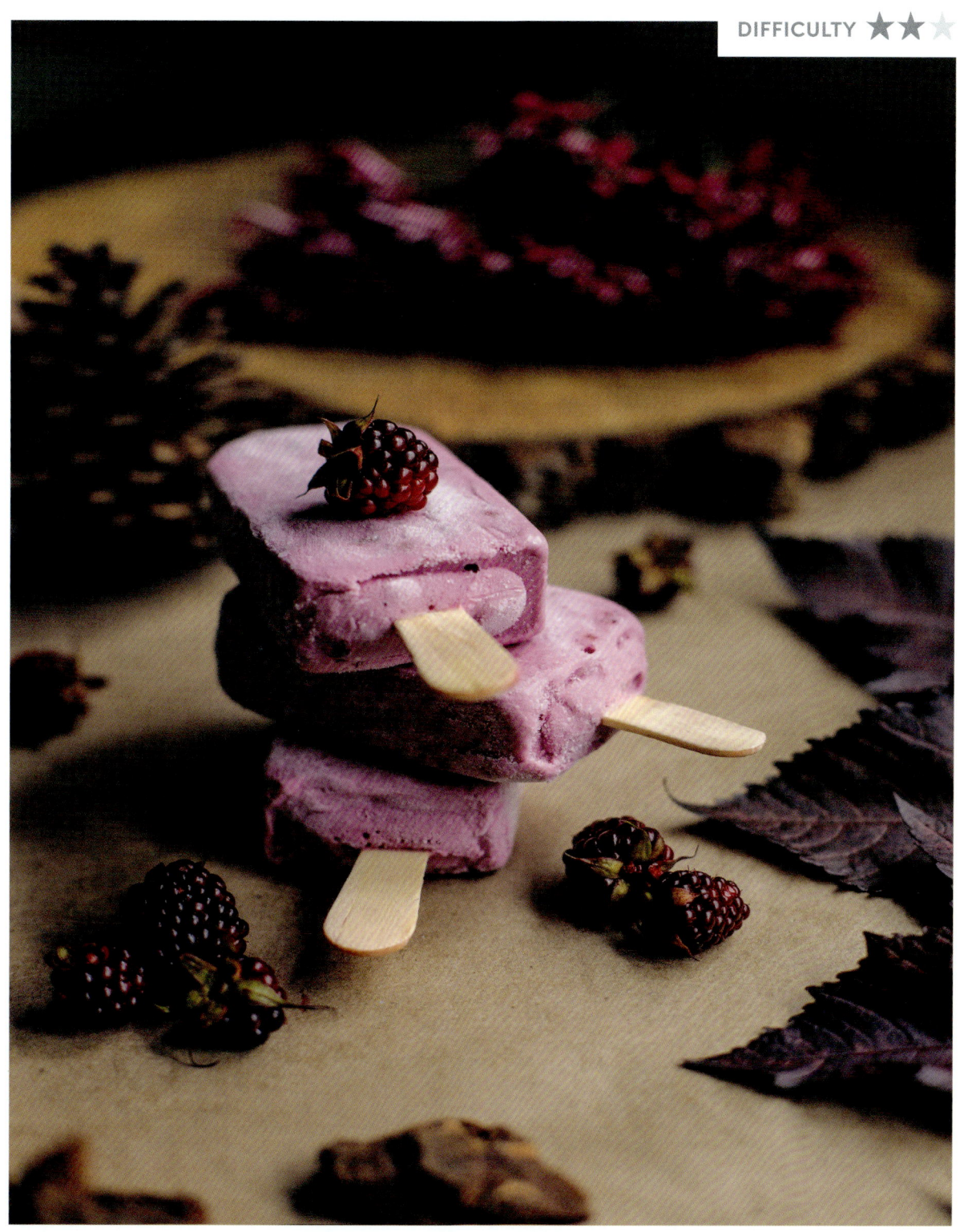

COOK UP A TASTY DISH 173

Camera settings

Although the aesthetic differences between food and product photography are stark, the settings used are virtually the same, with one obvious difference: aperture selection. When selling cosmetics or shoes, buyers want to see the entire product and every little detail, which requires a narrow aperture and a large depth of field. When photographing food, we can adopt a less utilitarian, more creative approach and use focus and blur to direct the viewer's attention to the main course, which requires a wide aperture and a shallow depth of field.

With the mode dial still set to aperture-priority (A or Av), select your kit lens' smallest f/number, which will typically be f/5.6. As we will be fully zoomed in and relatively close to our culinary arrangement (see below), your zone of sharpness will measure just a few centimetres (1 inch) from front to back, meaning that whichever part of the dish you focus on becomes the image's focal point by default. We can use this 'differential' focusing to our advantage by layering props and other adornments to create a sense of depth and add to the narrative.

WHY THIS SHOT WORKS

① The eye is immediately drawn to the tasty cherry ice cream bars in the centre of the frame, thanks to a shallow depth of field, careful focusing and a single 'key' light source, i.e., a window, illuminating the subject.

② The rest of the scene is more subdued, with darker tones and shadows used to increase contrast and further isolate the focal point. This is called low-key lighting, where a scene comprises very few midtones and whites.

③ The carefully placed berries, leaves, pine cones and flowers all contribute to the autumnal narrative without distracting from the star of the show. Note how cleverly these visual extras fill the empty spaces.

④ The muted hessian fabric and wooden chopping block create the perfect backdrop, with their rustic hues receding and allowing the colourful ice cream bars to leap out of the darkness.

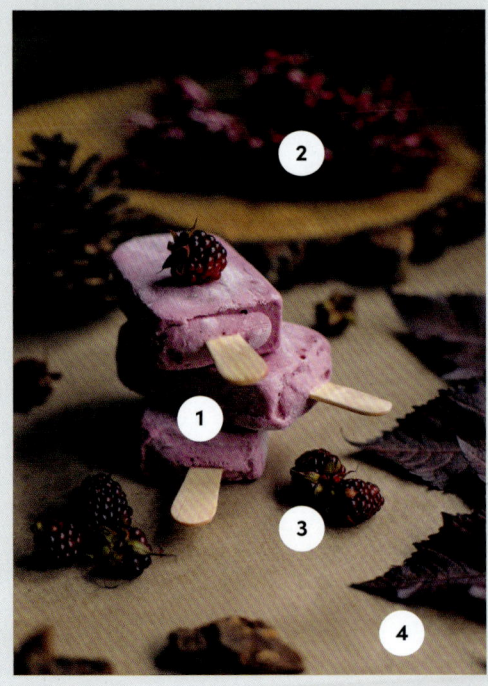

With the camera still attached to a tripod, there is no need to deviate from ISO 100. You should be fairly well acquainted with this tripod/ISO combo by now and, unless there is a very good reason to stray, this should be your default for all still life photography. Many new digital cameras feature an auto ISO mode, which, like semi-automatic modes such as aperture- and shutter-priority, entrusts ISO selection to the camera. Auto ISO is ideal when shooting action and wildlife, when quick reactions are essential, but not recommended for static subjects such as still life and landscapes.

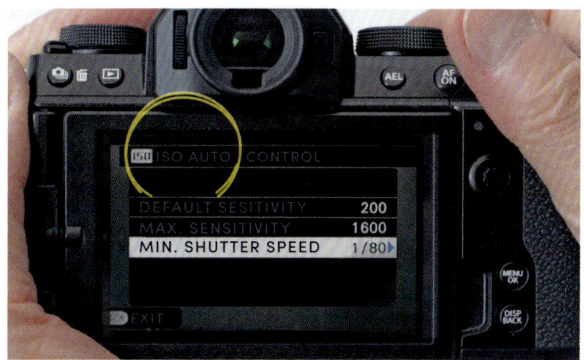

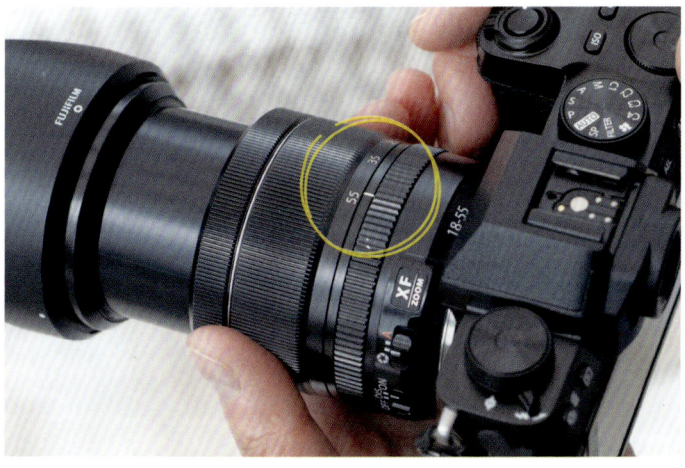

Lens settings

As with basic product photography, we want to zoom our lens all the way in to 55mm and leave it there. Not only does this short-telephoto focal length provide a distortion-free perspective, it also allows us to shoot from a comfortable working distance from the 'stage', close enough to fill the frame but far away enough to minimize the risk of us inadvertently disturbing the arrangement. Plus, it encourages us to use our zoom lens as we would a prime lens – a lens with a fixed focal length – and physically move closer or further away to fine-tune composition. This is good training for when we move beyond kit lenses and discover the world of fast primes.

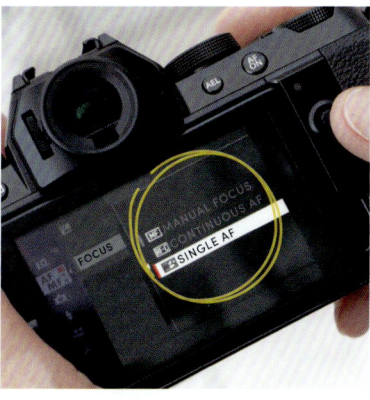

To focus, the exact same settings we used in the previous module will work perfectly. Just to remind you, they are: AF area – single-point AF; AF operation – single-shot AF; drive mode – self-timer (or single-shot if using a remote shutter release). I'd also recommend you activate Live View to aid composition and focusing – this saves having to squint into the viewfinder at an awkward angle every time you want to check sharpness and so on.

Technique

There are three viewpoints commonly used in foodography: directly above (which we'll explore on page 178), directly in front and at a 45-degree angle to the tabletop. Which you opt for will be determined by the shape, height and size of the food and the aspects you want to emphasize. Taller subjects may benefit from a side-on angle, while dishes with fillings hidden away inside pastry, for instance, may benefit from a top-down approach. Start at a 45-degree angle and revise your composition accordingly, using the upright 'portrait' format and the extra depth this orientation provides – as well as any lines and layers created by the various props – to help tell the story.

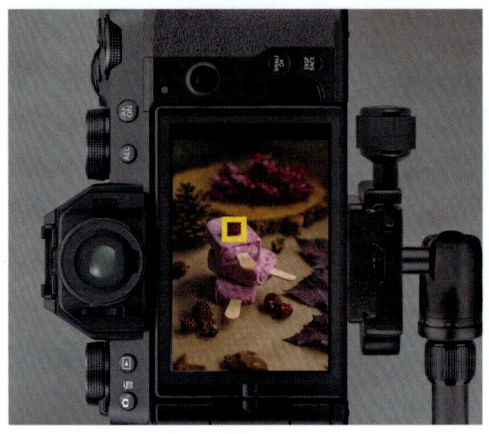

While our food and props will be of varying heights and distances, when it comes to focal point, we are only interested in the main 'hero' dish or desert, which should be positioned roughly a third of the way up the frame for balance and prominence. As we are working with a shallow depth of field, place the active AF point over the tallest part of the hero food nearest the lens – this will ensure that its 'face' is absolutely pin sharp while the rest of its mass further away from the lens will fall gently out of focus. Use white or black foam boards to fill or darken shadows – you may need an extra pair of hands for this – and use exposure compensation to lighten the overall composition if needed.

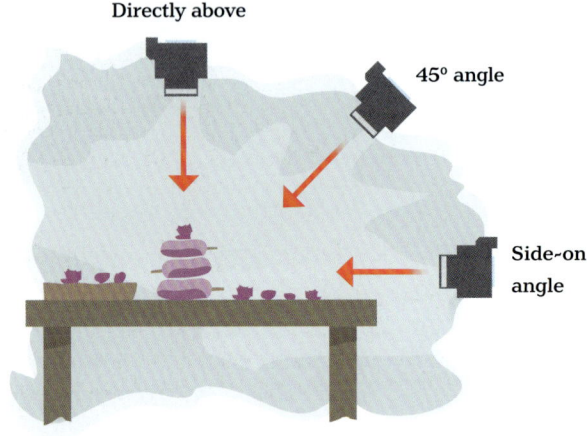

ABOVE **The angle you shoot from will depend on the size of your food and the story you want to tell.**

TIP

Professional food photographers use all kinds of tricks to keep their foods looking fresh and succulent. For instance, they lightly spray vegetables and salads with water using the same spray bottle we used for grass close-ups (see page 100) to give them that 'just picked' look, and slabs of meat are brushed with vegetable oil to make them look hot and steaming.

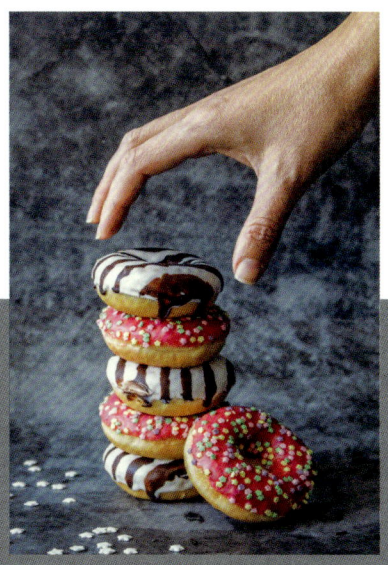
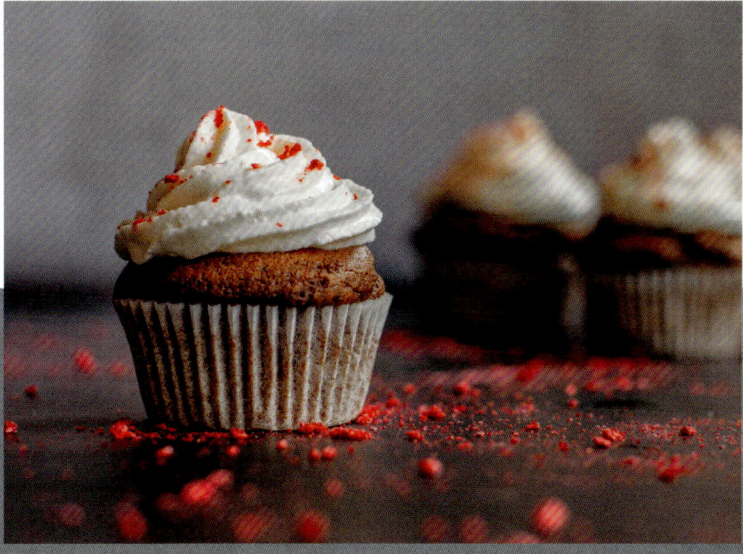
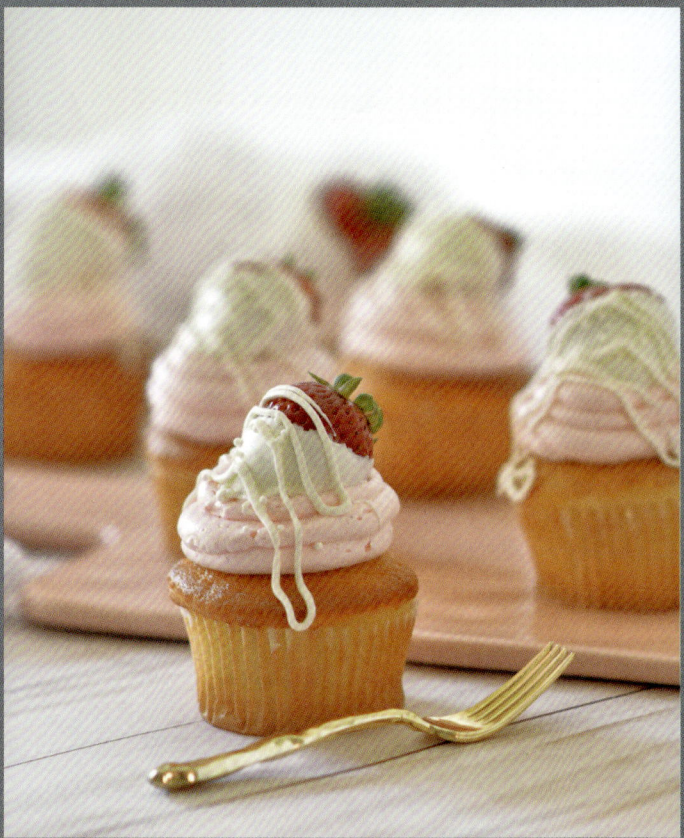

SHOOTING INSPIRATION

Food photography is a hugely challenging type of still life, but get it right and the results can be hugely satisfying – and very tasty.

ABOVE LEFT Including a reaching hand adds a touch of humour as well as a sense of scale.

ABOVE Filling areas of negative space with further points of interest can reinforce and expand your story.

LEFT Props such as cutlery add to the narrative but should never distract from the main subject.

COOK UP A TASTY DISH

Module 5.5
Shoot from above

Like food, flat lay is a style of still life that has enjoyed a meteoric rise in popularity thanks to Instagram and its loyal legions wanting to share their interests and adventures in a more creative way. At its simplest, a flat lay is a photograph taken from directly above a collection of objects carefully arranged on a flat surface. The most engaging examples tell an interesting visual story or convey a meaningful message, with a cohesive theme and/or colour scheme and a small number of key objects of varying sizes. Popular flat lay subjects include fashion, food and, judging by the number of Instagram images I stumbled on when researching this chapter, coffee.

Once you know what story you want to tell and have collected the objects you need to tell it, start with the background and build from there. Your backdrop should complement but not compete with your objects, and so neutral colours and textures are a safe bet – white bed sheets draped over a dining table or paper placed on a desk will provide you with a blank canvas on which to get creative. Wooden floorboards and marble worktops can also be very effective. Avoid materials or surfaces with distracting patterns or bold colours as they will overwhelm your flat lay.

Position your setup near a large window and start to arrange your objects. The viewer's eye will naturally be drawn to the largest, most prominent object so place this first and don't be limited by the constraints of the picture frame – in our example, the turntable is the 'hero' of the flat lay and part of this flows out of the frame, giving the impression that there is a larger scene beyond these four walls, encouraging the viewer to literally think outside of the box. Carefully arrange secondary props around your hero, filling the gaps and using lines, curves or a rule-of-thirds grid and its intersecting power points to achieve a balanced composition.

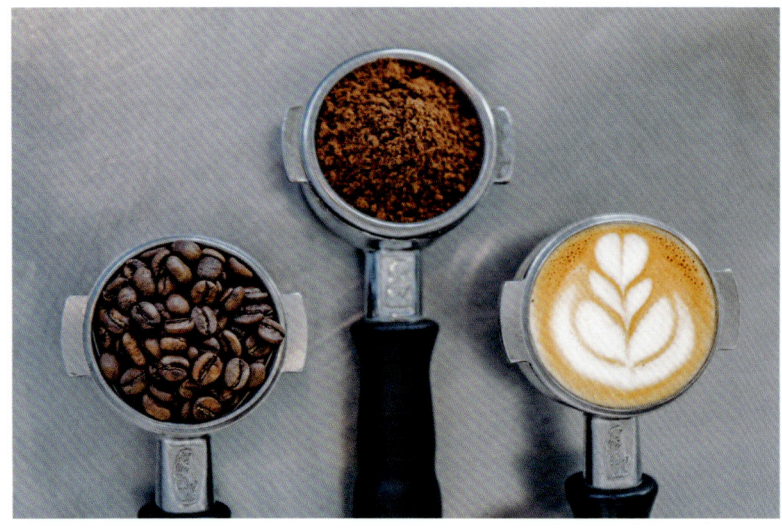

LEFT **A clever flat lay shot tells the story of coffee from bean to latte.**

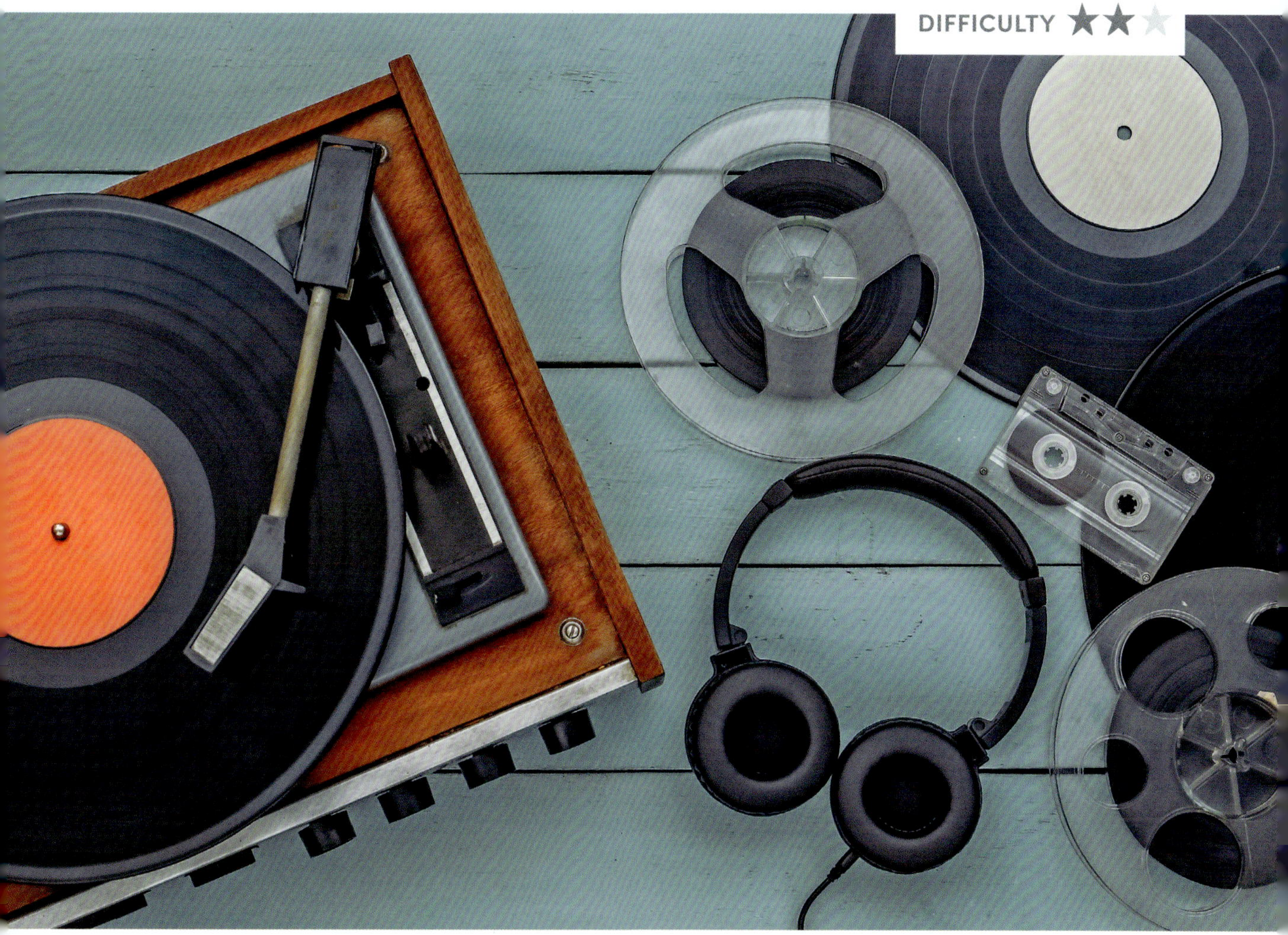

DIFFICULTY

ABOVE **This stylish flay lay arrangement pays homage to analogue sound and its various formats.**

RECOMMENDED SETTINGS

- Shooting mode: **Aperture-priority**
- Aperture: ***f*/8**
- Shutter speed: **1/125sec**
- ISO: **100**
- Focal length: **35–55mm**
- AF area: **Single-point AF**
- AF operation: **Single-shot AF**
- Drive mode: **Single-shot or self-timer**
- Metering mode: **Evaluative/matrix**
- White balance: **Auto or cloudy/shade**
- Picture style: **Standard**

SHOOT FROM ABOVE 179

Camera settings

Depth and depth of field are important considerations when photographing most subjects, still life or otherwise, but with flat lays we are dealing with a subject that exists on a single plane of focus. Of course, depending on their height, some objects will be closer to the camera than others, even if only by a few millimetres, but the clue is in the name: flat lay. This means that while we still need to capture front-to-back sharpness to tell our story, we don't necessarily need to use the narrowest aperture to achieve this.

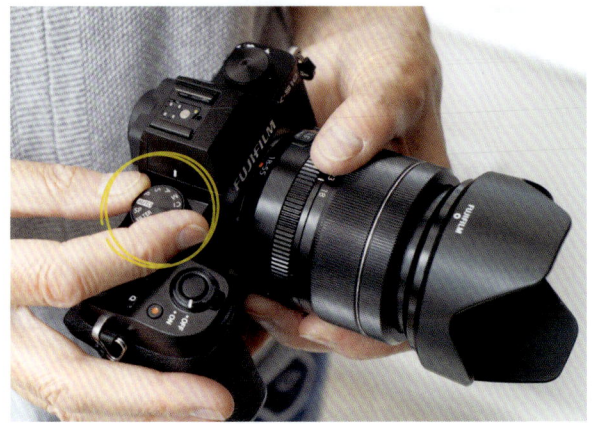

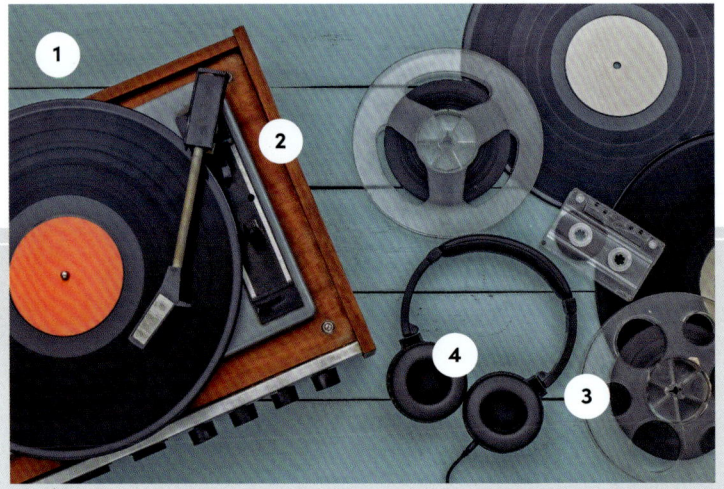

WHY THIS SHOT WORKS

1 The muted blue floorboards provide a neutral background and perfectly complement the props, allowing the turntable and records to stand out while also reinforcing the retro theme.

2 The wooden turntable is the 'hero' of the flat lay and grabs the viewer's attention first. It occupies a large part of the frame and also suggests that there is a world outside of it.

3 The extra props are carefully chosen, strategically positioned and kept to a minimum, with analogue sound being the theme that connects the narrative dots.

4 The natural light is soft, diffused and subtly directional, with the shadows beneath the turntable and headphones in particular adding depth and definition to the flat lay arrangement.

Still in aperture-priority mode, start at f/8 and only stop down to f/11 or f/16 to increase the depth of field if you have any particularly tall objects in your flat lay arrangement that you want to be in sharp focus. The DSLR in our example is roughly 10cm (4in) in height and I'd advise against including any props taller than this. That said, if you wanted to break the 'rules', you could use height to deliberately blur objects nearer the camera, such as flowers in a vase, to further emphasize the importance of the props that are rendered perfectly sharp.

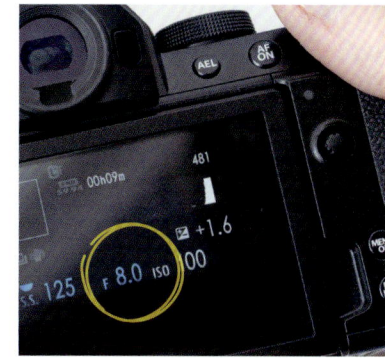

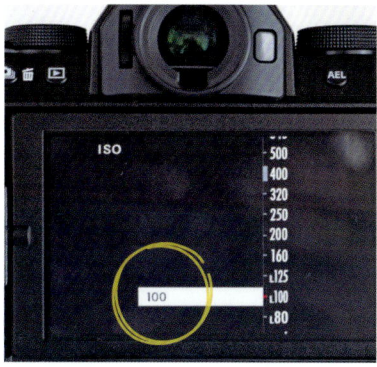

Set ISO to 100 and be mindful of shutter speed – if shooting handheld, shutter speed should always stay at 1/125 second or faster to combat camera shake. Increase ISO to 200 or 400 if the exposure drops below this level and activate your camera's image stabilization – depending on the camera, this innovative technology can allow for shutter speeds up to 5.5 stops slower than the 35mm equivalent focal length reciprocal, meaning that you could potentially shoot handheld at 1/4 second and still obtain sharp images. However, this is no excuse for poor technique, so elbows tucked in and stand with your feet shoulder-width apart for maximum stability.

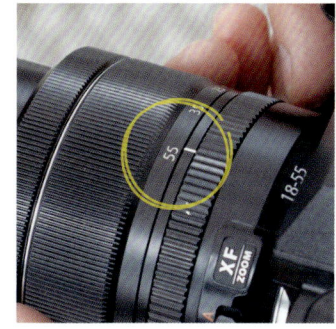 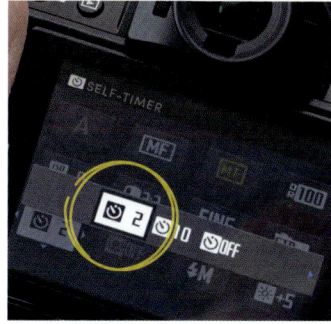

Lens settings

So far, we have used focal lengths between 35-55mm for our still life projects and flat lay is no different. This modest zoom range gives us a 35mm equivalent of around 52-83mm, a versatile short-telephoto sweep that helps us to maintain a relatively narrow angle of view while avoiding the potential for optical distortions associated with wider focal lengths such as barrel distortion – where the lines of a subject appear to bulge outwards. This is particularly important when shooting still life in which crisp lines play a pivotal visual role.

Focusing settings are mostly the same as for the previous module – single-point AF and single-shot AF – but make sure you change the drive mode to single-shot if shooting handheld (self-timer is fine if using a tripod). As before, Live View will prove invaluable when composing and focusing.

Technique

Whether you shoot your flat lay with the camera mounted on a tripod or handheld will depend on the height and dimensions of your arrangement. If your setup is on the floor and small in size, you may be able to position a tripod close enough without its legs appearing in the frame. Some tripods feature a tilting centre column, which will allow you to position your camera directly above the flat lay – just be careful that your tripod doesn't topple over due to the weight imbalance. If your setup is at table height and/or larger in size, you may need to stand on a chair or ladder to gain the necessary height, in which case a tripod is impractical.

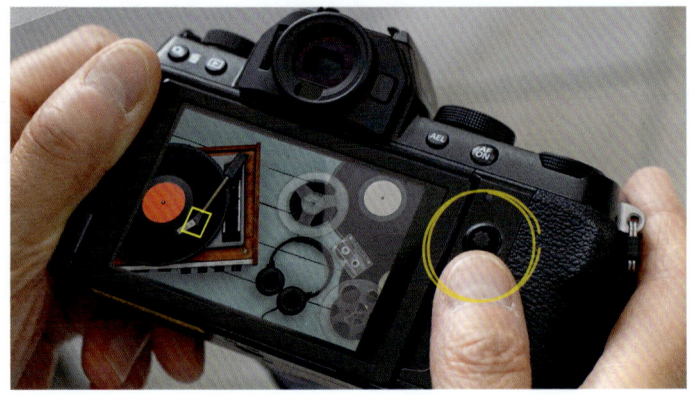

Use your camera's D-pad or joystick to position your AF point directly over the hero object and half-press the shutter button to obtain sharp focus. If using a tripod, flick the AF/MF switch to MF to 'lock' focus and use Live View to zoom in and check sharpness. A mid-range aperture such as $f/8$ will provide more than enough depth of field to ensure that every flat or near-flat item in your still life arrangement is sharp. If shooting handheld and standing on a chair or ladder, remember that any swaying or camera movement will not only affect composition but also focus so brace yourself against a wall if possible and always refocus whenever you have to recompose.

Use paper or fabric to diffuse and soften the natural light, angle your sheets of white and black foam board to fill or flag (lighten or darken) the shadows, and adjust exposure compensation to fine-tune overall brightness levels, keeping one eye on shutter speed at all times, as this is the setting the camera will use as its exposure variable when shooting in aperture-priority mode.

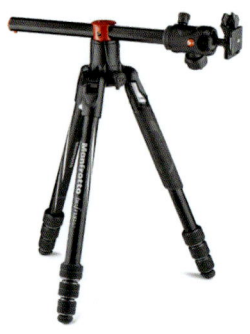

ABOVE **Tripods with tilting centre columns are particularly useful for flat lay photography.**

TIP

Simple concepts, minimal colour palettes and creative thinking are the keys to flat lay success. Coffee cups can be balloons, planets or stars; scattered flour can be mist, rain or the Milky Way; shoelaces can be words, hearts or arrows. And remember that less is often more – too many props can be a distraction.

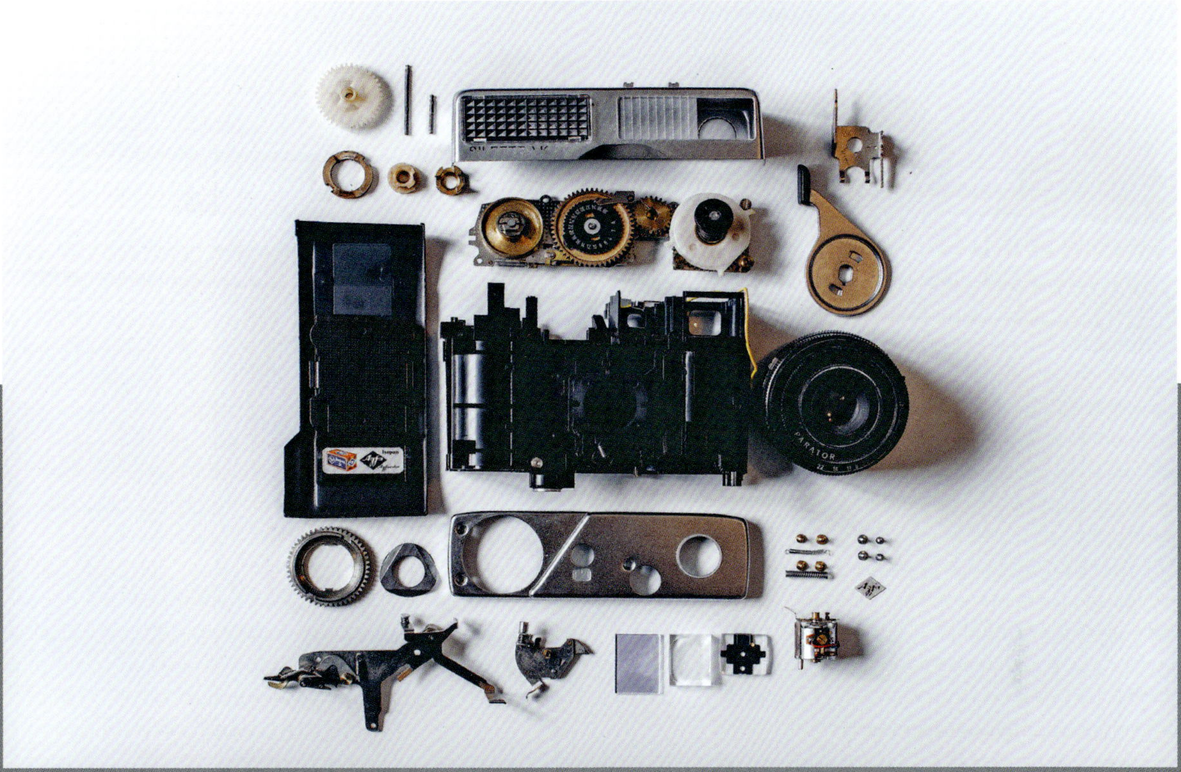

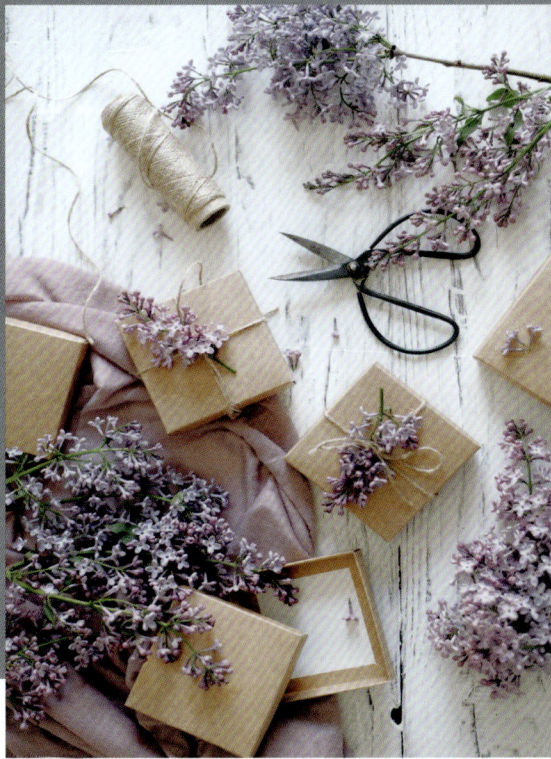

SHOOTING INSPIRATION

This simple yet versatile still life technique can be adapted and refined to suit, whatever your passion, interest or lifestyle.

ABOVE Deconstructions, in which an item's individual components are neatly arranged, make for fascinating flat lays.

LEFT Craft and hobbies are themes that readily lend themselves to flat lay photography's storytelling abilities.

Module 5.6
Get abstract with *bokeh*

The importance of sharp focus is drummed into us from the moment we first pick up a camera. For many, it is the visual and technical be-all and end-all, the only thing that matters. And more often than not it is – but not always. If you have ever explored the fascinating world of abstract art, you will be familiar with its fluid grasp of reality and its creative use of shapes, colours and forms to convey its meanings. Abstract photography is just the same, and is far more accessible than you might imagine. It also breaks pretty much every rule in the book, giving you free rein to unshackle your imagination and really express yourself.

Bokeh is a photographic term that refers to the aesthetic qualities of an image's out-of-focus areas. A Japanese word meaning 'blur', it is created when a lens is used at a wide aperture and is typically employed as a visual aid to add interest to backgrounds. However, for this project, we are going to make *bokeh* the star of the show, creating abstract art from nothing more than spectral highlights. All you need is a cheap fibre optic lamp – or a string of fairy lights, the kind you might decorate your house with on festive occasions – and a room that you can black out.

Place your lamp – or cluster of fairy lights – on a table, turn them on and, with the curtains closed, switch the main room lights off. The glowing fibre optic strands should now be the only visible source of illumination. To what degree these strands are abstracted will depend on how close you get, how much you zoom in and how far you turn the focusing ring. To visualize this, half-close your eyes, get close and look for shapes and patterns. Although art such as this can appear random and chaotic at first glance, there is almost always an underlying compositional foundation – triangle and grid designs, and positive and negative space, can all be effective.

RIGHT **A string of fairy lights and a wide aperture are all you need to create abstract *bokeh* art.**

RECOMMENDED SETTINGS

- Shooting mode: **Aperture-priority**
- Aperture: ƒ/**5.6**
- Shutter speed: **Any**
- ISO: **100**
- Focal length: **55mm**
- AF area: **N/A**
- AF operation: **Manual**
- Drive mode: **Self-timer or single-shot**
- Metering mode: **Evaluative/matrix**
- White balance: **Auto or daylight**
- Picture style: **Standard**

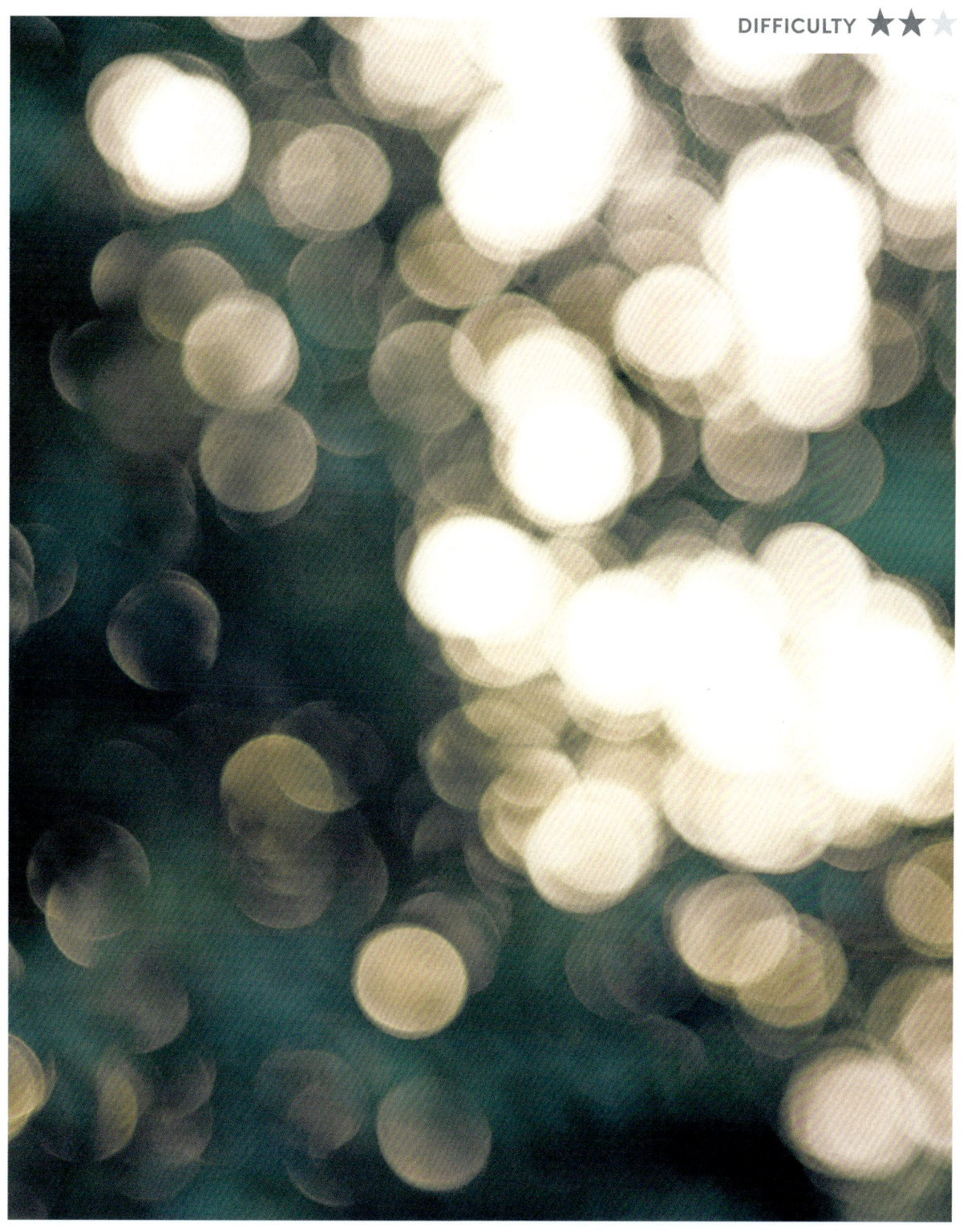

Camera settings

Due to the static nature of still life, you can shoot nearly all projects in either aperture-priority or manual mode. But while the latter gives you complete control of all exposure variables, using the former means you only have to worry about one, allowing you to get creative while the camera does the heavy lifting. With aperture such an important part of *bokeh*, it makes sense that we select aperture-priority here – although fibre optics tend to be relatively dim, which means that shutter speeds will almost certainly be upwards of 1 second, with the camera on a tripod and no moving parts in the scene, we can forget about exposure time entirely.

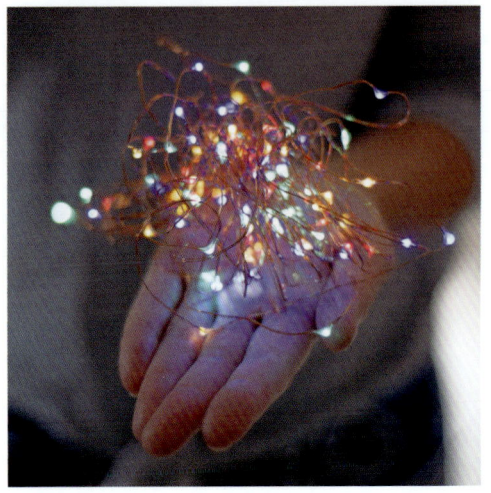

ABOVE **Your light source doesn't need to be overly bright, as your camera will be mounted on a tripod.**

WHY THIS SHOT WORKS

1 A wide aperture and careful defocusing has blurred the numerous pinpoints of light into large, glowing 'halos', giving us the perfect *bokeh* effect. Who said every photo needs a single focal point?

2 Shooting at a slight angle means that no two out-of-focus lights are the same density, with those in the top-right of the frame brighter and fuller than those in the bottom-left.

3 Although there is no single point of focus, the spectral highlights clustered in the top-right corner of the frame create positive space, while the emptier bottom-left part of the frame creates negative space.

4 The *bokeh* fills at least two-thirds of the frame, giving the viewer plenty to look at and explore without the image feeling cluttered and visually incoherent.

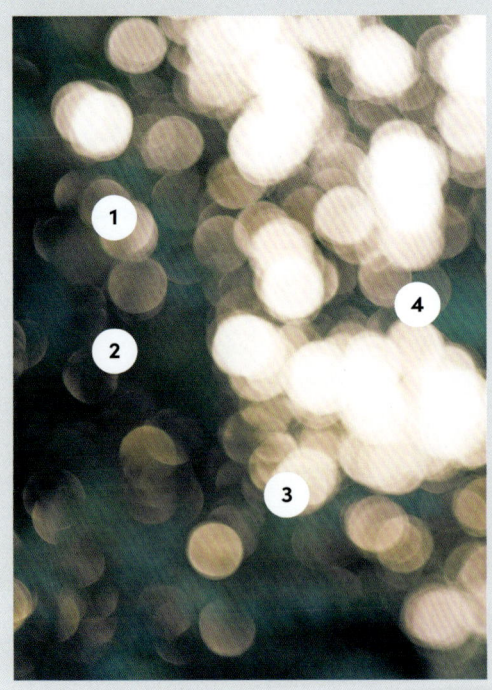

This magical technique demands that we use the widest aperture our lens allows for the shallowest depth of field possible. On most kit lenses this will be between $f/3.5$ and $f/5.6$ (to go wider, you would need to invest in a more expensive prime, or fixed focal length, lens, which is definitely next-level territory). Wide open, the fibre optic lights will blur from individual pin-points into large colourful circles, creating the all-important *bokeh* effect.

As with all still life/tripod-based projects, leave ISO at 100 for maximum image quality. This is incredibly important when shooting in low-light situations, when noise (the digital equivalent of film grain) is at its most visible in darker areas of an image. If you don't have a tripod to hand, the only alternative is to shoot handheld, which may require an ISO of 1600 or beyond to obtain a shutter speed of 1/125 second or faster, which would result in a noisy image full of unwanted coloured specks and dots in the shadows.

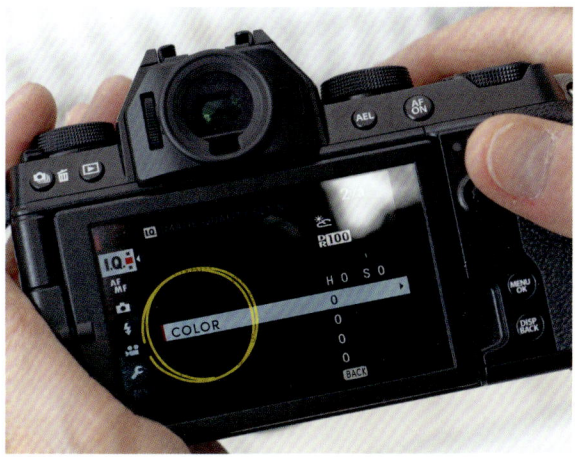

Plain white lights are absolutely fine for this technique, but if your fibre optic lamp changes colour, you may want to crank up the saturation for punchier results. One option would be to customize the standard Picture Style preset by maximizing the saturation slider, while another would be to create a user-defined setting, which is essentially a blank picture style you can call your own by adjusting sharpness, contrast, saturation and colour tone according to the subject and desired style. These are often referred to in the menu as User Def 1, User Def 2 and so on, so spend a few minutes refining your Picture Style once you have mastered the technique.

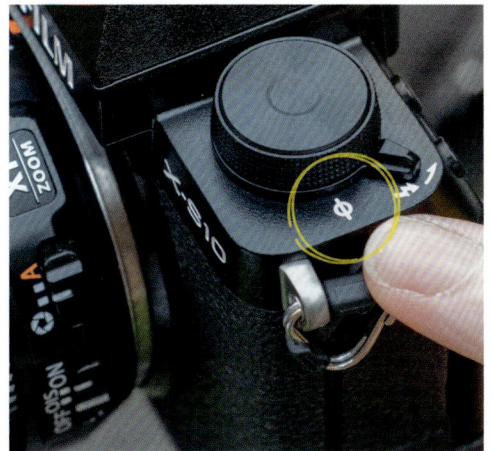

Lens settings

The larger the subject appears in the frame, the more pronounced the shallow depth-of-field effect (contrary to popular belief, focal length doesn't affect depth of field, just magnification and angle of view). So, we are going to zoom all the way in to 55mm and focus at our lens' minimum focusing distance, which will be around 25cm (10in) from the focal plane mark – a circle with a line through it – on top of the camera, rather than the end of the lens itself. Our aim is to fill at least two-thirds of the frame with out-of-focus lights, as this will provide us with lots of beautiful *bokeh*.

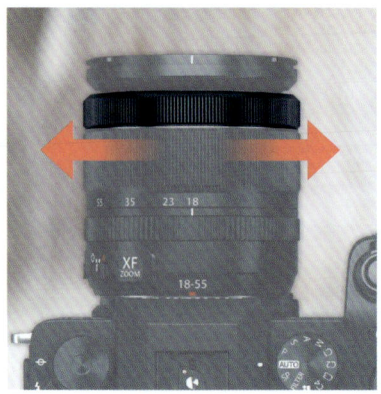

This is a strictly manual-focus-only project – AF will always assume you actually want to focus on something – so flick the AF/MF switch to MF and activate Live View so you can see the effects of defocusing in real time. Leave the drive mode set to self-timer (or single-shot if using a remote shutter release) and familiarize yourself with your lens' manual focusing ring – you'll be focusing in the dark so will need to know where it is instinctively.

Technique

With your fibre optic lamp or cluster of fairy lights placed on a table, think about the viewpoint you want to adopt. While the flat lay approach will allow you to fill the frame easily enough, the lights will all be very close together and on the same level, resulting in a rather flat image. A more dynamic angle would be at 45 degrees above the surface of the lamp's 'umbrella', as this will vary the distances between the individual lights and therefore the sizes at which they appear, resulting in more three-dimensional images with a greater sense of depth and recession. Which viewpoint you choose will dictate where and how you position your tripod.

Start with the focusing ring turned to its minimum focusing distance, using the measurements on the ring itself as a guide, and either nudge the tripod or move the lamp to fill the frame and fine-tune the composition. Draw the curtains and switch off any other lights. Using Live View to judge the effect, slowly rotate the focusing ring until you achieve the perfect balance between recognizable blur and artistic abstraction. Take a test shot, assess the result and use exposure compensation to lighten or darken the *bokeh* highlights. Don't worry about overexposing the brightest areas – this is an abstract technique, and formal rules are for wimps!

TIP

Although *bokeh* is polygonal by definition (the number of lines is determined by the number of blades that make up a lens' aperture), it can be manipulated into virtually any shape you want with custom stencils. You can make these stencils by cutting shapes into a thin sheet of black card and wrapping it over the end of your lens, or by buying pre-cut *bokeh* stencils online.

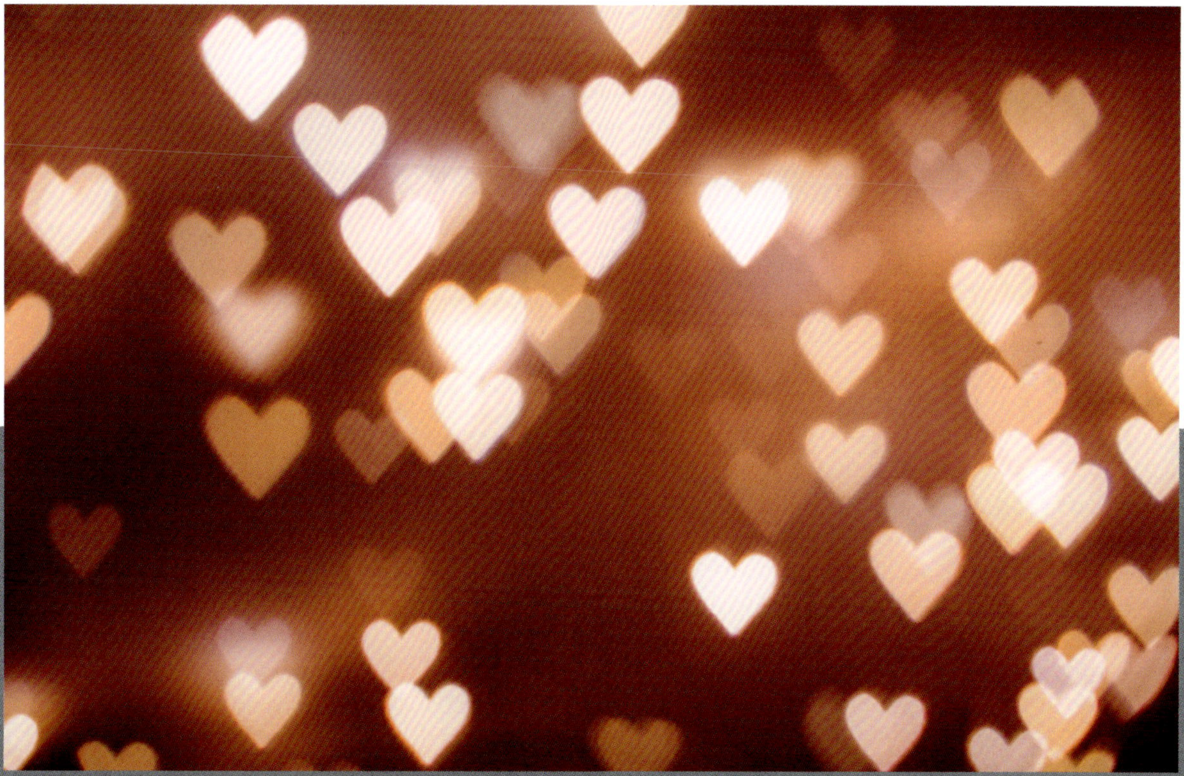

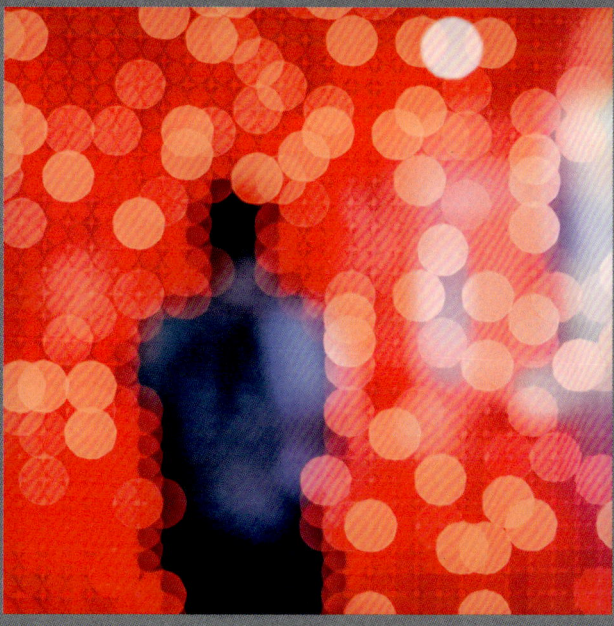

SHOOTING INSPIRATION

Colour, tone, shape, form and texture are all incredibly important aspects of any type of abstract art.

ABOVE Experiment with *bokeh* stencils and turn your out-of-focus highlights into glowing hearts.

LEFT A human presence adds context and a sense of scale to this otherwise abstract image.

Module 5.7
Create liquid art

Oil and water don't mix. You can shake a bottle full of both as much as you like, but as soon as you put the bottle down, the two liquids will separate immediately. This is because oil is less dense – something to do with polarity and hydrogen bonding, but that's for another book – and so floats on the surface, stubbornly refusing to dissolve. When viewed in detail, this inherent immiscibility (remember that word for your next pub quiz) creates some truly magical patterns that resemble the bubbles in a lava lamp or tiny molecules through a microscope. It also makes for an entertaining 'kitchen science' photographic experiment that everyone should try at least once.

The basic ingredients are simple enough: water, cooking oil, glass dish, colourful background and desk lamp. Olive, sunflower and vegetable oil all work well, and you may want to add a drop or two of washing-up liquid to break up larger oil bubbles and give them an added sheen. Casserole dishes make for perfect containers as they are deep enough to fill with enough water to increase the distance between the oil and background, and free of any textures or logos that may distract the eye. Coloured card, posters and even your favourite Hawaiian shirt can all be used for backgrounds – just remember that whatever you use will be blurred so don't obsess over small details. And the brighter the better for contrast and depth.

Place your background and glass dish on a stable work surface and fill the dish three-quarters full with water. Using a spoon or pipette, drop a small amount of oil into the water at a time (you can always add more, but it's virtually impossible to take any out). Large bubbles will form at first, creating distinct circles suspended in water. For smaller bubbles, use a spoon to stir the mixture – the more vigorously you stir, the more the oil will break up. Oil will refract light differently to water, adding highlights and defined edges for a more three-dimensional feel.

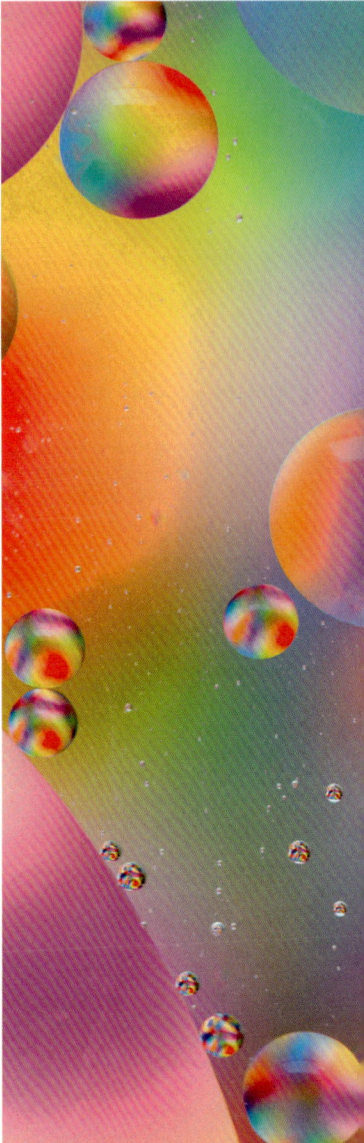

ABOVE **Brighter colours will create liquid art with intense contrast and defined contours.**

190 STILL LIFE

DIFFICULTY ★★☆

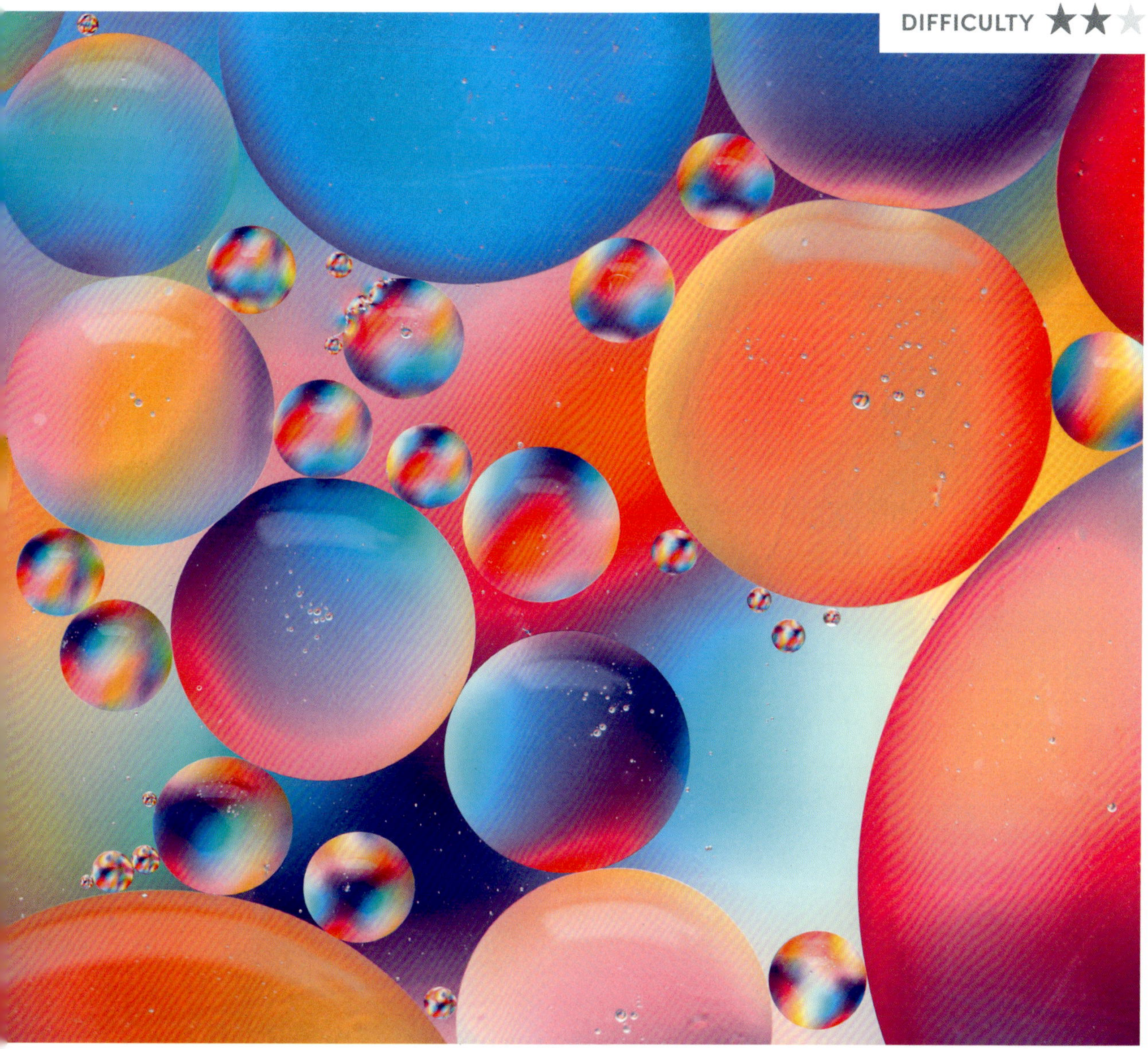

RECOMMENDED SETTINGS

- Shooting mode: **Aperture-priority**
- Aperture: **f/5.6**
- Shutter speed: **Any**
- ISO: **100**
- Focal length: **55mm**
- AF area: **Single-point AF**
- AF operation: **Single-shot AF**
- Drive mode: **Self-timer or single-shot**
- Metering mode: **Evaluative/matrix**
- White balance: **Auto, tungsten or fluorescent**
- Picture style: **Standard**

CREATE LIQUID ART 191

Camera settings

As we need to generate a very shallow depth of field to make sure the oil bubbles are sharp and prominent, but the background is blurred and unobtrusive, we need to select a wide aperture. So, still in aperture-priority mode, dial in your lens' lowest f/number – this will give us the surreal 'miniature world' look we want to achieve, but will also require very careful focusing due to the zone of sharpness being only a few millimetres wide.

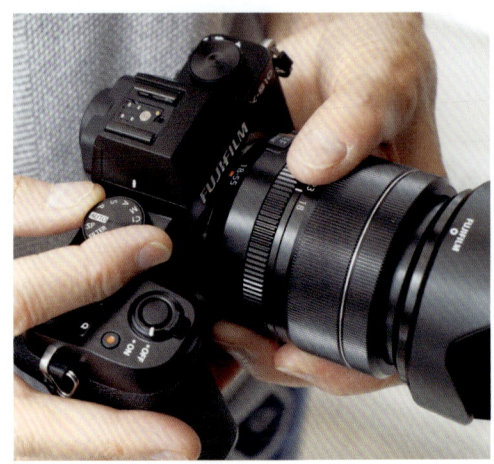

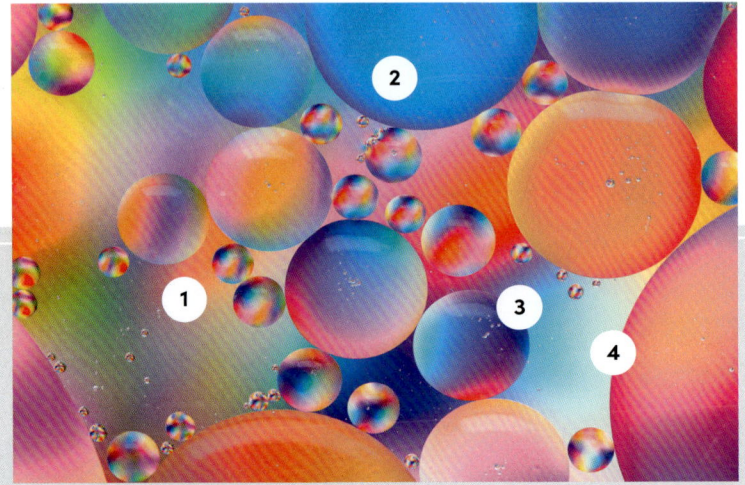

WHY THIS SHOT WORKS

1 A healthy mix of large and small bubbles, with some flowing out of the frame, and just enough negative space creates a pleasing visual balance that doesn't overwhelm the senses.

2 The right amount of water and good camera technique has ensured that the glass dish is invisible and the background is blurred, giving the shot a kaleidoscopic feel with bags of eye-catching vibrancy.

3 Look closely and you will see that each bubble has highlights and defined edges, which makes even the smallest shapes stand out. This is due to the fact that oil refracts light differently to water.

4 By keeping the lens' front element perfectly parallel to the surface of the water, the photographer has achieved sharp focus on every bubble, despite shooting with a wide aperture.

Such precision requires a steady hand, which is why I would strongly recommend you use a tripod for this project – while it is possible to shoot oil and water abstracts handheld, a tripod allows you to 'lock off' composition, set ISO to 100 and forget about shutter speed, freeing you up to get creative with the shape, size and placement of the oil bubbles. Just remember to switch off image stabilization, as this will unintentionally introduce blur. Get the technique right and any subject movement will be due solely to the oil moving, in which case simply wait a few minutes for it to settle.

Halogen lamps will have a colour temperature of around 3000K, while LED lamps will be between 2700–4500K. As we want to capture neutral colours here, select the most suitable white balance setting for your type of lamp, which will typically be either tungsten or fluorescent. To add extra punch and definition to your background and bubbles, navigate to the standard Picture Style sub-menu and ramp up the contrast and saturation sliders, being careful not to overcook it – vibrant is attractive; unnatural, not so much. Use your camera's evaluative or matrix metering mode to measure light from the across the entire frame.

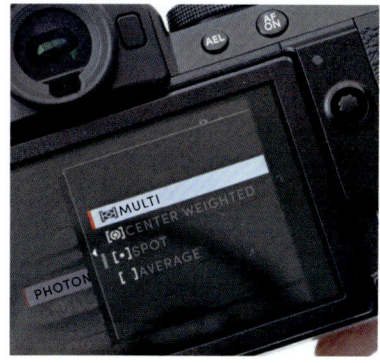

Use your camera's evaluative or matrix metering mode to measure light from the across the entire frame.

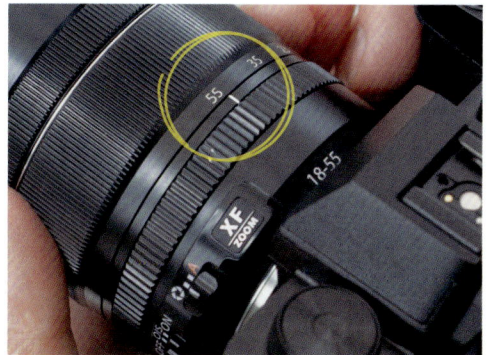

Lens settings

Most tutorials will tell you that you need a macro lens – a lens designed for extreme close-ups – to shoot oil-and-water abstracts, but this simply isn't the case. Rather, this is where a kit lens' ability to focus on subjects just a few centimetres (about an inch) from the end of its front element really comes into its own. Zoom your lens in to 55mm, remove the hood if you have one attached (I tend to leave mine in situ by default), and activate Live View – your camera will be pointed down and this feature will make composing and focusing so much easier than trying to squint into a small viewfinder from an awkward angle.

Flick the AF/MF switch back to AF as there will be plenty of defined edges for autofocus to lock onto. Set the AF operation to single-shot AF, the drive mode to self-timer or single-shot, depending on whether you are using a remote shutter release or not, and the AF area to single-point AF.

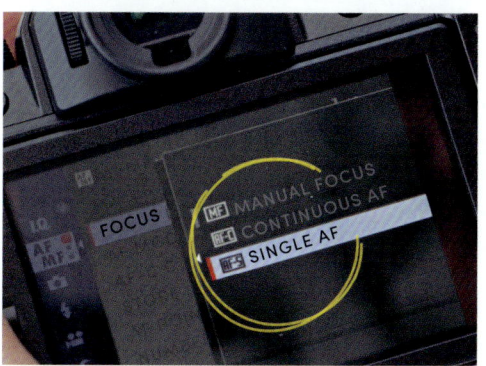

Technique

Position your lamp about 30cm (1ft) away from the glass dish, with the light pointing at the background so it shines up and through the oil for added vibrancy and definition. With your camera mounted on a tripod, point the lens down and make sure its front element is as parallel to the surface of the water as possible – with such a shallow depth of field to play with, this attention to detail will greatly improve your chances of capturing a sharp edge-to-edge image.

Move your single AF point so that it sits over the edge of the largest bubble and half-press the shutter to find focus. Once AF has locked on, flick the AF/MF switch back to MF to make sure focus stays in its current position. Using Live View, fine-tune your framing, looking for the perfect balance of large and small bubbles and positive and negative space – there is no magic compositional formula when it comes to oil abstracts, but as with flat lays (see page 178), it helps to include bubbles that flow out of the frame to create the impression that the scene is larger than it actually is.

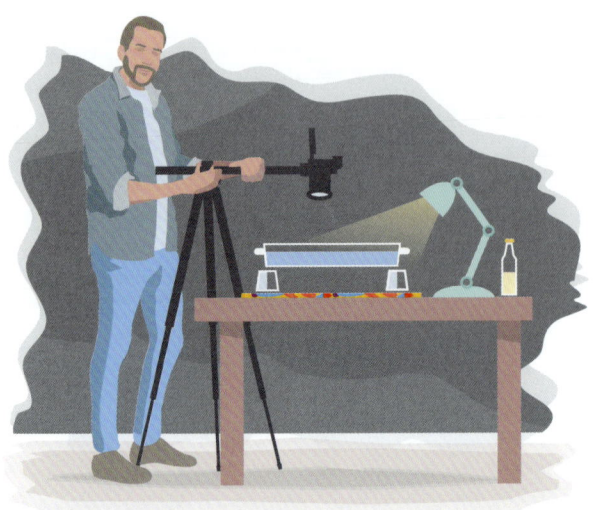

ABOVE **An articulated lamp, glass dish and tripod are the only accessories you will need to create a solid oil-and-water setup.**

If certain background details are still visible and distracting, either add more water or raise the height of your dish with some books to increase the distance between oil and backdrop. And experiment with different ratios of oil and water for completely different compositions – the more oil you add, the closer the bubbles will be; the more vigorously you stir, the smaller the bubbles will become. This technique is not an exact science and no two images will ever be exactly the same, but that is half the fun!

TIP

Don't just stop at cooking oils – try using other liquid substances such as milk and acrylic paints, adding a drop or two of washing-up liquid, to vary how the different ingredients react. Not all combinations will produce visually stunning images, but when they do, the results can be truly mesmerizing.

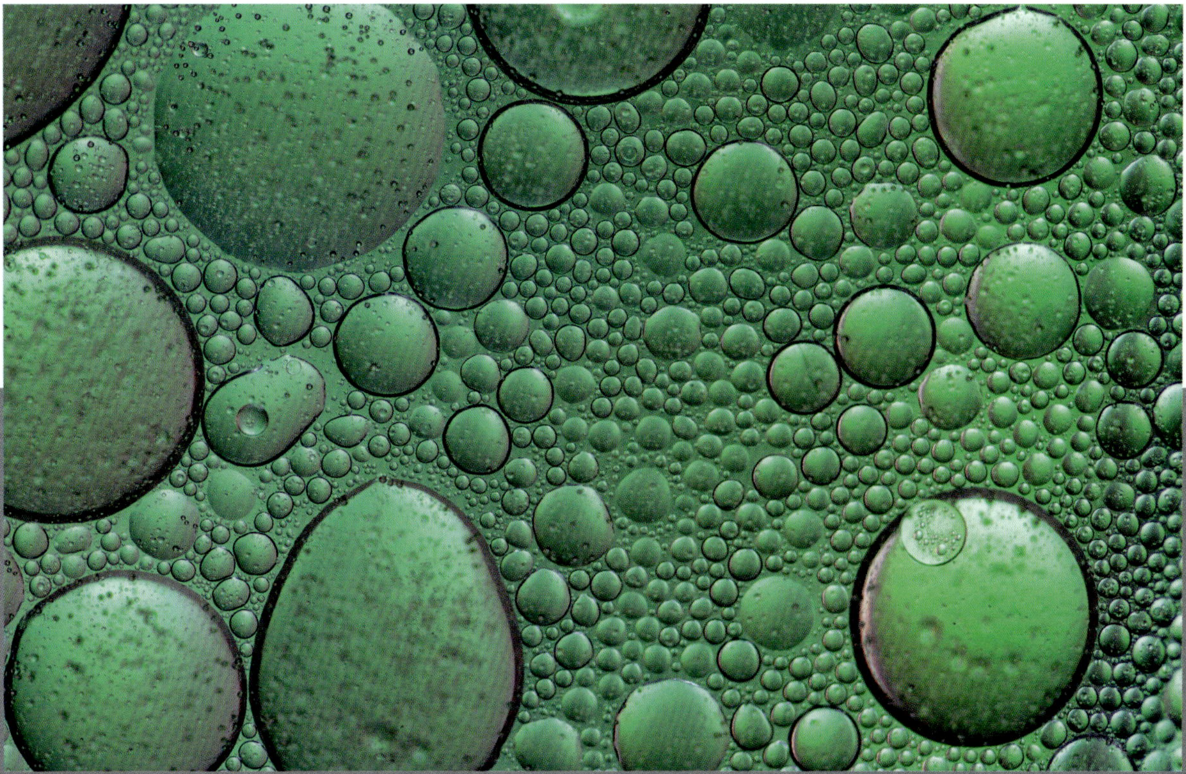

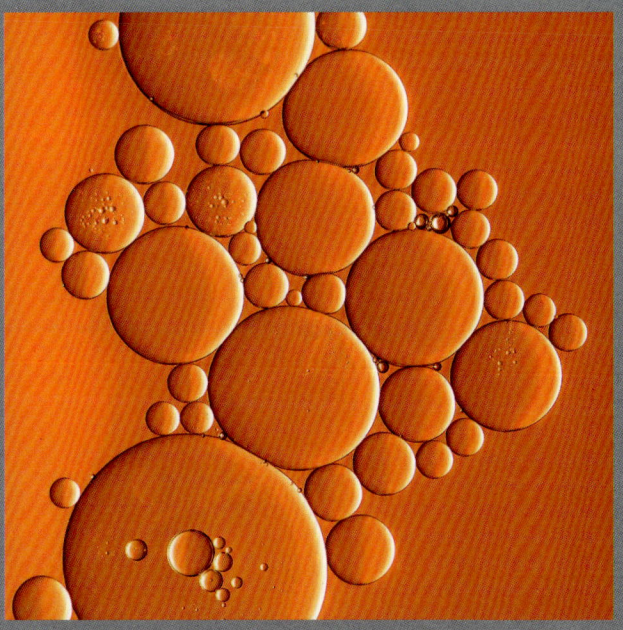

SHOOTING INSPIRATION

Experimentation is the key to finding the perfect balance between the number, size and proximity of bubbles.

ABOVE The more oil you add to the water, the more bubbles you will create and the closer they will be.

LEFT Not all oil and water images need kaleidoscopic backgrounds – a single colour can be just effective.

Module 5.8
Bend light

While we may not be able to fly or shape shift, we do all have one incredible superpower: the ability to bend light. When light passes from one transparent medium into another, it changes speed and direction according to the substances' relative densities. So, when it moves through air into water, for instance, it slows down and bends towards the 'path of least time' – essentially, the path of least resistance – because water is denser than air. This phenomenon is known as refraction and is the basic physics behind photographic lenses, magnifying glasses and rainbows. It is also the crux of this simple but fascinating 'rainy day' still life project.

Refraction is an increasingly popular avenue of creative photography, thanks largely to the availability of props such as prisms and glass balls. But before you go spending your cash on gimmicky items you will probably only use once or twice, give the technique a try using nothing more exotic than a cheap, plain tumbler or wine glass. These simple vessels are ideal, as the more spherical the liquid-carrying object, the more pronounced the effect. However, while the glass alone will bend the light, filling the glass with water – and therefore creating an area of denser mass – will completely invert it, reversing whatever happens to be visible through it.

Take advantage of this optical reversal by creating a suitably graphic background. Draw or print two identical linear patterns on A3 paper (A4 will work too – you will just need to zoom in a little more) and position them at right angles against a wall near a window, taking care to perfectly align any patterns. Vertical lines and stark monochrome work well, and I have also seen some very colourful harlequin-style designs used to great effect. Clean your glass thoroughly – or invest in a new one – and position it around 5cm (2in) away from the background, filling it almost to the top with water. You are now ready to bend light!

RIGHT **Make your viewers look twice with this simple light-bending optical illusion.**

RECOMMENDED SETTINGS
- Shooting mode: **Aperture-priority**
- Aperture: **f/11–f/16**
- Shutter speed: **Any**
- ISO: **100**
- Focal length: **18–35mm**
- AF area: **Single-point AF**
- AF operation: **Single-shot AF**
- Drive mode: **Self-timer or single-shot**
- Metering mode: **Evaluative/matrix**
- White balance: **Auto or daylight/cloudy**
- Picture style: **Monochrome**

DIFFICULTY ★★☆

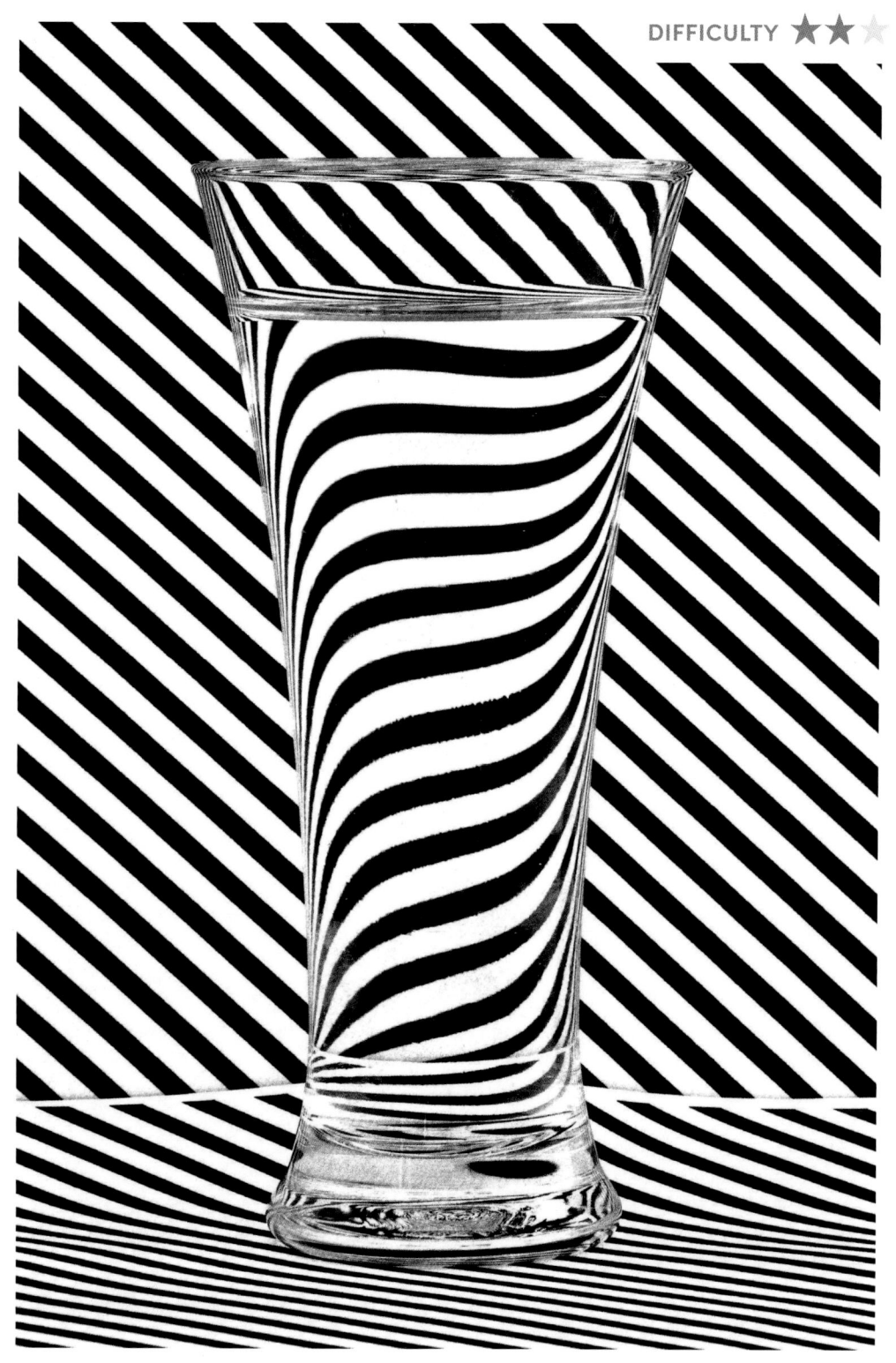

Camera settings

To enhance the graphic nature of the background and refraction effect, we want both the glass and background to be perfectly sharp, with the glass itself almost invisible among the stripes or patterns. To achieve this, we are going to need a larger depth of field, so leave the mode dial set to aperture-priority and select an aperture of $f/11$ or $f/16$ (as always, resist the urge to select the highest f/number due to diffraction). There are various creative approaches to this technique, some using a shallow depth of field for a more abstract look, which you may want to experiment with later.

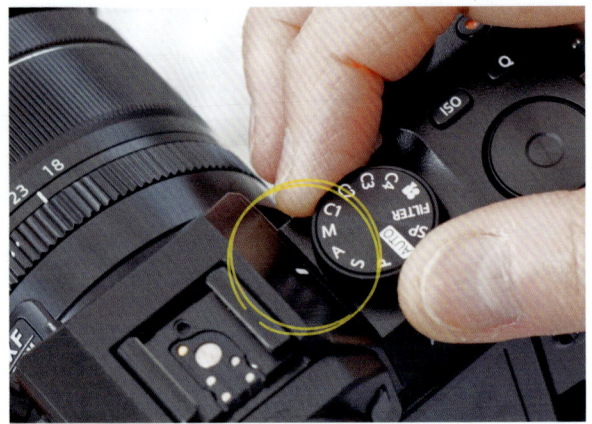

WHY THIS SHOT WORKS

1. A tall, shapely drinking glass provides the perfect frame-filling vessel for this project, allowing for a large volume of water and a generous surface area for the refraction effect to take centre stage.

2. The background design is simple yet so effective, with the vertical monochromatic lines interrupted by the light being inverted by the water, forcing the eye to grapple with the optical illusion.

3. With the glass positioned roughly 5cm (2in) from the background and a large depth of field generated by a narrow aperture, both the glass and graphic patterns are perfectly sharp.

4. Shooting in Monochrome mode has removed any unwanted colour casts caused by reflected objects, and also chromatic aberration, which can appear as coloured fringing around areas of high contrast.

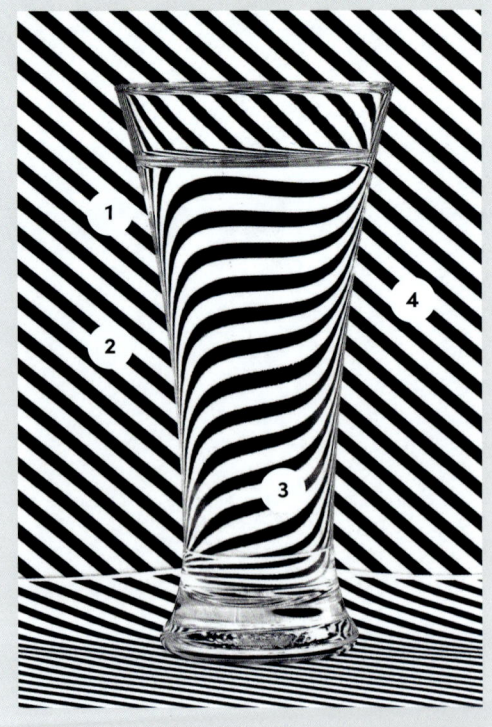

Shooting still life at ISO 100 should be second nature at this point. While digital noise is a contentious subject for some – just spend a few minutes reading a photography forum for evidence – it can actually enhance certain types of images, where the 'film grain' look can add a degree of warmth and texture. However, when detail and precision are important pictorial aspects, the lowest ISO will always give you the cleanest images. The only reason to use anything other than ISO 100 in this instance would be to introduce noise for artistic effect.

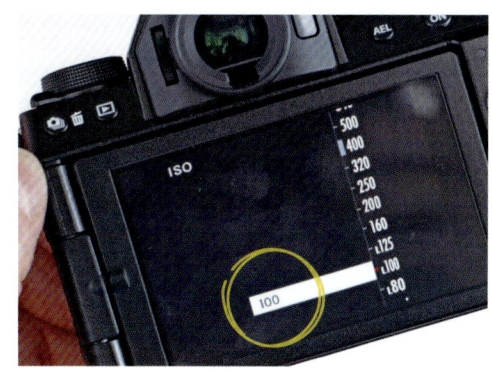

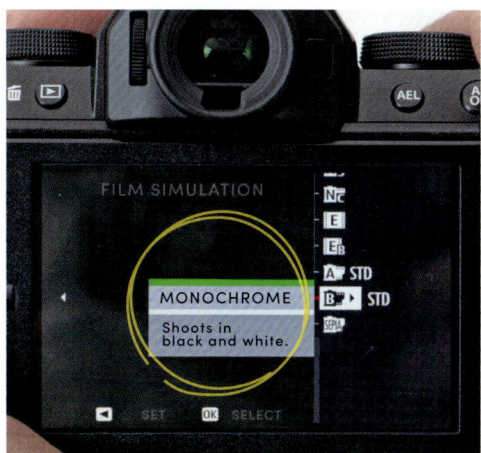

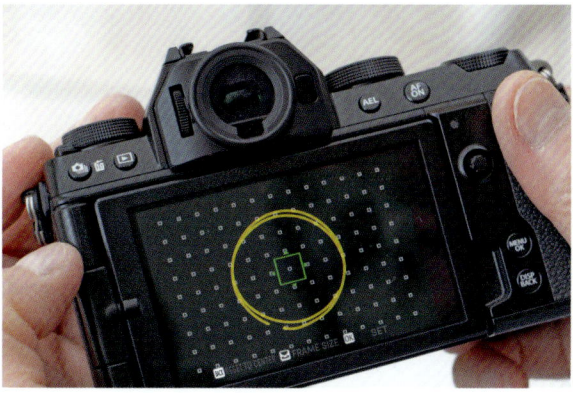

If you opt for a graphic black-and-white background, select the Monochrome Picture Style preset and increase the contrast, just as we did when shooting kitchen utensils (see page 160). Not only will this remove any unwanted colour casts, it will also neutralize any chromatic aberration, or colour fringing, which can occur around objects and areas of high contrast. If you opt for a more colourful background pattern, the Standard Picture Style preset with added contrast and saturation would give similarly striking results.

Lens settings

Focal length will largely depend on the size of your background. If you are able to print or draw your graphic patterns at A3, a wider angle of view can be used to exaggerate the effects of any stripes or patterns that are close to the lens' front element, without any extraneous detail showing outside of the 'stage'. However, if you are limited to A4, a narrower angle of view will allow you to fill the frame with the glass and background, only with a slightly less prominent foreground. Start at 18mm and slowly zoom in to find the perfect composition.

Single-point AF (AF area), single-shot AF (AF operation) and self-timer or single-shot (drive mode) are your go-to focusing settings.

Technique

If you have followed this chapter in chronological order, you will already have devised a small tabletop setup near a window. If not, see page 166. This is the perfect 'stage' for this project. With your background patterns in situ and perfectly aligned, position your tumbler or wine glass and carefully fill it with water (spillages could spoil your backdrop). Soft, diffused light is best as we don't want the glass to cast shadows across our vertical lines, so either wait for an overcast day or use sheer curtains, a bed sheet or similar to spread the window light more evenly.

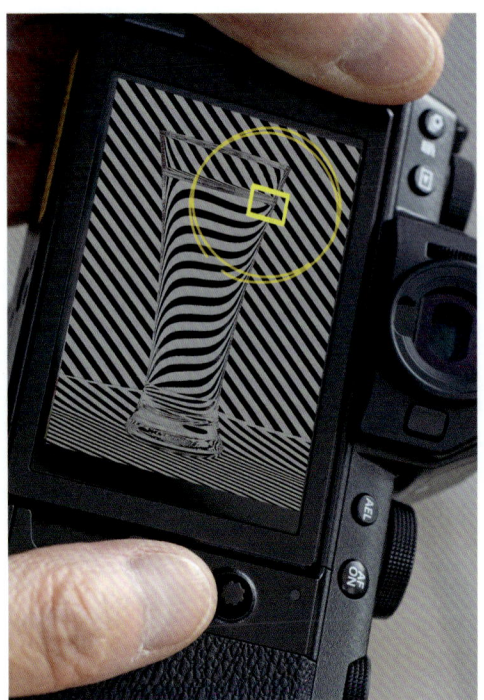

Your camera needs to be at the exact same height as the glass, so adjust your tripod accordingly and use Live View to fine-tune framing – ideally, the glass should occupy 50–75% of the frame for the refraction effect to be prominent enough. Position your AF point over part of the glass' rim, engage focus and flick the AF/MF switch back to MF, and take a test shot. You may find that the white areas of your monochromatic design are a tad on the grey side at first, in which case use exposure compensation to brighten them; +1 stop should be enough.

The greater the distance between glass and background, the more obvious the refraction 'bends', so once you have taken a shot of the original setup you are happy with, move the glass closer to the camera and experiment with both distance and depth of field – a wide aperture such as $f/5.6$ will start to blur the background. Of course, you will need to recompose and refocus each time you make a change, but the ever-changing geometry can be truly fascinating.

TIP

Large marbles and water droplets also make for great refraction photography subjects. You could even mix water with glycerine for natural-looking droplets that will last for hours. Try adding these droplets to a sheet of clear glass or a CD for another 'rainy day' still life experiment.

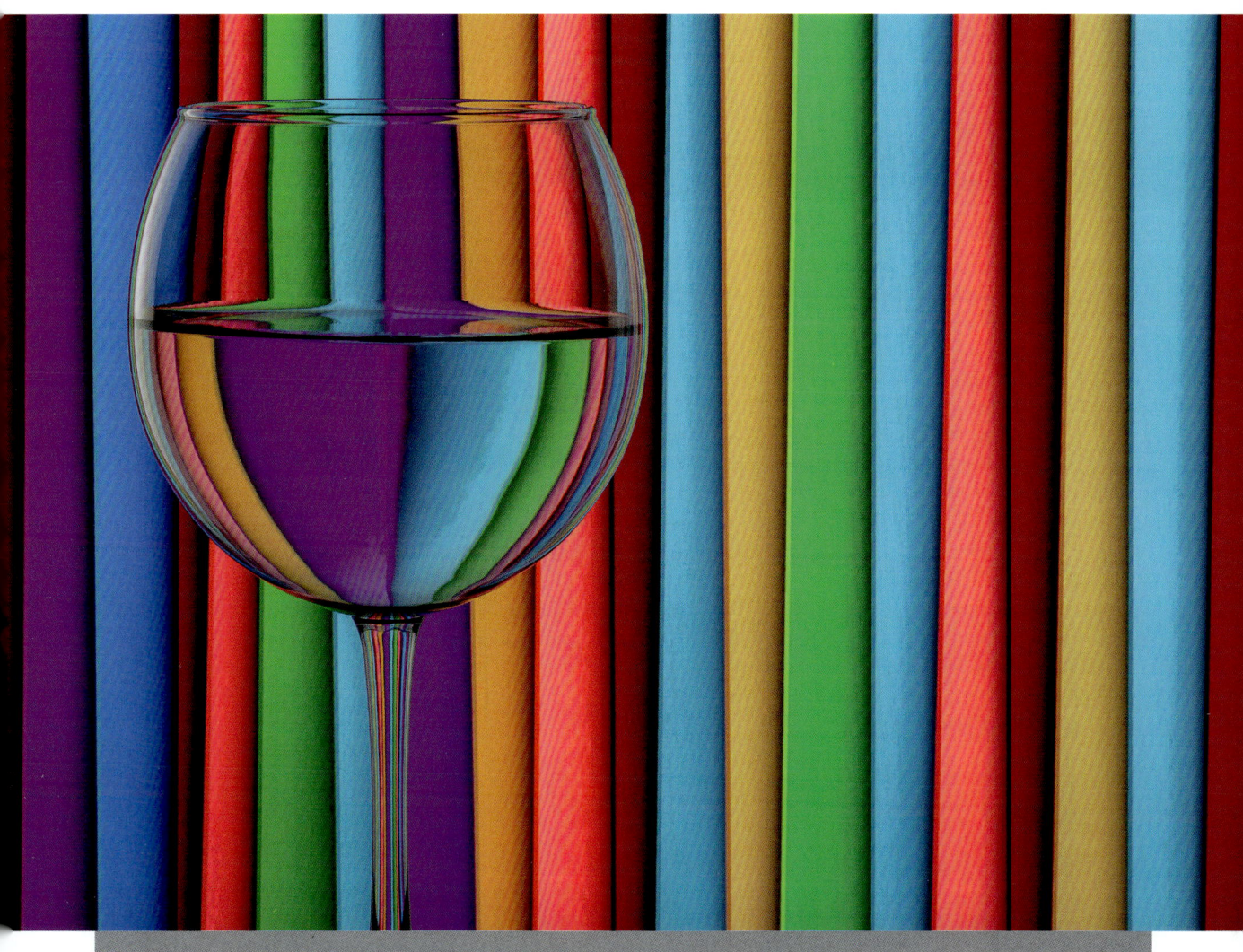

SHOOTING INSPIRATION

Graphic refraction-friendly patterns don't need to be exclusively monochromatic – colourful vertical and diagonal lines can be just as striking.

ABOVE The slightest elevation of the camera angle further exaggerates the refraction effect as the vertical lines meet the surface of the water.

Module 5.9
Freeze nature

Continuing the water theme, we are now going to take a very literal approach to the phrase 'freezing the moment'. Water is an endlessly fascinating photographic subject that can be interpreted in as many ways as your imagination allows. From cascading waterfalls and crashing waves to abstract reflections and tiny droplets, it is a creative theme that can be explored to dramatic effect on an epic scale and also in close up. For this sub-zero still life project, we are going to revisit the natural world, only this time our aim is to preserve a simple floral arrangement in a block of ice, using only subject matter and props that you will find in your garden and kitchen.

The type of objects you trap in ice is limited only by the size of your freezer and the container you freeze it in. Food, kitchen utensils and kids' toys are all worth considering (I once froze a Han Solo Lego minifigure for that authentic 'trapped in carbonite' look à la *Star Wars: The Empire Strikes Back*). However, the delicacy and vibrancy of a flower's stem and petals perfectly complements the ethereal appearance of frozen water. Additives in tap water can form icy clouds when frozen, reducing transparency, so always boil your water at least twice to purify it (or use distilled water) before pouring it into a wide, shallow plastic dish.

Arrange your flowers facedown, so that they sit on the surface of the water, and keep the number of stems and flowers to a minimum – elegant simplicity is the aim here. Basic colour theory may also come in handy, with red and green providing the greatest natural contrast. Pour just a few millimetres of water into your container and place it in the freezer – this small amount of water will freeze quickly, trapping the flowers in situ. After a few hours, pour another thin layer of water into the dish, up to a depth of around 5cm (2in), and return to the freezer and leave overnight. In the morning, you will have a beautiful floral masterpiece, frozen in a solid block of ice.

RIGHT **Even the most delicate of flowers can be frozen for a natural world study of a very different kind.**

RECOMMENDED SETTINGS

- Shooting mode: **Aperture-priority**
- Aperture: ***f*/5.6**
- Shutter speed: **Any**
- ISO: **100**
- Focal length: **35–55mm**
- AF area: **Single-point AF**
- AF operation: **Single-shot AF**
- Drive mode: **Self-timer or single-shot**
- Metering mode: **Evaluative/matrix or spot**
- White balance: **Experiment!**
- Picture style: **Standard**

DIFFICULTY ★★★

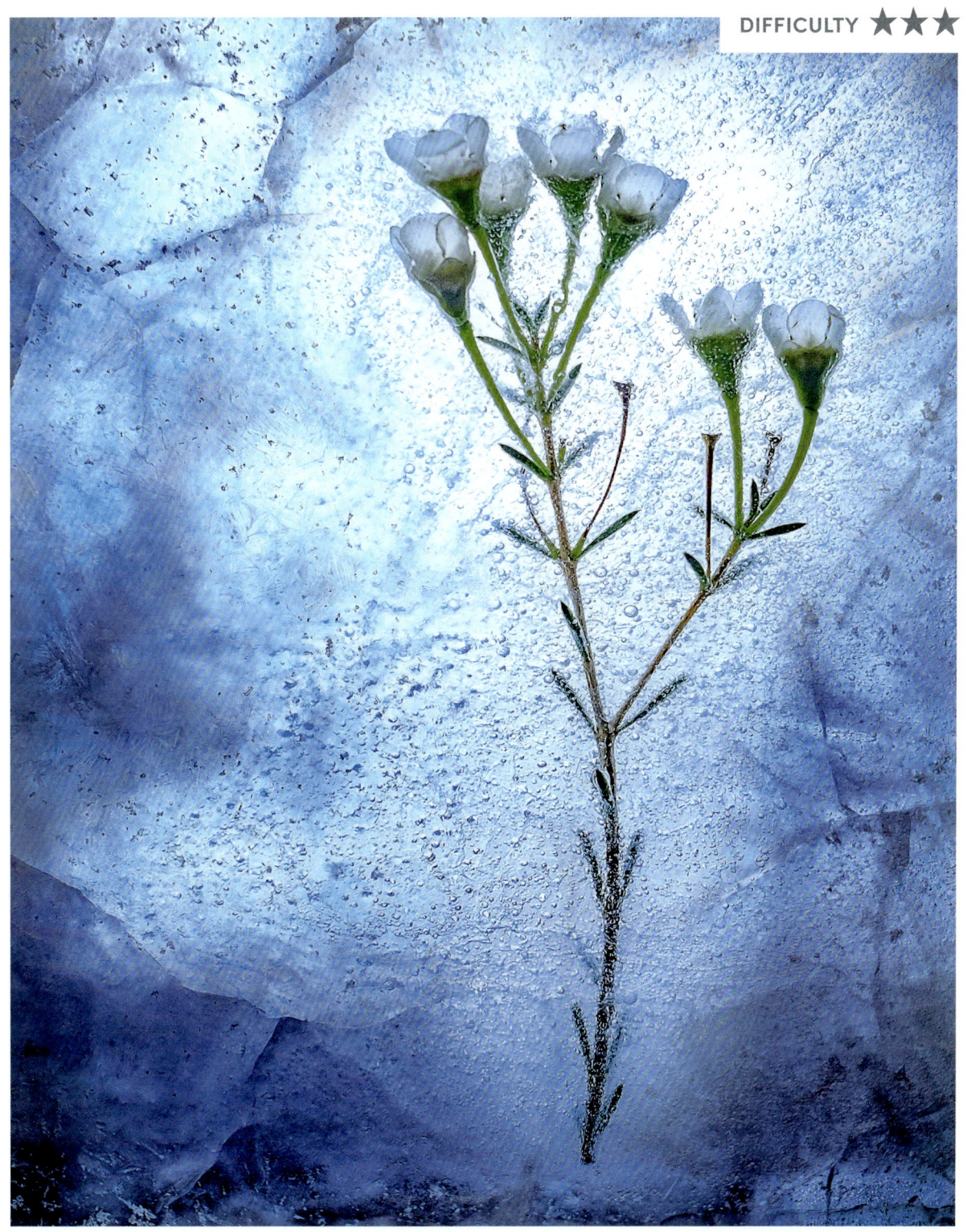

FREEZE NATURE 203

Camera settings

There are two ways to 'stage' your floral ice blocks: propped against a window and backlit by natural light, as per our main example, or positioned on an infinity curve and lit by torch or desk lamp. Whichever you choose, the settings needed are very similar to those we used for shooting oil and water (see page 190). This is because both projects require a shallow depth of field to subtly blur the parts of the stem and petals that are fractionally deeper into the ice than those on the surface.

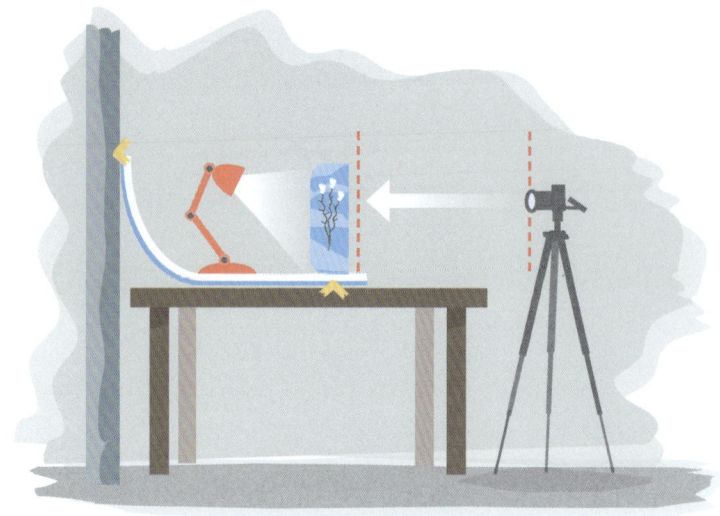

ABOVE **Keep your camera parallel to your ice 'face' to capture to ensure sharp edge-to-edge detail.**

WHY THIS SHOT WORKS

① With the emphasis on elegant simplicity, the subject matter has been kept to a minimum, with just a single, carefully positioned branch occupying the central part of the frame.

② Parts of the flowers and stems are flush with the surface of the ice, while others are trapped deeper within the block of ice, conveying a subtle sense of depth and intrigue.

③ The ice itself is full of tiny but fascinating details, from trapped air bubbles to hairline cracks, all of which are highlighted and accentuated by the natural backlighting.

④ The tonal range stretches from the deepest ocean blues in the bottom-left corner to almost pure whites in the top-right corner. Just looking at this photo makes you feel cold!

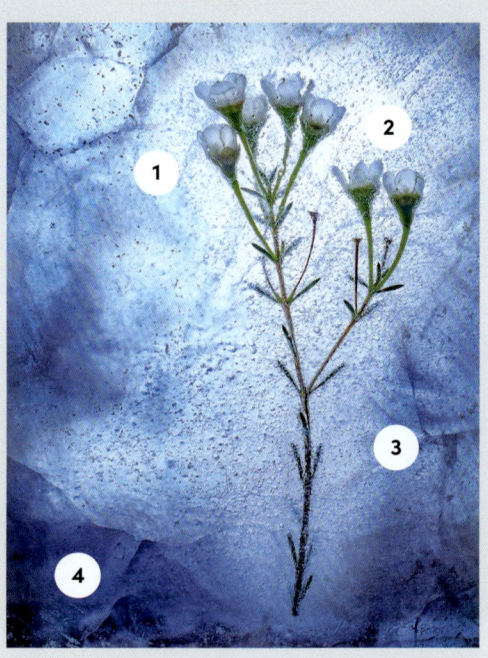

Turn the mode dial to aperture-priority mode, select your lens' smallest *f*/number and leave ISO set to 100. As always for still life photography, compositional precision is essential and so a tripod should be a standard part of your setup. However, if you don't have one to hand and need to shoot handheld, make sure the shutter speed stays at 1/125 second or faster, and switch on image stabilization to avoid camera shake. You may need to increase ISO to 400 or above, but noise will still be well contained at these moderately higher sensitivity settings.

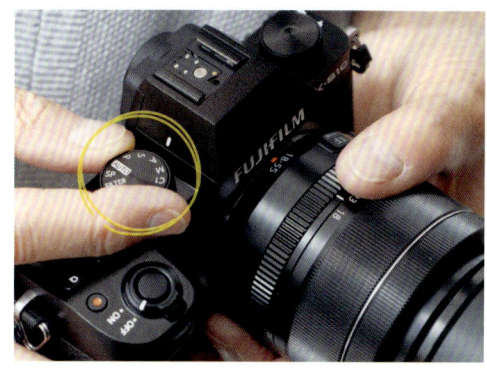

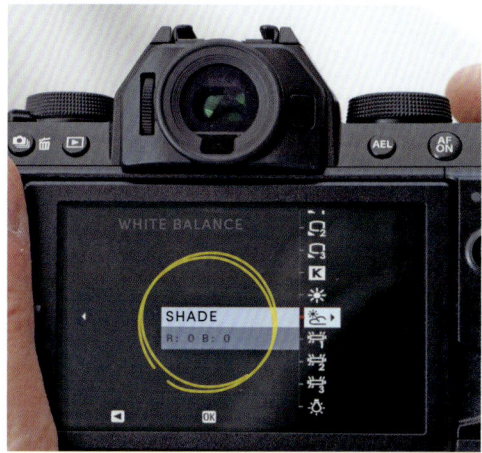

Which white balance preset you opt for will depend on which setup you choose. However, this is a project ripe for experimentation. If using natural light, daylight, shade and cloud will all give varying degrees of warmth or neutrality; if using artificial light, start with tungsten, but also try the fluorescent and flash settings. Each will give slightly different results, with subtle variations in contrast and highlight tonality. Use the same customized picture style preset as in the previous module, increasing sharpness for an extra degree of clarity and detail if needed.

Lens settings

'Standard' focal lengths – so called because they feature a similar angle of view to the human eye – are often preferred for still life as they capture a realistic perspective, so zoom out to between 35–55mm. Not only will this modest focal-length range provide you with a distortion-free view, it will also afford you a comfortable working distance, allowing you to fill the frame for maximum impact without getting too close, while also excluding any extraneous elements that may detract from the composition's minimalist elegance.

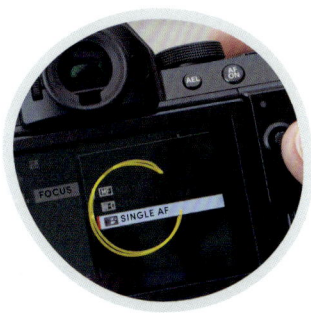

If your ice sculpture features clear, crisp details close to the surface that your camera's AF can lock onto, select single-point AF (AF area), single-shot AF (AF operation) and self-timer or single-shot (drive mode). If it is more abstract in design, switch to MF, activate Live View and zoom into a key area of the frame to focus by eye.

Technique

To remove the block of ice from its container, let it sit for a few minutes at room temperature before placing it facedown and running cold water over it. If extra persuasion is needed, push the back of the dish and gently force the block out. The ice will start to melt almost immediately so preparation and speed are of the essence – in my experience, you have 20 minutes or so until your frosty sculpture turns into a small puddle. Of course, the thicker the ice, the longer it will take to melt.

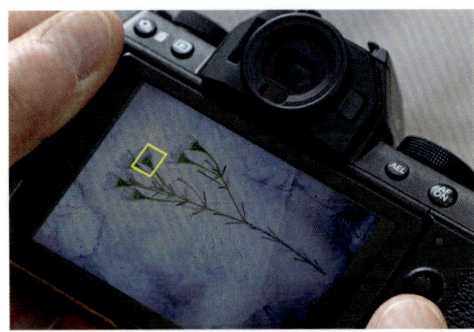

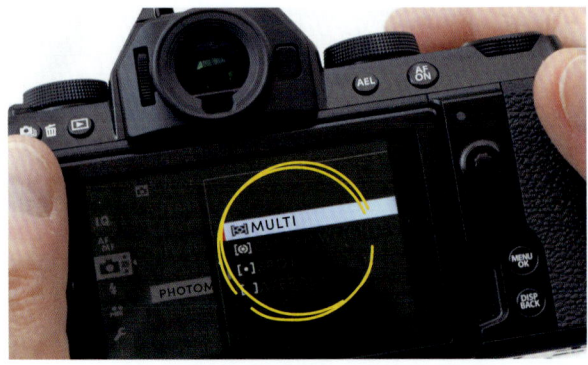

Ensure your lens is parallel to the ice 'face' and look for an area of crisp detail such as the edge of a petal on or near to the surface – this is where you want to position your active AF point. Coupled with a wide aperture, this will render all surface detail pin-sharp while any parts of the subject frozen deeper in the ice will fall out of focus, giving an ethereal sense of depth and mystery. If using a tripod, half-press the shutter to find focus and flick the AF/MF switch back to MF to lock it off; if shooting handheld, focus and shoot in one smooth movement to avoid any shift in the camera's position between actions.

Because our subject is backlit, we need to make sure that we are exposing for the frozen flower and not the background. Evaluative/matrix metering will calculate an average exposure from across the entire frame, and because our subject may only occupy a small portion of the overall composition, the 'correct' exposure may be too dark. In this case, use exposure compensation to brighten the finer details, +1 or +2 stops should be more than enough. Alternatively, use spot metering (see page 72).

TIP

Ice doesn't have to be neutral in tone – you could add a few drops of food colouring to your water before you freeze it, to either complement or contrast with the frozen subject matter. A subtle shade of blue will add to the chill factor, while fiery red will add a surreal warm glow.

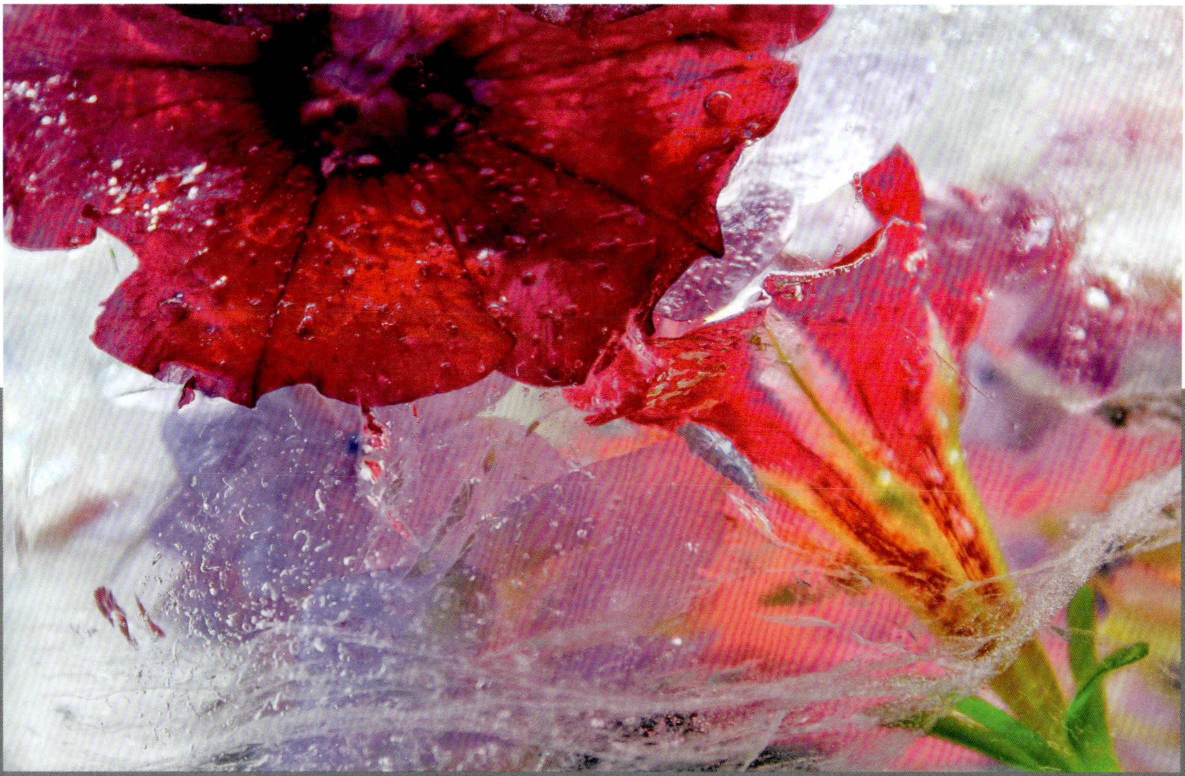

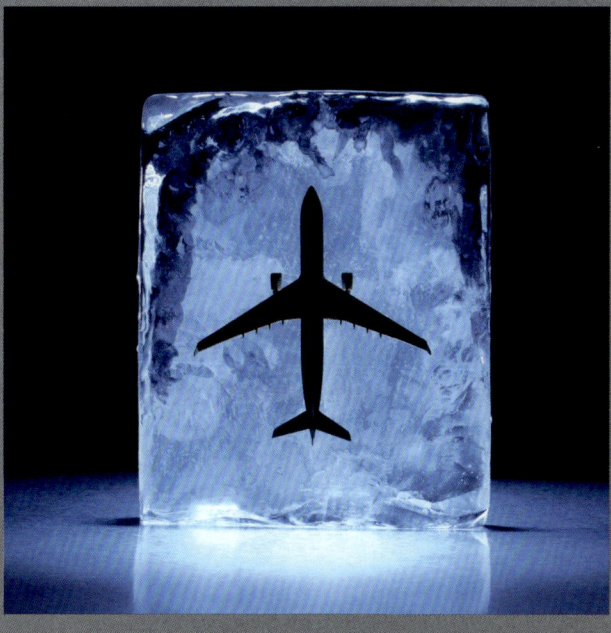

SHOOTING INSPIRATION

Freezing objects in ice is a fun and accessible technique – if it's small enough, or your dish is large enough, it can be frozen!

ABOVE Flowers are readily available subjects, but they don't always need to be delicate and subtly toned – sometimes bold and brash can be just as eye-catching.

LEFT Use strong backlighting to create bold silhouettes of instantly recognizable objects.

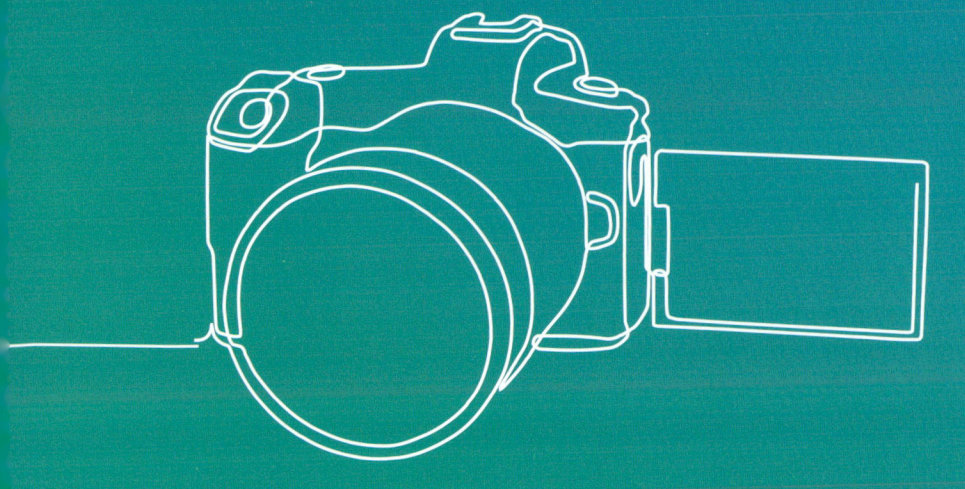

6 STREET & URBAN

Module 6.1
Shoot from the hip

Street photography has enjoyed a renaissance in the 21st century, largely due to the smaller, more discreet sizes of today's mirrorless cameras and the genre's accessibility. You can now walk along any high street, tiny camera in hand, shooting 'from the hip' while blending into the throngs of shoppers and commuters unseen. This cloak of invisibility allows us to capture natural expressions and documentary-style images of everyday life without our subjects knowing they are being photographed. 'From the hip' literally means taking pictures without the camera to your eye, which may seem unintuitive, but with some basic camera know-how and a multi-angle LCD screen, waist-level photography can be hugely rewarding.

Making sense of the chaos of urban life isn't always easy. Either our subjects are on the move or we are, street furniture such as bollards, benches and bins can get in the way, and too many colours can distract and confuse the eye. One way to simplify a scene is to shoot in black and white. This timeless medium has a unique ability to reduce an image to its core components, replacing colour with tone while emphasizing detail, texture and expression. Learning to 'see' in shades of grey takes time and practise, but whereas film-era street photography legends such as Henri Cartier-Bresson and Vivian Maier had to trust their eyes and instincts, we have the huge advantage of being able to view the world in mono in real time as we shoot.

Street photography requires a very different set of skills to most other genres. Patience and persistence are essential, as is an ability to visualize and anticipate what Cartier-Bresson called the 'decisive moment' – that split-second in which the subject, location and light perfectly interact. There's an expression among documentary photographers that neatly sums up the best way to approach street photography: '$f/8$ and be there'. In a nutshell, this means that so long as your camera is set up correctly and you are in the right place at the right time, good photographs will come to those who wait. It also suggests that opportunism is more important than technical perfection, although we are about look at a few techniques we can use to strike the perfect balance.

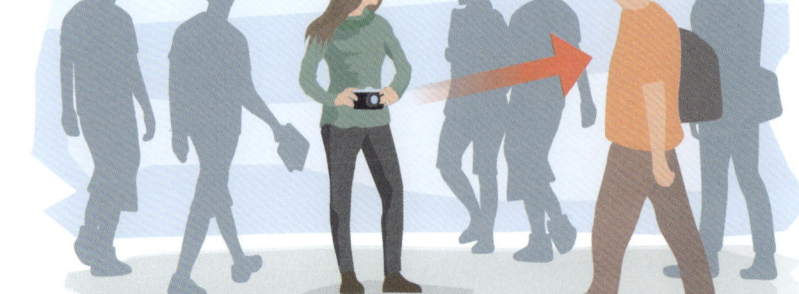

RIGHT **Shooting from the hip is a great way to blend into the crowd and capture spontaneous moments.**

DIFFICULTY ★★☆

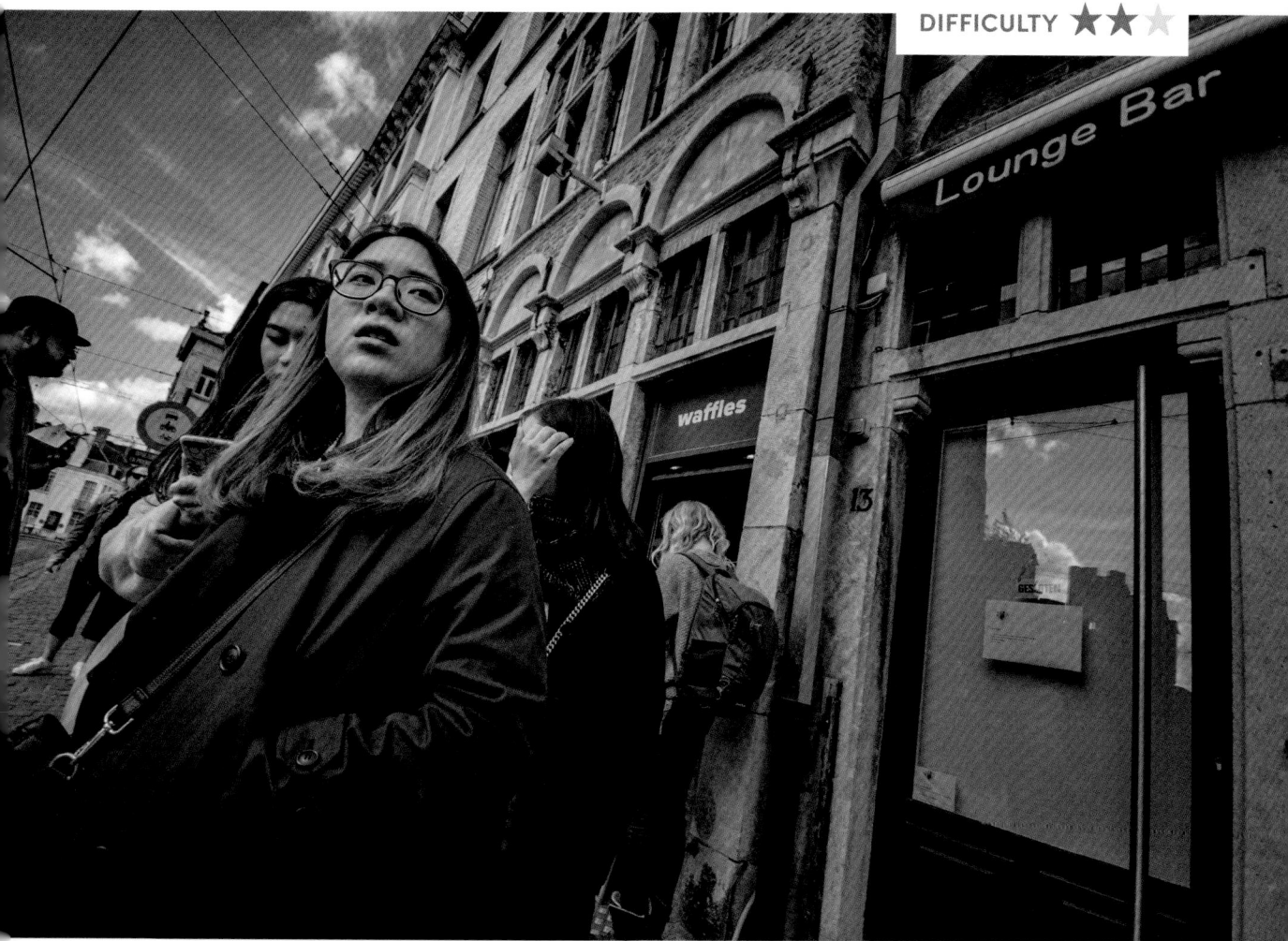

ABOVE **Black and white is a timeless medium that can simplify busy street scenes.**

RECOMMENDED SETTINGS

- Shooting mode: **Aperture-priority**
- Aperture: **f/8**
- Shutter speed: **1/250sec or faster**
- ISO: **100**
- Focal length: **18–35mm**
- AF area: **N/A**
- AF operation: **Manual**
- Drive mode: **Continuous**
- Metering mode: **Evaluative/matrix**
- White balance: **Auto or daylight/cloudy**
- Picture style: **Monochrome**

SHOOT FROM THE HIP

Camera settings

From-the-hip photography is a demanding shooting style that requires shutter speed, aperture and ISO to work in unison in order to freeze the moment. The right camera settings will not only increase your hit rate, but they will also make focusing easier (see below). Start by turning the mode dial to aperture-priority (A or Av) and selecting an aperture of f/8. This is a tried-and-tested 'walkabout' aperture that provides plenty of depth of field for images with greater context. It's also the 'sweet spot' – the point at which most lenses produce their sharpest results.

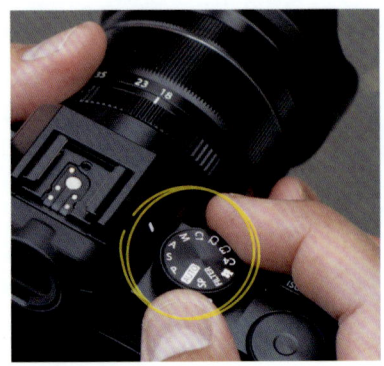

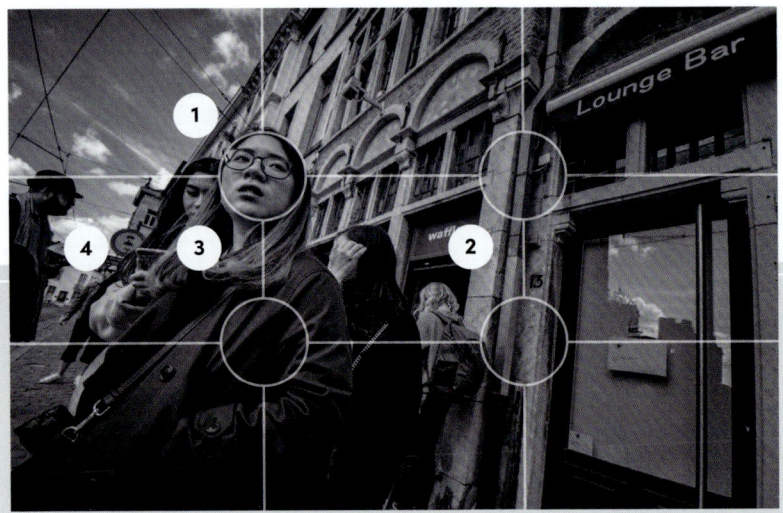

WHY THIS SHOT WORKS

1 The main subject's face is precisely positioned on a rule-of-thirds power point – a point where a vertical grid line and horizontal grid line intersect – which creates a strong focal point and a well-balanced street scene.

2 Any potential colour clashes and distractions have been nullified by the use of black and white, resulting in a candid image with lots of contrast, tonal variety, details and textures.

3 Shooting from the hip and being discreet has resulted in a natural facial expression that suggests that the subject was unaware she was being photographed.

4 By shooting at f/8 and using the zone focusing technique, the photographer has captured a sharp street portrait with plenty of depth of field to add context in the distance.

In terms of hierarchy, shutter speed and aperture are more important than ISO when it comes to street photography. That's not to say it doesn't have a part to play, but image quality isn't our primary concern here. Our aim is to facilitate a shutter speed fast enough to freeze potentially moving subjects, so start at ISO 1200 (or your camera's nearest setting – some will be ISO 1250). Don't worry about digital noise – modern DSLRs and mirrorless cameras control noise superbly well up to around ISO 6400, and as we're shooting in black and white, any visible noise will look like film grain and add to the character of your images.

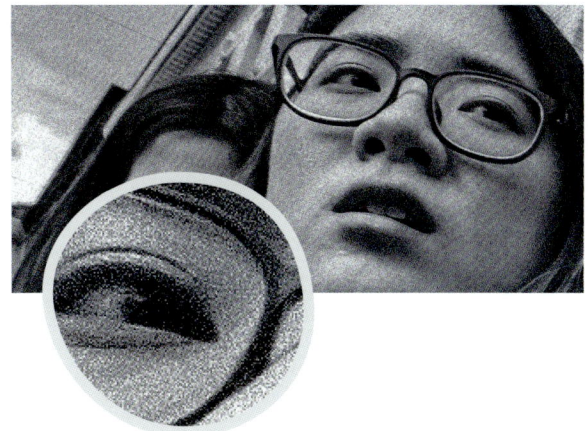

Although we're shooting in aperture-priority mode, which means that the camera will calculate the 'correct' shutter speed, the mid-range aperture and high ISO setting together should allow for a fast enough exposure. The perfect shutter speed for from-the-hip street photography is 1/250 second. Of course, 'perfect' is relative to how fast your subject is moving through the frame, but 1/250 second will freeze a person walking at an average speed of 3–4 miles (5–6km) per hour – any slower and your subject's limbs will start to blur. If your shutter speed isn't fast enough, simply increase ISO.

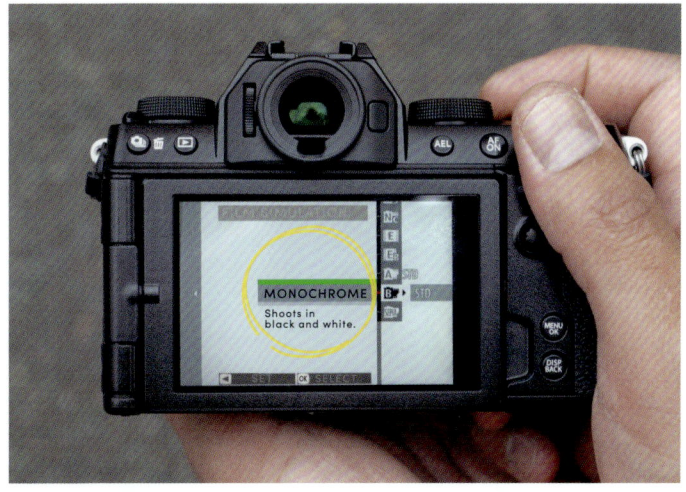

Dive into your camera's Picture Style menu and select the Monochrome option. Now, when you activate Live View, you will see the world in black and white. This is hugely beneficial as not all scenes that look great in colour translate so well to mono. Different colours can have the exact same tone – for instance, red and green are complementary colours on the colour wheel, but stripped of colour they can be the exact same shade of grey. Finally, although we're shooting in black and white, white balance is still important as it affects brightness so select either the auto or daylight/cloudy preset.

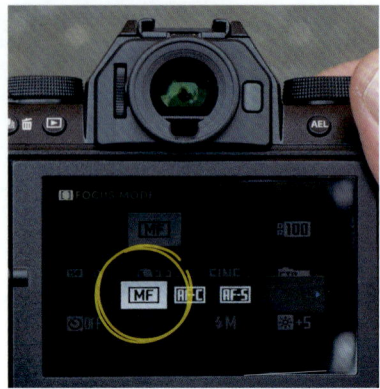

Lens settings

Street photographers tend to favour wide-to-standard focal lengths, particularly when shooting in crowded areas, so start at 18mm and zoom in to 35mm for a more natural perspective if needed (remember that 35mm equals 50mm-ish once the crop factor is applied). We want to take full control of focusing so switch to manual focus (MF). We also want to shoot in short bursts of images rather than single frames to improve our chances of capturing that perfect split-second moment so select the high-speed continuous drive mode.

Technique

We are going to use a technique known as 'zone focusing', which may sound complicated but is remarkably simple in practice. At a focal length of 18mm and an aperture of $f/8$ on an APS-C camera, if you manually focus 3m (9ft) away from you – some lenses feature a distance scale on the focusing ring – the depth of field will extend from 1.25m (4ft) from where you stand to infinity, giving you a huge plane of focus to play with. At 35mm, the depth of field will extend from 2.2m (4ft) from where you stand to just 4.75m (15.5ft) away, giving you a much smaller focal plane. So long as your subjects fall within these zones, they will be acceptably sharp. If in doubt, there's an excellent depth-of-field calculator at photopills.com.

To aid from-the-hip composition, flip your camera's rear LCD screen up and use your thumb rather than your index finger to press the shutter button, keeping it primed at all times. When you spot an opportunity that falls within your zone of focus, shoot in bursts of three to five images. Some cameras feature a silent shooting mode that minimizes the sound created by the shutter, so check your manual as this will help you to remain discreet. As always when shooting in a semi-automatic mode, use exposure compensation to fine-tune your exposure.

TIP

Always research and respect local privacy laws and be aware that some 'public' spaces are privately owned. In many countries, there is no right to privacy in public spaces, which means that you can photograph whoever and whatever you want to. However, airports, shopping centres and hospitals, etc., are private spaces and so photography is strictly prohibited.

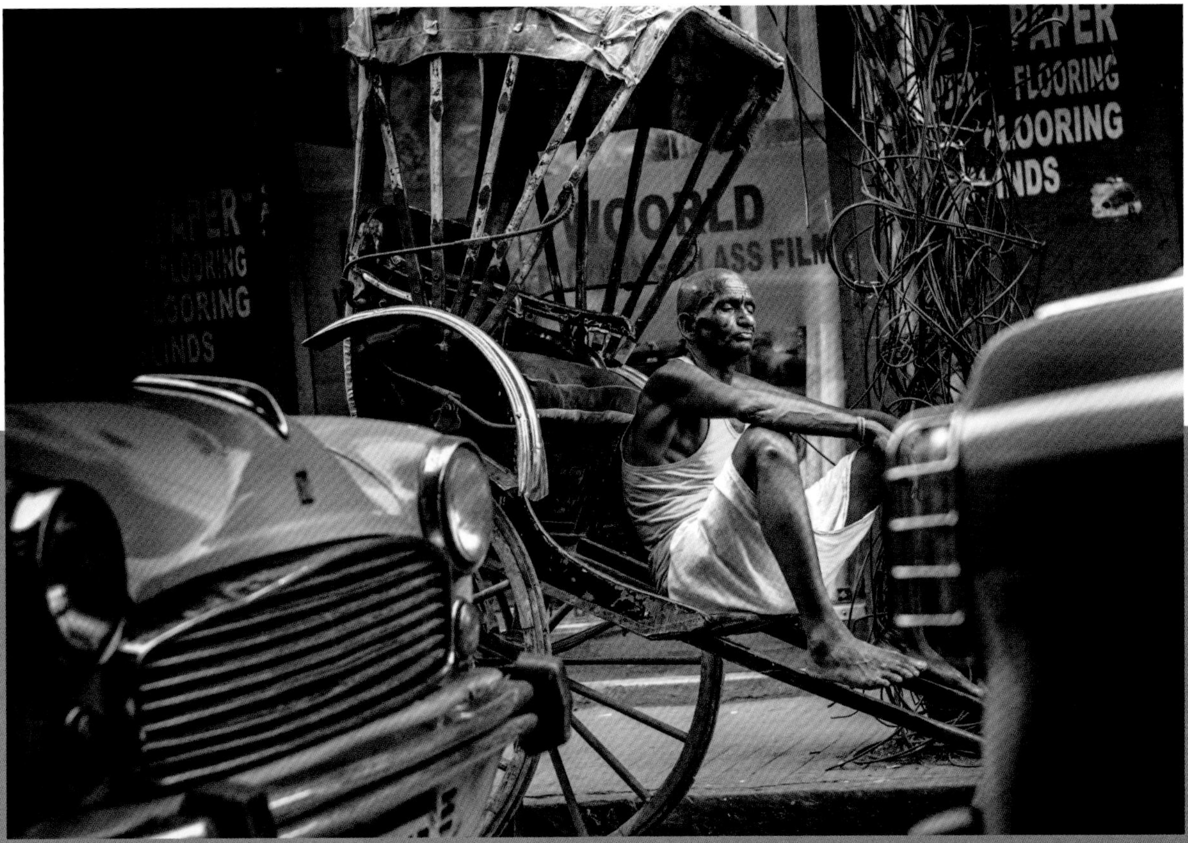

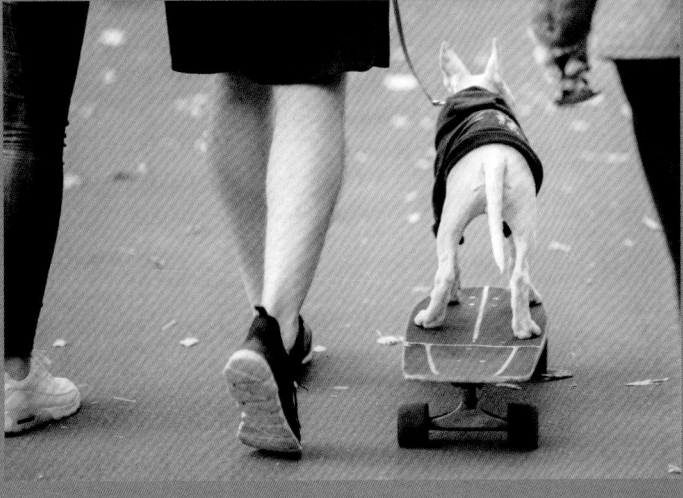

SHOOTING INSPIRATION

Street photography is 99% observing and 1% shooting.

ABOVE Look for moments of calm amid the urban chaos.

LEFT It takes a keen eye and quick reflexes to spot humourous moments in street photography.

SHOOT FROM THE HIP

Module 6.2
Focus on reflections

If you find pointing your camera at people and crowds intimidating, even from the hip (see page 210), there are different ways of 'seeing' the urban environment that move beyond the realms of straight documentary photography and into quieter, more interpretative territory. From shop windows and parked cars to wet pavements and fountains, towns and cities are littered with reflective surfaces, and with a keen eye and a little imagination, we can turn these urban mirrors into street scenes of a more abstract nature. Even the smallest puddles, when viewed from a particular angle, can become portals into another world, adding interest, depth and intrigue to an otherwise unremarkable urban landscape.

While Henri Cartier-Bresson was busy searching for decisive moments, contemporaries such as Saul Leiter and Ernst Haas adopted a more expressive style, often using reflections to portray a certain calmness – what author Martin Harrison described as a 'quiet humanity' – amid the chaos of the streets. In our main example, there could have been thousands of commuters marching to their offices, just inches from this tiny body of water, yet our scene depicts a perfect stillness, with the building's ornate embellishments crystal clear. This kind of creative abstraction encourages us to slow down and look – really look – at our surroundings to find the perfect pictorial ingredients.

These components include an instantly recognizable subject in your reflection and a low viewpoint – you may attract a few curious glances from passers-by as you circle the puddle looking for the best angle, but it is this kind of attention to detail that will help you identify a clear subject and create visual interest. In addition, for the most immediate images, it helps if the puddle is in shadow and the reflected subject is well lit – not only does this allow the subject to stand out, it also provides an area of contrast for your camera's autofocus system to latch onto. Ripples caused by wind and rain can add intriguing textures, though I'd recommend you wait for a still day after heavy rainfall to shoot your first reflections.

RIGHT **Abstract street scenes can be found in even the smallest of puddles.**

RECOMMENDED SETTINGS

- Shooting mode: **Aperture-priority**
- Aperture: **f/5.6**
- Shutter speed: **1/125sec or faster**
- ISO: **800**
- Focal length: **55mm**
- AF area: **Single-point AF**
- AF operation: **Single-shot AF**
- Drive mode: **Single-shot**
- Metering mode: **Evaluative/matrix**
- White balance: **Auto or daylight/cloudy**
- Picture style: **Standard**

DIFFICULTY ★★☆

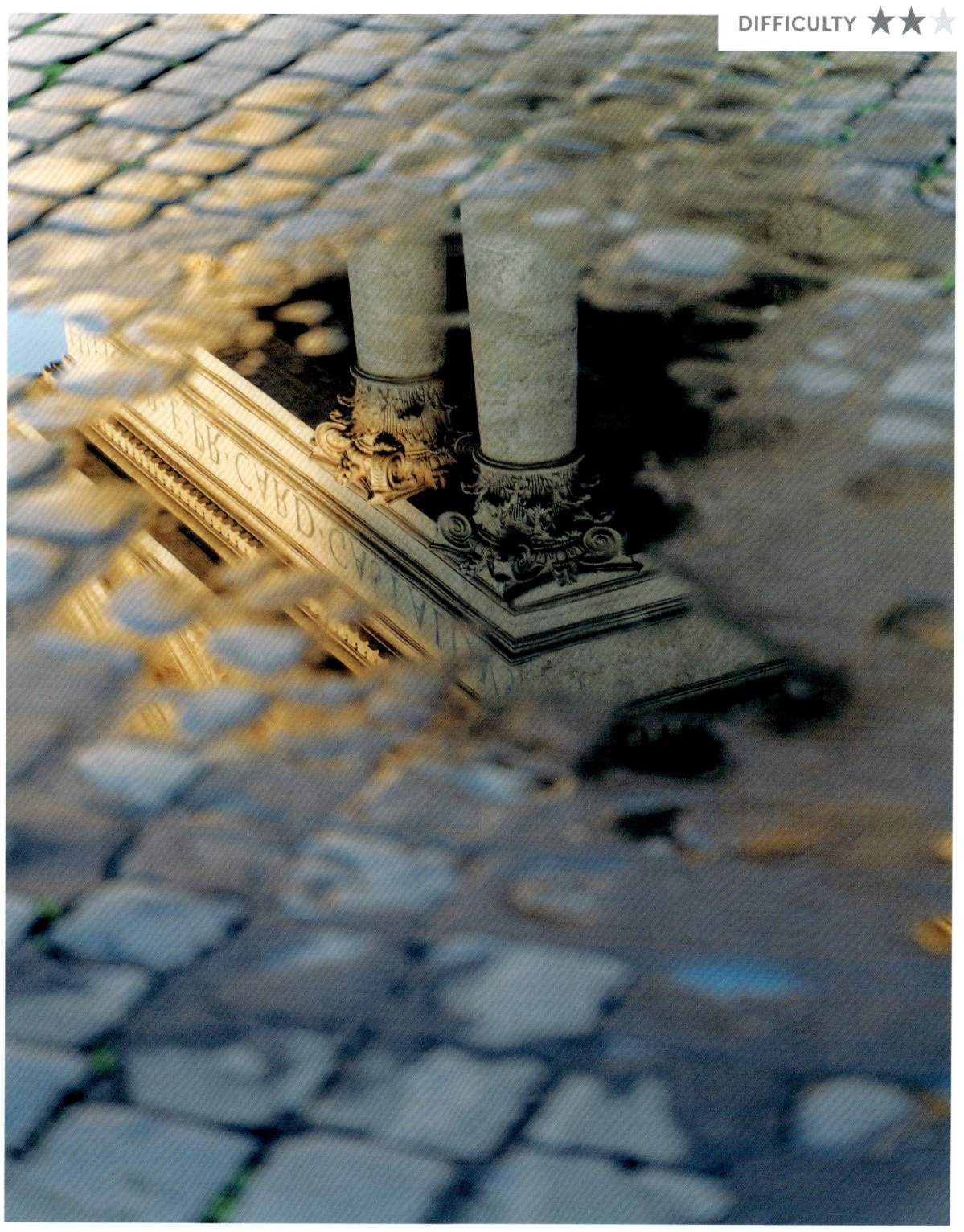

FOCUS ON REFLECTIONS 217

Camera settings

The contrast between sharpness and blur is the key to effective reflection photographs – the detail draws the viewer's eye while the out-of-focus area provides framing and context. We can use focal length and focusing to simplify and declutter a scene (see below), and we can also use aperture to generate a shallow depth of field, which means shooting in aperture-priority mode and selecting your lens' widest aperture. At $f/5.6$, the zone of sharpness will be just large enough to cover the width of the puddle and the reflected image, removing any potentially distracting details.

While I would usually endorse the use of a tripod for any type of photography that requires such a slow and methodical approach, there are two reasons why this is impractical here: setting up a tripod on a busy street can create a dangerous obstruction, and not all tripods allow you to shoot so low to the ground. So, our only option is to shoot handheld, which presents its own challenges, namely keeping shutter speed fast enough to avoid camera shake.

WHY THIS SHOT WORKS

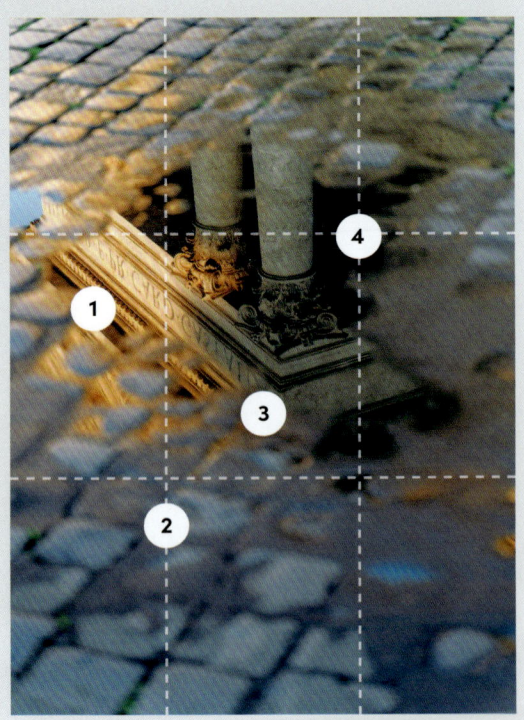

1 The reflected image within the puddle is pin-sharp, instantly recognizable and beautifully lit, jumping out of the picture amid the darker surrounding areas.

2 A low viewpoint and shallow depth of field have blurred the pavement around the puddle, simplifying the scene and diverting our attention to the sharp reflection.

3 Despite the strong contrasts between light and dark areas, the reflected image is perfectly exposed, with an incredible amount of detail captured in the building.

4 The puddle occupies roughly one-third of the frame while the pavement occupies roughly two-thirds, with the puddle straddling the upper horizontal rule-of-thirds grid line.

If we employ the rule of thumb that suggests that exposure time should match or exceed focal length (see page 61), at 55mm (which produces an effective focal length of around 80mm on an APS-C camera) we should aim for 1/125 second or faster. Of course, if your camera features image stabilization, this will help you shoot handheld at slower shutter speeds.

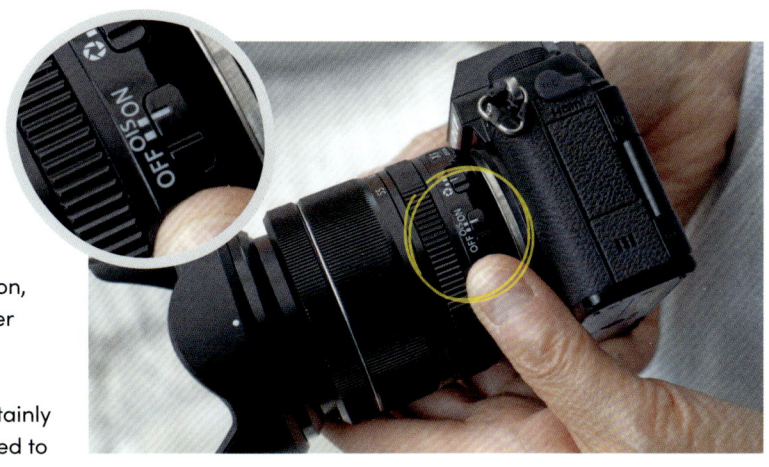

Shooting in shaded areas will almost certainly mean that higher ISOs will need to be used to maintain a fast enough shutter speed. Start at ISO 800 and increase it to ISO 1000 or 1200 if exposure times are too slow, and decrease it to ISO 640 or 500 if exposure times are faster than needed. As in the previous module, a little barely visible noise won't detract from a shot in which detail and contrast are the main talking points.

While black and white is an abstraction in itself, and an effective way to enhance detail and texture, in this instance the radiant warmth of the golden light as it hits the building would be lost if converted to mono. Which Picture Style you choose should depend on subject matter and personal preference, although if you are lucky enough to attract such incredible conditions, I would be tempted to switch back to the Standard preset and ramp up the contrast and saturation.

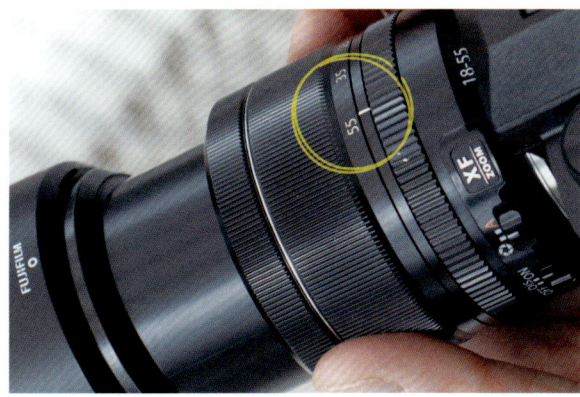

Lens settings

Reflections require tighter framing than general from-the-hip street scenes, so zoom in to 55mm and use your feet to fine-tune composition. Just as we used aperture to limit depth of field and focus the viewer's attention, so too can we use focal length to force a narrow angle of view and exclude unnecessary details around the reflection. Flick the AF/MF switch back to AF and set AF area to single-point AF, AF operation to single-shot AF and drive mode to single-shot. This combination will allow us to focus and shoot quickly and accurately – crucial skills when shooting on busy streets.

Technique

There is a simple formula that will help you compose well-balanced reflection images. While puddles tend to be haphazard in shape, which means that applying a strict rule-of-thirds approach to framing won't always work, a ratio of one-third reflection/two-thirds pavement (or vice versa) will always create visual harmony. If you can position the main point of interest on or near a horizontal or vertical rule-of-thirds grid line, all the better, as this will move it away from the centre of the frame, which rarely makes for interesting shots. Activate Live View and select the 3x3 Grid Display so you can visualize this formula in real time.

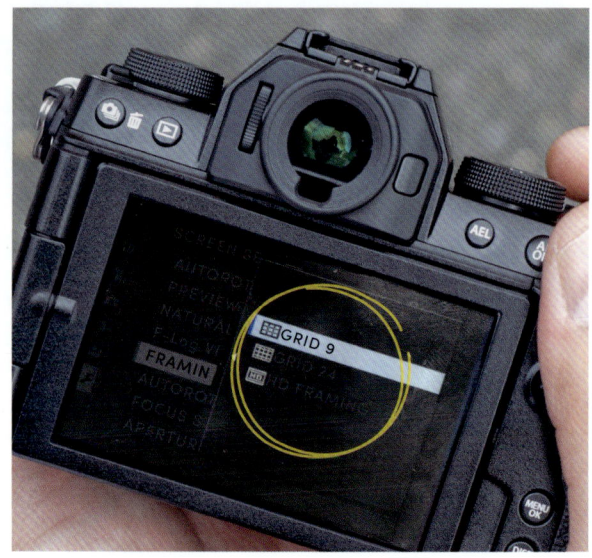

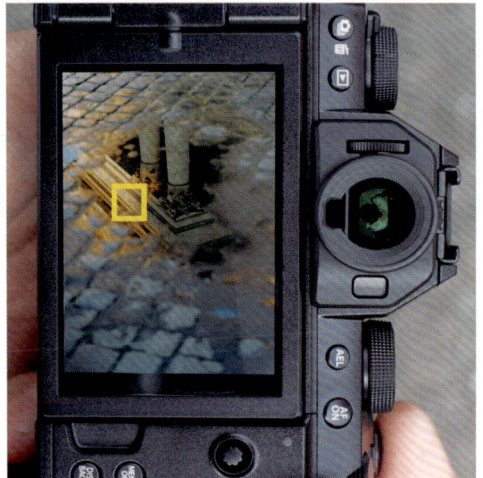

Once you have found your composition, move your single AF point over the area of strongest contrast within the reflection – in our example, this would be the area where the bright fascia meets the dark underside in the top-left of the frame. Gently half-press the shutter to engage autofocus and, once locked on, squeeze the shutter fully to take your shot. Don't be surprised if your first attempt is too dark – reflected light surrounded by a darker background can cause a camera's metering system to underexpose. If this is the case, dial in +1 stop of exposure compensation to override the camera's suggested exposure and brighten the darker areas.

TIP

If you want to practise this technique at home but don't want to wait for rain, create your own puddles by pouring water onto a level outdoor surface. Not only will you have plenty of time to get creative before the water drains away or evaporates, you also won't have to contend with busy passers-by while you get to grips with the settings and technique.

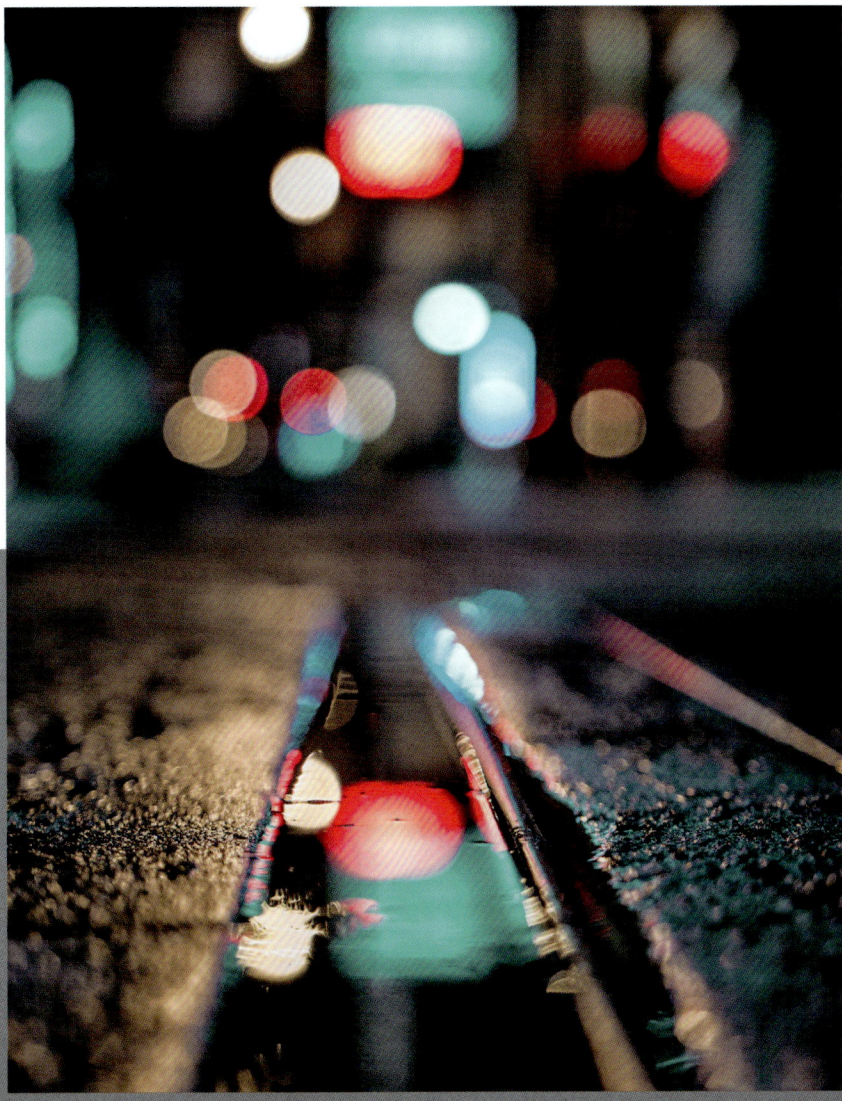

SHOOTING INSPIRATION

Reflections can be found in the most unlikely of places – and not all reflections need to be pin-sharp to be effective.

ABOVE Use a shallow depth of field to direct viewers' attention to a small area of the scene.

Module 6.3
Frame your scenes

Now that we have looked at the two extremes of street photography, we can start to explore the creative middle ground. Composition doesn't just describe the arrangement of objects or points of interest within the frame, it also refers to how we direct the viewer's eye through and towards certain areas and at what speed. In portrait and still life photography, we can direct or physically move the subject or object, adding and taking away to achieve a harmonious balance. However, in street photography, we have to work with what is already there, and frames within frames provide a very graphic means of highlighting certain people and events.

Similar to how we used trees and overhanging branches to frame our landscapes (see page 26), we can use windows, doorways and arches to frame our street scenes, providing a narrative gateway through which we can tell our story. But these devices are only half the visual equation – you also need to find an interesting focal point to position in the centre of the scene being framed. This could be a person, building or statue, and should be recognizable and fully contained – a subject cut off by the framing device will always look untidy. In the real world, this technique requires serious legwork and anticipation, though you could always cheat and use a friend to pose as though they were just passing through.

With two main elements to consider, knowing how to balance them is crucial, and helpfully we can use the one-third/two-thirds formula we used in the previous module (see page 220) to guide us. If the framing device and its surroundings occupy two-thirds of the frame, suggesting place and context, the focal point can then fill the remaining third, providing instant eye candy without dominating the scene. This is also a rare style that suits both off-centre and central compositions, the key difference being the immediacy of the viewer's journey: the latter will direct the eye straight to the focal point and hold it there with minimal effort, while the former will force the eye to navigate its way to the focal point, following any lead-in lines such as shadows, curbs or road markings like a detective following clues.

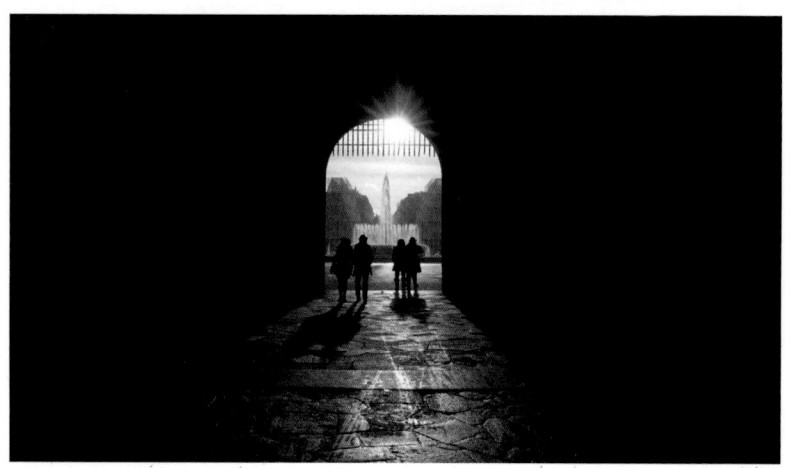

LEFT The central composition directs the eye straight to the framing device and the silhouettes within.

DIFFICULTY ★★★

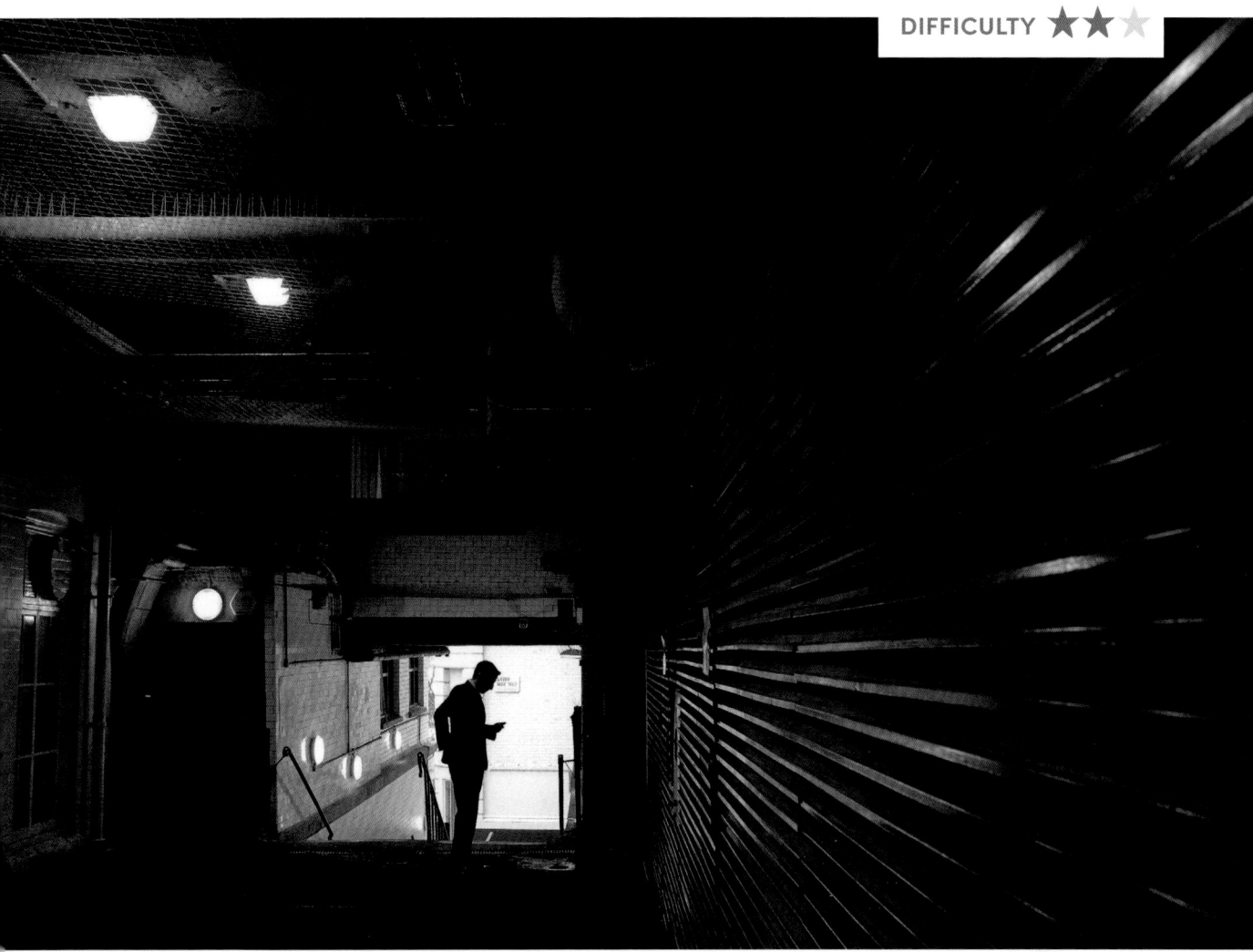

ABOVE **The lead-in lines on the right side of the frame point to the figure within the framing device.**

RECOMMENDED SETTINGS

- Shooting mode: **Aperture-priority**
- Aperture: **f/8**
- Shutter speed: **1/125sec (static subject), 1/250sec (moving subject)**
- ISO: **200–1200**
- Focal length: **23mm**
- AF area: **Single-point AF**
- AF operation: **Single-shot AF**
- Drive mode: **Single-shot**
- Metering mode: **Evaluative/matrix**
- White balance: **Auto or daylight/cloudy**
- Picture style: **Monochrome**

FRAME YOUR SCENES

Camera settings

Like shooting from the hip (see page 210), observational street photography requires control over aperture to ensure plenty of depth of field, and flexibility when it comes to ISO to ensure a fast enough shutter speed. Once again, this means shooting in aperture-priority mode, but instead of selecting our lens' widest aperture as we did for reflections, we need to dial in our 'walkabout' aperture of $f/8$. While not every part of our composition needs to be in sharp focus, we don't want the extreme edges to blur too much.

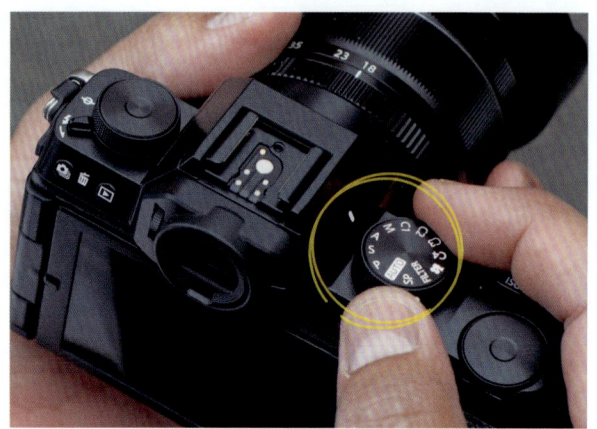

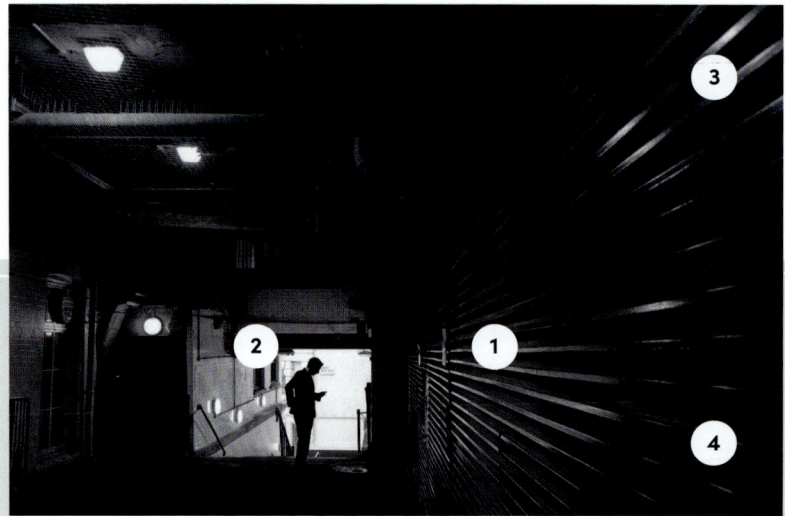

WHY THIS SHOT WORKS

1 The horizontal lines of the metallic shutters create the perfect lead-in lines, directing the viewer's eye towards the figure silhouetted in the centre of the framing device.

2 Although the figure occupies only a small portion of the frame, the stark contrast between the dark silhouette and bright background creates a very clear focal point.

3 A mid-range aperture has produced plenty of depth of field, ensuring that details are sharp from the edges of the frame to the bricks and stair rails behind the figure.

4 Shooting in black and white has simplified a potentially confusing scene, created a classic street image with extreme contrasts and lots of interesting textures and details.

Which ISO you use will depend on your surroundings. If you are shooting in a wide-open space with plenty of natural light, start at ISO 200 and increase to 320 or 400 if needed; if you are shooting in a built-up urban environment with tall buildings either side, start at ISO 800 and increase to 1000 or 1200 if needed; and if shooting indoors or from a subway, for instance, start at ISO 1200 and increase to 1600 or 2000 if needed. Just remember that ISO is a secondary concern here, so don't obsess over image quality and never use a wider aperture instead, as this will reduce the depth of field.

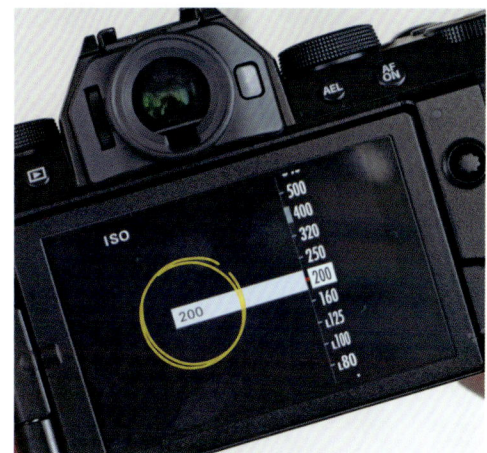

There are two default shutter speeds to aim for when framing subjects on the street – and which you choose will be determined by the nature of your central focal point. Static subjects, such as statues and trees, are easier to frame (and branches blowing in the wind are more predictable in their movement than people), so a handheld exposure time of 1/125 second will suffice. However, moving subjects, such as pedestrians, bikes and cars, are harder to frame and less predictable in their movement, in which case a faster exposure time of 1/250 second will be needed. As we are shooting in aperture-priority, you will have to keep a careful eye on this setting and adjust ISO accordingly.

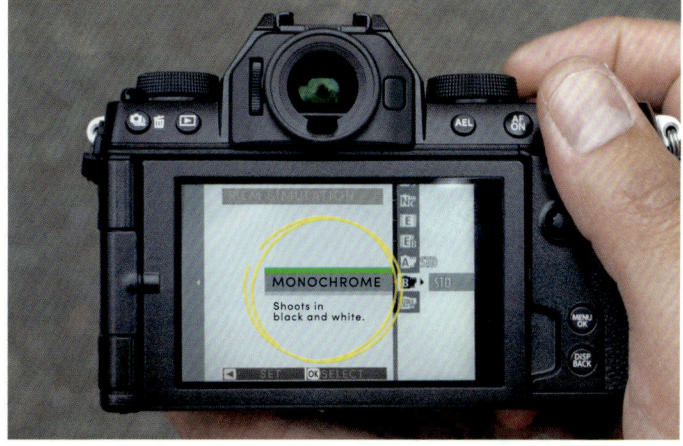

This is a classic style of street photography that screams black and white, and while the Monochrome Picture Style setting will help you visualize the world in shades of grey and help simplify potentially confusing scenes, we can also customize the preset by adding more contrast to enhance the mood and sense of grittiness. How you access a preset's individual settings will vary from camera to camera, so consult the manual if you are unsure. Alternatively, you could opt for one of the Monochrome preset's classic filter effects – the yellow filter will produce the most subtle contrast, while the red filter will add the most drama.

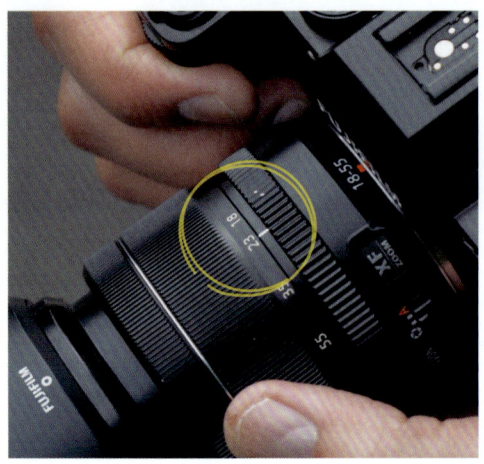

Lens settings

Your kit lens' widest focal lengths can produce barrel distortion, an optical imperfection in which straight lines appear to bulge outwards from the centre of the frame. As our framing devices will almost certainly feature straight lines, it is best to start with a focal length of around 23mm to capture a wide-angle view (this will give you an effective focal length of around 35mm on an APS-C camera). Zoom in to exclude extraneous details, or step back to include more of the scene rather than zoom out any further.

As we need to achieve accurate focus quickly and in a very particular part of the frame, flick the AF/MF switch back to AF and set AF area to single-point AF, AF operation to single-shot AF and drive mode to single-shot.

Technique

If ever there was a project designed to challenge your camera's metering system, this is it. There are two very distinct components to your framing image, one very bright and one very dark, but while the framing device is important, the viewer will move past this quickly and focus on the scene inside the frame. So, while a little underexposure around the edges of the frame is acceptable, the scene within absolutely has to be correctly exposed (if the framing object is correctly exposed, the scene inside will be overexposed). To darken the framed scene and avoid blowing the highlights where detail is needed, dial in up to -2 stops of exposure compensation, depending on how extreme the contrast is.

When it comes to focusing, mid-range apertures, such as $f/8$, are always going to be more forgiving than wide apertures such as $f/5.6$. However, accuracy is still a crucial part of this technique, so place your single AF point in the centre of the frame (or to one side if your subject is off-centre), compose your framed street scene and gently half-press the shutter. If your focal point is static, fully press the shutter to take your shot; if your subject is on the move, wait for it to enter the area where your AF point is positioned, and focus and shoot in one fast, smooth and steady action. With practise, you will soon learn to anticipate and capture those split-second moments where frame and subject perfectly interact.

TIP

Use Live View and your camera's tilting LCD screen to experiment with high and low viewpoints that would be awkward or impossible to achieve with a standard viewfinder. In particular, a ground-level viewpoint is a great way to enhance an image's foreground detail and sense of depth and intrigue.

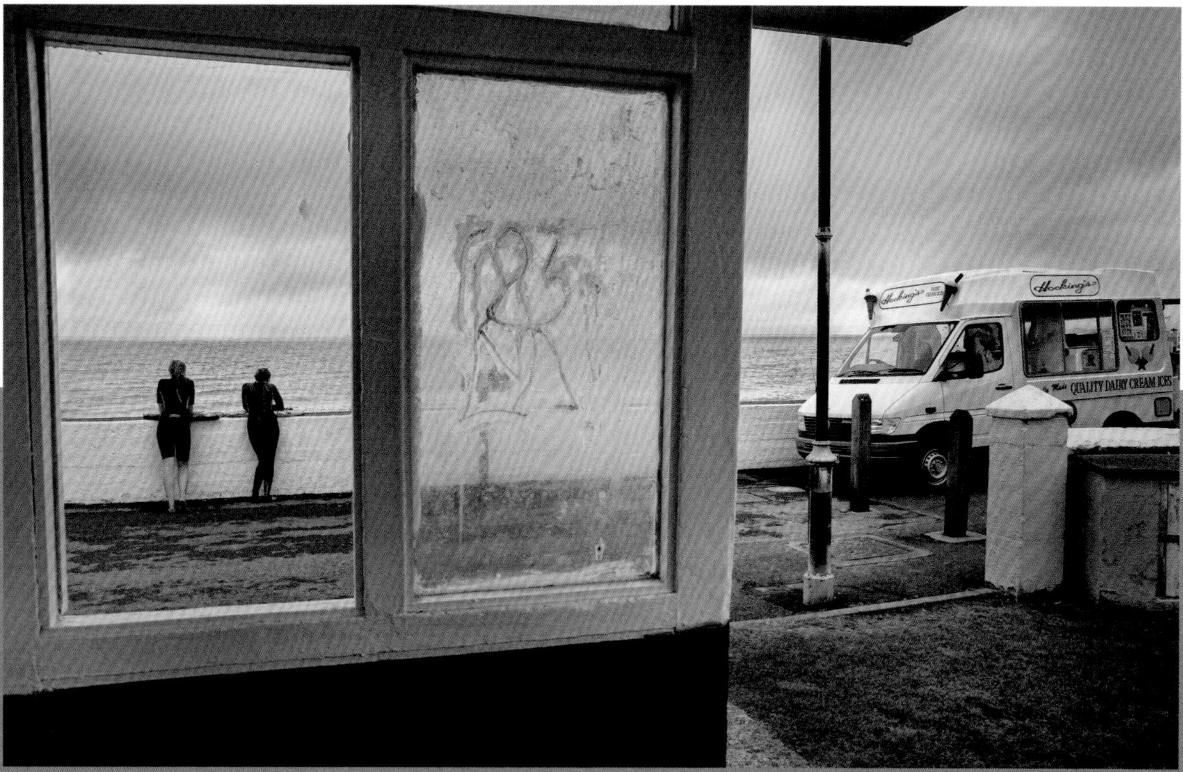

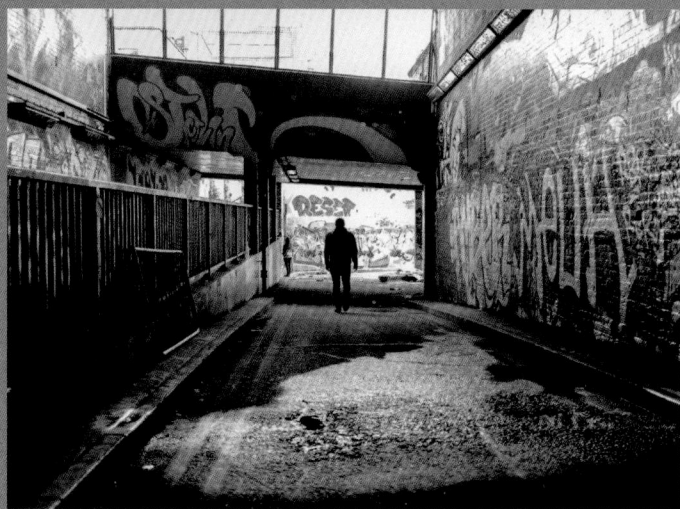

SHOOTING INSPIRATION

Frames within frames can be used to take the eye on a visual journey as well as direct it to a particular area of the frame.

ABOVE **Framing can be used to add narrative layers to your street scenes.**

LEFT **Railings, road markings and even graffiti create interest as well as structure.**

FRAME YOUR SCENES

Module 6.4
Play with shadows

Light and shadow are an inherent part of all artistic endeavours, but what happens when we make them the sole focus of our street photography? While this most egalitarian of subjects is rooted in realism in terms of subject matter, visually we are free to indulge our unique artistic visions and impulses, and shadow play provides a compelling way to enhance contrast, emphasize texture and add a sense of mystery. It is also an approach with its creative advantages: for stronger shadows, you have to shoot on sunny days, when the light is too harsh for most other subjects; and you don't have to point your camera at actual people, just the abstract suggestion of their presence.

Time of day is perhaps the most important consideration for this project. The lower the sun, the longer the shadows and the softer the light, so if you want to photograph shadows against a wall, for instance, the two hours after sunrise and before sunset are your windows of opportunity. Of course, if you want less subtle shadows, the middle of the day, when the sun is directly overhead, may be more appealing. If you want the shadows to fall away from you, shoot with the sun behind you; if you want the shadows to fall towards you, shoot with the sun in front of you (see page 70). If you opt for the latter, be prepared for lens flare.

As counterintuitive as it may sound, metering for the shadows will dilute the impact they have, as your camera's metering system will record them as a midtone grey if left in evaluative/matrix mode. As a result, the brightest parts of the scene will almost certainly be overexposed too. Instead, we need to meter for the highlights, as this will capture the most amount of detail in the brightest areas while reducing the darker areas to almost solid black, producing extreme contrasts and bags of mood, atmosphere and drama. The most precise exposure method for this project is to use spot metering, a technique we explored in detail when shooting backlit portraits (see page 70).

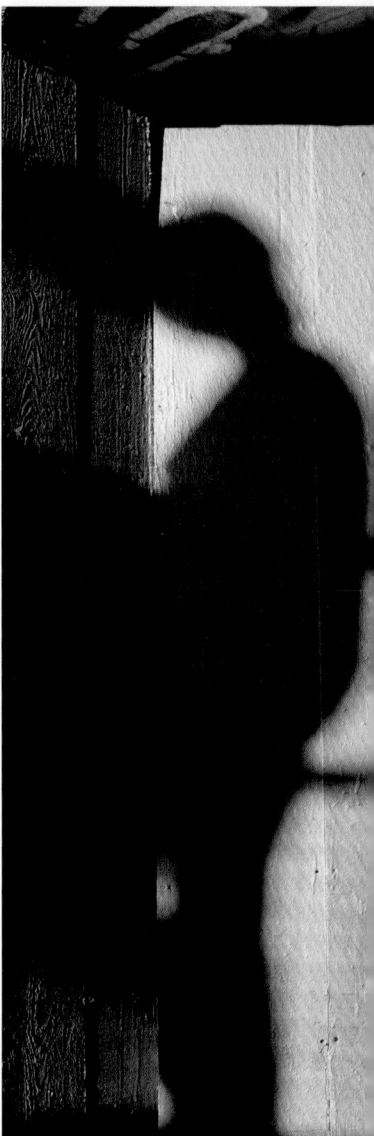

ABOVE **Sunny days and harsh shadows are perfect for this creative technique.**

DIFFICULTY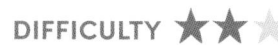

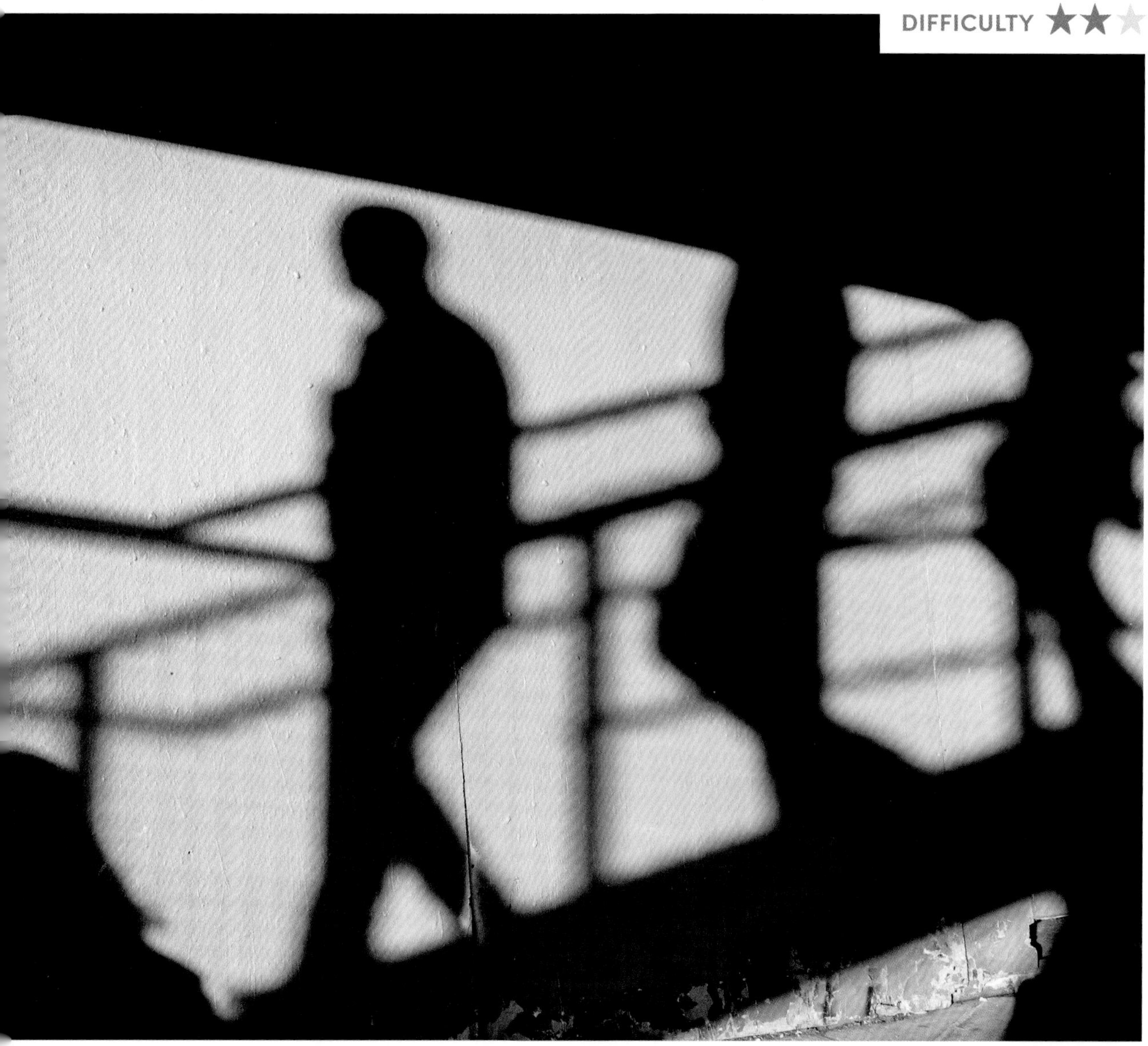

RECOMMENDED SETTINGS

- Shooting mode: **Aperture-priority**
- Aperture: **f/8**
- Shutter speed: **1/125sec**
- ISO: **200**
- Focal length: **35mm**
- AF area: **Single-point AF**
- AF operation: **Single-shot AF**
- Drive mode: **Continuous**
- Metering mode: **Spot**
- White balance: **Auto or daylight/cloudy**
- Picture style: **Monochrome or standard**

PLAY WITH SHADOWS

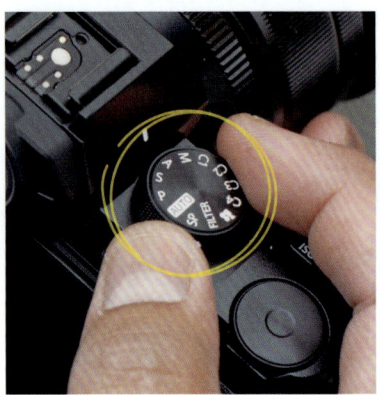

Camera settings

Experienced street photographers will tell you that shooting in manual mode and adjusting shutter speed, aperture and ISO on the fly is the only way to go, but with street photography's reliance on keen observation and fast reflexes, shooting in aperture-priority mode and letting the camera take at least some of the strain makes much more sense to me. So, turn the mode dial to A or Av and adopt the '$f/8$ and be there' rule (see page 210), as this will provide you with more than enough depth of field for front-to-back sharpness, regardless of whether you're shooting straight on or at an angle to the surface on which the shadows are projected.

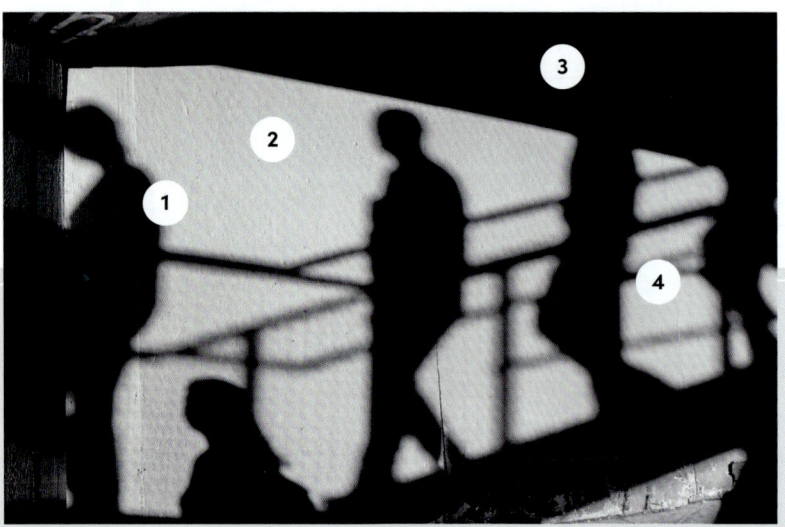

WHY THIS SHOT WORKS

1 Harsh light and bold shadows create a strikingly graphic yet abstract street scene absent of any actual people but alive with the suggestion of their presence.

2 The brightest parts of the scene have been perfectly exposed, emphasizing the wall's textures and details and ensuring that the shadows are suitably dark and pronounced.

3 The large areas of shadow in the top-right and bottom-right corners of the frame create a triangular wedge of light that frames the figures and creates a strong top-right to bottom-left diagonal line.

4 Shooting in black and white strengthens the contrast between light and dark, further defines the lines and shapes created by the shadows, and helps draw our attention to the human element.

As we are metering for the highlights, shutter speed is likely to be faster than it would be if we were metering for midtones or shadows, and so we can use a lower ISO than we would for standard from-the-hip street photographs. Start at ISO 200 and only increase to 400 and beyond if shutter speed drops below the 1/125 second handholding limit. Of course, if you opt to shoot in black and white, you may want to deliberately introduce a hint of noise to mimic the effects of film grain, in which case ramp ISO up to 800 for a subtle analogue feel.

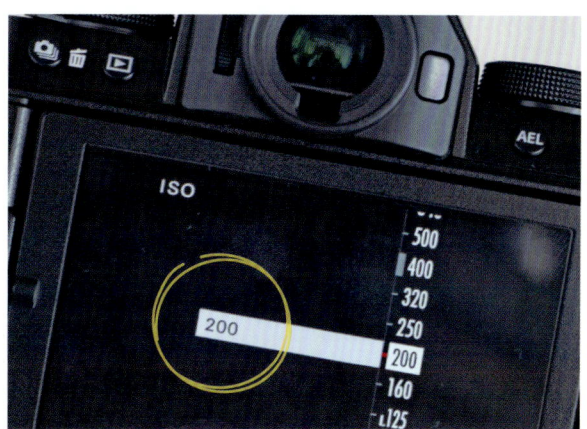

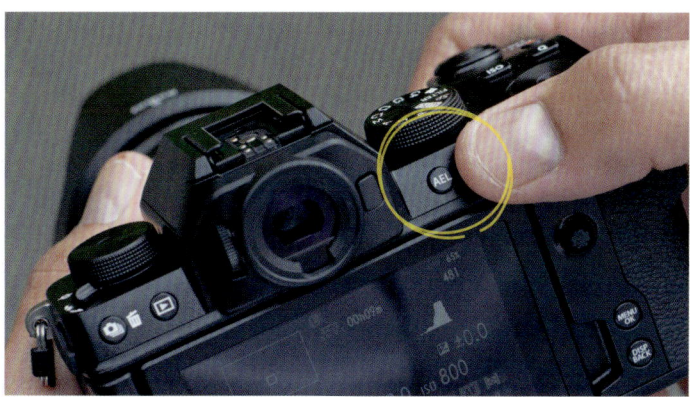

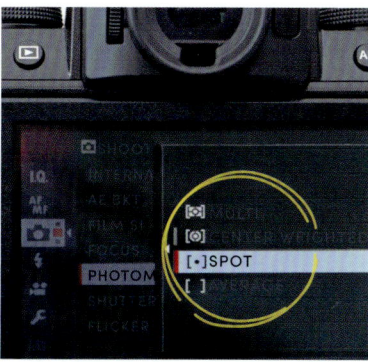

One handy feature that we haven't explored in this book yet is exposure lock, often abbreviated to AE lock. As we are dealing with extreme contrasts and a very specific method of metering, the area from which we meter is unlikely to be the area of focus, or focal point, so we need a way to meter, compose and focus without the exposure changing. To use AE lock, simply meter for the highlights then press the AE lock button to lock in the exposure setting, then recompose and take your shot without having to worry about your shadows being too light or your highlights not retaining enough detail. To take more shots at the same exposure, simply hold down the AE lock button until you are ready to move on.

Change the metering mode from evaluative/matrix to spot – this will either be via a selection button on your camera's top plate or a menu on the rear screen. To refresh your memory, spot metering measures light from just 1–2% of the frame, typically around your AF point, and is symbolized by a 'spot' icon. If you have completed the backlit-portrait project (see page 70), you will be familiar with its precision; if you haven't, I'd recommend a quick practice before you hit the streets.

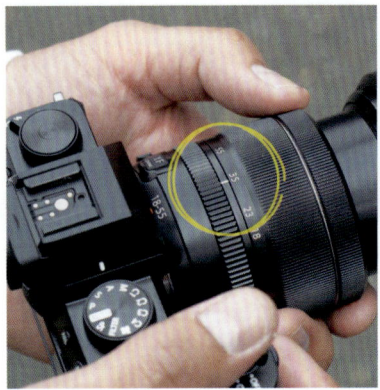

Technique

Framing a shadowy street scene is a lot like framing a rural landscape (see Chapter 1, pages 8–31) in that the shapes, lines and contrasts created by the interplay between light and dark can be used as compositional devices, just as we would use horizons, lead-in lines and focal points in more traditional pictorial scenes. Use guidelines such as the rule of thirds and power points to inform where you position key elements, look for strong diagonal lines that run from one corner of the frame to another, and remember that shadows are entirely transient and will constantly change as time passes and the quality of light mutates. Think of it as an abstract geometry – shadows are an absence of light and yet they can be used to sculpt incredibly graphic images.

Lens settings

Start at around 35mm and zoom in – or use your feet – to refine composition. Not only will this standard focal length give you a distortion-free perspective, it will also ensure that you don't get too close to your subjects. For speed and accuracy, leave the AF/MF switch set to AF, AF area set to single-point AF and AF operation set to single-shot AF, but change drive mode to high-speed continuous – this will allow you to shoot in short bursts (how many and for how long will depend on your camera and memory card speed), greatly increasing your chances of capturing at least one frame with shadows and subjects exactly where you want them to be.

Despite being a specialist metering mode with limited application, spot metering is surprisingly easy to use. Look for the brightest part of your scene – the area we want to be correctly exposed – half-press the shutter to both engage AF and take a meter reading, press the AE lock button, recompose and refocus, moving the AF point to where you want your focal point to be positioned. It may sound like a complicated process in writing, but in practice it only takes a few seconds and will become second nature after a day pounding the streets.

TIP

Large areas of shadow can be used to create negative space that helps draw attention to smaller illuminated areas, perhaps with a colourful character walking through the light. Think of shadows as framing devices and don't be afraid to go dark – after all, shadows formed an intrinsic part of the film noir genre's mysterious allure.

This is a style of street photography that can be just as effective in colour as it is in black and white, so you will need to choose based on location, subject and personal preference. The graphic simplicity and starkness of our main example – not to mention the lack of actual people – lent itself to high-contrast mono, but scenes in which colour is an integral part of the story and doesn't overpower the human element or location may be best captured in the standard Picture Style preset to help ground your images in reality. My preference would always be black and white, but shooting street scenes with a specific colour in mind can be a fun project in itself.

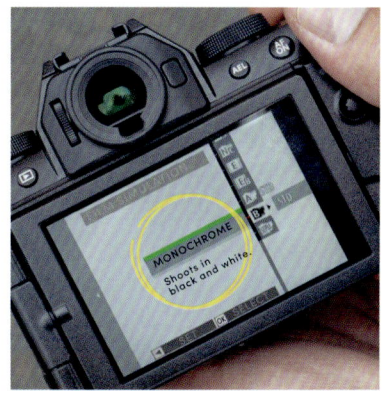

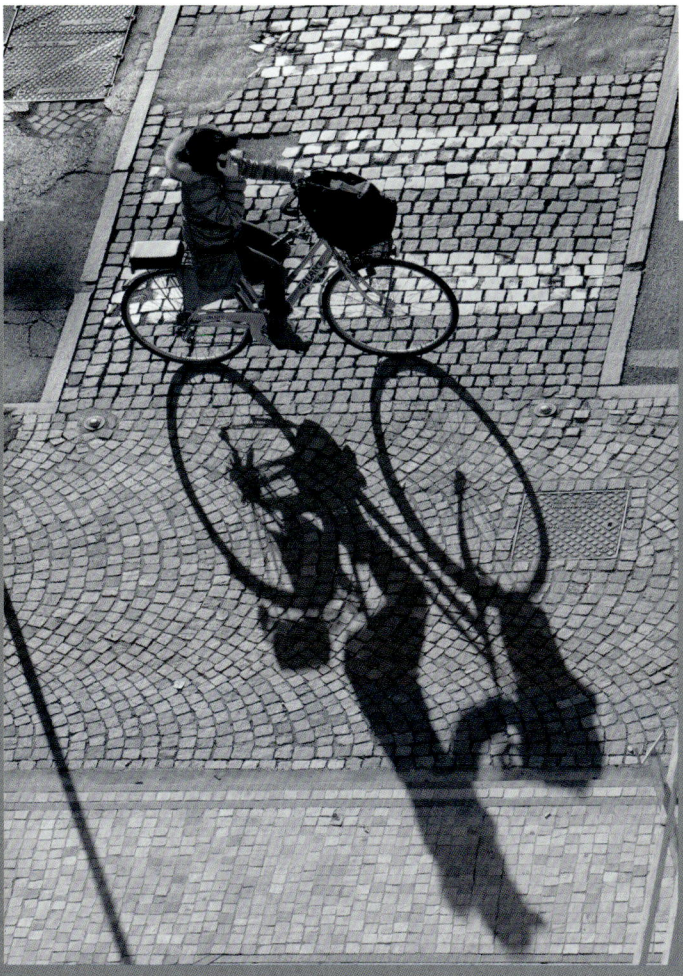

SHOOTING INSPIRATION

The busy urban environment, with all its lines, textures and patterns, is the perfect place to get creative with shadows. Consider the time of day, the viewpoint and the level of abstraction.

LEFT A high vantage point has helped the photographer to maximize the longer shadows created by late-afternoon light.

PLAY WITH SHADOWS 233

Module 6.5
Blur moving people

If your street photography adventures coincide with rush hour or weekend shopping, chances are you are going to be confronted by throngs of people muscling their way through dense crowds. To the naked eye, the sensory overload of this constant procession can be difficult to make visual sense of, but with a little artistic interpretation and a few simple camera skills, we can creatively blur these 'solid' crowds and render them as ghost-like human traffic trails, conveying a sense of elegant fluidity and a more poetic interpretation of the urban chaos. How much motion blur you generate will depend on light levels, camera settings, the speed of your subjects and their distance from the camera.

While photographing crowds in busy towns and cities is more challenging than shooting windswept grasses in tranquil rural settings (see page 32), the basic principles are the same. By venturing out just after sunrise and just before sunset, when the sun is lower in the sky, we can combine narrow apertures with lower ISOs to limit the amount of light entering our lens and force slower shutter speeds without the need for filters, creating longer windows of time for our crowds to move through the frame. Exposure time is critical: too fast and people and traffic won't have time to blur, and the sense of movement will be limited; too slow and they will become almost invisible, nullifying the motion-blur effect.

Your moving subjects should be prominent in the frame, which means choosing a viewpoint that is close enough yet not causing an obstruction. With a maximum reach of just 55mm at our disposal, this also means being discreet for the most natural results. There are various ways to become 'invisible' as a street photographer: use Live View rather than your camera's viewfinder – this way you are not holding a camera to your face and advertising the fact that you are about to take a picture; use a remote shutter release and hold it inside a jacket pocket so you can shoot unnoticed; avoid eye contact and gaze into the distance as you work; shoot from an elevated viewpoint so you are not in your subjects' line of sight.

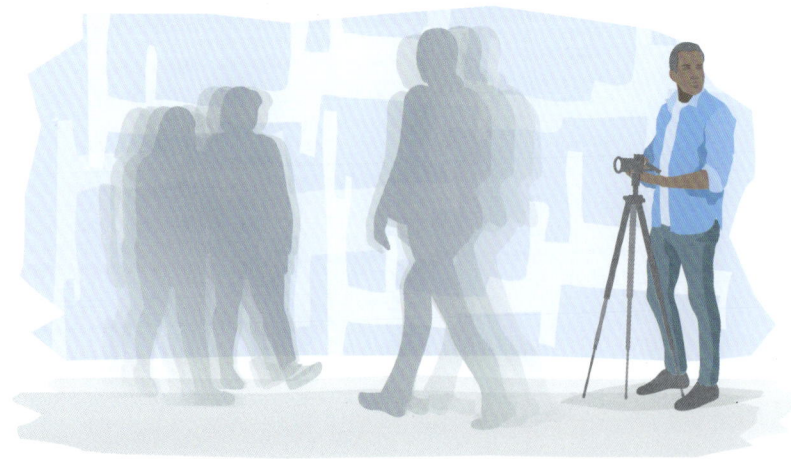

RIGHT **Use Live View at waist level** – this way you are not holding a camera to your face and advertising the fact that you are about to take a picture. Avoid eye contact with subjects for more natural shots.

DIFFICULTY ★★☆

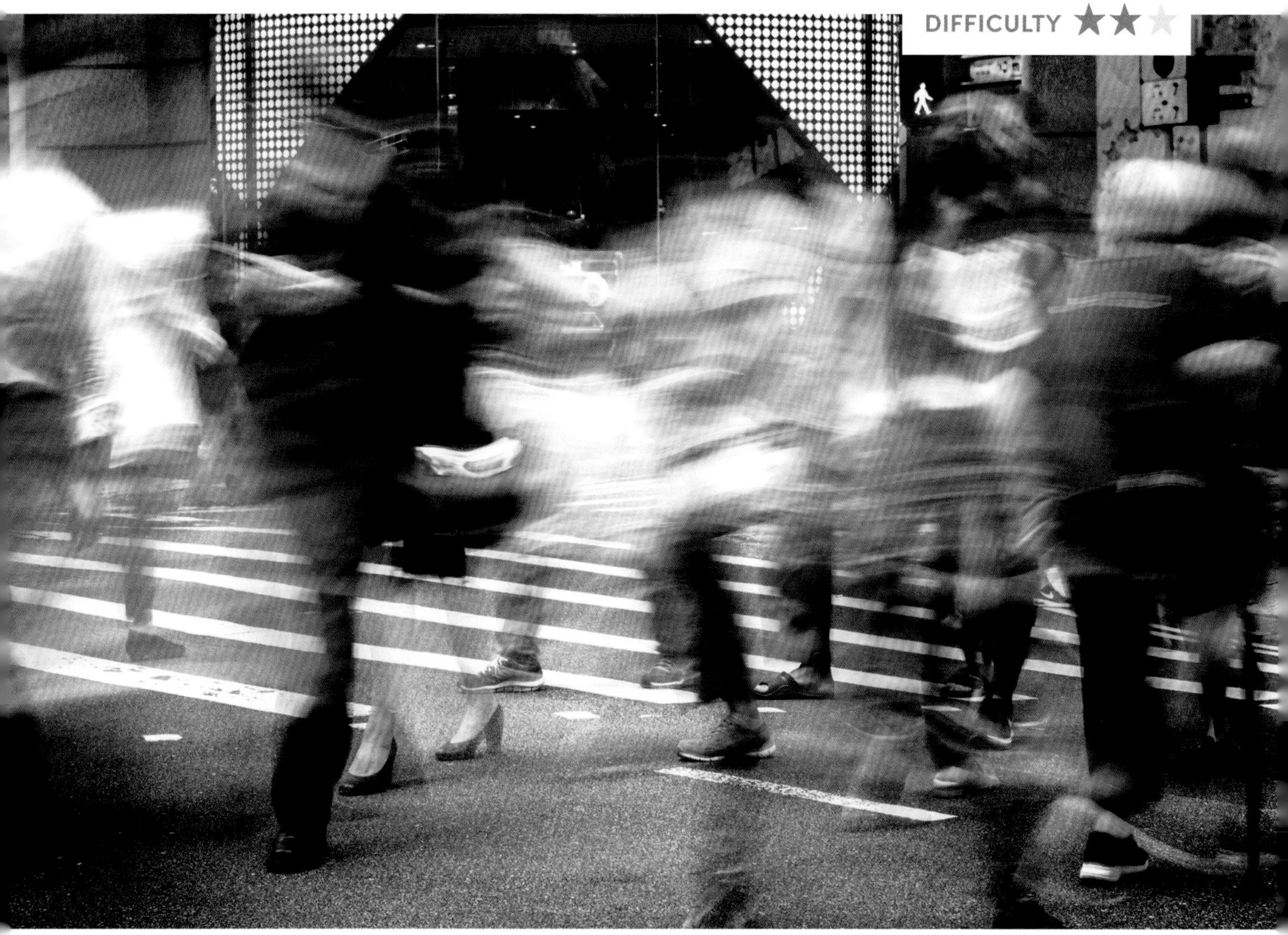

ABOVE **Road crossings on busy streets guarantee a steady flow of shoppers and commuters.**

RECOMMENDED SETTINGS

- Shooting mode: **Aperture-priority**
- Aperture: **f/16–f/22**
- Shutter speed: **1/60sec or slower**
- ISO: **100 (or 'L')**
- Focal length: **55mm**
- AF area: **Single-point AF**
- AF operation: **Single-shot AF**
- Drive mode: **Single-shot or self-timer**
- Metering mode: **Evaluative/matrix**
- White balance: **Auto or daylight/cloudy**
- Picture style: **Monochrome or standard**

BLUR MOVING PEOPLE

Camera settings

The narrowest aperture and lowest ISO will always produce the slowest shutter speed in any given situation, which is exactly what we want to achieve here. But while exposure time is critical for this technique, f/stops and depth of field are arguably more important, as we are effectively shooting a dynamic landscape, just with an urban spin. This is why we are still going to shoot in aperture-priority rather than shutter-priority, and why I would recommend you only select the latter mode when depth of field is an unimportant creative consideration; for example, when shooting ICM images (see page 38).

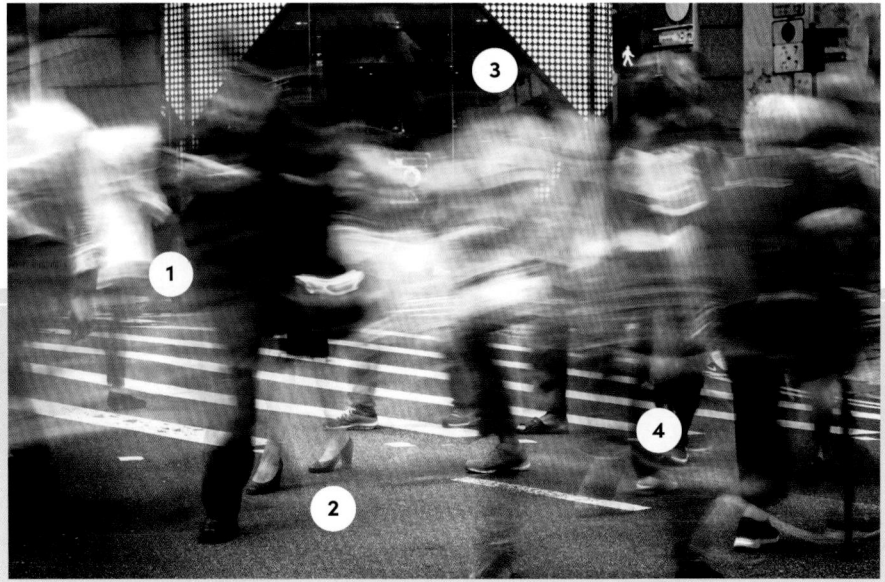

WHY THIS SHOT WORKS

1 A slow shutter speed has transformed the busy crowd into a ghost-like human traffic trail, with shoes and trainers being the only instantly recognizable parts of the shoppers.

2 A close yet discreet viewpoint has allowed the photographer to include the moving subjects prominently in the frame, with only the most essential visual information included.

3 A narrow aperture and careful focusing has ensured that the road, buildings and street furniture are perfectly sharp, enhancing the contrast between the static elements and the motion blur.

4 Black and white simplifies and minimizes a busy and potentially confusing street scene, removing the distraction of colour and helping the viewer to focus on the movement of the subjects.

Rules are made to be broken and here I'm going to break one of my own, which is never shoot at a narrower aperture than $f/16$. There are times when that extra stop of light will make all the difference and this could be one of them, so if you need to force a fractionally slower shutter speed to increase motion blur, close down to $f/22$. Just remember that diffraction – when light spreads from one pixel to another – will start to affect sharpness at this point, so which f-stop you choose becomes a creative trade off.

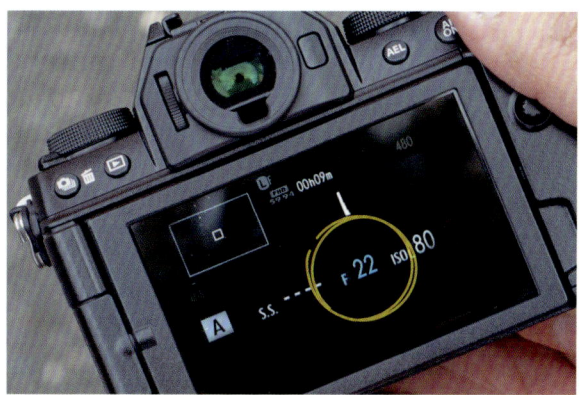

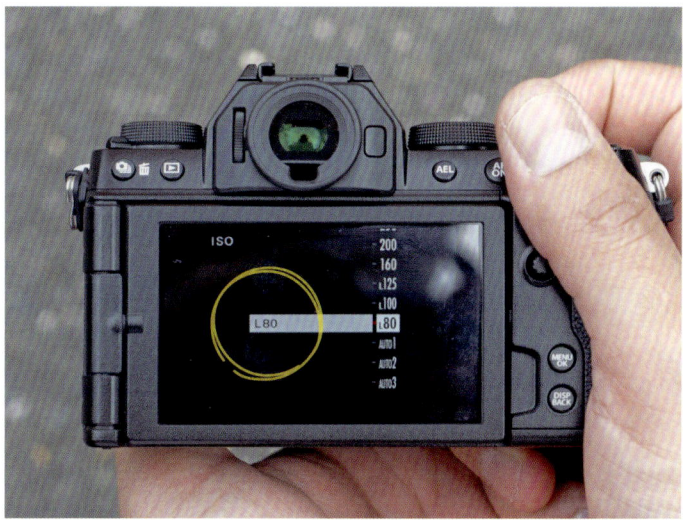

Your camera's lowest native ISO should suffice for this project, but if you want to increase exposure times and would prefer not to push aperture beyond $f/16$, consider using the extended low, or 'L', option. This will allow you to select ISO options beyond your camera's native range, which for some is ISO 80 and for others ISO 50. You may need to dip into your camera's menu to find this setting so check the manual for details. While occasionally useful when shooting JPEGs, it's worth noting that extended ISOs rely on software processing, which is effectively in-camera image editing.

The 'perfect' exposure time will fall somewhere between 1/60 second and 1/2 second and will depend on how quickly your subjects are moving, how close you are to them and how pronounced you want the motion blur to be. In my opinion, the effect works best when the subject is vaguely recognizable but with no distinguishing features or facial expressions, although I know plenty of photographers who opt for total abstraction, so it really is a question of personal preference. Experiment with shutter speeds, adjusting aperture and ISO accordingly, and remember that shutter speeds will always be faster on sunny days than overcast ones.

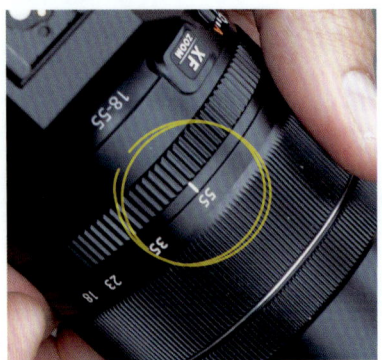

Lens settings

This is where urban and rural motion-blur images differ: with traditional landscapes, we typically want to capture an expansive view that encapsulates the widescreen splendour of an idyllic location, which means zooming out to 18mm; with gritty street scenes, we want to avoid clutter and distractions for cleaner compositions, which means zooming in to 55mm. Keep the AF/MF switch set to AF, AF area set to single-point AF and AF operation set to single-shot AF, but change the drive mode back to single-shot. Or, if you don't have a remote shutter release to hand, set your camera's self-timer drive mode to its shortest delay, which will typically be 2 seconds – timing is important, after all.

Technique

Find a location where a steady stream of people is guaranteed. Busy pedestrian crossings and station and subway entrances are likely to be packed with shoppers and commuters, particularly between 8 and 9 a.m. and 5 and 6 p.m. when rush hour is in full swing. Use every compositional device at your disposal to find order in the chaos: the rule-of-thirds grid will help you position buildings and horizons; power points will help you place important objects; road markings could act as lead-in lines; a ground-level viewpoint might emphasize any foreground interest.

The visual power of motion blur is the contrast between static location and moving subject and so we need to make sure that the static elements are perfectly sharp. Just as we did when shooting landscapes (page 36), once you have found your composition, position the single AF point roughly one-third of the way into the frame, half-press the shutter to obtain focus and flick the AF/MF switch back to MF to lock it off. Depth of field will always extend one-third in front of this point and two-thirds behind, which, at f/16, will ensure that all static objects near and far will be in focus.

Now all that's left to do is to wait, observe and anticipate. In the meantime, a few tips about shooting in busy towns and cities: take only the gear you need so you can travel light (and to limit the amount you'd lose were it lost or stolen); wear your camera bag on your front so it is visible at all times; be extra vigilant when looking through the viewfinder as you will be less aware of your immediate surroundings; never block or obstruct walkways with your tripod and always move on if asked to do so by police; and always take an 'assistant' with you if shooting after dark or in secluded areas.

TIP

Include cars and buses in your motion-blur street shots to add an extra layer of interest. As they move faster than people, they will travel further across the frame at any given shutter speed and so will blur more.

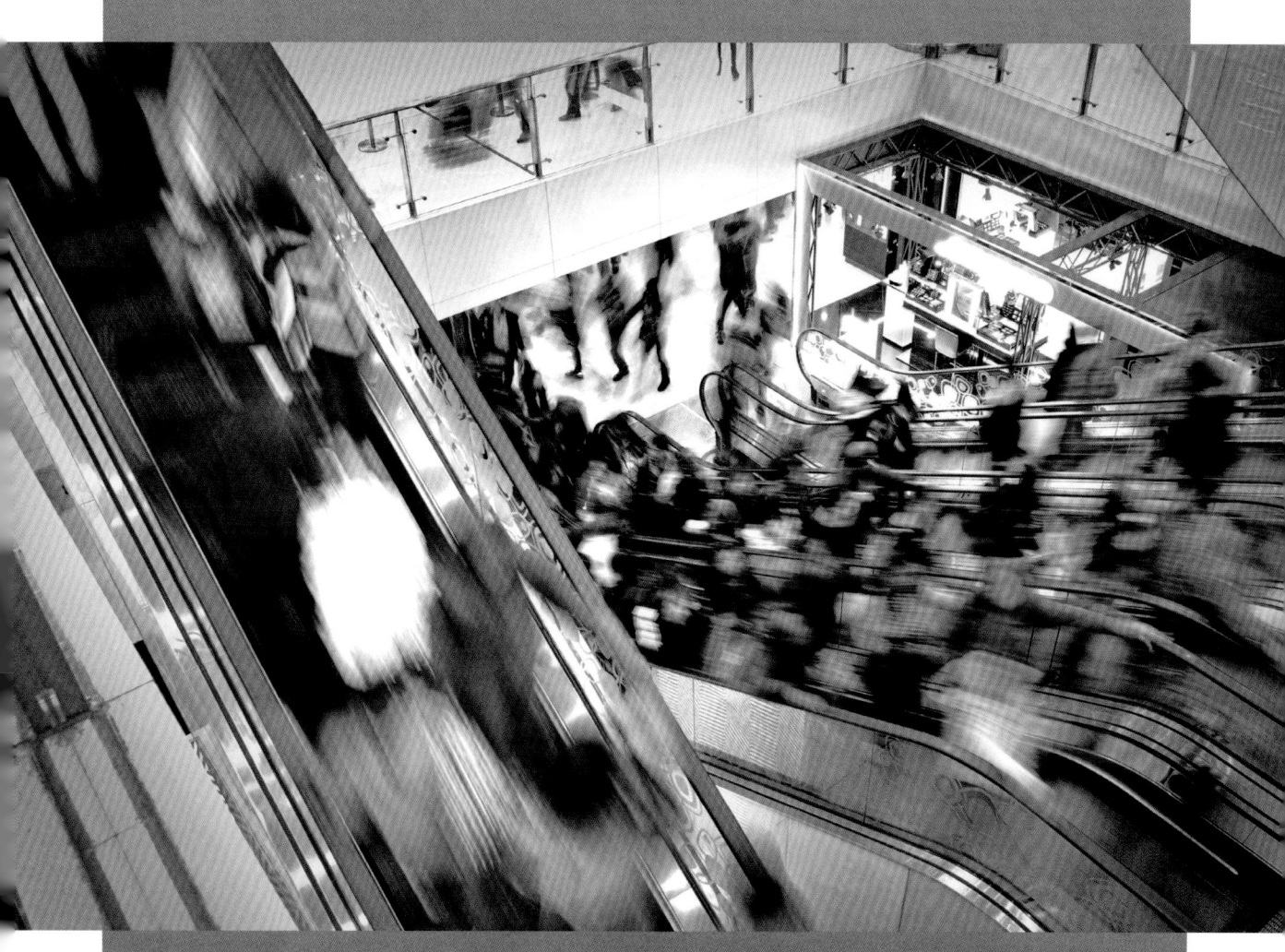

SHOOTING INSPIRATION

With the right camera settings and technique, you can turn oblivious passers-by into ghosts just about anywhere.

ABOVE An elevated viewpoint keeps you out of your subjects' line of sight and allows for some interesting compositions.

Module 6.6
Look for lines & shapes

Point your lens up and away from people and focus instead on buildings and you move from gritty street photography into the lofty realms of architectural photography. At its most literal, this fascinating sub-genre can be defined as the study of design and accurate representation, but dig deeper and you will unlock a less constrained interpretation more concerned with the arrangement of lines, shapes and the interaction of indoor and outdoor spaces. This more creative approach frees us up to explore structural elements of the urban jungle without having to worry about purist 'problems' such as converging verticals – when two parallel lines appear to get closer when you tilt the camera upwards.

It helps to divide architectural scenes into sections. Our main image contains three distinct components: the keyhole-shaped structure, the tubular skyscraper and the blue sky. Now imagine these sections are jigsaw pieces and ask how they can be best slotted together for the most aesthetically pleasing arrangement. In our example, the curvaceous foreground structure acts as a framing device, creating a hole in the centre of the frame; the diagonally placed building doubles as a lead-in line, pointing to this hole like an accusing finger; and the sky creates negative space around both, helping to define the other two sections. Although the top of the tower is where the eye finishes its visual journey, I'd argue that these three sections, and their associated lines and shapes, are the stars of the show.

It also helps to know that different geometric shapes convey different meanings and energies that will have an impact on how we interpret and explore a scene, a phenomenon often referred to as the 'grammar' of shapes. For instance, circles and ovals have no beginning or end and yet are regular, symmetrical and easily recognizable; they promote a free sense of movement and are used to convey community, unity and, dare I say it, femininity. Squares and rectangles, on the other hand, have right angles and so are less organic and less free-flowing; they are used to symbolize stability, solidity, order and, yes, masculinity. Triangles are changeable depending on the equality of their sides and whether or not they are sitting on their base; they can be used to communicate power and progression or tension and conflict.

RIGHT Use the 'grammar' of shapes to lend a sense of meaning and energy to your images.

CIRCLES & OVALS
Movement, freedom, unity community, femininity

SQUARES & RECTANGLES
Stability, solidity, order, masculinity

TRIANGLES
Power, progression, tension, conflict

240 STREET & URBAN

DIFFICULTY ★★★

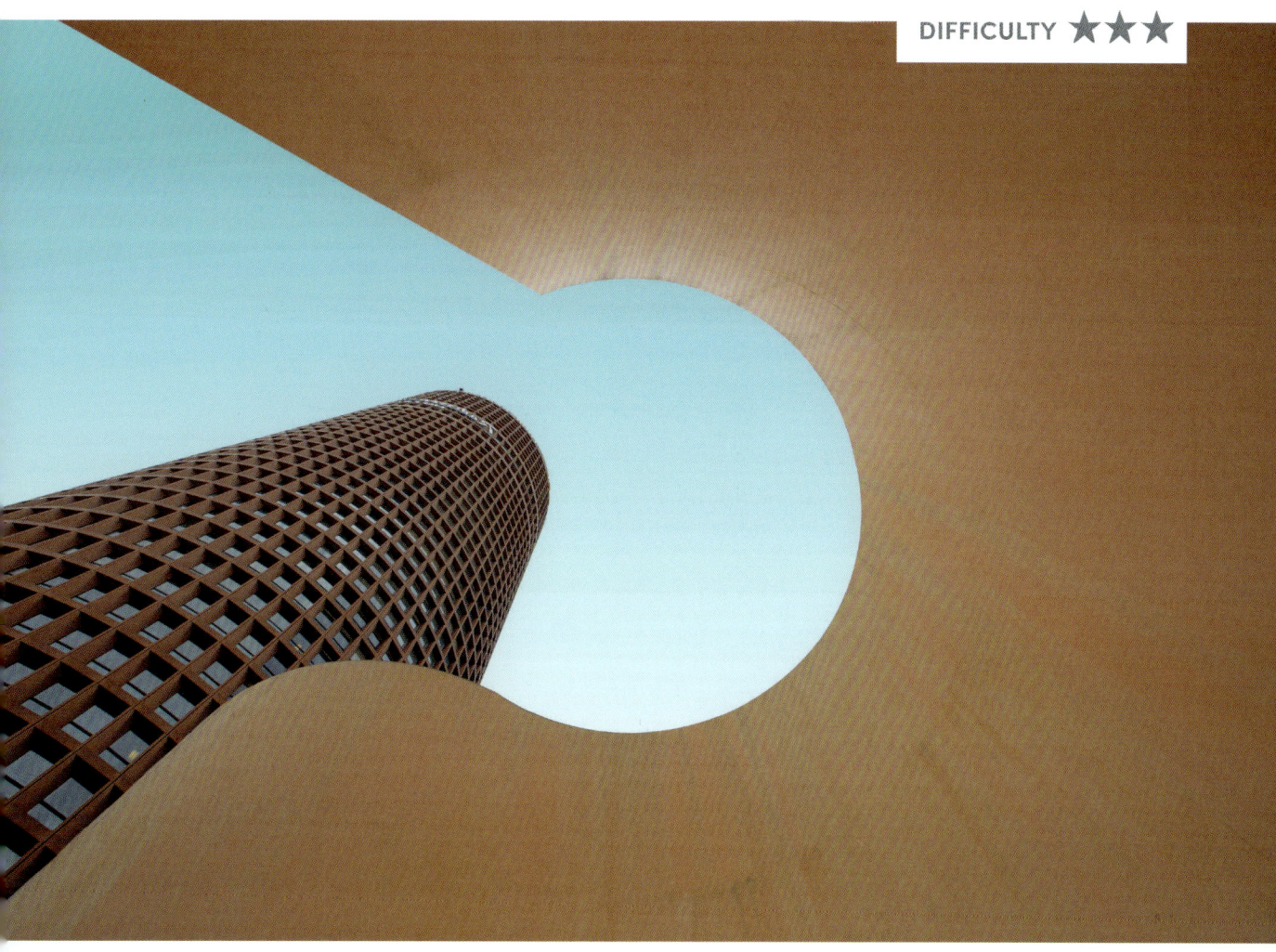

ABOVE **Curves, straight lines and negative space combine to create a fascinating architectural study.**

RECOMMENDED SETTINGS

- Shooting mode: **Aperture-priority**
- Aperture: **$f/8$–$f/16$**
- Shutter speed: **Any**
- ISO: **100**
- Focal length: **18–23mm**
- AF area: **Single-point AF**
- AF operation: **Single-shot AF**
- Drive mode: **Self-timer**
- Metering mode: **Evaluative/matrix**
- White balance: **Auto**
- Picture style: **Standard or monochrome**

LOOK FOR LINES & SHAPES

Camera settings

Aperture and depth of field are the most important technical considerations when shooting architecture, particularly when an image comprises key foreground and background details, so select aperture-priority mode and start with an aperture of ƒ/8. This is typically a kit lens' sharpest aperture – its sweet spot (see page 113) – and will provide plenty of front-to-back sharpness when shooting at wide focal lengths (see below). However, if you need to generate a greater depth of field due to the physical distance between structural elements, close down to ƒ/16.

ISO should always be set to 100. With strong lines and intricate features being such an integral part of a building's design, we want the highest possible image quality for the most amount of noise-free detail.

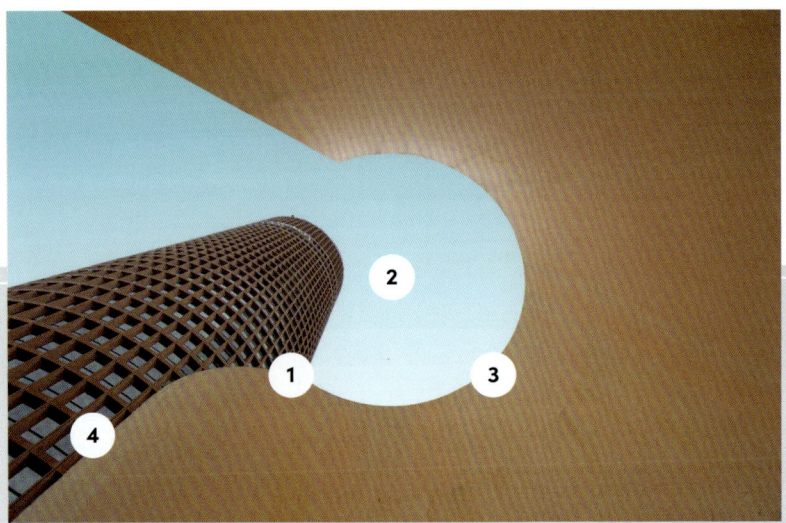

WHY THIS SHOT WORKS

1 The three pictorial components – the curved foreground structure, the skyscraper and the sky – slot together perfectly, with the tower pointing to the hole in the centre of the frame.

2 The tranquil sky creates negative space around the two structural elements, helping to define them while also adding depth and atmosphere.

3 The circular foreground shape contrasts starkly with the harder vertical lines of the skyscraper while mimicking its softer horizontal lines. This suggests both fluidity and stability.

4 By tilting the camera upwards to highlight the skyscraper's height, the photographer has exaggerated its converging verticals, which appear to get closer as they move further away from us.

Observation is the key to mastering both street and architectural photography, but while the former requires split-second reflexes, the latter encourages a more meditative approach. After all, your subject is unlikely to walk off any time soon! This means that shutter speed is of much less importance and we can let the camera determine exposure times without having to worry about it. As a result, a tripod is recommended, regardless of whether shutter speeds are 1/125 second or faster – not only will this eliminate camera shake, it will also encourage you to spend more time fine-tuning your compositions.

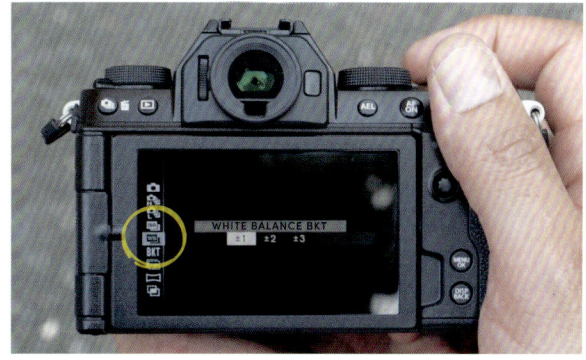

Architectural photography often involves mixed lighting – a combination of natural and artificial light sources – particularly if shooting around dawn or dusk, so the safest option is to set white balance to auto and use a rarely mentioned feature called white balance bracketing. This JPEG-friendly mode allows you to take multiple images at fractionally different WB settings – the first will be as your camera sees it, the second will be slightly warmer and the third will be slightly cooler. You can typically vary the increments by up to 3 stops. Of course, if you opt to shoot in black and white, WB is much less of an issue and auto white balance alone will suffice.

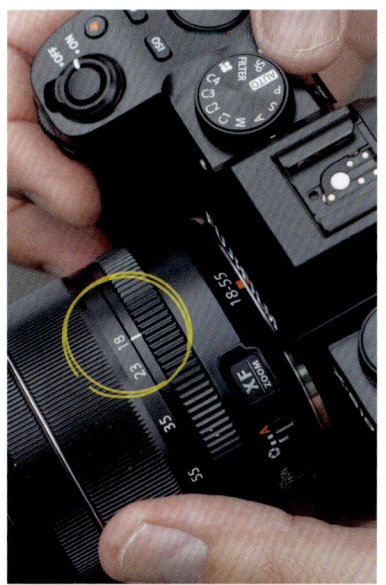

Lens settings

Professional architectural photographers will typically use a wide-angle lens for the majority of their work, as buildings tend to be rather large and wider focal lengths allow you to capture a larger part of a scene. They can also be used to exaggerate perspective and amplify the distance between objects, making them look further away from each other than they really are, which can be fun to play with so long as accurate representation isn't an important consideration. Zoom out to 18mm, but remember that barrel distortion can cause straight lines to bulge outwards from the centre of the frame so zoom in to 23mm if this is a problem.

Set the AF/MF switch to AF, AF area to single-point AF, AF operation to single-shot AF and drive mode to self-timer – the 10-second option will allow plenty of time for any camera shake to dissipate before the shutter is triggered.

Technique

Before you even take your camera out of its bag, take a moment to explore and observe your subject: which are its most interesting angles and features? What time of day will these aspects be beautifully lit? Does this light reveal new shapes and patterns? Where do the shadows fall? If possible, revisit your subject at different times of day and note how different types of light affect its appearance. Planning and timing will evolve your architectural images from opportunist snapshots into considered works of keenly observed urban art.

If you want to avoid converging verticals – which is a good idea when shooting symmetrical shapes and grid-like patterns – resist the urge to tilt your camera upwards and instead make sure your camera's sensor is parallel to the subject.

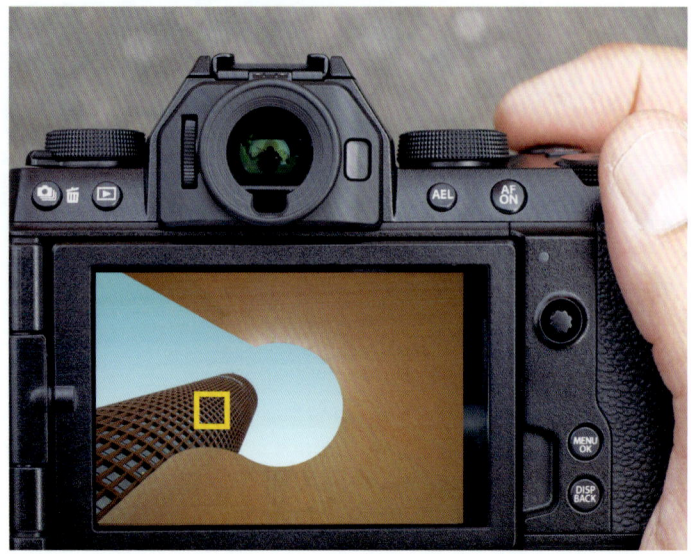

Move your single AF point over an area of contrast one-third of the way into the frame – in our main example, this would be a third of the way up the skyscraper – and gently half-press the shutter to engage autofocus. Now flick the AF/MF switch to MF so that the camera doesn't try to refocus every time you press the shutter. As always, when using semi-automatic exposure modes, use exposure compensation to lighten or darken your images.

TIP

You don't always need to include the whole building to create interesting architectural photographs – sometimes, a more abstract crop highlighting a particularly eye-catching feature or aspect of a structure is all you need. And not all images need sky – zooming in to 55mm can present you with a very different kind of composition.

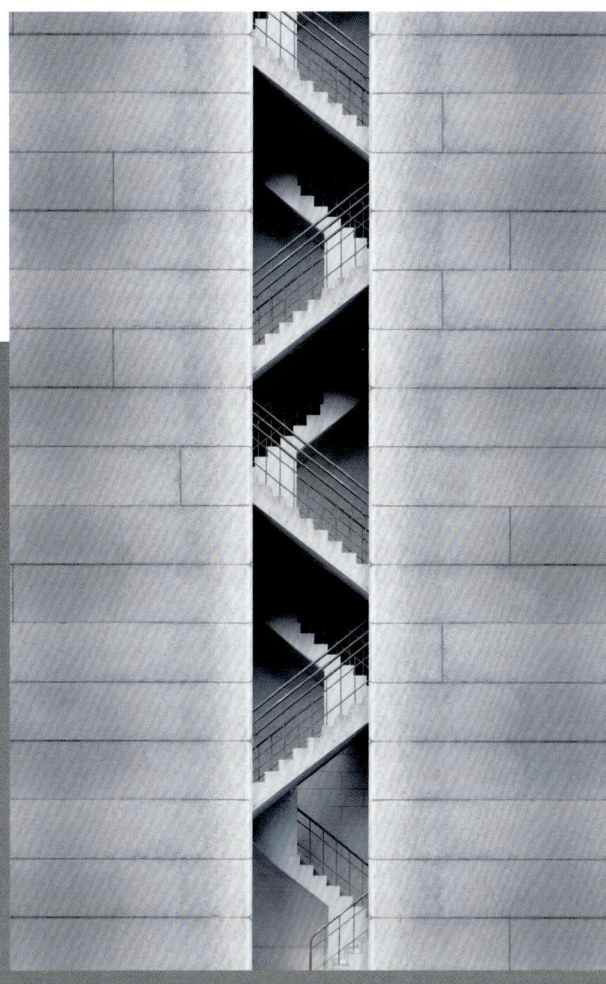

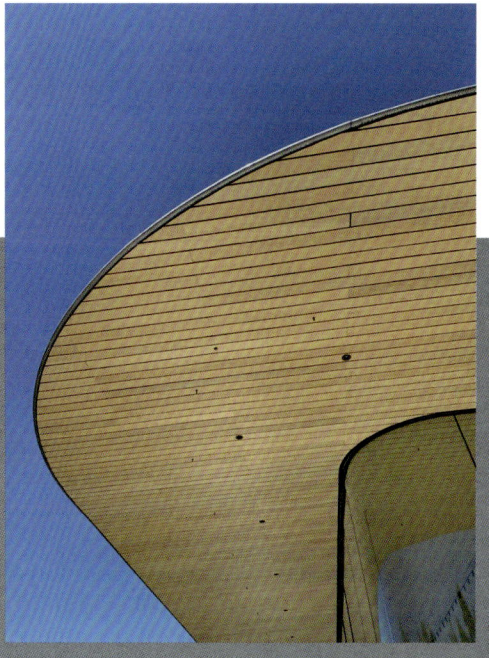

◯ SHOOTING INSPIRATION

A keen eye will be able to pick out interesting architectural details that can be either photographed in isolation or combined with other eye-catching elements.

ABOVE LEFT The stark contrast between vertical, horizontal and diagonal lines creates a very graphic composition.

ABOVE Isolate sweeping curves against saturated blue skies for an elegant simplicity.

LEFT Looking up reveals a futuristic mix of strong shapes, converging verticals and industrial tones.

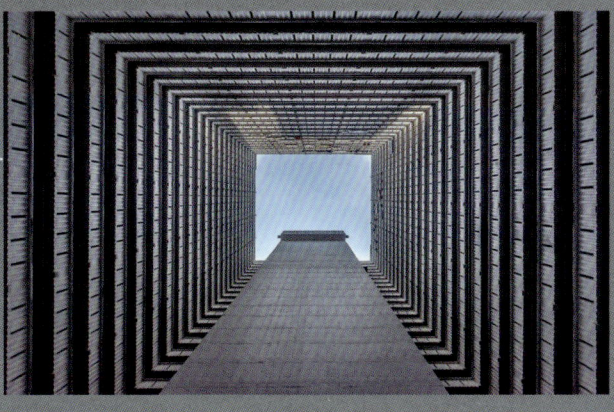

LOOK FOR LINES & SHAPES 245

Module 6.7
Isolate smaller details

What is minimalism and how does it affect our lives? Imagine you have to pack up and move house every six months: within a year or two you would develop a very clear idea of what you need and don't need to live a happy and mobile life, without the distraction of excess possessions. Now apply this scenario to photography: what do you really need to tell your story? What do you really need to capture the viewer's imagination? The answer is: only what really matters. In art, the 'less is more' approach requires careful consideration and an ability to know when to stop taking away. Find the perfect balance and not only will you be able to focus attention on a small number of elements, you will also be able to say a lot with very little.

Minimalism can be found in even the most cluttered towns and cities, from interesting patterns (check out the iconic Selfridges Building in Birmingham, England) to unusual windows (as in our main image) and beyond. It's a question of honing your creative eye and learning to isolate compelling details and to do this we can use a few simple visual tools: include negative space to frame and isolate your subject; employ the rule of thirds (see page 8) to position your subject and create balance, but don't be afraid to break the rules and opt for a central composition when the subject demands it; remove all other distractions by changing viewpoint and aperture (see overleaf); and restrict colour palettes for striking contrasts and subjects that 'pop'.

While architectural exteriors are the obvious places to start, wandering off the streets and into the buildings themselves can open up a whole new world of minimalist potential. Staircases, ceilings and even doorknobs can all be viewed and interpreted through reductionist eyes – often, it's the smallest and most seemingly inconsequential details that reveal the most about a building's construction and history. Of course, you won't be able to walk into any old building, but there are plenty of libraries, galleries and museums that are open to the public, and if there's a private space that catches your eye, you could always contact the owner and ask for permission.

RIGHT Less is most definitely more in this minimalist architectural study.

RECOMMENDED SETTINGS

- Shooting mode: **Aperture-priority**
- Aperture: ƒ/**8**
- Shutter speed: **1/125sec (handheld)**
- ISO: **100**
- Focal length: **55mm**
- AF area: **Single-point AF**
- AF operation: **Single-shot AF**
- Drive mode: **Self-timer or single-shot**
- Metering mode: **Evaluative/matrix**
- White balance: **Match to predominant light source**
- Picture style: **Standard or monochrome**

246 STREET & URBAN

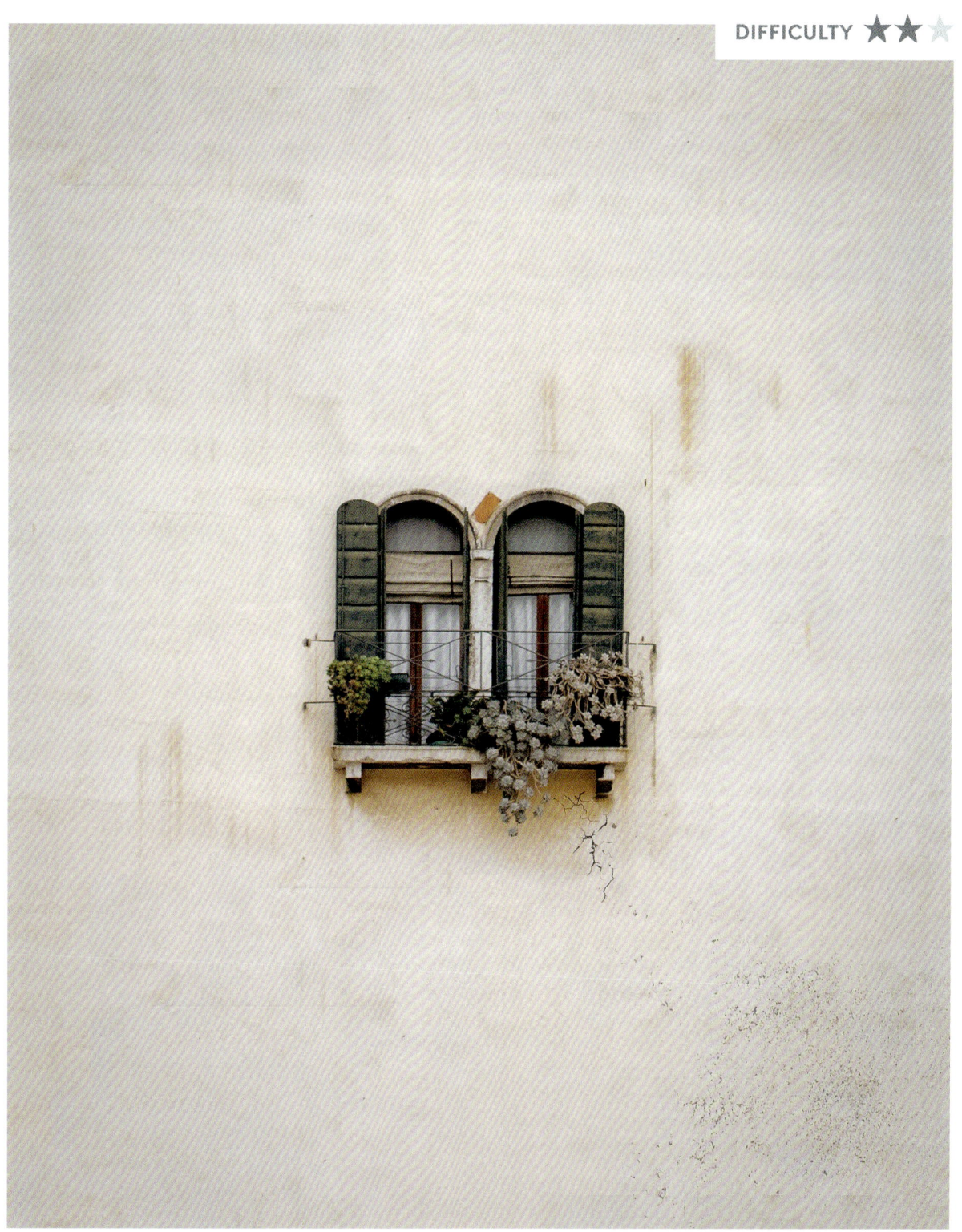

ISOLATE SMALLER DETAILS 247

Camera settings

As with wider architectural scenes, aperture should be our number one priority when shooting smaller details, although if framing up subjects that exist on a single plane, kind of like a real-world flat lay (see page 178), a mid-range aperture of f/8 should give us all the depth of field we need. Professional architectural photographers will use a tripod for every shot, unless it's physically impossible to do so, so follow suit and leave the mode dial set to aperture-priority and close down to f/11 or f/13 if you need a greater depth of field. Open up to f/5.6 if you have to shoot handheld for whatever reason and need to achieve a faster shutter speed, or if less depth of field would help blur a distracting element that can't be cropped out by zooming in or getting closer.

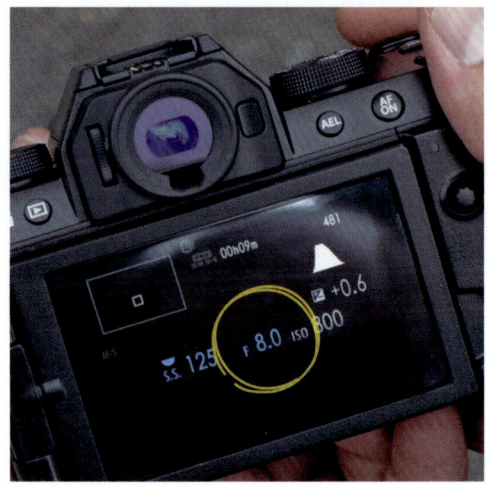

WHY THIS SHOT WORKS

1. Short of photographing a bare wall, there really is nothing else that can be stripped away from this scene, leaving only a beautifully rustic set of shuttered windows and a wonderfully muted colour palette.

2. This image is roughly 90% negative space, 10% positive space, a 'less is more' ratio that both frames and isolates the windows, drawing the viewer's eye while providing plenty of visual breathing room.

3. The negative space isn't as 'negative' as it first appears, with the cracks, textures and subtle variances in tone adding just enough 'background' interest without detracting from the key details.

4. Knowing when to break the rules is as important as knowing the rules in the first place. In this instance, a central composition suggests a certain calmness and honesty, while also emphasizing the space around the focal point.

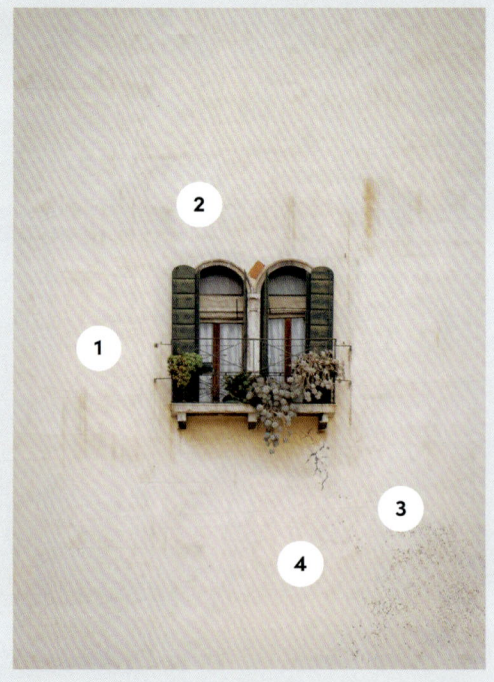

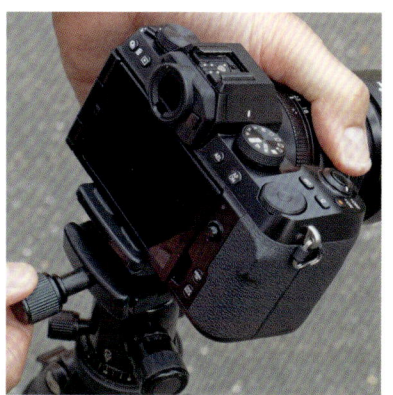

If you are using a tripod, ISO can simply be set to 100 and forgotten about, as can shutter speed. However, as tripods aren't always welcome or practical in enclosed public spaces or busy thoroughfares, use the lowest ISO possible to achieve an exposure time of 1/125 second or faster if handholding, and activate image stabilization if conditions are particularly gloomy. Remember the rule of thumb that suggests that shutter speed should be the reciprocal of the focal length (see page 61) – this means that if shooting at the 55mm end of your kit lens (which provides a 35mm equivalent focal length of around 80mm), a shutter speed of 1/125 second should be plenty fast enough to ensure a sharp image devoid of camera shake.

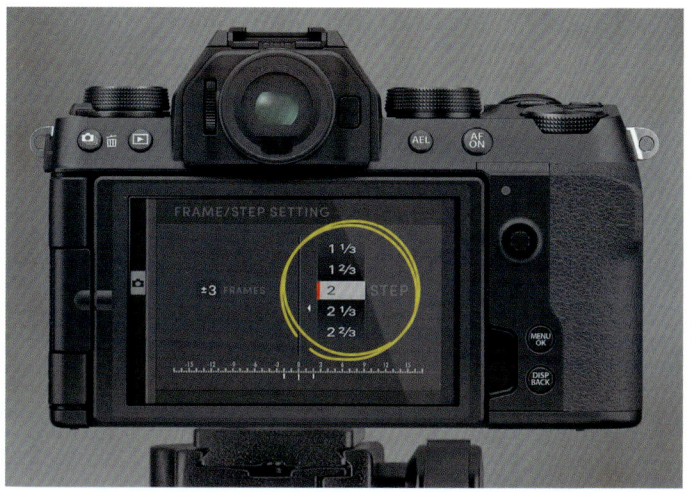

In the previous module (page 243), we looked at the lost art of white balance bracketing, and there's another form of bracketing that will greatly increase your chances of capturing at least one perfectly exposed shot in even the most challenging of situations. Exposure bracketing works in a similar way – you take the first shot at the camera's metered exposure and then deliberately underexpose one frame and overexpose another. Whether you vary the aperture or shutter speed will depend on which setting is least important – as we're shooting in aperture-priority, aperture will remain constant while shutter speed will change according to the parameters set by the user.

All digital cameras feature an auto exposure bracketing (AEB) function, which will be accessible in the main menu. This will allow you to set the exposure compensation range within which you under and overexpose, and then shoot a sequence of automatically bracketed images. Three exposures 1 stop apart will usually suffice, and so our 'bracket' would look like this: 1/125 second at $f/8$ (metered); 1/250 second at $f/8$ (1 stop underexposed); 1/60 second at $f/8$ (1 stop overexposed). AEB can be deployed when shooting any kind of static subject, but note that it doesn't automatically cancel itself once the sequence is complete, so always remember to switch it off before moving on to the next shot.

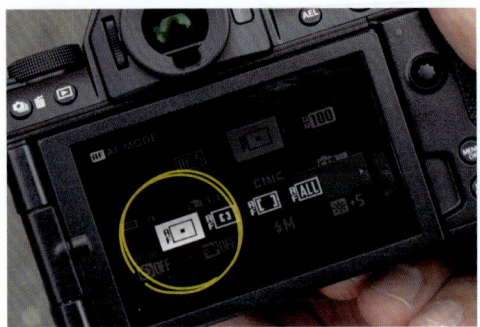

Lens settings

This is a project that will really test the limitations of a kit lens. Within reason, the longer the focal length the better when shooting architectural details, and typically I would recommend a 70–300mm telephoto zoom. However, as we are working within a modest focal-length range, we will have to zoom in to 55mm and let our feet do the heavy lifting. This is because we want to focus attention on a very specific aspect of a building, which will require a tighter crop and therefore a narrower angle of view. In a nutshell, if your lens can't get you close enough, your feet will have to instead.

Focusing follows the tried-and-tested formula that should be very familiar at this point: single-point AF (AF area); single-shot AF (AF operation); self-timer or single-shot (drive mode).

Technique

If shooting outside, use the tripod 'best practice' techniques we looked at in the Landscape chapter (see page 30) to ensure you have the most solid platform on which to shoot. Extend the thickest leg sections first, only use the middle sections if you need a higher viewpoint, and never extend the centre column (consider this an 'in case of emergency' option). Carefully adjust leg height according to terrain and make sure the tripod head is level and image stabilization features are switched off. Run through this quick checklist every time and you can't go wrong.

With the emphasis on minimalism and simplicity, it pays to scan around the edges of your compositions, looking for unnecessary distractions that may detract from the key details. I prefer to use Live View for this, as you can compose your image and then zoom in for a closer look without having to hunch over at an awkward angle to squint through the viewfinder. As in the previous module, if verticals and horizontals need to be, well, vertical and horizontal, now is the time to straighten them, keeping the camera's sensor parallel to the subject or surface you are photographing.

TIP

The golden hour (see page 19) isn't just for landscapes – this is the time of day when the quality of light will be at its warmest and most flattering, and when the sun will be lowest in the sky, enhancing textures and casting shadows that can be used to add pictorial interest and intrigue to even the smallest architectural detail.

Interior shots tend to be more complicated, as they often include mixed lighting that can play havoc with auto white balance. If possible, choose the WB preset that most closely matches the predominant light source and use the white balance bracketing technique we looked at in the previous module to ensure at least one image with neutral colours. Alternatively, if the subject lends itself to a more graphic or more tonally subtle interpretation, you may want to shoot in black and white, in which case accurate white balance becomes less of a concern.

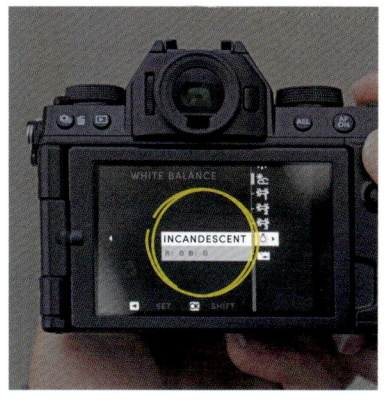

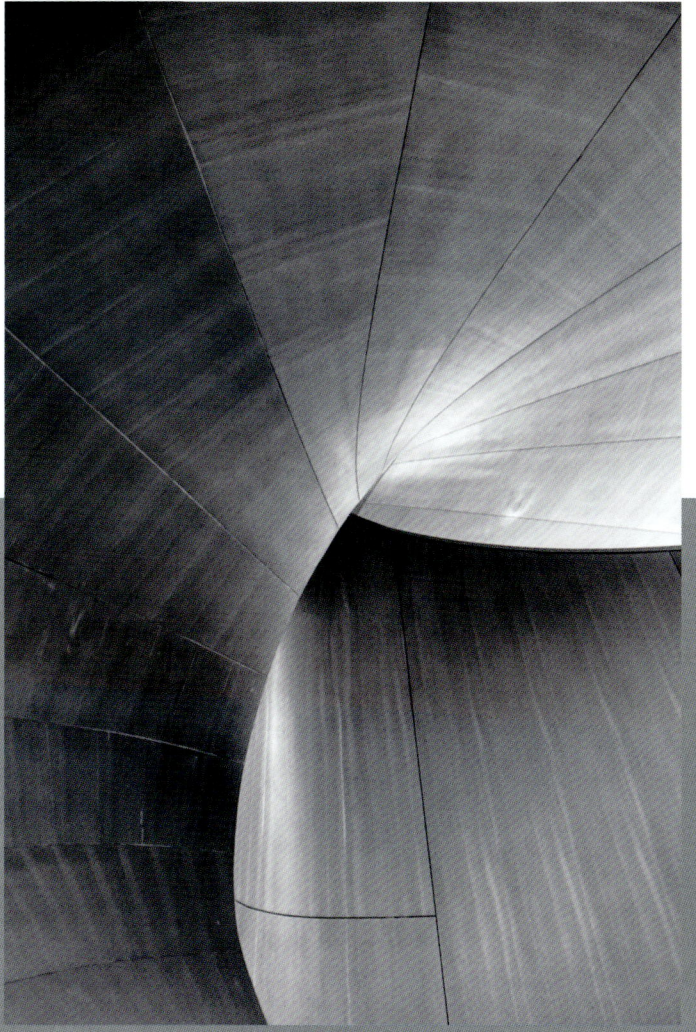

SHOOTING INSPIRATION

The key to this module is knowing when to stop taking away – find the perfect balance between meaning and minimalism.

LEFT Shooting in black and white will focus the viewer's attention on tone, texture, light and shade.

Glossary

While the tech speak is kept to an absolute minimum to make this book as accessible as possible, some words and phrases are unavoidable, and it's important that you understand what these mean before we venture further. We'll be exploring them all in relatable real-world scenarios as we progress through the course – and looking at how they interrelate to one another – but for now, here's a quick rundown of the most commonly used terms…

Aperture
In photography, an aperture is the hole that allows light into a lens and determines how much of a scene is in focus (see *Depth of field*). The larger the hole, the less the depth of field; the smaller the hole, the greater the depth of field. Apertures are measured in f-stops and, confusingly, the smaller the f-stop, the larger the physical hole and vice versa. A simple f-stop scale can be seen below.

Composition
A general term used in all creative arts from pottery to poetry, though in photography it specifically refers to how you frame an image and position its key pictorial elements. The camera's orientation, the height at which you shoot from, how much you zoom in and where you focus all play their part. We're using the rule of thirds as our compositional backbone – serious enthusiasts can get rather sniffy about this device, but it is tried and tested and can be applied to almost any subject.

Crop factor
Even in the digital era, camera sensors are compared to 35mm film in terms of size, and as entry-level DSLRs and mirrorless cameras feature APS-C sensors that are smaller than a 35mm negative, we have what's referred to as a crop factor. This means that we have to multiply a lens' stated focal length by the crop factor – typically 1.5x or 1.6x – to find its effective focal length. For instance, your average 18–55mm kit lens will provide an actual focal length range of 27–83mm when a 1.5x crop factor is applied.

Depth of field
This is a much-used term that refers to the amount of a scene in sharp focus. Depth of field is influenced by aperture, focal length and the distance between camera and subject. Wide apertures such as $f/4$ and $f/5.6$ produce a shallow depth of field while small apertures such as $f/16$ and $f/22$ produce a large depth of field. At any given aperture, two-thirds of the depth of field falls behind the point of focus and one-third falls in front.

Exposure compensation
When shooting in a semi-automatic exposure mode – aperture-priority or shutter-priority – exposure compensation can be used to lighten or darken an image. Like aperture, exposure compensation is measured in stops and is displayed on the camera's top LCD screen and also on the rear LCD screen when using Live View. Minus stops (i.e., -1) will darken an image while plus stops (i.e., +2) will lighten an image.

Focal length
Focal length defines a lens' angle of view. Lenses with a focal length below 35mm are known as wide-angles and lenses with a focal length above 80mm are known as telephotos. Lenses in the middle are known as standards. Your average 18–55mm kit lens covers all three bases – once the crop factor is taken into consideration (see crop factor) – making them a hugely versatile tool that is perfect for beginners finding their feet.

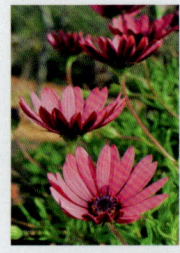 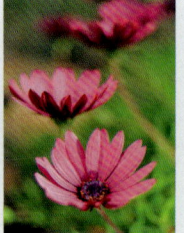

Aperture: $f/22$ Aperture: $f/5.6$

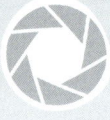     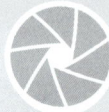 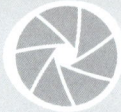

$f/2.8$ $f/4$ $f/5.6$ $f/8$ $f/11$ $f/16$ $f/22$

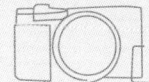

ISO
ISO simply refers to an image sensor's sensitivity. The lower the ISO, the less sensitive the sensor is to light and vice versa. Also, the lower the ISO, the less noise – the digital equivalent of film grain – is produced and so ISO also has a direct impact on image quality. Entry-level cameras start at ISO 100 and often stretch to ISO 6400 or higher, however unless there's a very good reason not to, we'll be shooting at ISO 100 to ensure noise-free images.

JPEG
Digital cameras allow you to save images in two formats: RAW and JPEG. RAW is a format that can't be used straight from the camera and requires editing software and know-how to bring to life. JPEGs, on the other hand, are a universal, beginner-friendly file format that can be used straight from the camera, and they can also be edited in camera via a range of Picture Style menus. As this book is about camera skills and not editing skills, we'll be shooting JPEGs throughout.

Live View
Perhaps the single greatest digital camera innovation of all is the ability to view scenes in real time via a rear LCD screen. Known as Live View, this feature displays any changes to exposure settings and even allows you to superimpose compositional grids and virtual horizons, as well as review images and zoom in and out. This gives photographers – beginner or otherwise – a huge advantage that makes the picture-taking process so much more intuitive than it was in the days of film and darkrooms.

Metering
Digital cameras feature internal light meters that measure the amount of lighting hitting the sensor. This allows us to choose the most suitable shutter speed, aperture and ISO for a 'correct' exposure (I use inverted commas because 'correct' is in the eye of the beholder). You'll see an exposure level indicator in the viewfinder, top LCD panel and Live View display, which looks like a dotted line with +/- numbers either side of a bold central marker. This marker shows what the camera considers to be the optimal exposure.

Metering modes
Today's DSLRs and mirrorless cameras feature hugely sophisticated metering systems that offer three main metering modes: evaluative/matrix, partial/centre-weighted and spot. Evaluative/matrix calculates an average exposure by measuring light from across the entire frame and is the most useful for most situations. It's also the mode we'll be using the most. Partial/centre-weighted calculates an average from the central area of the frame and is useful when shooting in high-contrast light. Spot measures light from just a very small area around the focus point.

Shooting modes
All DSLRs and mirrorless cameras feature four exposure modes, collectively known as PASM, and we're going to be using three of them throughout this book: aperture-priority (A or Av), shutter-priority (S or Tv for time value) and manual (M). The first two are semi-automatic modes that allow you to prioritize one particular setting while the camera takes care of the rest, and the third gives you full control of shutter speed and aperture. The P stands for program and is an automatic mode.

Shutter speed
Measured in fractions of a second or whole seconds, this term refers to the amount of time a camera's shutter stays open when taking a picture. Faster shutter speeds let in less light and slower shutter speed let in more light. Together with aperture and ISO, shutter speed forms one-third of the exposure triangle and plays a crucial role in how subjects are portrayed.

White balance
While the human eye can compensate for different colour temperatures, cameras cannot – unless we tell them to. White balance (WB) allows us to neutralize colour casts emitted from different light sources via a series of presets such as daylight, tungsten and fluorescent. Match the preset to the light source and you've got neutral colours. In most instances, the auto preset is reliable enough; however, in certain instances we'll need to take a more hands-on approach.

Index

abstract art (bokeh) 184–9
AE lock 231
AEB (auto exposure bracketing) 249
aperture
   architectural photography 241, 242, 246, 248, 249
   bokeh 184, 186
   flash 135, 136
   flat lays 179, 180, 182
   foodography 127, 174
   landscapes 29, 34, 47, 48, 147, 149, 150
   light painting 141, 142, 143
   moving subjects 129
   nature 90, 92, 97, 98, 101, 104
   portraits 52, 53, 54, 59, 60, 61, 63, 65, 70, 73, 83, 84
   refraction 196, 198, 200
   speed-with-blur 123, 124, 125
   still life 155, 161, 162, 168, 169
   street/urban scenes
      framing 223, 224, 226
      from the hip 211, 212, 213, 214
      motion blur 234, 235, 236, 237
      reflections 216, 218
      shadows 229
      traffic trails 111, 112, 113, 117, 118
aperture-priority 10
architectural photography 240–5

backlighting 70, 72, 104
bokeh 96, 98, 100, 101, 184–9

centre-weighted metering 69
children 64–9

depth of field
   architectural photography 242

   bokeh 187
   flat lays 180, 181
   landscapes 9, 10, 16, 17, 23, 28, 40, 48
   moving subjects 124, 125
   nature 90, 92, 98
   physiograms 149
   portraits 52, 54, 60, 74, 84
   refraction 204
   still life 156, 162, 163, 164, 168, 169, 174, 176, 198
   street/urban scenes 212, 214
diffraction 11

emotion, creating 70–5
environmental portraits 58–63
exposure compensation 12, 31, 81, 95, 126, 137
exposure lock 231
exposure time 234, 237

flagging 172
flash 134–9
flat lays 178–83
flowers 90–5, 202–7
focal length
   architectural photography 241, 242, 243, 246, 250
   flash 135
   flat lays 179, 181, 187
   landscapes 12, 14, 18, 24, 28, 29, 30
   light painting 141
   moving subjects 129, 131
   nature 91, 94, 97
   physiograms 147
   portraits 56, 59, 61, 62, 70, 77, 80, 83
   refraction 199

   still life 155, 158, 167, 175, 184, 191, 202, 205
   street/urban scenes 211, 214
framing 223, 226
   reflections 216, 218, 219
   shadows 229, 232
   traffic trails 111, 117
focusing ring 100
foodography 172–7
forced perspective 44–9

golden hour 19, 70, 250
grass 96–101

hands 82–7
household objects 160–5
Hyper-Focal-Pro 25, 28, 29
hyperfocal distance focusing 25, 28

ICM (intentional camera shake) 38–43, 47, 236
infinity curves 157, 164, 166, 168, 170, 204
ISO
   architectural photography 241, 242, 249
   auto 175
   bokeh 184, 187
   flash 135, 137
   flat lays 179, 181
   landscapes 9, 11, 16, 17, 23, 47
   light painting 141
   moving subjects 123, 125, 129, 131
   nature 91, 93, 98, 102, 105
   physiograms 147, 149, 150
   portraits 55, 61, 67, 78, 82, 85
   refraction 199
   still life 155, 157, 161, 162, 168, 175, 191,

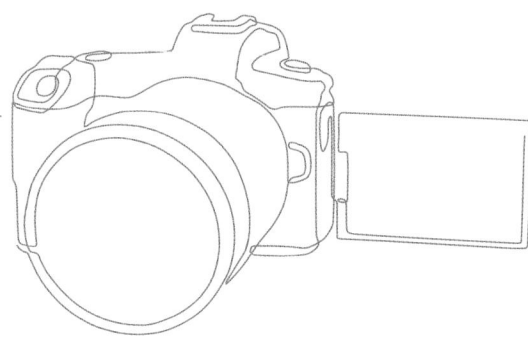

193, 203, 205
    street/urban scenes 211, 212, 213
    traffic trails 111, 112, 113, 117, 119

kit lenses 5, 12, 85, 90
kitchen utensils 160–5

landscape format 24, 62
landscapes 8–49
lead-in lines
    movement 110, 114, 122–3, 124
    nature 20–5, 26, 28, 34, 36, 48
    street/urban scenes 223, 224, 232, 238, 240
leaves 102–7
lifestyle photography 64–9
light painting 140–5
lines and shapes 240–5
liquid art 190–5

mise-en-scène 26
motion blur 122–7
    landscapes 23, 34, 35, 37
    speed 122–7
    street scenes 234–9
movement 110–51
    flash 134–9
    following a moving subject 128–33
    light painting 140–5
    motion blur 122–7
    physiograms 146–51
    traffic trails 110–21

nature 90–107

pets 76–81
PhotoPills 25, 28, 29, 37

physiograms 146–51
portrait format 24, 62, 176
portraits 52–87
power points 14, 16–19, 20, 22, 36, 48, 60, 62, 114, 122, 136, 178, 212, 232, 238
product photography 166–71, 172, 174
public spaces and privacy 214

rain 120
reflections 216–21
reflectors 158
refraction 196–201
retro classics 154–9
rule of odds 154–9
rule of thirds
    landscape 8, 10, 13, 14–19, 20, 26, 29, 36, 48,
    movement 114, 118–19, 122, 131
    nature 90, 92, 100, 106
    portraits 52, 54, 56, 60, 62, 68, 75, 80, 86
    still life 178
    street/urban scenes 212, 220, 232, 238, 246

shutter speed
    architectural photography 241, 243, 249
    bokeh 184, 186, 187
    flash 134, 135, 136
    flat lays 179, 181
    landscapes 9, 10, 11, 32, 35, 39, 40, 41, 47
    light painting 140, 142, 143
    motion blur 122, 125, 126
    moving subjects 128, 129, 130, 131
    nature 91, 93, 97, 98

physiograms 150
portraits 53, 55, 59, 61, 65, 66, 67, 70, 76, 77, 78, 83, 85
refraction 196
still life 155, 162, 167, 168, 172, 191
street/urban scenes 211, 212, 213
traffic trails 111, 112, 113, 117, 118, 119, 120
spot metering 72, 73, 74, 206
street scenes 228, 231, 232
still life 154–207
street/urban scenes 210–51

traffic trails 110–21
tripods 5, 30, 36, 126

waterproofing cameras 36, 37, 114
white balance
    architectural photography 241, 243, 250, 251
    landscapes 9, 11, 17, 23, 29, 41
    light painting 141, 143
    nature 93, 97, 102, 105
    physiograms 147, 149
    portraits 53, 55, 61, 65, 67, 70, 73, 78
    speed with blur 123
    still life 155, 161, 167, 172, 179, 184, 191, 202, 205
    street/urban scenes 213, 216, 223, 229, 232, 235
    traffic trails 111, 113, 117, 119

zone focusing 214
zoom burst 138

Picture credits & acknowledgements

Alamy Stock Photo agefotostock 167; Alex Ward Studios 211; Andrew Soundarajan 27; Andriy Bezuglov 123; Anita Nicholson 13 below; Anna Usova 155; Capture That - Landscapes 21; Carolyn Eaton 43 above; Cavan Images 65; Culture RM 53; David Lichtneker 43 below; Dawna Moore 191; diversbelow 26; Igor Goncharenko 49 below; Image Source 63; imagebroker 57 below; Mark Phillips 223, 227 above & below, 229; Mark Robertson 31 centre; Mattia Oselladore 233 below; mauritius images GmbH 222; Mike Sivyer 117; Nature Picture Library 107; Nicholas Eveleigh 207 below; romd 145 above; Sam Oakes 39; Stephen Emerson 19 below, 25 below; Steve Atkins 135; Steve Purnell 197; Tim Gartside 121; Tirthal Shankar Das 215 above

Dreamstime.com Alex N 215 below; Annausova75 159 below; Elena Schweitzer 13 above; Juan Moyano 90 & 252; Pavalache Stelian 9; Sara Winter 14; Yotka 159 above

iStock Andrea Izzotti 83; baratroli 15; estherpoon 239; Faina Gurevich 201; fergusowen 59; JoeyCheung 235; SeanPavonePhoto 111; Sterling750 122 right; Suriya Silsaksom 122 left; Vladimir Sukhachev 179; WoodysPhotos 129

Pexels Anna Shvets 171 above right; Avery Nielsenwebb 37 left; Ferbugs 165 below; Freestocksorg 189 above; Isaac Weatherly 145 below; Jeffrey Czum 247; Jun 95 below right; Laker 95 below left; 171 below; Leon Macapagal 221; Martin Damboldt 31 below; Mike Greer 207 above; Misha Voguel 57 above; Pixabay 87 above; Tijana Drndarski 177 above left; Vishal Shah 115; Zukiman Mohamad 37 below right

Shutterstock Creative Abel Tumik 161; Angel House Studio 139; Maarten Zeehandelaar 147; Mike Neilsen 151 above; Paulo Vilela 141; Pincasso 45; Sara Winter 32; Vasilev Evgenii 91

Unsplash Aaron Burden 101 above; absolutvision 165 above; Alvan Nee 76; Andrew Seaman 101 below; Aneta Voborilova 177 above right; Annie Spratt 106; Aron Visuals 185; Caique Silv 71; Chor Tsang 245 below; Clay Banks 103; Coline Beulin 241; Dan Roizer 127 above; Deva Williamson 177 below; Gabriella Clare Marino 217; Guillaume Bourdages 189 below; Henry Co 245 above left; Jessica Rockowitz 69 below; Joel Filipe 251 below; Jose Alejandro Cuffia 81; Jose Martinez 75; JP Valery 127 below; Kai Dahms 195 above; Mae Mu 171 above left; Mikah Sargent 245 above right; Mitul Grover 133 below; Nathan Dumlao 86, 178; Ochir-Erdene Oyunmedeg 97; Om Prakash Sethia 87 below; Pablo Merchan Montes 173; Ryan Stone 77; Shane Aldendorff 183 above; Sharon Pittaway 195 below; Sreekumar 49 above; Tetiana Shadrina 183 below; Zoltan Tasi 203

Camera views courtesy of Adam Atkins

Illustrations courtesy of Chris Robinson

Love, hugs and metal horns to Rachel and Beckett. I couldn't have written this book without your endless support, encouragement and patience. You rock.

Big thanks to Dad, for reading every word before anyone else – and for the daily Coryton Cove updates. Up the Villa.

Big thanks to Mom, for the many trips up and down the A1, the Spanish chicken and the lockdown survival packages.

Props to Richard, Rachel and the Ilex team, for having the gumption to ask me to write a book – and being daft enough to invite me back for a second. I hope I met the brief.

And, finally, sincere thanks to you, the reader, for picking up this hefty tome. I truly hope you find it useful and interesting in some way. Enjoy your photography.